J. G. Bourinot

A Canadian Manual on the Procedure at Meetings of Municipal Councils

Shareholders and Directors of Companies, Synods, Conventions

J. G. Bourinot

A Canadian Manual on the Procedure at Meetings of Municipal Councils
Shareholders and Directors of Companies, Synods, Conventions

ISBN/EAN: 9783337187682

Printed in Europe, USA, Canada, Australia, Japan

Cover: Foto ©ninafisch / pixelio.de

More available books at **www.hansebooks.com**

A

CANADIAN MANUAL

ON THE

PROCEDURE

AT

MEETINGS OF MUNICIPAL COUNCILS, SHAREHOLDERS
AND DIRECTORS OF COMPANIES, SYNODS, CON-
VENTIONS, SOCIETIES AND PUBLIC BODIES
GENERALLY

WITH

AN INTRODUCTORY REVIEW OF THE RULES AND USAGES OF
PARLIAMENT THAT GOVERN PUBLIC ASSEMBLIES
IN CANADA.

BY

J. G. BOURINOT, C.M.G., LL.D., D.C.L., D.L.

CLERK OF THE HOUSE OF COMMONS ;

*Author of Parliamentary Procedure in Canada; Manual of Canadian Constitutional
History; Federal Government in Canada; Canadian Studies in
Comparative Politics, etc.*

TORONTO:

THE CARSWELL CO. (Ltd.), LAW PUBLISHERS, ETC.

1894

TORONTO:
PRINTED BY THE CARSWELL CO. LTD.
22, 30 Adelaide St. East.

PREFACE.

SINCE the publication of the author's large work on Parliamentary Procedure some years ago, he has been in constant receipt of enquiries on various points of order that have arisen from time to time in municipal and other meetings, and has consequently seen the practical necessity that exists for a relatively short treatise that is directly adapted to the special wants of municipal councils, public meetings and conventions, religious conferences, shareholders' and directors' meetings, and societies in general. Such a treatise will necessarily supplement the large work just mentioned, which is exclusively devoted to parliamentary procedure and government, and to which reference can be made in those complicated and difficult cases which can alone be treated in such elaborate books. In the practice of many societies and public bodies in this country some confusion appears to exist with reference to the true meaning and object of "the previous question," and of such motions as "to lay on the table," "to postpone definitely," or "indefinitely," and "to reconsider," which are drawn from the procedure, not of our own legislative assemblies, but of assemblies in the United States. I have attempted in this treatise to give such explanations as will aid in preventing confusion or doubt in the application of these methods of procedure. In this way, the author hopes he will meet the wants of that large number of persons, who, in this country of popular institutions, are immediately interested in the methodical progress of business, and naturally wish to make themselves conversant, as easily as possible, with the principal rules and usages that should guide the proceedings of public assemblies of all kinds. At all events, if the numerous persons who have used a good deal of the author's time for years, will refer as a rule to this volume in ordinary cases instead of making personal application to him, he may expect to have more leisure than he has heretofore been able to enjoy. At the same time the author adds that he will be grateful for any suggestions that may make any future edition of this work as accurate and comprehensive as possible, especially in connection with the meetings of municipal councils, for whose proceedings the writer has suggested a uniform code of rules as desirable and easy of accomplishment.

In order that this work may be as comprehensive and as useful as possible to all practical men, the writer has divided it as follows :

1. A statement of the leading rules and principles of parliamentary procedure which lie necessarily at the basis of the proceedings and deliberations of all public assemblies and societies of this country.

2. Next an application of those rules and principles to the proceedings of Public Meetings, Societies, Conventions, Church Conferences and Synods, Companies' Meetings and Municipal Councils.

Comments are made on the special procedure of the various classes of meetings dealt with in full—especially of municipal councils in Ontario—and references are given throughout to the first part of the work in order to make that procedure as intelligible as possible, especially in cases of doubt.

The Index has been made as full as practicable, and a Table of Contents is given at the commencement of each of the Five Parts of the work.

J. G. BOURINOT.

CONTENTS.

FIRST PART.

RULES AND USAGES OF PARLIAMENT.

SECOND PART.

RULES OF ORDER AND PROCEDURE FOR PUBLIC MEETINGS AND SOCIETIES.

THIRD PART.

CORPORATE COMPANIES.

FOURTH PART.

CHURCH SYNODS AND CONFERENCES.

FIFTH PART.

MUNICIPAL COUNCILS.

FIRST PART.

RULES AND USAGES OF PARLIAMENT.

I.—GENERAL OBSERVATIONS.

II.—SUMMARY OF THE RULES AND USAGES OF
PARLIAMENT.

I.—GENERAL OBSERVATIONS.

1. Meetings of public bodies in the Dominion.—Since the time Canada was relieved from that system of absolutism and repression of all debate, which was a signal feature of the French regime, and became a country of English institutions, her people have raised a structure of government having at its basis freedom of speech and thought. We must place first those primary (a)· meetings which are called together from time to time to discuss public questions relating to the general, the provincial, or the municipal affairs of the country. Then come the meetings of the numerous municipal councils which are guided by certain statutory laws and rules of procedure, and are at once deliberative and legislative in their character. A story higher are the various legislative bodies of the several provinces, which have plenary jurisdiction within their provincial limits, and are themselves the creators of the municipal bodies immediately below them in the structure of government. The dome of the edifice is the parliament of the Dominion, having powers of legislation over the general affairs of the whole confederation.

In addition to this artificial system which has slowly evolved from the necessities of a community having the instincts of a self-governing people, there are numerous conventions, synods, conferences, literary, labour and benevolent associations, and directors' and shareholders' meetings, which have grown out of the requirements of all classes in these busy times.

2. **All public bodies governed by parliamentary law.**—The meetings of these several bodies, from the simple primary, ward, village or town assembly to the complicated session of parliament, are all, more or less, governed by the leading principles of the common law of parliament—those generally recognized rules which have had their origin in the parent state, the old home of the common law and of the parliamentary system of Canada and of all the English speaking peoples of the world. It is a well understood principle that the people of these dependencies, in adopting the common law of England, did not adopt it in its entirety, but only those parts of the system which are suited to a new colonial condition, very different from the state of society under

(a) I do not use the word "primary" here or elsewhere in the narrow sense customary in the political organizations of the United States, but I refer to a "public meeting" in the ordinary or common acceptation of the phrase; that is to say, an assembly of all persons interested in the object for which it is called, and not a legislative or representative or other body of limited membership, and subject to certain constitutional and other regulations.

which the usages of the common law grew up. On the same principle, the common law of parliament that governs in this country
is that system of rules and conventions which has been adapted
from the elaborate system of the great prototype of all legislative
assemblies, and established by usage and prescription in this
Dominion to meet existing conditions. As a matter of fact, the
differences of law and procedure are relatively few—the method of
putting amendments being one of those differences — but where
they do exist they should necessarily govern all assemblies that
have a permanent code of rules or by-laws for their guidance.

3. **Special rules necessary in certain cases.**—Every assembly of the character previously described in general terms, will, of
necessity, have its own rules adapted to its peculiar organization
and requirements, just as parliament itself has its special orders
governing its hours of meeting, its order of business and such
other matters as are essentially of detail. But each and all
should be, and are in fact, governed by those old rules which
regulate debate, the making and putting of motions, the introduction and passage of bills, the procedure of committees of the whole
and of select committees, and, in short, such other proceedings of
parliament as are well calculated to ensure calm deliberation, full
discussion and sound legislation.

The proceedings of deliberative, legislative and other public
bodies—that is to say, of those bodies which have a complicated
and elaborate procedure compared with the simple regulations of
primary assemblies and meetings—are governed by statutory
enactments as well as by ordinary rules of parliamentary usage.
The parliament and the legislatures of Canada, municipal councils,
public companies, religious conferences, courts and synods, and
the more important societies of the country at large, are all, in
certain essential particulars, governed by the rules of their respective constitutions or charters of existence. These statutory
enactments cannot be changed at the mere will of the body they
govern, but only by the superior legislative authority that enacted
them. But to all bodies, generally speaking, there are given either
in express terms, or by necessary implication, the right to make

such rules, regulations and by-laws as are essential to their use-fulness and very existence as legislative, deliberative, or business bodies.

4. How regulations can be changed.—All such rules, regu-lations and by-laws are left necessarily to be modified, amended or changed by these bodies themselves. As long as they remain in force, and are not in direct conflict with statutory enactment or in excess of the powers given by law, they must regulate the pro-ceedings of the bodies that have passed them. They cannot be changed or altered except in accordance with the methods laid down in the regulations or the law, and any violation of them may be prevented by any member asking the intervention of the chair under the rules.

5. Suspension of rules not to be encouraged.—At times, it may be necessary and convenient to suspend rules by unanimous consent, but this should rarely be permitted even in the society of the most humble object, and never, except in cases of urgency or routine business, in municipal or other bodies, regulated by law and immediately dealing with the rights and interests of indivi-duals. Every assembly having legislative and large responsibili-ties, should have a rule prohibiting a change of any fundamental rule, or by-law, except after exact notice of the proposed amend-ment. In the case of bodies having a corporate existence and dealing with the pecuniary and other important interests of individuals, no important amendment should be made except after such special notice, and with the consent of a certain majority —generally two-thirds—of all the members of the com-pany or body (b). In addition, the rules or by-laws of all municipal councils, conferences, synods and other important associations, should have a rule referring in all cases, not provided for expressly in those rules and by-laws, to the common law of parliament; that is to say, to the rules and practice of the house of commons of Canada (c).

(b) See rules of certain councils, etc., *Fifth Part* of this work, II. sec. 11.
(c) *Ibid*, II. sec. 12.

6. Meaning of session, sitting and meeting.—The business of every legislative and deliberative assembly, of every ecclesiastical assembly and synod, of every municipal council, of every association and of every body of men that meet for a certain object, is transacted at a "meeting," "sitting," or "session." An ordinary "meeting" means the interval of time between the assembling or convening of a body until the close of its proceedings by an adjournment. A "session," in a strict sense, means the duration of the several meetings of a legislative, ecclesiastical or other deliberative body which assembles at a fixed time, meets and adjourns from day to day, and finally after a week, month or longer period comes to a close by prorogation, or by such other usage as terminates the session. The meetings of an ecclesiastical body which sits for several days make up one session. In the case of bodies like municipal councils, companies' and directors' meetings, school boards and societies, which meet once, weekly, fortnightly, monthly, annually, or at other fixed and short periods, and transact their business at that particular time, the word "meeting" is practically synonymous with "session." If such a short meeting is adjourned until another day to conclude the matters for which it originally met, it is the same meeting, but not a session in the large sense. A "sitting" (d) is the word sometimes applied to the daily meeting of a session of parliament, or of any other important body.

7. The presiding officer.—Every body of men, assembled for the purpose of discussion, deliberation and the promotion of a certain object, must be, from the very nature of things, presided over by a particular person, who is called a chairman. It is his duty to maintain order, read motions to the meeting, so that they may be formally debated, decide questions of order and procedure, submit motions or resolutions to the final decision of the meeting or assembly by their voices, show of hands, or poll—or, as in parliament and other bodies, by a formal recording of yeas and nays—and finally adjourn the meeting when the business is con-

(d) Often called "sederunt" by a not very accurate application of a latin term.

cluded. This chairman is called by various titles according to the
usage, rule or law that governs particular assemblies and bodies.
The time-honoured name of speaker, which has come down to us
from the ancient parliaments of England, is still used with rigid
formality in all legislative bodies. President is generally the name
of the presiding officer of synods, societies and companies' meetings, appointed or elected for a fixed interval. Prolocutor is the
old English title of the president of the lower house of a church of
England general or provincial synod in Canada (e). Moderator
distinguishes the presiding officer of the Presbyterian courts.
Warden, mayor and reeve, are the titles derived from old English
local institutions, for the presiding officers of municipal councils.
The Masons, Odd Fellows and other fraternities have designations
peculiar to themselves. In addressing these several officers, it is
usual to call them by their special title, Mr. Speaker, or Mr.
Moderator, or Mr. President, or Mr. Mayor, though each is simply
a chairman in the general sense of the common law that governs
all assemblies. Frequently, provision is made for a deputy-
speaker, or vice-president, or other officer, to supply the place of
a presiding officer during his temporary absence.

8. **How presiding officers are chosen.**—Either law, rule or
custom regulates the selection of a presiding officer of an assembly, council or other body. The speaker of the Canadian and
English houses is elected on motion duly made by a mover and
seconder, with the clerk acting as temporary chairman. If two or
more candidates are proposed, the sense of the house is given on
the name of each candidate, in the same order in which it is proposed: that is to say, the first name is voted upon, and if rejected,
the second name, and so forth. It is not usual for a candidate to
vote for himself. In the case of all public bodies in this country,
it would be well to adopt the same practice and in this way ensure
uniformity from a primary up to a parliamentary assembly (f).

(e) See *Fourth Part*.

(f) See *below*, p. 27, for parliamentary rule respecting the election of speaker.

9. **Special statutory provisions in certain cases provide for chairman and other officers.**—An ordinary public or primary meeting elects its chairman on a motion duly made, seconded, submitted and agreed to by the meeting. In the case of assemblies governed by statute, rules and by-laws—like legislative, ecclesiastical and municipal bodies, special provision is made for the election or appointment of all the officers. The speakers of the house of commons and of legislative assemblies generally in Canada are elected by those bodies as provided by law. Wardens, mayors and reeves are chosen by the people of the municipalities or by the councils. The secretaries, clerks, treasurers, aud.tors and such other officers as are necessary to the transaction of the business of municipal councils, shareholders' and directors' meetings, and ecclesiastical bodies, are generally appointed by the bodies themselves in accordance with the constitution and regulations.

10. **Quorum.**—When any meeting or public body is regularly convened, and a chairman is elected in accordance with law or usage to preside over its debates and deliberations, the business before it can be regularly proceeded with. Every legislative and deliberative assembly with a certain number of members, has its quorum fixed by statute or by its own regulations. If there is no such provision in the constitution or regulations, then the common law requires a majority of *all* the members to give regularity to the proceedings of any meeting of that assembly. In case of a committee of the whole, the same rule prevails. A quorum is generally fixed by the appointing body for those smaller committees called "select" or "special." If no such quorum is fixed, then a majority of the committee must be present before any business can be transacted. As a rule it is important to have a fixed quorum for an assembly and its committees (*g*).

11. **Order of business.**—In every legislative or deliberative assembly of a permanent character, the rules generally provide for

(*g*) See *below*, p. 29, for parliamentary rule respecting quorum.

a regular order of business (*h*), which will be prepared for each meeting by the secretary or clerk, or scribe, or whatever may be the name of the recording officer, and should be called, item by item, by the chairman or clerk. It is absolutely essential to a proper discharge of the functions of every body that such an order should be regularly prepared and adhered to. In the case of an ordinary or primary or mass meeting, it should also be the duty of those responsible for its assembling and interested in its deliberations and debates, to arrange at the outset among themselves an order of proceeding, and not leave it to haphazard, and the confusion that would then probably ensue. All these matters, however, will be explained in their proper place, when we come to consider the proceedings of particular meetings.

12. **Notices of motions and proceedings.**—If this order of the day is to be effective and to carry out its main object of enabling each member of a permanent assembly or organized society to discuss every question that comes before it with some knowledge, it is necessary that the rules should provide as far as possible for a *notice* of every substantive motion or proceeding, in accordance with a fundamental principle of parliamentary procedure—questions of privilege and order, demanding the immediate interposition of the house, being the only exceptions. Such notices are especially important in the case of proposed changes in the constitution or by-laws of an incorporated body ; and it is well always to provide for such adequate notice as will inform all the members of the body of the precise terms of the amendment, and at the same time prevent it being made except by a vote of two-thirds of all the members (*i*) of the corporation, council, or assembly. The rules on these points should be very carefully framed. Notices are not, of course, as a rule necessary in the case of amendments relevant to a motion, though it is well to remember that questions may at times arise, especially in shareholders' and directors' meetings, how

(*h*) See *below*, p. 29, for parliamentary rule respecting order of procedure; also for that of city councils, *Fifth Part*, II. sec. 13:

(*i*) See *Fifth Part*, II. sec. 14, for rules of certain councils respecting notice.

far amendments are allowable in the case of motions of which special notice has been given (*j*).

13. **Minutes of proceedings.**—Every assembly and association has necessarily its minutes, or authorized record of its resolutions and proceedings generally, prepared by the clerk or secretary. In parliament the daily journal or record is signed by the speaker, but it is not now formally read and approved by the house, as it is regularly printed, and open to correction on motion duly made, or by an erratum in case of clerical error at the end of the proceedings of a subsequent day. In other bodies however, it is usual to read and approve the minutes at a later meeting of the same assembly or council, and to have it signed by the chairman—his signature, however, being only necessary for courts of law. These minutes may then be corrected, but it is not regular to raise a discussion on the policy or merits of a question when attention is called to an error in the entry. All remarks must be simply in reference to the particular error. The record of all business meetings should be, as in parliament, succinct and accurate minutes of the actual motions, resolutions, and results of the deliberations, and not a report of men's speeches (*k*). In the case of companies' meetings, a president's address, relating to the operations of the company, is generally considered as much a part of the business as a manager's statement or a committee's report. All such points will be explained in the proper place in this work (*l*).

14. **Proposal of motions.**—Every question submitted to a meeting must come before it in the form of a motion which is moved by one member of the assembly, and seconded by another. Then it is read by the chairman, so that the meeting is actually seized of the proposition. It is then debatable, and may be negatived, or accepted, or amended. Until it is proposed from the

---

(*j*) See *Third Part*, sec. 4, for the strict interpretation that is given to a rule respecting special notices in the case of directors', shareholders', and other meetings governed by statutory regulations.

(*k*) See *Third Part*, sec. 7, for mode of keeping minutes accurately.

(*l*) See *Third Part*.

chair it cannot be formally entered in the minutes by the recording officer. Each motion should be in writing, except it be a purely formal and well understood motion of routine, or one for the adjournment of the debate or of the meeting (*m*). When a motion in its original or amended form is adopted it becomes a resolution, that is to say, the decision or determination of the meeting on the particular subject under consideration. That every amendment must be relevant to the subject-matter of a motion is a fundamental principle (*n*).

15. How motions and amendments thereto are "put."—In all Canadian legislative and deliberative assemblies, public bodies and meetings, motions and all amendments thereto are put by the chair in the reverse of the order in which they are made and not in the more logical but less convenient form peculiar to the English houses (*o*). That is to say, if, in Canada, a motion is first proposed, then an amendment, and next an amendment to the amendment—the full limit of such a proceeding—the sense of the meeting is taken, first on the amendment to the amendment, then on the amendment, and finally on the main motion. This usage is intelligible to every one, and is now the common law of all assemblies in this country (*p*). It is only in the case of the election of speaker that the reverse of this practice obtains (*q*).

16. How sense of an assembly is taken on a question.— The common law of parliament also provides certain methods of coming to a conclusion on any question submitted in the way just stated. When the chair is of the opinion that the meeting is ready to close the debate, he will first submit the question to the voice of the meeting (*r*), and give his opinion whether the "yeas" or

(*m*) See *below*, p. 30.

(*n*) See *below*, p. 33, for parliamentary rule respecting motions.

(*o*) See Sir Reginald Palgrave's remarks on this point, cited in Bourinot's "Parliamentary Procedure," 2d ed. p. 387, *n*.

(*p*) See *below*, p. 34, for parliamentary rule as to the putting of questions and amendments thereto.

(*q*) See *above*, p. 8; and *below*, p. 27.

(*r*) For taking "voices," see *below*, p. 41.

"nays" prevail. If he cannot decide by the voices, then the rules of parliament require that five members rise, and the names of the yeas and nays be duly recorded in accordance with the method in vogue. In ordinary public meetings a show of hands (s) is only necessary as a rule, and a poll, or a recording of the names (t), is peculiar to more formal assemblies governed by strict rules. Municipal councils, generally speaking, follow the practice of legislative bodies. In some assemblies and societies, a ballot is required (u) by the rules. All of which will be explained in the proper place.

17. **Debate of a motion or question.**—Every member of an assembly has a right to discuss every question in accordance with the rules and usages of the body. The common law of parliament gives no limit to the length of a speech, but it is expedient in public bodies, whose meetings are held only at fixed periods, and the transaction of business should be expedited, to fix the duration of speeches on questions (v). It is a well understood rule that a reply should be allowed only to the mover of a *substantive* question— that is to say, a main question, to which amendments can be proposed—and not to the mover of an amendment, though if a new question is proposed—the adjournment of the debate, or a new amendment—then the member who has not spoken to those questions can speak again (w). The old common law of parliament still exists in Canada and the closure in the form now adopted in England has not yet reached the house of commons of the Dominion.

18. **The previous question.**—In the parliament and legislative assemblies of Canada the previous question, as it long existed in the English commons—an ingenious method of avoiding a direct vote on a question—is still in force. No form of proceeding is less understood in public assemblies generally than

(s) For a "show of hands," see *below*, p. 70.

(t) For "yeas and nays," see *below*, p. 76.

(u) For "ballot," see *below*, p. 77.

(v) See *Fifth Part*, II, sec. 6; Toronto Rule 20, etc., for limitation of speeches in certain municipal councils.

(w) See *below*, p. 38, for parliamentary rule on this subject.

this method of bringing a meeting to a direct vote on a particular question (x). If a question is before a meeting, a member may prevent any amendment by proposing that the "question be now put." The chairman will propose the motion like any other, but this does not mean that the meeting is precluded from continuing the discussion on the main motion, unless there is a special rule limiting the practice of parliament. On the contrary, the debate goes on as before under our general parliamentary law, and it is only when the meeting proceeds to give a final decision that the effect of the previous question is at once felt. If the meeting decide by a majority vote that "the question be now put," then a vote must be immediately taken without amendment or debate on the original question; or, if the meeting negative the motion that "the question be now put," then no vote can be taken at all on the original motion, since the house has decided that the question shall *not now* be put—in other words, it is practically effaced for the time being (y). This suspending or removal from debate of the main motion in case an assembly negative the previous question is rarely understood in public bodies and municipal councils, some of which, like that of Toronto (z), entirely change the parliamentary rule and allow debate and amendment on the main motion if the majority reject the previous question, " Shall the main motion be *now* put ? " Such debate and amendment are clearly irreconcilable with the decision of the majority and the origin and purpose of the previous question. As the object generally of moving the previous question is to prevent a decision on the main motion or question, the mover and seconder may vote against their own motion for the previous question in order to swell the vote against the original and objectionable motion. The ancient form of the previous question, "That the question be not put," is preferable and would prevent such an anomaly as just stated ; and in fact, it

(x) See *below*, p 36, for parliamentary form of the previous question.

(y) See Bourinot, p. 398 ; May's Practice (8th ed.) p. 283 ; Cushing's Practice, (large ed.), p. 551 ; Roberts' Rules of Order, p. 52.

(z) See *Fifth Part*, II. sec. 16, Rule 37.

is now the form in the English commons. The previous question, however, cannot be moved in a committee of the whole (a).

But the all important point to be impressed on those who use the previous question as practised in parliament, without being thoroughly conversant with its nature, is that, while it prevents any amendment on the main motion—that is to say, if an amendment has been already proposed, the previous question cannot be moved except that amendment be first withdrawn—it does not stop discussion on the main subject under consideration until the meeting comes to a vote.

The misapprehension that generally exists, as to the proper use, and the necessary consequence of the previous question, has arisen from confusing the rules of legislative assemblies of the United States with the common parliamentary law of Canada, alone applicable to this particular matter. In the United States the previous question takes precedence of every debatable question, is not debatable, and cannot be amended. When a member calls for the previous question, the chair must immediately put the question, "Shall the main question be now put?" If this is carried by a two-thirds vote, all debate instantly ceases, and a vote is forced at once on the question under discussion. If the previous question is negatived, then the main question is again debatable. The previous question in United States assemblies can also be asked and ordered upon a single motion, a series of motions allowable under the rules, or an amendment or amendments. In case of an amendment the form of the question may be, "Shall the amendment be now put?" If adopted, debate is closed on the amendment only. After the amendment has been voted upon, the main question is again open to debate and amendments. So in the same way it can be moved on an amendment to an amendment. In fact, all questions are put to vote in order and without debate. It will therefore be seen that the previous question among our neighbours is moved under conditions very different from those in practice among us.

(a) See *below*, p. 37.

In all those cases, the moving of the previous question is under special rules and cannot be otherwise applied in Canada, where the common parliamentary law, as explained in the first two paragraphs, can alone govern. If there is to be no debate when the previous question is proposed, the rule must so specifically state (b). *In the absence of this or other definite rule of closure, the law of parliament in this country must prevail.*

19. Object of all rules—due deliberation.—The primary object of all parliamentary rules is to ensure due deliberation and the orderly discussion of every question. Hence, notice is necessary of all substantive motions, but not of amendments or of motions for adjournment or for the previous question or other subsidiary or dilatory motions. All measures involving the expenditure of public money cannot be hastily adopted, but should be initiated in committee of the whole and pass through their necessary stages on different days (c). No two stages of any bill should be taken at the same sitting except on urgent occasions, of which the house or assembly must be the sole judge; and every bill should be considered in committee of the whole where each clause can be separately discussed with that freedom which is best calculated to ensure accuracy in the details of the measure (d).

20. Relevancy of debate.—To prevent a waste of time and ensure a decision as soon as possible on a question at issue, it is the duty of the chair to maintain the relevancy of debate, and keep members to the subject under discussion. All acrimonious personal attacks and the attribution of unworthy motives are

(b) It will be seen hereafter that in the majority of cases the rules of municipal councils and other assemblies make the previous question undebatable.

For cases of parliamentary rule, *i.e.*, the previous question debatable: see *Fifth Part*, II. sec. 16.

For cases where the previous question is not debatable, and the closure is practically in force, see *Ibid.*

I give also in the *Fifth Part*, III. sec. 9, a form that might be advantageously used according as it is wished to have the previous question debatable or undebatable.

(c) See *below*, p. 47, for parliamentary rule governing money votes and committee of supply.

(d) See *below*, p. 53, for parliamentary rules on bills.

promptly repressed. No one can interrupt a speaker except with his own consent or by rising to a question of order which must be succinctly stated, and decided by the chair with promptitude. Every rule or usage that governs debate mean due deliberation, courteous speech and relevancy of argument (*e*).

21. Question once decided not renewable as a rule in same session.—A question once decided cannot be brought up in the same session, but the rules provide for the rescinding of a resolution passed in the affirmative, after due notice of a motion to that effect, to be taken up and considered at a subsequent meeting. A question once decided in the negative cannot be brought up in the same terms, though there are instances in parliamentary history of an evasion of the rule by such an alteration of the original motion as to give a sort of justification of a procedure most questionable however in principle (*f*). These few exceptions, however, only prove the rule. In the case of bills, every stage is open to an amendment, whether accepted or negatived in a previous stage, as the great object of parliament is to give every possible facility for the discussion and consideration of bills which may become the law of the land.

22. Reconsideration.—The " reconsideration " of a question already decided, is, however, provided for in the rules of legislative and other assemblies in the United States, and in not a few public bodies in Canada. Consequently the rule admits not only of rescinding, as with us, a motion passed in the affirmative, but also of reconsidering a vote passed in the negative. The practice that generally prevails is to make a motion to reconsider on the same day, when the question was decided, or upon the following day, or at the succeeding meeting, but not necessarily to act upon the motion to reconsider on the same day. In fact, notice is practically given for reconsideration at another meeting. It is well to adhere as far as possible in this country to the usages of parliament; but, as it must be admitted there may at times be a necessity to reconsider a

---

(*e*) See *below*, p. 37, for parliamentary rules respecting debate.

(*f*) See *below*, p. 32, for parliamentary rule respecting the renewal of a ques. tion in same session.

hasty action of public bodies, whose meetings or sessions are relatively short and not always able to give that ample discussion usual to legislative assemblies, the rules should provide a power to that effect, but the conditions and circumstances under which the reconsideration should take place must be carefully indicated in the regulations. Hence the rules of municipal councils and other bodies, with limited sessions, generally provide that, after any question has been decided, " any member may at the same, or at the first meeting held thereafter, move for a reconsideration thereof; but no discussion of the main question shall be allowed unless reconsidered, and there shall be no reconsideration unless notice of such consideration be given at the meeting at which the main motion is carried ; and after such motion is given no action shall be taken by the council on the main motion until such reconsideration is disposed of." It is also wisely provided in some rules that a motion for reconsideration shall not be allowed unless a majority at least, or even two-thirds, of the meeting agree to such reconsideration ; and again, that " no question shall be reconsidered more than once nor shall a vote to reconsider be reconsidered." An American authority (Roberts) suggests very properly that " where a permanent society has meetings weekly or monthly, and usually only a small proportion of the society is present, it seems best to allow a reconsideration to hold over to another meeting so that the society may have notice of what action is about to be taken." *If an assembly has no special rule, then*, as Cushing states very properly in his manual, " *a motion to reconsider must be considered in the same light as any other motion, and as subject to no other rules.*" That is the reason why I urge a clear rule on the subject in every society or assembly (*g*).

(*g*) See special rules of Hamilton, London, Ottawa, and other city councils for reconsideration, *Fifth Part*, II. sec. 24. Dr. Neely, Parliamentary Practice, p. 68, says, that the motion "must be made, excepting when the vote is by ballot, by a member who voted with the prevailing side ; which may be a minority of more than one-third on a question requiring a two-thirds vote, or where there is a tie vote, by the negative."

The following citations from American authorities on other points will be useful to those Canadian bodies which adopt the American practice in its entirety :

23. **Committees of the whole and select committees.—** Every legislative or deliberative assembly has the right to form itself in committee of the whole body with a chairman to preside over its proceedings instead of the speaker, or permanent presiding officer, and to appoint small select committees of a fixed number of members to give particular consideration to certain matters to the details of which the whole assembly cannot so conveniently attend. The great advantage of committees of the whole is the free discussion of details, without members being confined to one speech on a question. It is important, however, that in these committees the rule of relevancy should be maintained and the

" When the previous question has been partly executed, it cannot be reconsidered. The motion to reconsider can be applied to votes on all questions, excepting on motions to *adjourn* and to *suspend the rules*, and affirmative votes on motions *to lie on the table* or *to take from the table.*

" When the motion is applied to a vote on a *subsidiary motion* [for subsidiary motions, see *below*, p. 25n.], it takes precedence of the *main question.*

" It yields to *incidental motions* and all *privileged questions*, [see for such questions note *below*, p. 25n.], except for the *orders of the day*. A vote on an amendment, whether carried or lost, which has been followed by a vote on the motion to which the amendment was proposed, cannot be reconsidered until after the vote on the original motion has been reconsidered.

" When the motion to reconsider properly applies to a vote, it cannot be made during the day on which said vote was taken, when any other business is before the house, even when another member has the floor, or the meeting is voting on the motion to *adjourn*, but action on the motion cannot be taken to interfere with current business, but must be deferred until the business then before the house is disposed of.

" In such a case the motion is made and seconded and entered upon the minutes, then the business before the house proceeds, and the motion to reconsider is held over to be called up at any time before the close of the session. As soon as the subject interrupted has been disposed of the reconsideration, if called up, takes precedence of all other motions, except to adjourn and to fix the time to which to adjourn."—Neely.

" The effect of making this motion is to suspend all action that the original motion would have acquired until the reconsideration has been acted upon ; but, if it is not called up, its effect terminates with the session, provided that, in an assembly having regular meetings as often as monthly, if there is not held upon another day an adjourned meeting of the one at which the reconsideration was moved, its effect shall not terminate till the close of the next succeeding session. But the reconsideration of an *incidental* or *subsidiary motion* (except where the vote

members kept as strictly as possible to the subject of each particular clause of the bill, or item of a resolution that is before it. In bodies like municipal councils, ecclesiastical bodies and associations generally, where time is of special value, it is frequently of advantage to have a rule limiting each member to remarks of five or ten minutes on each question as it presents itself. When every line of a clause or resolution is a question, it is evident that sufficient latitude would be given to every member to express his views in case of a limitation of speaking (*h*).

24. **Importance of standing and special committees.**— Standing and special committees in legislative and deliberative bodies—especially in municipal councils—have very useful and important functions to perform. The report of every committee must be signed by the chairman, and be the report of the majority —minority reports as such being unknown in parliament (*i*).

to be reconsidered had the effect to remove the whole subject from before the assembly) shall be immediately acted upon, as, otherwise, it would prevent action on the main question."—Roberts.

" The motion to reconsider cannot be amended, and it is debatable or not, just as the question proposed to be reconsidered is debatable or undebatable. If debatable, then it opens up for debate the entire subject which it is proposed to consider. If the *previous question* is ordered while this motion is pending, it affects only the motion to reconsider. The motion to reconsider can be laid on the table, and, in such instances, the last motion cannot be reconsidered. If laid on the table, the reconsideration can, like any other motion, be taken from the table, but possess no privilege.

" When the motion to reconsider is laid on the table, it does not carry with it the pending measure. If this motion prevails then the question which the meeting has decided to reconsider is in the exact position it held just before the vote was taken, and, if debatable, it can be discussed as though no vote had been taken. Hence, if, in the former discussion, a member exhausted his privilege of debate, he cannot discuss it further without permission, but he may manage to present his views during the consideration of the motion to reconsider."—Neely.

" A reconsideration of a vote in committee shall be allowed regardless of the time elapsed, only when every member who voted with the majority is present when the reconsideration is moved."—Roberts (p. 70), who adds in a note : " No improper advantage can be taken of the privilege, as long as every member who voted with the majority must be present when the reconsideration is moved."

(*h*) See *below*, p. 44, for parliamentary rules regulating committees of the whole.

(*i*) See *below*, p. 48, for parliamentary rules regulating select committees.

Neither a committee of the whole nor a select committee has any other authority except what is given it in its power of reference by the body that constitutes or appoints it; and all its acts must be duly ratified or sanctioned by an assembly before they can legally bind the same.

25. **Reports of committees.**—The reports of committees of the whole, and of standing and special committees, are made to the assembly by the chairman, or in his absence by a member of the committee; and motions for its reception, consideration, and adoption should be proposed in regular form. On bringing up a report, the chairman of the committee—or the clerk of the assembly as a rule—should read it at length unless the document is printed—like a manager's or director's report—and in the hands of every member, when the reading can be dispensed with if the meeting so order. After the reading, a motion should be made "That the report of [*subject*] be considered immediately," or at some future time. Ordinary reports can be taken up on the same day they are made, but those involving important points of policy or constitutional changes, or matters of expenditure or taxation ought to be considered at a subsequent meeting as a rule. When it is under consideration, a motion can be made for its adoption as a whole; or it can be taken up resolution by resolution, or paragraph by paragraph, if it should contain separate recommendations or propositions, on each of which the sense of the meeting can be most conveniently and regularly taken (*j*).

26. **Dilatory motions for adjournment, etc.**—The motions for adjournment of the house, adjournment of the debate—two motions as a rule, always in order on a question—and the previous question, are well known methods by which decisions on a question are delayed or superseded for the time being. In committees of the whole, motions, "That the chairman do rise and report progress," or "That the chairman do leave the chair," are also dilatory and superseding motions, and are equivalent to the motions for the adjournment of the debate and of the house. The motions for the adjournment of the

(*j*) See *below*, p. 50, for parliamentary rules respecting reports from committees.

house and for the chairman to leave the chair, supersede the question entirely, though it can be renewed again on a subsequent day. If the chairman leaves the chair no report is made, and there is no question before the house. While these several motions are, generally speaking, "always in order," they are also subject to certain restrictions which are explained in a later place (*k*).

To lay on the table.

In addition to these well known rules of parliamentary procedure, many municipal councils, companies and associations have adopted from the procedure of the United States, motions "to postpone" a question, or "to lay it upon the table" or to "commit it," which are also of a dilatory nature (*l*).

According to American authorities, as I am for the moment leaving the domain of Canadian parliamentary law, a member who wishes to carry a question to the table, that is to say, prevent its consideration until a majority vote to resume it, will move, "That the question be laid on the table." This motion cannot be debated, or reconsidered when it is adopted in the affirmative, or interrupted by any amendment or subsidiary motion. If the motion "to lay

(*k*) See *below*, p. 46, for parliamentary rule respecting such dilatory motions in committee of the whole; for adjournment of the house, *below*, p. 33, for adjournment of the debate, *below*, p. 33.

(*l*) The American (U. S.) books (see Roberts, p. 28) place the following among "subsidiary" or "secondary" motions, because they can be "applied to other motions for the purpose of most appropriately disposing of them." They take precedence of a principal question, and must be decided before the principal question can be acted upon. They yield to "privileged" and "incidental" questions (for meaning of such questions see *below*, p. 25*n*,) and are arranged in the following order of precedence ;—

1. Lie on the table.
2. The previous question.
3. Postpone to a certain day.
4. Commit.
5. Amend.
6. Postpone indefinitely.

Roberts adds that "any of these motions (except to amend), can be made when one of a lower order is pending, but none can supersede one of a higher order." For meaning and operation of "precedence" of one of these motions over another, see *Fourth Part*, II., Methodist Conference, Rule 10.

on the table " is decided in the negative, the business proceeds as
if no motion had been made. If decided in the affirmative, the
effect, in general, is to remove from before the assembly the principal motion and all other motions, subsidiary or incidental, that are
connected with it (*m*). When it is desired to take up a question
thus tabled, a member will move that the assembly do now
proceed to consider the question laid on the table (its nature and
time of tabling should be specified) and this motion, which is
undebatable, and not open to amendments or subsidiary motions,
must be submitted to the decision of the assembly, a majority of
whom alone can order the consideration asked for.

To postpone to a specified time.

To postpone to a certain time, or to postpone indefinitely, are
two other forms of proceeding which are practically equivalent to
the ordinary motions for the adjournment of a debate, or the
adjournment of the house, or for laying on the table. According
to American authorities, if the motion to postpone for a specified
time is decided affirmatively, the subject to which it is applied
is removed from before the body with all its appendages and
incidents. The motion can be amended as respects the time, is
open to the previous question and is debatable not as respects the
merits of the subject of the original question, but only as respects
the advisability of the proposed postponement. If the motion is
carried, the matter cannot be taken up before that specified time
except by a two-thirds vote ; but when it is reached, it is a question
having the priority over all questions except those that are
privileged. Questions postponed to different times, but not then

(*m*) Dr. Neely (pp. 44, 45) adds : " There are a few exceptions, thus : as a
question of privilege does not adhere to the subject it interrupts, it does not carry
with it to the table the question pending when it was raised ; an appeal laid on the
table does not carry with it the original subject ; a motion to reconsider, when laid
on the table, leaves the original question where it was before the reconsideration
was made ; an amendment to the minutes, being laid on the table, does not carry
the minutes with it. It is in order to lay upon the table the questions still before
the body, even after the previous question has been ordered and up to the moment
of taking the last vote under it." See also Roberts, ss. 19, 57b, 59c ; Spofford's
Parliamentary Rules, p, 137.

taken up shall, when considered, be taken up in the order of the times to which they were postponed (*n*).

To postpone indefinitely.

To postpone indefinitely has the object and effect of superseding or suppressing a question altogether, without coming to a direct vote. The motion cannot be amended, but it opens to debate the entire question it proposes to postpone. If the previous question is ordered when this motion is pending, the previous question is applicable only to the same (*o*).

These two motions of postponement are chiefly useful in legislative and deliberative assemblies that have a session for a considerable time. In such assemblies the motions cannot extend beyond the present session—one session cannot bind the next. In the cases of municipal councils, or societies, or of companies' meetings, that have limited sittings on one day, a motion to postpone indefinitely cannot have any effect, and the only one of practical value is to postpone for the particular meeting, or until the next assembling or session—here synonymous terms, as before explained (*p*). The question thus postponed comes up with the unfinished business of the previous meeting, and consequently should take precedence of new business. If the meeting at which the motion "to postpone" simply is carried, should be only adjourned, the question could not be taken up at the adjourned meeting, since it would seem that the meeting would be one and the same. If it is desired to hold an adjourned meeting to consider a special subject the time to which the assembly shall adjourn should be first fixed before making the motion to postpone the subject to that day (*q*).

To commit in American practice.

Another subsidiary motion, subject in American assemblies and societies to special rules, is "to commit" or "recommit" a subject

(*n*) See Neely, p. 49 ; Roberts, pp. 53, 156.

(*o*) See Neely, p. 53 ; Roberts, pp. 59, 160.

(*p*) See *above*, p. 7.

(*q*) See Roberts, p. 54.

with the view of considering and amending it more in details than is possible in the whole body. As I have previously shown (*above*, p. 19) a reference to committees is a common and useful parliamentary practice; but in United States and (a few) Canadian assemblies the motion is subject to certain conditions like the other subsidiary motions I have been just dealing with. This motion takes precedence of the motions to amend or indefinitely postpone, but yields to such "privileged" questions as to adjourn, call for orders of the day, fixing the time to which the body shall adjourn, questions relating to the rights or privileges of the assembly; also to such "incidental" (*r*) questions as appeals or questions of order, objection to the consideration of a question, reading of papers, suspension of rules, leave to withdraw a motion; and also to the motion to lie on the table, or for the previous question, or to postpone to a certain day. It can be amended by altering the committee or giving it instructions. It is debatable and, like a similar motion in parliament, opens up the merits of the whole question which it is proposed to refer (*s*).

27. General remarks on the foregoing motions.—All these motions to reconsider, to lay on the table, to postpone to a specified time or indefinitely, and also to commit under the conditions just stated are, as I have already said, not drawn from the practice of our parliament, and it is consequently obvious that questions of doubt that may arise in Canadian assemblies that have adopted the procedure in simple terms cannot be solved by reference to our parliamentary law. Under these circumstances, it is customary to

(*r*) Roberts (pp. 29, 30) explains that in American practice "incidental questions" are such as arise out of other questions and take consequently precedence of and are decided before those questions to which they are incident. They yield to privileged questions and cannot be amended. Excepting an appeal they cannot be debated. "Privileged questions" are such as, on account of their importance, take precedence of all other questions whatever, and are consequently undebatable except in cases relating to the rights of the assembly or its members. I give in the text the incidental and privileged questions mentioned by the same American authority. They all form part of a very complicated procedure which has no status in Canadian assemblies unless formally adopted.

(*s*) Roberts, pp. 54, 155.

refer to United States authorities, but as this reference may not be always conclusive on account of the procedure being mixed up with "incidental," "privileged," "subsidiary" and other motions peculiar to American practice, it is advisable, when our councils or other public bodies adopt it, to frame these special rules so as to make them workable and intelligible under all circumstances (*t*).

I repeat emphatically : *Unless the rules are made clear in every particular and there is a general reference in all cases of doubt to recognized United States authorities, like Roberts, or Neely, or Cushing, all such dilatory and subsidiary motions, as I have been reviewing in the foregoing paragraphs, can only be subject to the rules that govern all motions in Canadian parliamentary procedure and to none other (u).*

28. **Importance of rules of order.**—The writer need only add, in closing these general observations, that his long experience of parliamentary and public bodies generally has taught him the wisdom of adhering as closely as possible to those rules and usages that illustrate the common sense and business habits of Englishmen and their descendants, as well as their desire to give every opportunity for the discussion of public questions and measures. Laxity of procedure is antagonistic to the successful prosecution of business.

So far, I have only attempted to give a short review of those leading principles that govern, generally speaking, assemblies. In the following pages the reader will find *a summary of those rules and usages which are common to all legislative assemblies in this country, and may be properly called the common law of parliament,* to which reference can be made by those bodies which find their own regulations insufficient to solve the questions of doubt that must constantly arise in practice.

(*t*) By reference to other parts of this work (see especially *Fifth Part*, II. sec. 15) it will be seen that many assemblies, municipal councils and other bodies have special rules on these dilatory and superseding motions, giving them certain precedence and making them undebatable in particular cases.

(*u*) See *above*, p. 18.

II. A SUMMARY OF THE RULES AND USAGES OF PARLIAMENT.

(Applicable to public bodies generally.)

References are given throughout to Bourinot's Parliamentary Procedure, 2nd ed.

1. ELECTION OF SPEAKER (*a*).

A member, addressing himself to the clerk, proposes another member then present to the house for their speaker, and moves that such member "do take the chair of this house as speaker."

The motion being seconded, and after debate thereon, if no other member be proposed, the question is put by the clerk, and the member thus proposed is elected *nemine contradicente*.

If more than one member be proposed as speaker, a motion is made and seconded regarding each such member, "that he do take the chair of this house as speaker," etc.

(*a*) For election of speaker in full, see Bourinot, pp. 274-277.

A question is then put by the clerk that the member first proposed " do take the chair of this house as speaker," which is resolved in the affirmative or negative, like other questions.

If the question be resolved in the affirmative, the member is conducted to the chair; but, if in the negative, a question is then put by the clerk, that the member next proposed "do take the chair of this house as speaker," and, if the question be resolved in the affirmative, the member is conducted to the chair.

The speaker elect, being conducted to the chair by the members who proposed and seconded the motion for his election, stands on the upper step of the chair and returns his acknowledgments to the house for the great honour they have been pleased to confer upon him.

2. Duties of Speaker (b).

The speaker shall not take part in any debate before the house.

See *below*, p. 42, for speaker's vote in case of an equality of votes.

The speaker shall preserve order and decorum, and shall decide questions of order, subject to an appeal to the house; in explaining a point of order or practice, he shall state the rule or authority applicable to the case.

Whenever the speaker is of opinion that a motion offered to the house is contrary to the rules and privileges of parliament, he shall apprise the house thereof immediately, before putting the question thereon, and quote the rule or authority applicable to the case.

It is the duty of the speaker to interrupt a member who makes use of any language which is clearly out of order.

3. Attendance of Members (c).

Every member is bound to attend the service of the house, unless leave of absence is given to him by the house. Leave of absence may be given by the house to a member, on account of his

(b) For duties of speaker, see Bourinot, pp. 213-215.

(c) See Bourinot, pp. 190, 191.

own illness, or of the illness or death of a near relation, or of urgent business, or for other cause, stated to and deemed sufficient by the house. While he has leave of absence, a member is excused from service in the house or on a committee.

4. QUORUM (d).

Whenever the speaker shall adjourn the house for want of a quorum, the time of the adjournment, and the names of the members then present, shall be inserted in the journal.

When the attention of the speaker has been called to the want of a quorum, (twenty members including the speaker), he proceeds to count the members present, while the bells are being rung. Members are counted as they come in. If there is no quorum, the clerk takes down the names, and records them in the journal, with the time when the speaker so adjourned the house.

For procedure in committee of the whole, see last paragraph *below*.

If the house should be suddenly adjourned in consequence of the absence of a quorum, a question then under consideration of the house will disappear from the order paper for the time being.

But a question may be revived after notice, and taken up at the stage where it was temporarily superseded. Some municipal councils provide for such cases by a special rule. The same rule applies to the case of a question superseded by an adjournment : see *below*, p. 33.

If it be shown by a division or otherwise that there is not a quorum present in a committee of the whole, the chairman will count the members and leave the chair, when the speaker will again count the house. If there is not a quorum present, he will adjourn the house ; but if there are twenty members in their places, the committee will be resumed.

5. ORDER OF BUSINESS (e).

The clerk of the house shall place on the speaker's table, every morning, previous to the meeting of the house, the order of the proceedings for the day.

(d) See Bourinot, pp. 298, 299.

(e) See Bourinot, p. 301 *et seq.*

A motion, even in reference to the business of the house can be taken out of its appointed order only by "universal assent" (*f*).

Such a rule is necessary to prevent members being surprised in their absence by a change of orders. One member objecting can prevent the change in parliament.

6. MOTIONS (*g*).

When a member proposes to bring any matter before either house with the view of obtaining an expression of opinion thereon, he must make a motion of which he must give due notice for consideration on some future day, unless it be one of those questions of privilege, or urgency which, as it will be shown hereafter, may be immediately considered.

For questions of privilege, see *below*, p. 40.

A motion may be made by unanimous consent of the house, without previous notice.

Such motions relate to the business of the house or some matter of urgency. No rule can be suspended except by notice or unanimous consent.

All motions shall be in writing, and seconded, before being debated or put from the chair.

Such motions of routine business as " That a bill be read a first or second or third time," etc., or " That the house do adjourn," or " That the debate be adjourned," are rarely written in parliament, nor is the motion for the previous question. Every other motion should be written.

A motion that is not seconded may not be proposed from the chair, or debated, and no entry thereof is made in the " votes."

That is to say, in the short daily record or journal called "votes and proceedings." The clerk who keeps the minutes at the table only recognizes the orders of the chair. It is only when the speaker has read or proposed a motion to the house that the clerk enters it on the journal. He takes no note of members' speeches.

No motion is regularly before the house until it has been read, or, in parliamentary language, proposed from the chair, when it

(*f*) See Bourinot, p. 308.

(*g*) See Bourinot, pp. 366-375.

becomes a question. When the house is in this way formally seized of a question, it may be debated, amended, superseded, resolved in the affirmative, or passed in the negative, as the house may decide.

See previous note, as to the duty of the clerk when a question is thus formally before the house.

The speaker reads the question at length: "Mr. A. moves, seconded by Mr. B., That, etc." And having read it, he adds, "Is it the pleasure of the house to adopt the motion?" The house is now in a position to debate the subject-matter of the motion or question thus formally proposed.

All motions should properly commence with the word "That." In this way if a motion meets the approbation of the house, it may at once become the resolution, vote, or order which it purports to be.

For instance, "That the house do adjourn," or "That in the opinion of this house it is desirable to proceed to the order of the day for the consideration of the bill providing for simultaneous voting at elections." A preamble is objectionable in any motion or proposed resolution or series of resolutions. Bills only have preambles commencing with "Whereas." When a motion is agreed to, it becomes a resolution; until then it is only a proposed resolution. It is a common practice in America to prefix such preambles to a set of resolutions, but it is at variance with correct parliamentary usage, and can be easily avoided by a careful framing of the motion.

Motions are frequently proposed and then withdrawn, but this can be done only "by leave of the house, such leave being granted without any negative voice."

A single voice can prevent such withdrawal. If there are a motion, and amendment, and an amendment thereto, all at once before the house, each must be withdrawn in due order. That is to say, the first amendment or the main motion cannot be withdrawn if the last amendment is persisted in.

In case a motion has been withdrawn, it may be again proposed as the house has not previously determined the question, and it is only in the latter event that the same question may not be revived. If an amendment has been negatived, a similar amendment cannot be proposed on a future day.

Any member may require the question under discussion to be read at any time of the debate, but not so as to interrupt a member while speaking (*h*).

Such a rule is necessary for the intelligent consideration of a question under debate, but the speaker or chairman of any assembly should not allow it to be obviously used to delay the progress of business and for the purpose of obstruction. His own judgment must be exercised in such cases to expedite business by a judicious interposition of the influence and authority of the chair.

By the rules of the house, it is irregular to propose any motion or amendment which anticipates a matter already appointed for the consideration of the house (*i*).

No question or motion can regularly be offered, if it is substantially the same with the one on which the judgment of the house has already been expressed during the current session (*j*).

But orders of the house are frequently discharged and resolutions rescinded. The latter part of the thirteenth rule of the house of commons provides: "No member may reflect upon any vote of the house, except for the purpose of moving that such vote be rescinded." In such a case, the motion will first be made to read the entry in the journals of the resolution, and when that has been done by the clerk, the next motion will be that the said resolution be rescinded, or another resolution expressing a different opinion may be agreed to (*k*).

If a motion has been negatived, it cannot be afterwards proposed in the shape of an amendment.

The only means by which a negative vote can be revoked is by proposing another question, similar in its general purport to that which had been rejected, but with sufficient variance to constitute a new question; and the house would determine whether it were substantially the same question or not (*l*).

(*h*) See Bourinot, p. 422.
(*i*) See Bourinot, p. 308.
(*j*) See Bourinot, pp. 401-403.
(*k*) See Bourinot, p. 401.
(*l*) See Bourinot, p. 402.

A motion to adjourn the house is always in order, and if carried supersedes the question under consideration. See *above*, p. 29.

A motion of this kind, when made to supersede a question, should be simply, " That the house do now adjourn," and it is not allowable to move an adjournment to a future day, or to propose an amendment to the question of adjournment (*m*).

A motion for the adjournment of the house may be made while a matter is under discussion, or in the interval of proceedings. In the first case, such a motion is in the nature of a dilatory or subsidiary motion and in the other it is a substantive motion to which a reply is permitted to the member who makes it (*n*). If the motion is negatived it cannot be renewed until after an intermediate proceeding.

A motion for the adjournment of the debate should be pure and simple, like the motion for the adjournment of the house (*o*).

7. AMENDMENTS (*p*).

Amendments must be relevant to a motion or question.

If they are on the same subject-matter with the original motion they are admissible, but not when foreign thereto (*q*).

Every member has the right of moving an amendment to a motion without giving notice thereof. This amendment may propose :

1. To leave out certain words ;

2. To leave out certain words, in order to insert or add others ;

3. To insert or add certain words.

But such an amendment is subject to the condition of the rule with respect to order of business, *above*, p. 30 ; for otherwise the house might be surprised into considering a question set down for another and later day.

(*m*) See Bourinot, pp. 395, 396, 413-415.

(*n*) See Bourinot, pp. 413-416.

(*o*) See Bourinot, p. 396.

(*p*) For amendments, see Bourinot, pp. 385-394.

(*q*) See Bourinot, p. 392.

When it is proposed to amend a motion, the question is put to the house in this way: The speaker will first state the original motion, "Mr. A. moves, seconded by Mr. B., that, etc." Then he will proceed to give the amendment: "To this Mr. C. moves, in amendment, seconded by Mr. D., that, etc." The speaker will put the amendment directly in the first place to the house: "Is it the pleasure of the house to adopt the amendment?" If the amendment be negatived, the speaker will again propose the main question, and a debate may ensue thereon, or another amendment may then be submitted. On the other hand, if the house adopt the amendment, then the speaker will again propose the question in these words: "Is it the pleasure of the house to adopt the main motion (or question) so amended?" It is then competent for a member to propose another amendment: "That the main motion (or question), as amended, etc., be further amended, etc."

But such amendments are subject to the limitations set forth in the three ollowing rules.

An amendment once negatived by the house cannot be proposed a second time.

When the house have agreed that certain words shall stand part of the question, it is irregular to propose any amendment to those words, as the decision of the house has already been pronounced in their favour, but this rule would not exclude an addition to the words, if proposed at the proper time.

In the same manner, when the house have agreed to add or insert words in a question, their decision may not be disturbed by any amendment of these words; but here again other words may be added.

When an amendment to the main motion has been proposed, it is competent for any member to move an amendment to the same.

8. Sense of House taken on Motions and Amendments thereto (r).

When there are a main motion, an amendment, and an amendment thereto, the speaker will ·submit the three motions in

(r) See Bourinot, pp. 388-392.

the reverse of the order in which they are made, and first take the
sense of the house on the last amendment: "Is it the pleasure of
the house to adopt the amendment to the amendment?." If this
second amendment is rejected, it is regular to move another (provided, of course, it is different in purport from the one already
negatived) as soon as the speaker has again proposed the question:
"Is it the pleasure of the house to adopt the amendment to the
main motion (or original question)?"

Only two amendments can be proposed at the same time to a
question. In other words, there can only be three questions at
one time before the house: the main motion, an amendment,
and an amendment thereto. But the motion for the adjournment
of the house or of the debate is always in order under such circumstances. See *above*, p. 33.

When a proposition or question before the house consists of
several sections, paragraphs, or resolutions, the order of considering and amending it is to begin at the commencement and to proceed through it in course by paragraphs; and when a latter part
has been amended, it is not in order to recur back, and make any
amendment or alteration of a former part.

Sometimes it may be necessary to refer to a previous paragraph incidentally
for the purpose of explaining or illustrating an argument on the second paragraph; but a continuance of the former discussion would be out of order.

If an amendment be resolved in the affirmative, it will not be
competent to move that it be struck out, in whole or in part.

Amendments may, however, be proposed to add words to the
main motion, or amendment, as amended.

No addition can be made to a question after the house has
decided that the words proposed to be left out should stand part of
the question.

9. DIVISION OF A QUESTION (s).

The ancient rule that when a complicated question is proposed
to the house, the house may order such question to be divided, is
applied as follows: When two or more separate propositions are

(s) See Bourinot, p. 371.

embodied in a motion, or in an amendment, the speaker may put
the question on such propositions separately, restricting debate to
each proposition in its turn.

10. PREVIOUS QUESTION AND DILATORY MOTIONS GENERALLY (t).

The previous question, until it is decided, shall preclude all
amendment of the main question, and shall be in the following
words, "That this question be *now* put." If the previous question be resolved in the affirmative, the original question is to
be put forthwith without any amendment or debate.

This parliamentary rule allows debate to continue on the main motion,
after the previous question has been proposed.

This important and not always understood motion is fully explained elsewhere in this work. See

1. General remarks on the subject of the previous question, *above*,
   p. 13.
2. Rules of city and other councils which stop all amendment and debate
   when the previous question is once proposed, *Fifth Part*, II. sec. 16.

No amendment may be proposed to the motion for the previous
question.   Neither can it be proposed when there is an amendment
under consideration.   If the previous question has actually been
proposed it must be withdrawn before any amendment can be
submitted to the house.   If an amendment has been first proposed,
it must be disposed of before a member can move the previous
question.

The motion, "That the house do now adjourn," can be
made to the motions for the previous question and for reading the orders of the day.   But such a motion cannot be made
if the house resolves that the question shall now be put.   It is
also perfectly in order to move the adjournment of the debate on
the previous question.   When a motion has been made for reading
the orders of the day, in order to supersede a question, the house
will not afterwards entertain a motion for the previous question,
as the former motion was of itself in the nature of a previous
question.   It is allowable to move the previous question on the
different stages of bills.

(*t*) See Bourinot, pp. 394-400.

While it is not allowable to move the previous question in a committee of the whole on a bill or resolution, a motion " That the chairman do leave the chair" (see *below*, p. 46) has practically the same effect as the previous question of anticipating and preventing a decision on a question under consideration. See Bourinot, p. 486 ; May, p. 433 (9th edition).

A motion to commit a bill or question, until decided, shall preclude all amendment of the main question.

That is to say, if it is proposed to commit a bill or question, it is not regular to move before committal to amend that bill or question ; but it is quite in order to reject the motion to go into committee thereon, or to propose a motion against the principle of such bill or question, which, when carried, would prevent committal. The object of going into committee is to amend the details or subject-matter of the question there considered.

11. RULES OF DEBATE (*u*).

Every member desiring to speak is to rise in his place, uncovered, and address himself to Mr. Speaker.

By the special indulgence of the house a member, disabled by sickness or infirmity, is permitted to speak sitting and uncovered.

When two or more members rise to speak, Mr. Speaker calls upon the member who first rose in his place ; but a motion may be made that any member who has risen " be now heard," or " do now speak."

In such a case, the house determines as in the case of any other question submitted to its decision. First, by the voices, and secondly, by a division, if necessary.

A new member, who has not yet spoken, is generally called upon, by courtesy, in preference to other members rising at the same time.

A member is not to read his speech, but may refresh his memory by reference to notes.

No member is to allude to any debate of the same session upon a question or bill, not being then under discussion, except by the indulgence of the house for a personal explanation.

Every member who addresses the house should endeavour to confine himself as closely as possible to the question under consid-

(*u*) See Bourinot, c. 11, pp. 404-443.

eration. If the speaker, or the house, believes that his remarks are not relevant to the question he will be promptly called to order by the former.

No member may refer to a member by name.

The rule requiring that speeches should be relevant to the motion immediately under consideration has never been yet applied in the Canadian houses to motions for the adjournment of the house or of the debate.

No member may speak twice to a question, except in explanation of a material part of his speech, in which he may have been misconceived, but then he is not to introduce new matter. A reply is allowed to a member who has made a substantive motion to the house, but not to any member who has moved an order of the day, an amendment, the previous question, or an instruction to a committee (*v*).

A "substantive" means the main or first motion or question, to which amendments may be moved. If, when there is no substantive motion before the house, in other words, no subject under debate, a member moves "That the house do now adjourn," for the sake of bringing into discussion some question of urgency, that motion is "substantive," and the mover has a right to reply, but should there be a question under consideration, and a member moves "that the house do now adjourn," this is a dilatory or incidental motion simply, and the mover has no reply.

When the speaker is putting a question, no member shall walk out of or across the house, or make any noise or disturbance; and when a member is speaking, no member shall interrupt him, except to order, nor pass between him and the chair; and no member may pass between the chair and the table, nor between the chair and the mace when the mace has been taken off the table by the serjeant-at-arms (*w*).

No member shall speak disrespectfully of her majesty, nor of any of the royal family, nor of the governor or person administering the government of Canada; nor shall he use offensive words against either house, or against any member thereof, nor shall he

(*v*) See Bourinot, p. 417.

(*w*) See Bourinot, pp. 405, 406.

speak beside the question in debate. No member may reflect upon any vote of the house, except for the purpose of moving that such vote be rescinded (x).

A member may rise to speak "to order," or upon a matter of privilege suddenly arising (y).

A member called to order shall sit down, but may afterwards explain. The house, if appealed to, shall decide on the case, but without debate. If there be no appeal, the decision of the chair shall be final (z).

See mode of appeal under such circumstances, *below*, sec. 12.

Every member against whom any charge has been made, having been heard in his place, should withdraw while such charge is under debate (a).

The charge may be embodied in a motion or in a statement made by a member in his place. If such a motion or statement, involving the character or conduct or language of a member, is to be made, due notice should be given him that he may be present to reply. When he has made his statement, then he withdraws.

See also *below*, p. 44, for withdrawal when it is a question of his vote.

12. CALL TO ORDER (b).

It is the right of a member to rise and call another member to order. He must state the point of order clearly and succinctly, and it will be for the speaker to decide whether the point is well taken.

When a member rises to a point of order—that is when he believes a rule or usage has been violated by a motion or in a speech—and in the latter event he may interrupt a speaker—he should say " I rise to a point of order." The speaker will say, " Please state your point of order." The objecting member must do this "succinctly," and no member can attempt under cover of his objection to discuss the subject-matter under debate. The speaker in case of special difficulty may ask opinions of members, but when he decides he should

(x) See Bourinot, pp. 410, 411.

(y) See *below*, p. 40.

(z) See Bourinot, p. 432.

(a) See Bourinot, pp. 430, 440-442.

(b) See Bourinot, p. 432.

not argue but simply give his opinion authoritatively. If a member is not satisfied with the decision he should rise and say, " I appeal from the decision of the chair," The speaker will then put the question, which is undebatable (see *above*, p. 39) by first giving the terms of his decision, and the point or appeal, and add, " The question is now, shall the decision of the chair stand as the judgment of the house? Those who are in favour of the motion will say aye." Then when the voices have been given for the ayes he will say, " Those who are against the motion will say no." If the voices are doubtful and the names are demanded by five members, he will again submit the question and the roll will be called in accordance with usage. It may be added that when the speaker is on his feet every member should sit down until the former concludes what he has to say on the point of order.

13. Questions of Privilege (c).

A motion directly concerning the privileges of the house, which calls for its present interposition on a matter which has recently arisen, takes immediate precedence of all other business before the house, and is moved without notice.

Questions of privilege refer to all matters affecting the rights and immunities of the house collectively, or the position and conduct of members in their representative character.

14. Breaches of Parliamentary Decorum (d).

When a member has been called to order by the speaker, for a breach of parliamentary decorum, it is his duty to bow at once to the decision of the chair, and to make an apology by explaining that he did not intend to infringe any rule of debate, or by immediately withdrawing the offensive and unparliamentary language he may have used. In case, however, a member persists in his unparliamentary conduct, the speaker will be compelled to *name* him, and submit his conduct to the judgment of the house.

In such a case the member whose conduct is in question should explain and withdraw, and it will be for the house to consider what course to pursue in reference to him.

(c) See Bourinot, pp. 375-379.
(d) See Bourinot, pp. 433, 434.

15. Words Taken Down (e).

When a member makes use of any disorderly and unparliamentary language, it is the right of another member to move that it be taken down.

When a member objects to words used in debate, and desires that those words be taken down, he repeats the words to which he objects, immediately after they have been uttered, stating them exactly as he conceives them to have been spoken. Whereupon Mr. Speaker, having ascertained that the sense of the house is in accord with the demand, directs the clerk to take down those words.

When the words have been taken down at the table and the clerk has read the words to the house, the member should explain and withdraw, and then the house will proceed to consider what course to take with reference to him.

16. Putting the Question—Divisions (f).

When a debate on a question is closed, and the house is ready to decide thereon, the speaker proceeds to " put " the question. If the question has not been heard he states it again to the house.

That is to say, the speaker says, " Is the house ready for the question?" The sense of the house being unequivocally in favour of closing the debate, and no member rising to speak, the speaker again reads the motion ; in other words he " puts " the question for a final decision thereon.

Having read the question on which the decision of the house is to be first given he takes the sense of the members by saying, " Those who are in favour of the question or amendment will say yea, those who are of the contrary opinion will say no." When the supporters and opponents of the question have given their voices for and against the same, the speaker will say, " I think the yeas have it ;" or " I think the nays (or noes) have it ;" or " I cannot decide." If the house does not acquiesce in his decision, the yeas and nays may be called for.

(e) See Bourinot, pp. 434-437.

(f) See Bourinot, chap. XIII. pp. 446-459.

In the house of commons, the speaker says, " Those who are in favour of the motion (or amendment) will please to rise." The clerk has before him a list of all the names printed alphabetically, and places a mark against each name as it is called. The assistant clerk calls out the name of each member as he stands up.

When the members in favour of the motion have all voted, the speaker says again :   " Those who are opposed to the motion (or amendment) will please to rise ; "   and then the names will be taken down in the manner just described.

When all the names have been duly taken down, the clerk will count up the votes on each side, and declare them ; the speaker will then say: "The motion is resolved in the affirmative;" or "passed in the negative," as the case may be.   If the motion on which the house has decided is a motion in amendment, then the speaker proceeds to put the next question, on which a division may also take place.

In case of an equality of votes, Mr. Speaker, or the chairman, gives the casting voice, usually in such a manner as not to make the decision of the house final (g).

Generally he gives his reason for his vote.   In municipal councils in Ontario a mayor or other head of the council or any person acting in his place, votes as a member, and in case of an equality of voices the motion is to be considered negatived.

No member may speak to any question after the same has been fully put by Mr. Speaker.

A question is fully put when the speaker has taken the voices both of the yeas and of the nays.

No member is entitled to vote upon a question upon which he has a direct pecuniary interest, not held in common with the rest of the subjects of the crown, and the vote of any member so interested will be disallowed.   The vote of such a member in a division taken in a committee of the whole house, is adjudicated upon by the committee.   A standing committee also has the like power of determining the question of a personal interest in a vote.

(g) See Bourinot, pp. 453-455.

If a member is believed to have a direct pecuniary and personal interest in a question, his attention will be called to the matter through the speaker, and, if his explanation is not satisfactory or sufficient the house will decide by voting on a motion " That A.'s vote be " disallowed." If it is disallowed the clerk will erase the vote from the record.

The rule relating to the vote upon any question in the house of a member having an interest in the matter upon which the vote is given, applies likewise to any vote of a member so interested in a committee (h).

If a member was not present in the house when the question was put by the speaker, he cannot have his vote recorded.

If he should vote under such circumstances, the speaker will ask, " Was the honourable member present in the house, and did he hear the question put ? " If he replies in the negative, his vote must be struck off the record.

If a member of the commons who has heard the question put does not vote, and the attention of the speaker is directed to the fact, the latter will call upon him to declare on which side he votes, and his name will be recorded accordingly.

Every member must vote unless he comes under the disqualifications of the foregoing rules.

If a member who has heard the question put in the commons should vote inadvertently, contrary to his intention, he cannot be allowed to correct the mistake, but his vote must remain as first recorded.

If a member's name is entered incorrectly or is inadvertently left off the list he can have it rectified should the clerk read out the names, or on the following day when he notices the error in the printed votes.

(h) See Bourinot, p. 455, for full explanation of what constitutes an interest not in common with the rest of the subjects of the crown. For instance, he may vote for an increase of pay to members of the house, but not for a direct pecuniary grant to himself alone.

In case of confusion or error concerning the numbers reported, unless the same can be otherwise corrected, the house proceeds to a second division.

When a doubt exists as to the right of a member to vote, he should be heard in explanation and then withdraw before the usual motion is made, " That the vote of ——— be disallowed " (i).

While the house is dividing members can speak, sitting and covered, to a point of order, arising out of or during the division.

17. QUESTIONS PUT TO MEMBERS (j).

A question put to ministers or members may not contain imputations, epithets, ironical expressions and hypothetical cases; nor may a question refer to debates, or answers to questions in the same session. A question cannot be placed upon the notice paper which publishes the names of persons, or statements not strictly necessary to render the question intelligible, or containing charges which the member, who asks the question, is not prepared to substantiate. Nor can the solution of an abstract legal case be sought by a question. A question cannot be made a pretext for a debate, and when a question has been fully answered it cannot be renewed.

18. COMMITTEES OF THE WHOLE (k).

A committee of the whole house is appointed by a resolution, " That this house will," either immediately, or on a future day, " resolve itself into a committee of the whole house."

In forming a committee of the whole house, the speaker, before leaving the chair shall appoint a chairman to preside, who shall maintain order in the committee; and the rules of the house shall be observed in committee of the whole house, so far as may be applicable, except the rule limiting the number of times of speaking.

(i) See Bourinot, p. 457.

(j) See Bourinot, pp. 381-385.

(k) See Bourinot, c. 15, pp. 475-490.

. When the order for committee has been read, the speaker says, Mr. A. moves " That the house do now resolve itself into a committee of the whole to consider (here state subject-matter)." An amendment may be moved against the principle of the proposed resolution or question, (see *above*, p. 37), or the motion for committee may be negatived. If the motion is agreed to, the speaker calls a member to the chair—in the commons, the chairman of committees, if he is in the house.

A committee may consider such matters only as have been referred to them by the house.

In committee, members may speak more than once to the same question.

A motion made in committee is not seconded.

The same order in debate is to be observed, as in the house itself.

Every question in committee is decided by a majority of voices.

In case of an equality of voices, the chairman gives a casting voice.

In case of a division being called for, the members rise and the assistant clerk counts and declares the number on each side, and the chairman decides the question in the affirmative or negative, ust as the speaker does in the house itself. No names are recorded in committee.

Questions of order arising in committee of the whole house shall be decided by the chairman, subject to an appeal to the house ; but disorder in a committee can only be censured by the house, on receiving a report thereof.

If any sudden disorder should arise in committee, Mr. Speaker resumes the chair, without question put.

When the matters referred to a committee have been considered, the chairman is directed to report the same to the house.

Until such report is made, no reference may be made thereto, nor to the proceedings of the committee.

Resolutions reported from a committee are read a first and second time, when amendments may be moved.

Such amendments, like all other amendments, must be relevant to the subject-matter of the resolution or resolutions.

The resolutions are then agreed to or disagreed to by the house, or agreed to with amendments, or recommitted, or the further consideration thereof postponed.

When a committee of the whole house, except the committees of supply and ways and means, has partly considered a matter and has reported progress, the speaker, when the order for the committee is again read, leaves the chair forthwith without putting any question, and the house thereupon resolves itself again into such committee.

19. DILATORY MOTIONS IN COMMITTEE OF THE WHOLE (*l*).

If it is proposed to defer the discussion of a bill or resolution in committee of the whole, the motion may be made: "That the chairman do report progress and ask leave to sit again;" and if this motion (which is equivalent to a motion for the adjournment of the debate) be agreed to, the committee rises at once, and the chairman reports accordingly. The speaker will then say: "When shall the committee have leave to sit again?" A time will then be appointed for the future sitting of the committee. But if a member wishes to supersede a question entirely, he will move: "That the chairman do now leave the chair." Such a motion is always in order and takes precedence of any other motion in the committee. If this motion (which is equivalent in its effect to a motion for the adjournment of the house) be resolved in the affirmative the chairman will at once leave the chair, and no report being made to the house, the bill or question disappears from the order paper. Two motions to report progress cannot immediately follow each other on the same question; but some intermediate proceeding must be had. Consequently, if a motion to report progress be negatived a member may move that "the chairman do leave the chair," or *vice versa*. In the case of a chairman making no report, and of a question having been in this way superseded, the original order of

(*l*) See Bourinot, pp, 485-487.

reference still remains, though the superseded question may not appear on the order paper, and it is competent for the house to resolve itself again, whenever it may think proper, after notice, into committee on the same subject.

20. MONEY VOTES—COMMITTEE OF SUPPLY (m).

The sole function of the committee of supply is to grant, reduce, or refuse the supplies set forth in the estimates.

The rules that obtain in other committees prevail also in this. Each resolution will be formally proposed from the chair, and amendments may be made thereto.

Each resolution must be proposed and discussed as a distinct question, and when it has been formally carried, no reference can again be made thereto. Neither is it regular to discuss any resolution before it has been formally proposed from the chair. Each vote or resolution is necessarily a question in itself to be proposed, amended and put as any motion or bill in the house.

It is irregular to discuss any matters in committee which are not relevant to the resolution under consideration.

By an ancient order declared, 3rd November, 1675, but since modified in practice, when there comes a question between the greater and lesser sum, or the longer or shorter time, the least sum and the longest time ought first to be put to the question (n).

Some municipal councils and other assemblies in this country, for some unintelligible reason, reverse this rule by giving precedence to the *largest* sum. See *Fifth Part* II. sec. 17.

Reports of resolutions from the committees of supply and ways and means, are ordered to be made on a future day, in accordance with the usage which forbids the taking of two or more stages of a money bill during one sitting of the house (o).

(m) See Bourinot, c. 17, p. 530 *et seq.*

(n) See May's Parliamentary Practice, 8th edition, p. 619. The practice is obsolete in the Canadian Commons.

(o) See Bourinot, pp. 558, 559.

Resolutions of the committees of supply and ways and means, reported to the house, are read a first and second time, and agreed to; or may be amended, postponed, recommitted, or disagreed to.

21. STANDING AND SPECIAL COMMITTEES (p).

At the beginning of a session certain standing or sessional committees are struck by a small committee appointed on motion of the leader of the house. The report of this committee must be adopted by the house, and then the standing committees are regularly organized in the way hereinafter set forth.

Special or select committees are also appointed in the course of a session on motion made after notice, for the purpose of considering particular subjects.

A member intending to move for the appointment of a select committee, must endeavour to ascertain previously, whether each member proposed to be named by him on such committee, will give his attendance thereupon.

A member who moves for a select committee is generally appointed the chairman thereof, but this is a matter entirely within the discretion of the committee itself. Rules of many municipal councils and other assemblies make such appointment imperative.

A committee is bound by, and is not at liberty to depart from the order of reference.

If it be found necessary to extend the inquiry, authority must be obtained from the house in the shape of a special instruction.

An instruction to a committee directs the order and course of the proceedings thereof, or extends or restricts the order of reference in such terms, whether mandatory or otherwise, as may be prescribed according to the discretion of the house. Notice of the instruction must be given.

A majority of the members of a committee compose a quorum, but it is now usual, on the appointment of standing or special committees, to fix it at a certain number immediately.

Committees are governed for the most part in their proceedings by the same rules which prevail in the house, and which

(p) See Bourinot, c. 16, pp. 491-525.

continue in full operation in every select committee. Every question is determined in a committee in the same manner as in the house to which it belongs. In case a difference of opinion arises as to the choice of a chairman, the procedure of the house with respect to the election of a speaker should be followed. That is to say, according to correct practice the clerk puts the question and directs the division in the same way as is done on that occasion by the clerk of the house. The name of the member first proposed will be first submitted to the committee, and if the question is decided in the affirmative, then he takes the chair accordingly, but if he is in a minority in the division, then the clerk puts the question on the other motion.

The committee having met, and a quorum being present, the members will proceed to elect a chairman. If there is no quorum present this proceeding must be deferred until the requisite number are in attendance ; or the organization of the committee may be delayed until another day. It is the duty of the chairman to preserve order and enforce the rules.

The names of the members present each day at the sitting of any committee are to be entered on the minutes of the proceedings of the committee, and reported to the house on the report of such committee.

If at any time during the sitting of a committee, the quorum of members fixed by the house be not present, the clerk of the committee is to call the attention of the chairman to the fact, who is thereupon to suspend the proceedings of the committee until a quorum be present, or to adjourn the committee to some future day.

The same rules obtain with respect to divisions in committees as in the house itself.

In the event of a division taking place in any committee, the question proposed, the name of the proposer, and the respective votes thereupon of each member present, are to be entered on the minutes of the proceedings of the committee and reported to the house on the report of such committee.

The chairman of a committee can only vote when there is an equality of voices.

A committee may adjourn from time to time; and, by leave of the house, from place to place.

A committee, having power to send for persons, papers and records can, without first obtaining leave of the house, report their opinion and observations, together with the minutes of evidence taken before them, and also make a special report of any matters which they may think fit to bring to the notice of the house.

Subject to the above rule, a committee must obtain the leave of the house to report their opinion or observations from time to time, or to report the minutes of evidence, or proceedings from time to time.

Committees should be regularly adjourned from day to day, though in the case of select committees particularly, the chairman is frequently allowed to arrange the day and hour of sitting, but this can only be done with the consent of all the members of the committee.

Committees are not permitted to sit and transact business during the session of the house. If a committee finds it absolutely necessary to meet on an important and urgent matter of enquiry, it must obtain authority from the house.

If a committee neglect to attend to its duties, the house can intervene and order it to meet and report (q).

When a committee is examining witnesses, it admits or excludes strangers at its pleasure; but always excludes them when deliberating.

The report submitted to the house is that of the majority of the committee. No signatures should be affixed to a report for the purpose of showing any division of opinion in the committee; nor can it be accompanied by any counter statement or protest from

(q) See Bourinot, pp. 743, 744.

the minority, as such a report is as unknown to Canadian as to English practice (r).

A minority report may appear in the appendix to the report of the committee; but such a paper of course can only be added in this way with the consent of the committee as a part of their proceedings.

A sub-committee cannot report directly to the house, but only to the committee from which it obtains its authority, and it is for the latter to order as it may think proper with respect to the report of this sub-committee (s).

Reports containing certain opinions, recommendations or resolutions are concurred in on motion.

When the report contains a series of resolutions or recommendations, each is formally and separately concurred in, or otherwise disposed of as the house may deem expedient.

But when the report does not contain any resolution or other propositions for the consideration of the house it does not appear that any further proceedings with reference to it, as a report, are necessary.

Every report must be regularly signed by the chairman.

The report of a committee is brought up by the chairman; it lies upon the table and is dealt with as the house may direct.

A report may be referred back to a committee for further consideration or with instructions to amend the same in any respect. In this way a committee may regularly reconsider and even reverse a decision it had previously arrived at.

No notice may be taken of the proceedings in a committee of the whole house, or of a select or standing committee, on a bill or other matter until the committee have made a report thereon to the house.

(r) See Bourinot, pp. 512, 513.
(s) See Bourinot, p. 513.

22. PETITIONS (*t*).

Petitions to the house shall be presented by a member in his place, who shall be answerable that they do not contain impertinent or improper matter.

Petitions may be written or printed in English or French. They must be free from erasures or interlineations, and the signatures must be written, not printed, pasted upon, or otherwise transferred. They must not have appendices attached thereto, whether in the shape of letters, affidavits, certificates, statistical statements, or documents of any character.

The house will refuse to receive a memorial containing no prayer. Every petition should have the signatures of "at least three petitioners on the sheet containing the prayer." But this rule is never interpreted as precluding a single petitioner from approaching the house, it simply refers to petitions signed by a number of individuals.

All petitions should be respectfully and temperately worded. The house will refuse to receive them if they contain any reflections on the queen or her representative in Canada, or on the action of parliament, or on any of its committees, or on the courts of justice, or affect "the legal and social positions of individuals." A document distinctly headed as a "remonstrance," even though it conclude with a prayer, cannot be received. Neither can any paper in the shape of a declaration be presented as a petition. Any forgery or fraud in the preparation of petitions will be considered a serious breach of privilege and severely punished.

A petition forwarded by telegraph cannot be received, inasmuch as "it has no real signatures attached to it." When a petition has contained a number of signatures in the same handwriting, these signatures have not been counted. Petitions of corporations aggregate must be under their common seal; and if the chairman of a public meeting sign a petition in behalf of those so assembled, it is only received "as the petition of the individual, and is so

(*t*) See Bourinot, c. 8, pp. 314-328.

entered in the minutes, because the signature of one party for others cannot be recognized."

If it shall be found on enquiry that the house has inadvertently received a petition which contains unbecoming and unparliamentary language, the order for its reception will be read and discharged (*u*).

In case of urgency, a petition may be immediately considered, but the grievance must be such as to require a speedy and urgent remedy. Petitions affecting the privileges of the house will at once be taken into consideration in accordance with parliamentary usage in all cases of privilege.

23. PUBLIC BILLS (*v*).

Every bill shall be introduced upon motion for leave, specifying the title of the bill; or upon motion to appoint a committee to prepare and bring it in.

A member moves : " That Mr. A. have leave to introduce a bill to "—(give title at length). On this motion being seconded and read by the chair, it is debatable and amendable (see Bourinot, p. 590), but after it is agreed to, the next question : " When shall the bill be read a first time ?" must be agreed to without amendment or debate, though the house may divide thereon and refuse the reading of the measure.

No bill may be introduced either in blank or in an imperfect shape.

If a member has broken the rule, the speaker calls attention to the fact, and if, by some inadvertence, leave has been given to introduce the bill, the order must be rescinded.

All measures involving a charge upon the people, or any class thereof, should be first considered in a committee of the whole.

(*u*) See Bourinot, p. 326.

(*v*) See Bourinot, c. 18, pp. 582-662. Only public bills, or in other words, bills relating to matters of public or general interest are here considered. Special rules govern the consideration of private bills, or bills relating to the interests of private individuals or corporations. See Bourinot, cc. 19-21, inclusive, for private bills.

When a bill has been read the first time, an order is made forthwith, that the bill be read a second time on a future day, or immediately, if the bill be passed with unusual expedition.

Every public bill shall be read twice in the house before committal or amendment.

On the order of the day being read for the second reading of a bill, a motion is made, and a question put : "That the bill be now read a second time."

The second reading of a bill is that stage when it is proper to enter into a discussion and propose a motion relative to the principle of the measure.

Amendments to bills also, like amendments to the orders of the day, "must strictly relate to the bill which the house, by its order, has resolved upon considering."

The question, "That the bill be now read a second time," may be superseded by an amendment which leaves out all the words of the question after the first word "that," and which substitutes for those words a resolution stating the object and motive on which opposition to the bill is based.

Amendments may be moved to that question by leaving out "now," and by adding at the end of the question, "three months," "six months," or any other time.

A bill, having been read a second time is ordered to be committed to a committee of the whole house, or to a standing, or to a select committee.

When the bill has been read a second time, the speaker puts the question : "When shall the house resolve itself into a committee of the whole on the said bill?" The house, on motion or call of a member of the government, if it is a government measure, or of the member in charge, generally speaking, will fix the day ; and when the order is duly reached and read by the clerk, the speaker will put the question : "Mr. A. moves that the house do now resolve itself into committee of the whole to consider the said bill" (*or* give title in full). This motion is debatable and amendable within limits of rule given *above*, p. 37. It may also be deferred for three or six months, as in the case of a second reading ; if the house agree to commit the bill, the speaker calls a member to the chair.

In proceedings in committee of the whole house upon bills, the preamble shall be first postponed, and then every clause considered by the committee in its proper order; the preamble and title to be last considered.

It is usual for the chairman to read each clause, and put the question formally thereon: "Shall the clause stand part of the bill?" It is then debatable or amendable, line by line, or word by word. If it is amended, then the question is again put: "That the clause, as amended, stand part of the bill." When one line has been amended and disposed of, it is not regular to go back and amend it further. A question once passed or negatived in the committee cannot be reconsidered except by an instruction from the house at a subsequent stage after report.

It is not unusual, however, in the Canadian commons, by unanimous consent, to reconsider clauses after a bill has passed through committee, as a matter of convenience or necessity, though such a proceeding is not strictly in order, as the rule shows.

Amendments to clauses of a bill may be made provided the same be relevant to the subject-matter of the bill, or pursuant to an instruction.

The house, by instructions, can empower a committee to make amendments to a bill not otherwise within the capacity of the committee.

Notice of the terms of an instruction must be given.

A clause may be postponed, unless upon an amendment thereto a question has been fully put from the chair.

Postponed clauses are considered after the remaining clauses of the bill, and before new clauses are brought up.

If a clause be disagreed to, a new clause in lieu thereof may be brought up after the remaining clauses of the bill have been disposed of.

When every clause and schedule has been agreed to, and any new clauses or schedules have been added to the bill, the preamble is considered, and a question is put. "That this be the preamble of the bill."

When all the clauses of a bill have not been considered, the chairman is directed to report progress, and ask leave to sit again.

When a bill has been fully considered, the chairman is directed either to report the bill without amendment to the house, or to report the bill with amendments.

The chairman in pursuance of the directions of the committee, reports the bill forthwith to the house; and when amendments have been made, a day is appointed for the consideration of the bill as amended by the committee.

A bill, after consideration as amended, is read the third time forthwith ; or is ordered to be read a third time on a future day.

Bills of an urgent nature are passed, with unusual expedition, through several or all of their stages on the same day.

The stages of bills imposing taxation, or appropriating the supplies for the year, are, by usage, not taken in succession, but are set down for a future day.

While a bill is in progress, no alteration whatever can be made in its provisions except by the authority of the house. If it should be found that a bill has been materially altered since its introduction it would have to be withdrawn and a new bill embodying the alterations formally introduced (v).

When a bill is read in the house, the clerk shall certify upon it the readings and the time thereof. After it has passed, he shall certify the same, with the date, at the foot of the bill.

24. Conferences Between Two Houses.

The commons may communicate matters to the senate, or have matters communicated to them at a conference.

In desiring a conference the subject-matter thereof is to be stated.

A conference is desired by message.

When the commons shall request a conference with the senate, the reasons to be given by the house at the same shall be pre-

(v) See Bourinot, p. 638.

pared and agreed to by the house before a message shall be sent therewith.

No conference is to be desired concerning any bill, or other matter depending in the other house. A conference is required by that house which, at the time of the conference demanded, shall be possessed of the bill or other matter.

Conferences, so frequent in old times of conflict before responsible government, between the assemblies and the legislative councils of the provinces, have become practically obsolete, through a better understanding of the constitutional relations between the two houses, and more simple methods of procedure in case of disagreement on a bill or other matter. Reasons of disagreement are communicated to the house from whom an amendment has come. It must either withdraw the amendment or send back a message insisting on the same for reasons. These latter reasons are again considered by the house first disagreeing, and a determination arrived at. If no agreement can be reached by various messages in this way, it is practically useless to ask for a conference. Still the rules and usages that regulate such conferences are in existence, and may be used to meet some contingencies. See Bourinot, pp. 463-466, for conferences. For reasons, pp. 466, 628.

26. Joint Committees of the Two Houses (z).

A committee of one house is occasionally appointed to join with a committee of the other house, and is called a "joint committee."

When such committee is desired by the commons, they appoint a committee of a certain number of members to join with a committee of the senate. A message is sent to the senate acquainting them therewith, and requesting the senate "to appoint an equal number of senators to be joined with the members of this house."

(z) See Bourinot, pp. 466, 467.

SECOND PART.

RULES OF ORDER AND PROCEDURE

FOR

PUBLIC MEETINGS—POLITICAL CONVENTIONS— SOCIETIES—LABOUR ORGANIZATIONS.

PUBLIC MEETINGS—POLITICAL CONVENTIONS— SOCIETIES—LABOUR ORGANIZATIONS.

1. GENERAL OBSERVATIONS ON PUBLIC MEETINGS.

1. Right of assembling in public.—The statute books of some of the provinces of Canada contain a law (*a*), the preamble of which declares in emphatic language that it " is the undoubted right of her majesty's subjects to meet together in a peaceable and orderly manner, not only when required to do so in compliance with the express direction of law, but at such other times as they may deem it expedient so to meet for the consideration and discussion of

(*a*) R. S. O. c. 187 ; R. S. Q. Arts. 2946-2961 ; see *below*, p. 63.

matters of public interest, or for making known to their gracious sovereign or her representative in this province, or to both or either of the houses of the imperial or dominion parliaments, or to the provincial legislature, their views respecting the same, whether such be in approbation or condemnation of the conduct of public affairs."

A high authority says with much force that "the right of assembling is nothing more than a result of the view taken by the courts as to individual liberty of person and individual liberty of speech." The English constitution does not give a specific right.of public meeting to the people at large, and any number of persons who block up a sidewalk or highway, or occupy a common, so as to interfere with the ordinary rights of citizens under the common law, subject themselves to the charge of creating a nuisance or committing a trespass (b). It is, however, well understood that as long as a number of persons assemble for a lawful purpose, and do not infringe or break any law, they should not be interfered with by other persons who do not approve of the object of the meeting. Any interference or breach of the peace on the part of those who disapprove of and assemble to break up a meeting peaceably and properly held, will be considered not so much "an invasion of the public right," but rather "an attack upon the individual rights of A. and B., and must generally resolve itself into a number of assaults upon definite persons, members of the meeting." The courts will, in such a case, recognize the personal rights that each individual has, under the law, to be protected from assault or injury on the part of those who differ from them on some question which he is attempting to discuss and promote by perfectly lawful means (c).

2. **Unlawful assembling.**—On the other hand, "the mode in which a meeting is held may threaten a breach of the peace, and therefore inspire peaceable citizens with reasonable fear; and in

(b) Some of the provinces have statutes against obstruction of highways or sidewalks. See R. S. N. S. App. A. c. 162.

(c) See Dicey, " The Law of the Constitution," 3rd ed., c. 7, and App. IV.

that case the meeting may be unlawful." The criminal law of Canada attempts to define (*d*) in the following specific terms what constitutes " an unlawful assembly." ·

" An unlawful assembly is an assembly of three or more persons who, with intent to carry out any common purpose, assemble in such manner, or so conduct themselves, when assembled, as to cause persons in the neighbourhood of such assemblies to fear, on reasonable grounds, that the persons so assembled will disturb the peace tumultuously, or will, by such assembly, needlessly and without any reasonable occasion provoke other persons to disturb the peace tumultuously.

" Persons lawfully assembled may become an unlawful assembly if they conduct themselves with a common purpose in such a manner as would have made their assembling unlawful if they had assembled in that manner for that purpose.

" Every member of an unlawful assembly is guilty of an indictable offence and liable to one year's imprisonment."

3. **Ontario and Quebec statutes on public meetings.**—Without dwelling on legal questions of public meetings, which can be only decided by the courts, in each case as it presents itself, I may again recur to the statutes of Quebec and Ontario which have been passed to give protection to public meetings duly called under their provisions (*e*).   The notice or summons for a public meeting called by a sheriff, a mayor, or other chief municipal officer, or by two or more magistrates resident in the district, on the requisition of twelve or more freeholders, citizens, or burgesses, must contain the information that the meeting and all persons in attendance are under the protection of the statute.   The notice must be issued at least three days before the proposed meeting, and shall set forth the names of the requisitionists in whole or part, besides the statutory authority under which it is issued.   It is also provided to meet other cases that should information be laid before any justice of the peace that a great number of persons will be present at a public meeting, two

---

(*d*) Criminal Code, Statutes of Canada, 1892, ss. 79, 81.   See on this point Dicey's admirable exposition of an interesting subject in App. 4.   Also N. B. C. S. c. 147, " Of offences against the public peace."

(*e*) R. S. O. c. 187; R. S. Q. Arts. 2946-2961.   These two Acts were originally passed by the legislature of the old province of Canada.   See C. S. C. c. 82.

justices of the peace, resident in the district, may give due public notice of such meeting and declare the same to be under the protection of the statute, (see *below*, pp. 64, 65, for public notices issued by the sheriff or justices according to the statute).

The authorities who call such a meeting shall continue at or near the place appointed for holding the same until it has dispersed, and are bound to afford such assistance as may be necessary for the preservation of the peace. Every person required by law, or chosen in the usual manner to preside over the meeting, shall at the commencement of the proceedings read the requisition, or the declaration setting forth the fact that the meeting is under the protection of the statute. The chairman has full authority to keep order, and may remove all disorderly persons who disturb the meeting and have them punished by due process of law.

4. Notices of public meetings issued in accordance with R. S. O. c. 187.

SCHEDULE A.—(Section 5.)

"To the inhabitants of the county of A., (*or* as the case may be), and all others her majesty's subjects whom it doth or may in anywise concern :—

"Whereas I, A. B., sheriff of, etc., or we, C. D. and E. F., two (*or* whatever the number may be) of her majesty's justices of the peace for the county (*or* district) of A., resident within the said county (*or* district) having received a requisition, signed by I., J., K., L., etc., etc. (inserting the names of at least twelve of the requisitionists and as many more as conveniently may be, and mentioning the number of others ; thus) and fifty-six (*or* as the case may be) others, who (*or* twelve of whom) are freeholders of the said county (*or* district) (*or* citizens of the said city) having a right to vote for members to serve in the legislative assembly in respect of the property held by them within the said county (*or* district or city, etc., as the case may be) requesting me (*or* us) to call a public meeting (here recite the requisition) : And whereas I (*or* we) have determined to comply with the said requisition ;

"Now, therefore, I (*or* we) do hereby appoint the said meeting to be held at   (here state the place) on   , the   day of   next (or instant), at   of the clock in the   noon, of which all persons are hereby required to take notice. And whereas the said meeting has been so called by me (*or* us) in conformity with the provisions of R. S. O. c. 187, entitled 'An Act respecting Public Meetings,' the said meeting, and all persons who attend the same, will therefore be within the protection of the said Act, of all which premises all manner of persons are hereby, in her majesty's name, most strictly charged and commanded, at their peril, to take especial notice, and to govern themselves accordingly.

"Witness my hand (*or* our hands) at   , in the   of   ,
this   day of   , 18 ."

> A. B., sheriff.
> or C. D., J.P.
> E. F., J.P.

R. S. O. 1887, c. 177, Schedule A.

SCHEDULE B.—(Section 6).

"To the inhabitants of the county of A., (*or* as the case may be), and all others her majesty's subjects whom it doth or may in anywise concern :—

"Whereas, by information on oath taken before D. E., esquire, one of her majesty's justices of the peace for the county of C. (*or* city or district, or as the case may be), within which the meeting hereinafter mentioned is appointed to be held, it appears that a public meeting of the inhabitants (*or* householders, etc., as the case may be) of the county of G., (*or* as the case may be), is appointed to be held at   , in the said county (*or* as the case may be) on   ,
the   day of   next (*or* instant), at   of the clock in the noon (*or* at some other hour on the same day), and that there is reason to believe that great numbers of persons will be present at such meeting ; and whereas it appears expedient to us C. D. and E. F., two (*or* whatever the number may be) of her majesty's justices of the peace having jurisdiction within the said county (*or* as the case may be), that, with a view to the more orderly holding of the said meeting, and the better preservation of the public peace at the same time, the said meeting and all persons who may attend the same, should be declared within the protection of R. S. O. c. 187, entitled 'An Act respecting Public Meetings.'

"Now, therefore, in pursuance of the provisions of the said Act, and the authority in us vested by virtue of the same, we, the said justices, do hereby give notice of the holding of the said meeting, and do hereby declare the said public meeting, and all persons who attend the same, to be within the protection of the said Act.

" Of all which premises all manner of persons are hereby, in her majesty's name, most strictly charged and commanded, at their peril, to take especial notice, and to govern themselves accordingly.

" Witness our hands at   , in the   of   this   day of   , 18 ."

C. D., J.P.
E. F., J.P., &c.

R. S. O. 1877, c. 177, Schedule B.

----

5. Ordinary notice of public meeting.

" Robert J. Fleming, Mayor of Toronto.

" To all whom these presents may concern :

" Whereas I, the said mayor, have received the following requisition :

" We, the undersigned electors of the city of Toronto, hereby request your worship to convene a public meeting, to be held in St. Paul's hall, Yonge street, at 8 o'clock p.m. on Tuesday, the 19th day of September, 1893, for the purpose of considering the objects and propositions of the ' Toronto Aqueduct Company,' more particularly in relation to the construction of a ship canal and power aqueduct between Georgian Bay and Lake Ontario, with its afflux at Toronto." (Here follow twenty-five signatures.)

" These are therefore to make known that in compliance with the above requisition, I do hereby convene a public meeting to be held in

ST. PAUL'S HALL, YONGE STREET,

ON TUESDAY, 19TH INST., AT 8 O'CLOCK, P.M.

" In witness whereof I have caused this proclamation to be made public at Toronto, this 15th day of September, A.D. 1893.

[Signed]   ROBERT J. FLEMING,

Mayor of the City of Toronto.

Mayor's office, Toronto, Sept. 15th, 1893.

2. THE PROCEDURE AT A PUBLIC MEETING.

As soon as a number of persons duly assemble at a certain place and at a fixed time in accordance with a requisition under the statute just mentioned, or in conformity with public advertisement for the purpose of discussing a matter of public import, it is the duty of any person, when so required by law, to take the chair; but in the numerous cases of ordinary or primary public assemblages—for the discussion of municipal, political or other matters—it is incumbent on some one responsible for calling the meeting, or otherwise directly interested in its purpose, to call it to order, and to move himself "That Mr. A. or B. do take the chair." This motion should be seconded and formally put to the meeting, like all other motions (see *above*, pp., 30, 31 for form and putting of motions). If another candidate be proposed—a rare occurrence in such primary or ordinary meetings—then the names are proposed in the order of nomination (see *above*, p. 8), the same person continuing to act as temporary chairman until the permanent chairman is elected.

When the meeting has chosen a chairman, he will call the same to order, and call upon it to appoint a secretary to keep a record of the proceedings. A member will move, and another will second the motion, "That Mr. C. do act as secretary of this meeting. When a secretary has been chosen in the same mode as a chairman, he will assume his duties and keep a record of all motions, amendments, divisions and proceedings generally (see *above*, p. 11).

No motions for the previous question, or for an adjournment, or irrelevant to the motions for the election of a chairman or a secretary, should be permitted.

The meeting being now regularly organized by the election of a chairman and secretary, it is able to proceed with the business for which it was called.

It is the duty of the chairman to read the requisition calling the meeting, or the declaration declaring the same to be under the protection of the statute (see *above*, pp. 63, 64). Or, in cases of most ordinary occurrence the chairman should read the notice or advertisement, if any (see *above*, p. 66), or in the absence of such notice inform the assembly in a few words of the object, and call upon such gentlemen, as he knows are especially interested, to address the meeting.

When the meeting is a ward or district, county or other meeting, called to discuss municipal or political questions, it is well that an arrangement should be made between the leaders of both sides—if such are represented—as to the order and length of speeches. Such an arrangement should be embodied in a motion, duly made, seconded, and put by the chairman, whose duty it is to see that it is observed. In all cases of political meetings it is well to limit the length of speeches to an hour or less, according to the time at disposal of the meeting, and the importance of the occasion.

In case the meeting is one for a definite purpose—to express an opinion on a question of the day, or to promote some charitable, benevolent or other public object—the promotors should always be ready with a motion or series of propositions (commonly called "resolutions," though not really so until adopted) which will enable the assembly to come to a conclusion on the matter discussed.

Each motion, or proposed resolution, should commence with the word "That," and amendments may be made thereto in proper form (see *above*, p. 31 for forms). In case the proposed motion contains separate paragraphs, or propositions, the sense of the meeting can be taken on each, if it is so desired, by a motion duly put by the chair, each paragraph being a distinct question to be amended, debated and voted upon (see *above*, p. 35).

Firmness, courtesy, tact, impartiality and willingness to give every one an opportunity to express himself on the subject under consideration, are the qualities essential to every chairman. If he finds the audience unruly, and the speakers inclined to that invective and personal acrimony which prevent fair deliberation and debate he should at once interpose and make such appeals to the meeting as his judgment will dictate. If his authority is set at nought, and the meeting gets beyond his control, it may be necessary to leave the chair and declare the assembly at an end. This will be the best course open to him in ordinary municipal and other meetings of heated local controversy. At meetings held in accordance with the statutory authority already mentioned, the chairman has large powers, and can have the assistance of the law to maintain order (see *above*, p. 64), but even in such cases, when it is obvious the meeting is under the control of an unruly faction, and order is impossible, it will be better to adjourn the body at once, than to evoke the interposition of the law, but all these are matters entirely to be governed by the judgment of the chairman in each case as it arises. No positive rules can be laid down to meet every exigency.

The chairman, in the case of ordinary meetings for the purposes of public discussion, should occupy an entirely independent position—like the speaker of a legislature—and should take no active part in the debate. In board, business and society meetings, it is necessary that he should be entrusted with the general conduct of affairs, and the explanations of measures and questions affecting the body, but, as it is well observed by a judicious writer, (*f*) "in the case of a large assembly, called for public purposes, this arrangement is wholly inapplicable, as the antagonistic responsibilities that attach to the leader of the debate and the chairman who controls the debaters cannot, even under the most favourable circumstances, be united without risk." "And," continues the same writer, "as it is of paramount importance to maintain, with the utmost strictness, the absolute impartiality of the chair, the limitation of the chairman to a single vote, given only, when an equality of votes occurs, is the most expedient course."

When a subject has, in the opinion of the chair, been fully discussed, and the sense of the meeting is obviously in favour of coming to a vote, he will ask, "Is the meeting ready for a vote ?" If there is no doubt on this point, he may, in the case of public meetings of a general character, ask for the voices as already explained (see *above*, p. 41, for mode of putting questions in parliament). But, as a rule it is best for him to ask for a show of hands ; and for the secretary to count them, and announce them when completed on both sides. If there should be an

(*f*) Palgrave, p. 9.

equality of votes, then the chairman should vote, and if necessary explain the reason of his vote (see *above*, p. 42). The secretary
should always vote, by holding up his hand, on completing the
vote on the side which he supports. Sometimes, in important cases,
tellers are appointed to count the show of hands. The chairman
will say, " Those in favour of the motion will hold up their hands."
Each member will then hold up his right hand. The secretary or
tellers will count them. Then the chairman will say, " Those
against the motion will hold up their hands," and the hands will
be counted as before. The secretary or tellers, having added their
own votes, will announce the result of the vote on each side ; and
the chairman will declare the motion carried or negatived. In
case a member holds up his hand by mistake, he should so declare,
and have the error rectified before the chair declares the final
decision on the question ; otherwise the vote cannot be changed.
If a number of persons give their voices for the yeas or nays, they
should so vote. If they vote otherwise, even in a show of hands,
and it is so shown to the chair before the decision on the total vote
is announced, their hands must be counted with the side on which
they had previously declared themselves by their voices (*g*).

Sometimes a vote will be taken in assemblies where everybody
is seated by calling upon members to rise in their places, and the
secretary or tellers, as in the case of a show of hands, will, by the
order of the chair count the votes on each side. In mass and
general meetings, however, a show of hands is the only convenient
method of arriving at the sense of the assembly on a question.
Names are recorded in legislative, municipal and other permanent
and regularly organized bodies only when there are special.rules to
that effect. A ballot can be taken only, as a rule, in exceptional
cases of nominations for offices and legislative seats, when secrecy
is considered expedient (see *below*, p. 76). It is not often feasible
or necessary in mass or ordinary public meetings.

When the business of a meeting is clearly finished, the chairman
should ask, " Is there any other matter before the meeting ? " If
there is none, then he should formally declare the meeting closed

---

(*g*) See on this point, Palgrave, p. 56.

and leave the chair. In all important meetings, however, the business is practically closed by some one formally moving a vote of thanks to the chairman for his impartial and able conduct as presiding officer. Some one, for this purpose, is called temporarily into the chair, and when the motion is duly made and approved by the meeting, the chairman may express his thanks, and then resuming the chair declare the business at an end, as just explained.

3. POLITICAL CONVENTIONS.

The organization and meeting of conventions, summoned to nominate certain persons for public offices to be elected by the people, or for representatives in the state legislatures, or in the national house of representatives, or for nominating presidential or vice-presidential candidates, have reached a completeness in the United States that no country in the world can in the least degree approach. This system of conventions necessarily arises from the fact that democracy is the form of government, and that it has necessarily required, for its perfect action, a complete machinery which will give the fullest possible expression to the voters in every ward, town, city, county, state, and in the republic at large (h).

In Canada the same complex machinery has not yet been established either in municipal or political affairs. A considerable development has, however, of late years taken place in the organization and operations of the political caucus and convention to nominate candidates for seats in the provincial or dominion legislatures, and to advance the objects of the respective parties. Under these circumstances, the procedure that should govern a convention of delegates, called for such a purpose seems necessary in a work of this character, which it is wished to make as comprehensive as possible. The rules laid down, however, will be understood to apply, generally speaking, to any large convention, or assembly, or conference for other special objects, not necessarily political.

As a rule, when it is necessary to nominate candidates for the provincial legislature, or the dominion parliament, and to express

(h) See Professor Bryce's "American Commonwealth," 2nd ed. of 1889, vol. II. pp. 80-89, and note in the app. to that excellent work.

opinions on the questions of the day, delegates are elected in every district to a convention, called for a certain time and place by the party association of the city, county or other district. The number of delegates to the convention from each voting precinct or division in a city or county is fixed generally by the central association and .they are elected by a meeting in each such precinct or division duly called for that purpose. Each delegate should have his certificate of election duly signed by the chairman or secretary (or by both) of the meeting that has elected him. It is also advisable that the "alternates" or "substitutes" chosen by the several district or primary meetings, to act in the absence of the delegate, should be prepared with their certificates in the proper form. It is always advisable that such substitutes be appointed to prevent a delegation from being incomplete at a convention, and the district consequently not adequately represented.

When the convention meets, generally at the call of the central party committee or association, the first duty is the appointment of a chairman.

The chairman of the committee in question will, as a rule, with the permission of the meeting, call it to order and preside temporarily. A gentleman may also be asked to act as temporary secretary, generally the secretary of the committee in question.

The chairman of the committee or association is himself often chosen as the permanent chairman of the convention on a motion duly made, seconded and put to the meeting by the chair (for form of motion, see above, p. 27). It is preferable that the convention should always have the choice of electing its own chairman. In case of opposition to a candidate for the chair, a motion should be proposed in due form, and the vote is taken on each in order of nomination ; that is, if the first name is rejected, then the second is submitted to the decision of the meeting (see above, p. 27).

The vote can be taken in this case, first by the voices (see above, p. 41), and then if the chair cannot decide, by a show of hands (see above, p. 70).

When the permanent chairman is chosen, he calls upon the meeting to appoint a permanent secretary—generally the acting officer. In case, however, of opposition, the procedure in the case of the chairman should be followed. If necessary, an assistant secretary can be appointed when there is a good deal of business to be transacted besides nominating candidates for parliament.

When the convention has been thus properly organized, and the meeting is likely to be of some duration, it is well that it should be agreed, by resolutions formally adopted (for form of such, see *above*, p. 31), that all speakers be limited to a certain time, and that the rules of debate in parliament be followed as far as practicable in such a body. This rule would prevent fruitless discussion and limit all members to one speech of a certain length on each motion or question (see *above*, p. 13).

If the chairman of the association is chosen chairman of the meeting, he may then call attention to the object for which they were called (see *below*, p. 74), and to the necessity of first examining the credentials of the various delegations. That is to say, before proceeding to deliberate action on the business before it, it must be known if the meeting is properly and fully constituted. Sometimes it is considered sufficient if each delegate or substitute presents his certificate to the secretary, and has it duly recorded. But the better practice is to follow that in vogue in the United States and appoint a small committee to examine and report on the credentials (*i*). Such a committee in the United States is generally appointed by the chairman in accordance with congressional usage, which gives the speaker that important power. In Canada, however, the parliamentary law requires that a member of the convention should move, and another should second, a motion in some such form as this :

"That Messrs. [name the members, generally three or five] be appointed a select committee to examine and report as soon as possible on the credentials of delegates to this convention."

(*i*) See procedure in a labour organization, *below*, p. 89.

This motion, when proposed, is debatable, and open to amendment by the substitution of other names. But when a name has
been once agreed to and inserted, it cannot be struck out by the
insertion or substitution of another (see *above*, p. 34). It is,
however, competent to make any addition to the number of the
committee on a motion duly proposed and put (see *above*, p. 34).

When the committee has been chosen, it should at once proceed to discharge its duty of examining the credentials of delegates
and substitutes, and enquiring into the merits of disputed claims—
not an unusual occurrence in important conventions. It is not
unusual for the permanent chairman of such conventions as
we are considering, like a president of a literary, scientific or
business society, to take the opportunity, while the committee
is occupied, to deal with those public questions which interest
the meeting. If, however, he should prefer to address the meeting
immediately on his taking the chair, then, on the appointment
of the committee he can adjourn the meeting, for a certain
time, or at the call of the chair—that is to say, until the committee has notified the chairman that it is ready to report. Then
the chairman calls the meeting again to order, and the committee,
through its chairman—generally the mover of the motion for its
appointment—brings up the report which is at once considered,
and adopted in its entirety or amended in any particulars. In
case of difference of opinion, and consequent division on any contested case or other part of the report, only members whose right
to their seats is undisputed can vote. As a rule the meetings, like
legislative bodies, will accept the report of the committee to which
it has made a special reference of matters of detail and investigation (for consideration of report of a committee see *above*,
p. 51).

After the committee's report has been properly disposed of,
and the meeting has been fully constituted, the chairman will
call upon the members to proceed to the nomination of candidates
for the constituency.

It would be advisable to follow the practice of some municipal
councils in cases of the election of wardens and other officers (see

Fifth Part of this work, I. sec. 8), and have a rule that nominations be made within an hour, or less time.

When the nomination of candidates has been formally begun, a member will rise and propose a name with such remarks as he thinks necessary in advocacy of his nominee. A seconder will follow and support the nomination. The motion should be duly proposed by the chairman who will, at the same time, ask if there are other names to be submitted. If there are no other candidates he will at once take the sense of the assembly upon the motion by asking for the voices (see *above*, p. 41, for form), and if they are given unanimously—as will most probably be the fact in such a case—he will declare the candidate the unanimous choice of the convention. It will then be in order for members to congratulate the candidate and for him to express his acceptance, and give his opinions on the questions of the day. In the event of this address it is always competent for the chairman to ask for him an extension of time should he exceed it.

If there are other candidates, then each is formally proposed, as in the first case, the chairman proposing each motion regularly, and asking for further nominations until they are completed.

When all the candidates are nominated it is for members to discuss the merits or claims of each. In this case each member should be confined to the rules of debate—the time limit (when any) and one speech; for though there may be half a dozen or more nominations the only question really before the body is the nomination of a candidate. It is also not unusual for candidates themselves, when present, to say a few words, accepting the nomination in formal terms. It frequently happens then, or before the vote is taken, one or other of the candidates will decline the nomination, either personally or through some friend authorized to speak for him. In such a case the chairman should put the ' question whether the member who proposed the name should have leave to withdraw the motion—a permission always accorded under the circumstances.

A vote may be taken by a show of hands, a ballot, or even the recording of the yeas and nays. When, under exceptional conditions, the meeting is fully constituted and the secretary has in his possession the roll of delegates duly authorized by the meeting on the report of the committee, it is always possible to adopt the ballot or even record the names with some accuracy. Accordingly the meeting should at an early part of the proceedings when the organization is complete and some rules of procedure are adopted, provide the methods of voting by a formal resolution. The ballot is preferable in cases of nominating for officers or for parliament.

When the meeting is ready for a vote the chairman will proceed to take the yeas and nays, in case that is the method required. He must put the question on the name of the candidate first proposed as in the case of the speakership of the commons (see *above*, p. 27). The secretary, having a list of the delegates before him, will call each name alphabetically, and members will answer yea or nay, and be so recorded. After all of the delegates present are so called, it is advisable to read over the names on each side in order that members may be able to correct any inadvertent mistakes. The total number of yeas and nays will be announced by the secretary, and the chairman will declare the motion carried or negatived. In the latter case, the chair will proceed to the next motion which will be decided in the same manner.

But the taking of yeas and nays is cumbrous and unsuited to ordinary conventions of this character, and it is expedient, as a rule, to adopt the ballot as more expeditious since the meeting has an opportunity of coming to a decisive vote immediately by one ballot. Two methods of taking the ballot may be used in conventions. The chairman may appoint two tellers, who are also scrutineers, and distribute slips of paper (*k*) furnished and initialled by the secretary, upon which each member of the convention, including the chairman, writes his vote. The votes are then collected, counted by the tellers, and the result reported to the chairman,

---

(*k*) It would be well if such slips of paper contained the names of all the nominees of the convention, so that each delegate could affix his cross X as at public elections, but such a practice would be hardly feasible, as in small bodies like municipal councils unless the convention gave time to the clerk to prepare the ballots in this more regular way. A proper box should be also provided.

who announces the result of the vote in some such words as these: "The whole number of votes cast is ——; the number necessary for an election is —— ; Mr. A. received —— ; Mr. B. —— ; Mr. C. ——. Mr. B., having the required number, is the candidate duly elected by the convention to contest the constituency." Or, in case no candidate has received the required number of votes—generally a majority of all the votes cast—another ballot must be taken, and the balloting must be continued until a decision is reached.

Where there is only one candidate for an office, and the regulations require the vote to be by ballot, it is a common practice to authorize the secretary to cast the vote of the assembly for such and such a person, but this is not regular, since secrecy is the essence of the ballot; it is better to move a suspension of the rule for the ballot, and ask that a candidate be elected unanimously.

In counting the ballots all blanks are ignored.

Another and more accurate mode of taking a ballot at a convention may be suggested. The clerk or secretary, at the time the ballot is called for, can call the roll of the delegates alphabetically and each delegate or substitute should come to the table, and having been handed a slip of paper, should record his vote, fold the same, and hand it to the clerk who will affix his initials thereon, and placing a check simply against the voter's name, deposit it in a box. In this way each vote may be duly recorded, and when the ballot is concluded, the secretary will open and count the votes in the presence of two scrutineers, appointed by the chairman, who, as in the previous method just described, will announce the result. This method is less expeditious than the other, but it is more reliable and ensures secrecy besides.

The chairman should not take any part in the debates of the convention after his address at the commencement of proceedings, except to fill the necessary functions of chairman ; inform the meeting on points of order, or the ordinary course of proceeding when it is advisable to do so, or at times, instead of ruling motions out of order at once, suggest how the desired object can be accomplished in order to facilitate the business of the meeting. As an eminent authority (*l*) has said, " the great purpose of all rules and forms is to subserve the will of the assembly, rather than to restrain it ; to facilitate and not to obstruct the expression of their deliberate sense."

The chairman, as a member of the body, has the right to vote when the vote is by ballot, but if he neglects to vote before the ballots are counted, he cannot then vote without the permission of the meeting, and it is very doubtful if it should be granted even then. In case he wishes to vote, his ballot should be first given to the secretary. In the majority of cases, however, it is not unusual for the chairman to refrain from voting, even in a ballot. In case the vote is by yeas and nays, the chairman should follow the parliamentary practice and vote only in case of a tie. The secretary should vote, as he may deem expedient, in every case.

When the convention has made a choice in any way, the successful candidate, if present, will thank the meeting formally, and addresses will be in order (as before stated on p. 75).

The convention, I have briefly described, is one for the nomination of candidates, but the rules and usages will apply to any body of larger scope. In case it is intended to adopt a platform or series of resolutions, embodying certain opinions on political and other questions, it is sometimes expedient to appoint a small committee simultaneously with that on credentials to draft such proposed resolutions and report them for the consideration of the meeting. When the report is brought up, it may be considered as a whole or paragraph by paragraph—the more convenient course when there are a series of propositions for debate. Each paragraph is then a question to be adopted, negatived, or amended, according to the sense of the meeting (see *above*, p. 51, for procedure).

It is not absolutely or always necessary, however, that such resolutions should be initiated by a committee in ordinary conventions and assemblies, but only on occasions when it is advisable to consider with great care and deliberation the principles of party action, or the leading details of some measure then agitating the

(*l*) Cushing, p. 990.

public mind. Each assembly is the best judge of the procedure expedient in its own case. In the majority of cases, motions embodying certain views on public topics may be conveniently brought up by individual members and immediately debated without the intervention of a committee.

When the business of a convention is understood to be concluded, the thanks of the body will be unanimously voted to the presiding officer and secretary for the efficient discharge of their duties. The chairman, having temporarily vacated the chair while this is being done, with another member presiding, will deliver a short address, thanking the assembly for their kind appreciation of his services, and at the same time make some general remarks on those features of the meeting that require his comment. Having done this, the chairman will declare the convention adjourned *sine die*, and leave the platform.

4. ORGANIZATION AND MEETING OF BENEVOLENT, LITERARY, SCIENTIFIC AND OTHER SOCIETIES.

Prefatory remarks.—I come now to refer briefly to the formation, constitution and regulations of those somewhat numerous societies that exist in Canada for the purposes of common study and investigation or for the promotion of benevolent, charitable, or other objects. When it is proposed to establish such an association, notices should be published in the newspaper press of the locality, and sent to those persons most likely to take part in the project, of the time and place of meeting.

First meeting for organization.—As soon as a sufficient number of persons are assembled, one of the promoters should be moved into the chair, and a secretary appointed for the purposes of the meeting until a permanent organization has been completed (see *above* p. 67, for procedure as in ordinary meetings).

When the temporary officers are appointed, the chairman should read the notice summoning the meeting, and call upon any one interested in the matter to address them. The secretary should keep the minutes as in all cases of public or other meetings (see *above* p. 11, for form). For the discussion of this informal meeting, no rules need be laid down, as it may be considered rather in the nature of a committee of the whole, when the object in view can be best promoted by a full and free debate. Good sense and relevancy are the qualities necessary on the part of the speakers ; tact and judgment are, as usual, the requisites of the chair. But it is essential that no discussion shall commence, and be allowed to proceed, until a member has proposed, and another has seconded, a motion as a basis of consideration and debate. Such a motion should briefly set forth :

" That in the opinion of this meeting, it is desirable to form a society in this city (*or* other place) to encourage studies and investigations in literature and science," or whatever may be the special object of the proposed association (see *above*, p. 30, as to the form and putting of motions).

After ample discussion of this motion, it should be put by the chair, and if carried, it should be at once the duty of a member of the meeting to propose another for the formation of a select committee in these terms :

" That Messrs.   be a committee of   members to frame a constitution for a society to encourage studies and investigations in literature and science, and to report thereon at a meeting to be called at   o'clock, p.m. (*or* a.m., *as the case may be*), on the   day of   instant in this hall (*or* such other place as may be most convenient).

As a rule the name of the society may be most conveniently left to the committee. If, however, a special name has been suggested and approved in the course of the debate, it can be formally moved after the general resolution for the formation of a society has been adopted. In that case the motion for the committee will set forth the designation of the proposed association.

Then a committee having been agreed to, the business of the meeting for the time being is at an end, and the chairman will formally adjourn it until the hour and day already fixed.

Subsequent meetings.—The meeting having resumed at the time and place to which it had adjourned, the same presiding officer and secretary will occupy their respective places. Should they be unable to attend, two other members will at once be appointed.

The chairman will call the meeting to order, and ask the secretary to read the minutes of the previous sitting. When the reading is completed it is open to members to make corrections in case of errors; and then the chairman will ask, "Shall the minutes be confirmed (*or* approved)?" When this motion is agreed to, it is usual, though not necessary, for the chairman to sign the minutes (see *above*, p. 11, as to minutes generally).

The chairman will then enquire, "Is the committee appointed to report a constitution for the proposed society ready to report?"

If the report is ready, the chairman of the committee will bring it up, and either read it himself or have it read by the secretary—the usual parliamentary course. The report should be that of the majority, be duly signed by the chairman, and no minority report is in order (see *above*, p. 50), should one be submitted.

The report, in all cases, should commence with the order of reference as follows :

"The committee appointed to frame a constitution for a society to encourage studies and investigations in literature and science (*or* whatever the object may be) respectfully submit the following as a recommendation :

Then should follow the draft of the constitution.

The chairman should formally move "That the report be now considered," and when the meeting has agreed to such a motion the document will be open to debate, amendment and adoption, (see *above*, p. 51, as to committee reports). The most convenient course is always to consider such a report in detail—that is to say, paragraph by paragraph, each being a separate motion or question (see *above*, p. 51), to be discussed, amended, accepted or negatived, as the meeting may finally determine.

The report should contain the constitution of the proposed society—that is to say, its fundamental law, setting forth the object, name, character of the membership, and designation of principal officers, with such other details as may properly be therein embodied.

When the constitution is adopted, then the chairman will call
upon the persons present who wish to become members to sign a
roll of membership prepared by the secretary, and for this purpose
the meeting can be adjourned definitely for a certain time, or at
the call of the chair.   That is to say, the chairman will either say,
"Is it the pleasure of the meeting that it do adjourn for half an
hour?" and he will formally put the question for adjournment; or
he may simply ask the assembly to resume in half an hour, when
he will again take the chair.

On resuming, the acting chairman will take the sense of the
meeting—strictly speaking of the members of the new society as,
they appear on the roll duly signed—whether it should proceed at
once to the election of officers.   If this is agreed to, a motion
should be made for the appointment of each officer designated in
the constitution.   These officers are generally a president, one or
more vice-presidents, a secretary, a treasurer and a council; or
otherwise.   The question should be put on each motion for the
appointment of officers.   In case of a difference of opinion on any
proposed name, the rules that prevail in parliament in similar
cases should be followed (see *above*, p. 8), and the motions for
each appointment taken in their due precedence.   The sense of
the meeting will be taken almost invariably in these preliminary
meetings by the voices or show of hands ; and it is rarely that the
ballot will be used, and then only by a formal motion to that
effect before the meeting proceeds to a nomination of officers.

When the officers are duly appointed, the temporary chairman
and secretary should vacate their places, and the new officers elect
assume their duties.   After thanking the meeting for the honour
conferred upon him, the president, or whatever may be his designation, should ask if members have other business to propose.

It is in order then to make a motion for the appointment of a
select committee of three or more members—a small number being
preferable, as a rule—to draft a code of rules of procedure and
order for the society.   Frequently the same committee that framed
the constitution will be appointed for this purpose.   Indeed, it is

not unusual to give them authority in the first instance to frame a constitution and regulations, and, in such a case, both will be embodied in the one report and considered at the same time. But it is more convenient, and indeed more regular, to frame a constitution in the first place ; in other words, to lay down the governing principles of the new association ; and when these have been agreed to, and the society has been formally organized, it is the proper time to adopt the necessary rules of procedure.

When the committee has been appointed in this way, it appears most convenient to adjourn until a later time that sufficient opportunity may be given to the committee to perform their important duties. Before the adjournment, other business that may be absolutely necessary can be conveniently disposed of, but not such as may evoke controversy. The constitution and rules of procedure should be necessarily determined before the society or association proceeds to discuss the subjects which come under its purview.

Accordingly the meeting will be adjourned on a motion duly made to a later hour or day.

At the meeting for the consideration of the regulations, the permanent officers will occupy their respective places at the fixed time. The chairman will call the meeting to order, if he is of the opinion that there is a majority of the members on the roll—the common law of such bodies requiring a majority of the whole in the absence of express provisions for a less number. When there is a quorum, the minutes will be first read and confirmed as in the previous meeting, and the chairman will then ask if the committee on rules and regulations is ready to report and the reply being in the affirmative, the chairman will bring it up and read it himself, or hand it to the secretary for that purpose.

The report will be in conformity with the rules applicable to all such reports (see *above*, p. 50), and will commence with the words :

"The committee appointed to draft a code of regulations respectfully submit the following as a recommendation to the society."

Then should follow the rules and regulations in a series of numbered paragraphs.

The report, having been taken into consideration, will be read and discussed paragraph by paragraph, as in all similar cases (see *above*, p. 51). It is always advisable for the chairman to have the report in print, when it is practicable, so that every member may be able to discuss it intelligently. Be that as it may, the regulations must be very carefully discussed. When each paragraph has been discussed and disposed of in due order it is not necessary to put a question on the whole report.

At these several meetings for organization, the rules that prevail in committees of the whole may conveniently govern all the debates and proceedings, but when the regulations are under consideration, either in the select committee or in the society itself, it is necessary to consider whether special rules should not be made for limiting the debates of the association.

All societies and associations that are of a permanent character should, at the earliest practicable date, obtain from the proper legislative authority an act of incorporation (*n*) embodying their constitution and giving them power to hold and sell property and dispose of such moneys as may be bequeathed or granted to them. Such acts of incorporation are initiated as private bills and do not require the notices in the dominion or provincial gazettes and in the local papers that are necessary in other cases of legislation for companies and undertakings formed for pecuniary gain and advantage. It is also usual for the legislature to refund the ordinary fees in the case of all scientific, literary and purely charitable or benevolent associations (*o*).

The procedure I have here sketched out may apply to all societies whatsoever, and not to one class necessarily.

(*n*) For form of incorporation of a literary and scientific society of a dominion character, see Act incorporating "The Royal Society of Canada," Dom. Stat. of 1883, c. 46. For constitution and regulations of the same, see Transactions, vols. I. and IX. The statute books of the dominion and provincial legislatures contain numerous Acts that form a guide for all classes of associations. But in every case a solicitor should be employed to draft the Act embodying the constitution of the society.

(*o*) See Bourinot, p. 730.

5. MUTUAL BENEFIT AND PROVIDENT ASSOCIATIONS.

The " Grand Council of the Catholic Mutual Benefit Association of Canada," incorporated by Act of parliament of Canada in 1893, 56 V., c. 90, has a very elaborate constitution and code of by-laws and regulations, and is in these respects a model for other benevolent and provident societies.

The general principles of the parliamentary law regulate order and decorum in this association, as in all other assemblies.

An appeal is allowed (without debate) against a decision of the chair, when seconded by two members in good standing, and put in the form, " Shall the decision of the chair stand as the judgment of the council (*or* branch)?" The chairman may succinctly explain his decision, and necessarily cite authorities. A two-thirds vote of those present can alone reverse the decision of the chair (for parliamentary rule of putting such questions of appeal, see *above*, p. 39).

All motions must be duly seconded and "stated," that is proposed by the chair ; and each shall be written at the request of the chair, the secretary, or any two members—a departure from the strict rule of parliament, hardly in the interest of business or order, since it may lead to loose practice. All motions should be written, except those of a purely routine character (see for parliamentary rule, *above*, p. 30).

No member shall speak more than once on a question until all others have had an opportunity of doing so ; nor more than twice, nor more than five minutes at any one time without permission of the chair or of the meeting, *i.e.*, of a majority of the meeting.

Another rule gives greater latitude than in parliament, viz. :

" 8. A member presenting a motion or [proposed] resolution may preface it by a few remarks bearing distinctly thereon ; this shall not preclude him from speaking on the question the same as other members, and he may close the debate."

On the call of three members, yeas and nays may be taken and recorded ; voting, as a rule, is in the usual way, by voices, by such

signs as holding up hands, by yeas and nays, or otherwise, as the
meeting may determine; but in the case of election for officers it
must be by ballot (for mode of taking the ballot, see *above*,
p. 77). The chairman has always a vote like any other member in
the council meeting, but the rules give him no casting voice; on
the other hand the president of a branch can vote at the election
of officers or on the balloting for candidates, and when the members are equally divided on other questions he has a casting voice.
He can, however, vote *on any question* in a branch (see sec. 197 of
"Constitution and By-laws"), "when he is one of only seven
members." Rule 24, which applies to all meetings, requires every
member to vote and serve on committees and accept nominations
unless excused by a majority vote or otherwise incapacitated.
Direct personal interest would be a disqualification in this sense
(see *above*, p. 43).

The following are :

6. "Privileged questions ":—When a question is before the meeting no
motion shall be received, unless it be :

1. To adjourn (see *below*, R. 28).
2. To lay on the table (see *below*, R. 29).
3. The previous question (see *below*, R. 12).
4. To postpone indefinitely (see *below*, R. 11).
5. To postpone to a certain time.
6. To refer.
7. To recommit.
8. To amend.

"And these motions shall take precedence in the order enumerated. The
first four shall be decided without debate."

For precedence, see *below*, Methodist Conference, r. 10.   A
"privileged question" means a question which is always in order,
and has a certain precedence, as stated in the rule above (see a
definition by the American authority Roberts, *above*, p. 25*n*).

The same rule is subject to the following limitations :—

11. When a subject has been indefinitely postponed, it cannot again, during
the same session, be taken up and considered ; nor can a subject which the
meeting has refused to consider be taken up that session.

For meaning of " session," see *above*, p. 7.

By rule 6 *above*, the previous question is privileged, undebatable and has precedence over all other motions therein enumerated, except to adjourn or lay on the table.   A later rule provides :

12. "On motion, a majority of the meeting may demand that the previous question shall be put, which shall be always in this form : ' Shall the main question be now put?" and until it is decided all further motions, amendments and debates shall be precluded."

That obviously means the previous question, as practically used in the United States (see *above*, p. 15) ; it can be proposed and put on amendments, but when it is once proposed no further motions are allowable.   But it is clearly subject to rule 6 above, which gives precedence, 1st, to adjourn (undebatable) ; and 2nd, to lay on the table (undebatable) which are privileged and consequently always in order.   It must be also subject to the ordinary parliamentary rule, as to the effect of a vote carrying or negativing the previous question (see *above*, p. 14).

The following rule makes other limitations with respect to adjournment and laying on the table :

28. "Adjournments.—A motion to adjourn shall always be in order except, 1st, when a member is in possession of the floor; 2nd, when a vote is being taken ; 3rd, when it was the last question or motion put ; 4th, when it has been decided to act upon the last question ; 5th, when a motion to consider a question, which could not be legally considered at a subsequent meeting is before the meeting.   A motion to adjourn shall be decided without debate, but, if decided in the affirmative, it is no adjournment until the meeting is closed in due form."

29. "Table.—A motion to lay on the table shall be decided without debate and cannot be reconsidered at same meeting."

In rule 28 *above*, the first three limitations to the putting of a motion of adjournment are according to parliamentary rule (see *above*, pp. 33, 38).   The meaning of No. 3, " when it was the last question put," is obviously that, once negatived, it cannot be again moved unless some other question or business has first intervened (see *above*, p. 33).

The rules also provide for reconsideration as follows :

17. "After any question has been decided, any member who has voted in the majority may at the same or next regular meeting move for a reconsideration thereof, but no discussion of the main question shall be allowed until the motion for reconsideration has been carried. When a subject has been indefinitely postponed or a reconsideration thereof refused, it shall not be again taken up during the same session."

The last sentence seems an unnecessary repetition of rule 11, given above. A motion to lay on the table can only, under rule 29 (see *above*, p. 87), be reconsidered at a regular meeting next after the one where it passed.

A subsequent rule gives another opportunity to annul a proceeding when reconsideration is not in order, viz. :

35. "Repeal or rescind.—A motion to repeal or rescind a motion shall be offered in writing and announced at a regular meeting at least one week before action shall be taken thereon, and shall only be in order when the motion to reconsider is no longer available."

6. TRADES AND LABOUR ORGANIZATIONS.

The industrial development of Canada has given rise to an immense army of workmen who have of recent years formed themselves into various associations for the purpose of protecting the interests of their particular trades, and at the same time asserting the claims of labour to just consideration. These associations can be organized in the way explained in the foregoing section in relation to societies generally. In addition to the constitution and by-laws which govern their special interests, they have necessarily adopted rules of order and procedure for their respective meetings.

1. **Trades and Labour Council of Toronto.**—The following code, taken from the constitution of this council, will sufficiently for my purpose illustrate the nature of the rules that are generally in vogue among the numerous industrial associations of the Dominion. As a rule these organizations are governed by the general principles of the parliamentary law given in the first part of this work, in the absence of special rules or usages regulating their proceedings.

It is the duty of the president to preside at all meetings, and in the case of the absence or the resignation of that officer, the vice-president performs his duties in the chair (see *below*, rule 19). The other officers are the recording and corresponding secretary, financial secretary, treasurer, librarian and serjeant-at-arms, all of whom are elected by a majority of votes cast by ballot. The following is a copy of the rules of procedure with such remarks as suggest themselves after any rule :

1. "The meetings of the organization shall be opened at the appointed time."

The constitution fixes the regular meeting on the first and third Friday of each month, at and from the hours of 8 p.m. to 11 p.m., and at such place as the majority may from time to time determine. The time may be extended with the consent of two-thirds of the members present. See article 3, sections 1, 2, of constitution.

2. "The business of each session shall be conducted in the following order :

(i) "Calling the roll of officers by the secretary."

A special rule of this society.

(ii) "Reception of credentials and report of credential committee."

The president appoints (article viii. section 6, of constitution) at each session this committee consisting of three members, whose duty it is to examine the credentials of all delegates seeking admission, and see they are properly signed, and sealed, and accompanied by the address of the delegate, and of the secretary of the organization sending him (see *above*, p. 72).

(iii) "Reading of the minutes of last meeting."

See *above*, p. 13.

(iv) "Calling of roll of delegates. This order shall not be suspended except with the consent of two-thirds of the members present."

This should be done alphabetically.

(v) "Election and installation of officers."

See article vi. section 1, and *above*, pp. 8, 27.

(vi) "Reports of standing committees read and disposed of."

Four standing committees of five members each, "legislative, municipal, educational and organization," are nominated and elected at the last regular meeting in January and July—each member to have a majority of votes cast. Each committee must report in writing. No member can be appointed on a committee unless he was present and consented to serve at the time of appointment (see *above*, for parliamentary rules, pp. 48-51, as to committees).

(vii) " Reports of special committees read and disposed of."

See parliamentary rules of committees, *above*, pp. 48-51.

(viii) " Receiving and disposing of communications from local organizations and other correspondence."

The secretary should have all such documents arranged and endorsed ; the endorsation should be read as a rule, unless a member wishes a paper read at length (see *above*, p. 52, as respects petitions in parliament).

(ix) " Unfinished business."

The secretary should have a docket ready for the meeting.

(x) " New business."

This must be such business as can be presented in accordance with the rules and usages of the council.

(xi) " Report of receipts."

A special procedure necessary to all such organizations.

(xii) "Adjournment."

At the hour of 11 p.m. the meeting must adjourn, unless two-thirds of the members agree by a vote to extend the time (see *above*, p. 89). An adjournment will throw over all business until next meeting when it must be taken up under head of "unfinished business," as above.

3. " The regular order of business may be suspended at any time by the president to receive the report of the credential committee or by a two-thirds' vote for the transaction of special business."

This is a privileged proceeding like messages from the crown or senate in parliament. Business is immediately resumed at the point where it was interrupted under this rule (see Bourinot, p. 461).

4. " Every motion and resolution shall be made in writing at the request of the chairman, except merely formal resolutions."

This leaves the matter practically in the discretion of the chairman who should, however, never fail to follow parliamentary usage, as *above*, pp. 11, 30, and demand written motions. The merely formal motions are to adjourn, lay on the table, commit, recommit, previous question (see *above*, p. 30).

5. "No question shall be stated unless moved by a member and seconded."

See *above*, p. 30. When so moved and seconded, and proposed from the chair a motion becomes a question.

6. "When a question is before the council, no motion will be in order except :—

(1) " To amend (see *above*, p. 32).

(2) " To refer or recommit (see *above*, pp. 24, 25).

(3) " To postpone (see *above*, pp. 23-25).

(4) " The previous question (see rule 7 and 16, *below*).

(5) " To lay on the table (see *above*, pp. 22, 25).

(6) " To adjourn (see *above*, p. 33).

" And shall have precedence in the order they stand herein— the last three of which shall be decided without debate."

For rule governing precedence, see Fourth Part II. Methodist Conference, rule 10. The motions, "That the house do now adjourn," "I move to lay (state subject) on the table," "That the main question be now put," are undebatable. As soon as they are proposed they must be submitted to the decision of the council. See *below*, rule 7 as to previous question.

7. "After the previous question shall have been stated, no amendment shall be entertained, and no explanation shall be allowed to be made or offered by any member, and all debate shall cease, and the council shall proceed forthwith to vote."

This goes further than the ordinary motion for an undebatable previous question since it does not even allow an explanation. Otherwise the rule is hardly necessary, since the previous rule (6) makes the previous question undebatable, and consequently prevents any amendment being made. The word "stated" in this and other rules, means the parliamentary term "proposed" from the chair obviously. See rule 29, *below* ; also *above*, p. 14, as to result of a vote carrying or negativing the previous question and the result in each case on the main motion.

8. "Any member voting in the majority may, during the same meeting, move a reconsideration."

A common rule (see *above*, p. 17).

9. "Any member, feeling himself aggrieved by the decision of the chairman, may appeal therefrom; and in such cases the question shall be: "Shall the chair be sustained?" and shall be decided without debate."

See the parliamentary form of proceeding which is identical, *above*, p. 39.

10. "When a blank is to be filled, the question shall be taken first on the highest sum or number and the longest time."

This is the reverse of the old parliamentary principle (see *above*, p. 47, for remarks on the subject).

11. "Any member may call for a division of the question when the sense will admit of it."

The parliamentary rule, *above*, p. 35.

12. "Any member wishing to address the council must rise, and if more than one rise at the same time the president shall decide which has the floor, and the other shall speak next in order."

The parliamentary rule *above*, p 37, excepting the concession of the floor to the next in order.

13. "During the reading of the minutes, reports, communications or other papers, and when a member is addressing the council, silence shall be observed, and no one shall be allowed to retire or otherwise disturb the meeting" (see *above*, p. 38).

A parliamentary rule of order, but it goes much further if it is to be interpreted as preventing a member from retiring while another is speaking. The convenient interpretation must be, no one should make unnecessary disturbance or interruption in retiring. His retiring, in fact, should not be noticeable.

14. "No member shall interrupt another member when speaking, except to raise a point of order, which shall be definitely stated, and the president shall decide it without debate."

See parliamentary rule, *above*, p. 39, limited by allowing no debate after a definite statement of the point of order.

15. "Any member who shall misbehave himself during the meeting, and disturb the harmony thereof, by abusive, disorderly or profane language, or who shall refuse obedience to the president,

shall be admonished by that officer, and if he offend again he shall be excluded from the room for the evening, and afterwards dealt with as the council may determine."

In accordance with parliamentary rules which permit members to be admonished, reprimanded or suspended, or even expelled, according to the gravity of the offence (see Bourinot, pp. 249, 434, 439).

16. "The previous question shall be stated in the following form : ' Shall the main question be now put ? ' "

The previous question is not debatable, see rule 7 above. If the council decide the previous question in the affirmative, the vote must be taken at once on the main motion. If it is decided in the negative, then the motion disappears (see *above*, p. 14).

17. "Each speaker on any question before the house shall be allowed *ten minutes*, and no member shall speak more than twice on the same question except by the unanimous consent of the council."

A wise limitation to debate in assemblies where time is valuable (see *above*, p. 13). If *one* member object, no member can speak twice on a question.

18. "The chairman shall not be permitted to speak on any subject, while in the discharge of his duty as president, except on matters of order, in which he shall have precedence ; when the council has occasion for facts within his knowledge, then he may, with leave, state the matter of fact."

A convenient and proper rule, permitting the chair not to debate, but to make such explanations and state such facts as are necessary for the satisfactory transaction of public business (see *above*, p. 69).

19. "The president shall have the right in the absence of the vice-president, to name any member to perform the duties of that chair, who shall be during such time invested with all the powers of the vice-president."

A necessary rule.

20. "A member shall not be interrupted while speaking, except on a privileged question, a call to order, or for the purpose of explanation."

The parliamentary rule, as *above*, pp. 38, 39.

21. "If a member, while speaking, be called to order, he shall, at the request of the chairman, take his seat until the question is determined, when, if permitted, he may proceed."

A parliamentary rule, as *above*, p. 39.

22. "Each member when speaking shall be standing, and respectfully address the presiding officer, confine himself to the question under debate, and avoid all personalities, indecorous or sarcastic language."

The parliamentary rule, as *above*, pp. 37, 39.

23. "When a question is put every member shall vote, unless the council shall for special reasons excuse him."

A parliamentary rule, as *above*, p. 43.

24. "On a call of one-third of the members, the yeas and nays shall be ordered, when every member's name and manner of voting shall be recorded on the minutes."

Otherwise, the decision of the meeting shall be given by the voices or show of hands. Yeas and nays in all assemblies are only ordered on the demand of a certain number of members (five in the Canadian commons). The way of voting is explained *above*, p. 41.

25. "The first person named on a committee shall act as chairman until the committee is called together, when they may choose any one of their number they may think proper."

The parliamentary rule, as *above*, p. 48.

26. "No committee shall be discharged until all debts contracted by it shall have been paid."

A special rule requiring no comment here.

27. "When there is no question before the council, no debate whatever shall be allowed, save questions asking for information, which shall be at the option of the president to retain."

Embodying a parliamentary principle which requires the assembly to be seized of a question before a debate can go on (*above*, p. 11). Questions on matters of importance or interest are always allowable as *above*, p. 44.

28. "All questions of order as to the propriety of entertaining the consideration of any subject may be debated."

A special rule to prevent the discussion of troublesome questions and to save the time of the assembly.

29. "The president, when in the chair, shall state every question coming before the council, and immediately before it is put to vote shall ask, 'Are you ready for the question?' when it shall be open for debate."

A parliamentary rule in effect, as *above*, p. 41. It would be better placed after rule 3.

30. "The president need not rise from his seat to state a question; but must rise to put a question."

In parliament the speaker rises both to "state" (propose) and put a question. I do not see why even in assemblies of less importance a similar procedure is not considered necessary.

31. "When the chairman has arisen to put the question all debate shall cease, and he shall immediately proceed to declare the result of the vote on the question, which has been under consideration."

The parliamentary rule in effect, as *above*, p. 42. Before declaring the result, the chairman should, however, gather the sense of the meeting by the voices or a show of hands, or by the yeas and nays as provided for in rule 24 above, under exceptional circumstances. Though there is no express rule to that effect, it must be understood that in all unprovided cases the council must refer to the parliamentary law of Canada so far as it can be made applicable to their circumstances.

The rules, it must be assumed, can only be suspended at any time by unanimous consent, which should be done only under exceptional conditions (see *above*, p. 6). If it is necessary to change or adopt a rule, notice thereof should be given at a regular meeting previous to that where it is considered. The constitution very wisely provides (article ix), as all constitutions of similar bodies should (*above*, p. 6), that it "shall not be altered, amended or suspended, except at a regular meeting of the council, and with the concurrence of a two-thirds vote of the members

present. Notice of any amendment or alteration of this constitution must be given in writing at a previous regular meeting. If
this notice is not general, but in definite terms, the meeting can
alone consider the amendment as it is actually given in the
notice (see on this difficult question, *below*, pp. 117, 118). It would
not be competent to alter its purport or effect. It must be either
rejected or adopted.

2. **Trades and Labour Council of Hamilton.**—The rules of
this association are the same as those of the preceding council with
the following exceptions in the copy before me:—

Rule 2, (s. iv): "Calling roll of delegates," not suspended "by
consent of two-thirds of the members present;" consequently it is
not suspended except under conditions of rule 3, given *above*,
p. 90.

Rule 32 added: "The president shall have the casting vote on
all questions resulting in a tie vote."

The president has, consequently in Hamilton, a vote first as a
member, and secondly a casting vote in case of an equality of
votes. The Toronto president, in the absence of such a provision,
can only vote once as a member.

3. **Builders' Labourers' National Union, No. 1, Toronto.**—
General principles of parliamentary order and debate govern this
as other associations (see *above*, pp. 37-39).

A president occupies the chair, maintains order, states and puts
every question practically as in parliament (see *above*, pp. 30, 31), or
as in rules 29, 30 and 31 of Toronto Council (see *above*, p. 95).

Each speaker is allowed ten minutes on any question; no one
can speak more than once on the same question until all members
have had an opportunity to do so; nor more than twice without
permission of the chair.

Yeas and nays may be called for by two members before the
chairman rises to take the question, but it requires the assent of
one-third of those present to take such a division. A member may

be excused from voting without debate, but he must have a personal interest in a question or his union must be interested in the same, or he must have other equally sufficient reasons for being so excused.

An appeal lies to members generally from the chair's decision as in all other assemblies (see *above*, p. 39). When the person appealing has stated his reasons, the question must be put, without debate, " Shall the decision of the chair stand as the judgment of the union ? "

The following special rules are given in full :

12. "When a question is before the union no motion shall be received unless :

    (1) To adjourn (see *below*, rule 24).

    (2) To take previous question (see *below*, rule 15).

    (3) To lie on the table.

    (4) To postpone to a definite time.

    (5) To refer.

    (6) To amend.

"And they shall have precedence in the order herein arranged, the first three of which shall be decided without debate."

For meaning of precedence, see Fourth Part, II., Methodist Conference, rule 10. Only first three are undebatable, and consequently not amendable, since to amend is practically to speak and commence debate.

14. "The motion to close debate may be made by any two members and shall be put in this form : ' Shall the debate now close ? ' and, if adopted, the president shall proceed to take the question on the resolution and amendments thereto, according to priority without allowing further debate."

15. "The call for the previous question may be made by any six members and shall be put in this form : "Shall the main question be now put ? " If adopted, the effect shall be to take the question on the original resolution, to exclusion of all debate, and [of] all the amendments which have not been adopted."

On a mere superficial reading it would seem as if these rules had the same practical effect, but it is not so. Rule 14 simply

B.M.P.—7

provides for taking the question at once on a motion and any amendments thereto in order when the majority decide by voting that "the debate now close." But the rule does not strictly preclude a discussion going on until that vote is taken. In that respect it is the previous question in the house of commons. Rules of some councils more logically (see *below*, p. 102) make such a motion undebatable. If the assembly negative the motion "to close the debate," then the discussion goes on.

Rule 15, evidently means that when six members demand the previous question it is put at once, since rule 12 makes the previous question undebatable. If adopted all debate must cease on the main question which is taken immediately, to the exclusion of all amendments that have not been adopted. The rule is a little vague, and "of," as marked above in brackets, should apparently go before "amendments" if the rule is to have any positive meaning in their regard. If the previous question is negatived then the parliamentary rule (see *above*, p. 14) is to suppress the main question for the time being.

The following rule makes strict provisions respecting reconsideration (see *above*, pp. 17, 18):

16. "All votes other than on amendments to the constitution or rules, may be reconsidered at the same or next succeeding regular meeting upon a motion made and seconded by two members who voted in the majority, provided the union agrees thereto, but after a motion to reconsider has been once lost, it shall not be renewed."

Art. 11 of the constitution (p. 7 of Constitution and By-Laws) and rule 3 provide very strict regulations with respect to any amendment or repeal of the constitution.

A majority of the union must agree, if required, to the reconsideration of any question, for "assent" necessarily means a majority vote in such cases.

By rule 24, a motion to adjourn, when negatived, cannot be again proposed until fifteen minutes have passed.

4. **International Building Labourers' Protective Union of America.**—Same rules as preceding National Union of Toronto, *above*, p. 96.

5. International Typographical Union, No. 91.—General parliamentary rules respecting order and debate prevail. Presiding officer maintains order and an appeal lies against his decision, as in all other assemblies (see *above*, p. 39).

All motions, "unless merely affecting the order of business," must be in writing. Motions may be withdrawn previous to amendment or final decision with consent ; that is, by a vote, if necessary, of a majority of the members present.

. No member can speak more than twice on any question, nor more than ten minutes at any one time, without consent—that is, of a majority of the union.

Any member may demand a division or the chairman may order same ; yeas and nays are recorded on call of five members ; such call shall not preclude amendment before main question is put (for putting questions correctly, see *above*, p. 41). A member may explain his vote during call, if the union consent thereto unanimously ; every member must vote except excused for sufficient reasons, such as personal interest in a question.

No rule can be suspended, except by consent (without debate) of two-thirds of members present.

The following are special rules :

12. "When a question is under debate, no motion shall be received but :

(1) To adjourn.

(2) To lie on the table.

(3) For the previous question (see *below*, rules 26 and 27).

(4) To postpone to a certain day.

(5) To commit.

(6) To amend.

"Which several motions shall have precedence in the order in which they stand arranged. The motion for adjournment shall be always in order ; that and the motion to lie on the table shall be decided without debate."

For meaning of precedence, see Fourth Part, II., Methodist Conference, rule 10.

Only to adjourn the union or to lay a question on the table are undebatable under the rule. The moving of the previous question does not, according to strict reading of rule 27, *below*, prevent a debate on the advisability of agreeing to such previous question, but only on the main question.

26. "A motion for the previous question shall not be entertained unless seconded by seven members of the union."

That is to say, when the previous question is moved, seven members, without the mover, must stand up."

27. "When so made, the question shall be put in these words : 'Shall the main question be now put?' and until decided shall preclude all further amendment and debate of the main motion. When there shall be pending amendments, the question shall be first taken upon amendments in their order, and then on the main question, without debate."

Each amendment must be voted upon in order : " Shall the amendment now be put ? " (see *above*, p. 15, for United States, practice, which here applies). If the previous question is carried then a vote must be taken at once on the amendment ; if it is negatived, then there is no amendment, since it is practically suppressed by the decision that it shall *not now* be put (see *above*, p. 14). The same remarks apply to all further amendments and to the main motion.

The following is a special rule :

13. "A motion for the 'order of the day' shall take precedence of all other business except a motion to adjourn or a question of privilege."

This is practically the parliamentary rule (see *above*, p. 36) which makes such a motion equivalent to the previous question. For a motion to adjourn (see *above*, rule 12) ; and a question of privilege, which has always priority (see *above*, p. 40).

6. **Toronto Typographical Union, No. 91.**—General parliamentary rules of order and debate prevail. A president maintains order in accordance with parliamentary usage (see *above*, p. 28).

No member shall speak more than once on same question, except mover and seconder of a resolution, (which is, of course, only " a motion," or " question," or " proposed resolution " at that initiatory stage see *above*, p. 31), who may speak twice ; nor more than ten minutes without permission (*i.e.* of a majority of those present).

Any member may call for a division; voices are first taken, and if that is doubtful, or a division is called for, members for and against rise and are counted in order by the recording secretary, first in the affirmative and then in the negative. The president shall announce the result.

The following are special rules :

6. " When a question is before the union, no motion shall be received but—

(1) To adjourn.

(2) To lie on the table.

(3) For previous question (see *below*, rule 19).

(4) To postpone.

(5) To amend.

" Which several motions shall have precedence in the order they here stand arranged." [For meaning of precedence, see Fourth Part, II., Methodist Conference, rule 10].

" The following shall be considered privileged questions and are not debatable :

(1) To adjourn.

(2) To lie on the table.

(3) For the previous question.

(4) To read a paper or document pending a question.

(5) To reconsider.

(6) All incidental questions of order arising after a motion is made for the previous question, and pending such motions whether, an appeal or otherwise, with this understanding, that the motion to adjourn be unconditional, and shall always be in order, except—

(1) When a member is speaking.

(2) When a vote is being taken on any question.

(3) A motion to adjourn, being negatived, cannot be renewed until some other motion is made or business transacted."

The last paragraphs, 1-3 inclusive, embody simply parliamentary usages (see *above*, pp. 38, 89).

The previous question, when moved, is not debatable under the foregoing and the following rule :

19. " The previous question shall be put in this form : ' Shall the main question be now put ? ' and, until it is decided, it shall preclude all amendments

and all further debate.   It shall only be admitted when demanded by a majority of the members present."

Consequently the chairman, if necessary, must take a vote to find if a majority wish " to admit," *i.e.* " allow " the moving of the previous question ; if there is such a majority, then the previous question is formally put.   If it is carried, then the vote is taken on the main question, as in all cases (see *above*, p. 14), if it is negatived, then, as in parliament, the assembly has declared that the vote on the main qestion shall *not now* be put (see *above*, p. 14), *i.e.*, it is practically effaced for the time being.   This is the strict interpretation of the rule.   Adjournment may be moved on the previous question under rule 6 *above*.

The following rule provides for a reconsideration :

16. "When a motion has been made and decided upon, it shall be in order for any member voting in the majority, at the same or the next meeting, to move for a reconsideration thereof; but no discussion of the main motion shall be allowed."

By previous rule 6, such a rule is privileged and not debatable.

7. **Bricklayers' and Masons' International Union of America.**—The same to all intents and purposes as the "International Building Labourers' Protective Union of America " or "Builders' Labourers' National Union, No. 1, Toronto," on pp. 96, 98, *above*.   The only important difference is that the constitution is not as strict concerning notice of amendments (Art. 23, p. 30, of Constitution and Rules of Order).

8. **Iron Moulders' Union of North America.**—Same as " Builders' Labourers' National Union, No. 1, Toronto " (see *above*, p. 96), except " To close the debate " is made a preferred motion, and " To postpone indefinitely" is added in rule 12, of foregoing union, which consequently should read as follows for the Iron Moulders' Union of North America :

11. "When a question is before the union no motion shall be received, unless :

(1) To adjourn.

(2) To close the debate.

(3) To take the previous question.

(4) To lie on the table.

(5) To postpone indefinitely.

(6) To postpone to a definite time.

(7) To refer.

(8) To amend.

" And they shall have preference in the order herein arranged, the first four of which shall be decided without debate."

Rules 12, 13 and 14, "to close the debate," " the previous question," and " to reconsider," respectively, are the same as rules 14, 15 and 16 (see *above*, p. 97, 98) of the Toronto union mentioned ; but the constitution has a very strict rule respecting amendments of the constitution (see Art. 16, s. 1 of Constitution and Rules of Order, p. 28).

THIRD PART.

—

CORPORATE COMPANIES.

DIRECTORS' AND SHAREHOLDERS' MEETINGS.

DIRECTORS' AND SHAREHOLDERS' MEETINGS.

1. INTRODUCTORY REMARKS.

A corporation has been well described as a legal *persona*, that is to say, a distinct person existing in contemplation of law, but having no physical existence (*a*). It can sue and be sued, and holds its existence in every respect under the legal conditions of the charter or enactment that clothes it with powers to promote the object or objects for which it was formed. Each corporation in exercising its powers is subject to,—

1. The provisions of the Act under which it was formed.

2. The decisions of the courts relating to public companies.

3. The rules of the common law respecting public companies or corporations where special or general statutes are not applicable.

Incorporated companies or joint stock companies are composed of a number of individuals, called shareholders, who subscribe and own a certain portion of the common stock or capital of the company. These shareholders are not responsible individually for the company's debts or engagements, and their property is affected only to the extent of their interest in the company.

(*a*) See Palmer's Company Precedents, 1.

In all the provinces of Canada, and in the Dominion itself, there are general statutes under which a certain number of persons —not less than three in any case—by complying with certain legal conditions, may obtain corporate powers. These powers are granted under what are known as letters patent in the Dominion and the provinces generally, except in British Columbia where the English system of registration is still in operation (*b*). Not a few companies exercise their rights as legal entities by virtue of particular statutes of the proper legislative authorities of Canada, incorporating them specially.

The affairs of all public companies are administered under legal regulations or by-laws at certain meetings, viz.:

General or shareholders' meetings;

Board or directors' meetings;

Which will be described in due order. In this review of the proceedings of public companies the writer is necessarily confined to the general laws under which charters are given to joint stock companies in the Dominion and to the leading principles that are admitted in special as well as in general statutory enactments on the subject. But, while reference is not made to the general statutes which relate to railways, banks, insurance, and other business and trading companies for which there is special legislation provided (*c*), the methods of procedure laid down in this work for the conduct of meetings of companies are for the most part applicable to all such corporations. But in every case care must be taken to consult the special regulations of such corporate

(*b*) R. S. C. 1886, c. 119, amended by c. 20 of 1887. R. S. O. 1887, c. 157; also c. 178; c. 26 of 1889; cc. 32, 33, 34 of 1891; c. 35 of 1892. R. S. Q. 1888, arts. 4694 *et seq.*; amended by c. 42 of 1889. S. N. B. c. 9 of 1885; amended by c. 7 of 1888; by c. 5 of 1889; by c. 20 of 1890; by c. 15 of 1892. R. S. N. S. 1884, c. 79; amended by c. 18 of 1885; by c. 30 of 1886; by c. 42 of 1889; by c. 35 of 1890: by c. 36 of 1892; c. 36 of 1893. C. S. Man. 1880-81, p. 218, ss. 226 *et seq.*; amended by c. 41 of 1883; by c. 20, s. 1 of 1884; by c. 11 of 1886; by c. 3, s. 15, of 1888; by c. 5 of 1892. S. B. C. 1890, c. 6; amended by c. 3 of 1891; by cc. 6, 7 of 1892. R. Ord. N. W. T. 1888, c. 30. Warde (pp. 285, 306) calls attention to the fact that the British Columbia Act of 1888 c. 21, C. S., has not been repealed and may be considered still in force.

(*c*) See Bourinot, pp. 695, 696*n*.

companies. All I can do is to lay down those principles which govern generally all meetings.

2. REGULATIONS OR BY-LAWS OF COMPANIES.

All corporate or joint stock companies are regulated in the exercise of their powers by certain regulations or by-laws, generally made by the directors, with the aid of a solicitor to the company (see *below*, p. 113), and duly authorized by the shareholders at general meetings. The term, by-law, is, as a rule, used in Canada as designating the legislative action of municipal bodies or a rule obligatory over a particular municipal district, authorized by the statutory and common law, and not at variance with the general laws of the Dominion or a province. In a more restricted sense, it is applied to the permanent regulations or laws which regulate and define the relations of the members of local companies and corporations towards the corporation, and between themselves, under powers conferred by charter or Act of the legislature, dominion or provincial. A by-law differs from a resolution in the respect that the latter applies to a single act of the corporation, while the former is a permanent and continuing rule of action for all occasions when business of the company has to be transacted.

Every by-law or code of regulations, like a public or private statute, has a preamble declaring that it is expedient to make certain regulations for regulating the affairs of the corporate body, and setting forth the authority of the charter or statute under which the company acts. Then follow the enacting clauses or sections setting forth in clear and definite terms the regulations governing the company. These regulations should be drafted by the legal adviser of the company, and provide, as a rule, for the following objects :

The holding of directors' and shareholders' meetings, ordinary and extra-ordinary, at such times as may be deemed necessary.

Management of the affairs of the company by a certain number of directors duly qualified.

The election of president or vice-president and other necessary officers, and their tenure of office, fitting up offices, salaries, etc.

Record of proceedings of directors and shareholders.   ·

Corporate seal.

The keeping of books and accounts.

Decisions of questions at directors' meetings.

Decision of questions by a certain number of shareholders, in person or proxy.   '

The voting of shareholders for themselves or by proxy.

Powers with respect to issue of stock.

Calls upon stock.

Forfeiture of shares.

Transfer of shares.

Appointment of solicitors and auditors.

And such other matters as relate to the objects of the company, and for which statutory authority has been given. The following section on directors shows their powers under general statutes to make regulations. The regulations of every company should incorporate all the statutory enactments relating to by-laws.

3. DIRECTORS' MEETINGS.

The shareholders of a joint stock company, at a general meeting of the same, duly convened by proper notice to each shareholder, elect the directors, whose business it is to manage the affairs of the company, under the Act or charter of incorporation. Until a permanent organization is effected and directors regularly elected at such a general meeting, the persons named in the charter or statute constituting the company, temporarily manage its affairs, but these provisional directors should lose no time in summoning a general meeting for the purpose stated.

A person to act as director should be a *bona fide* owner of stock absolutely in his own right and not in arrears in respect of any call thereon. Elections are yearly and by ballot as a rule. At the end of their term all the members retire, and if otherwise qualified are qualified for re-election. The directors elect the president, one or more vice-presidents, manager and other officers required by the law and the regulations. Vacancies occurring in the board of directors are, as a rule in companies, unless the regulations otherwise direct, filled for the unexpired remainder of the term by the board from among the qualified shareholders of the company. In the Quebec and Dominion general or companies' Acts, it is required that a majority of the directors reside in Canada. The Ontario Act is silent on this point. If the statutes under which the company is incorporated has no express provision in this respect, then the directors need not reside in Canada *ex necessitate*.

The number of directors on a board vary—from not more than fifteen in the Dominion Act to not less than three in the Ontario Act—but nine or five appear to prevail in the majority of companies. They must act and vote as a board, and not separately. They cannot act or vote by proxy. A majority of the board constitutes a quorum. A majority of a quorum, in the absence of express regulations to the contrary, even when a minority of the whole board, bind the board and company, provided, of course, their action is in accordance with the legal powers granted to the company. It is usual, however, in the regulations to fix the quorum with reference to the number of directors ; that is to say, if there are five, three is the proper quorum ; if seven, four ; if nine, five. In most cases, the powers and duties of the board are delegated to a manager, director or secretary, and when such is the case, the reasons for having such a large board or quorum of the same are lessened in importance. But directors, under any circumstances, are bound to meet periodically under well framed regulations, and assume complete supervision over the affairs of the company.

The general laws of the Dominion, Ontario and Quebec for the incorporation of public companies set forth the duties of directors.

The regulations of directors, as a matter of course, vary considerably, according to the character and object of the company. As an example of regulations, the following is given by Palmer (d):

(d) The Shareholders' and Directors' and Voluntary Liquidators' Legal Companion, a Manual of Every Day Law and Practice, etc., 13th ed. p. 29. In addition to this useful little work, the following authorities have been frequently consulted by the present writer : Palmer's Company Precedents, 5th ed.; Buckley on " The Companies' Acts," 6th ed.; Warde's Shareholders' and Directors' Manual, 6th ed., Toronto, 1892.

1. A board meeting shall be held every ――――― day at ――――― o'clock. Such meetings shall be called ordinary board meetings. Other meetings shall be called special.

2. Every meeting shall be held at the registered office of the company.

3. Any director may, and upon the requisition of any director, the secretary shall convene a special meeting ; not less than ――――― hours' notice shall be given thereof to each director.   Every such notice shall be given in the following form (*give form*) and state the time fixed for the meeting.

4. The quorum of an ordinary meeting shall be ――――― directors, and of a special meeting ――――― directors.

5. If all the directors are at any time present at any one place they may constitute themselves a board meeting for the transaction of business.

6. The common seal shall be placed in the custody of the president or chairman, or in that of the secretary or manager, and shall be kept in a box with two locks, whereof each of said officers shall have one key.

7. The common seal shall not be affixed to any document, except in pursuance of a resolution for a board, and the sealing shall be attested by two directors and countersigned by the secretary.

The regulations for board meetings should be formally adopted, on motion made, seconded and put, and finally entered with the resolution of adoption in the minute book of the board.

When a board has met in accordance with the regulations at the fixed time and place, the members present shall enter their names, and the regular chairman, or in his absence another member called to preside *pro hac vice*, will take care that a quorum is present (see *above*, p. 111) ; and if that be the case he will call upon the secretary to read the minutes of the last meeting (see *below*, p. 125, for form of minutes).   When these have been corrected, whenever necessary, confirmed by the meeting and signed by the chairman, the latter will direct attention to the business that is to be considered.

All well conducted societies will have an order of business, or *agenda*, as it is called, which should be always entered on the left hand page of the minute book and on the opposite page the chairman will note the determination of the meeting on each proceeding.   Each item of business, as a rule, should be taken up in order.   All matters of importance should be disposed of by resolutions duly made and put to the meeting by the chair. If it is found expedient to give priority to a particular item, some member should so move, but if there is one dissentient voice the order of business cannot be disturbed (see parliamentary rule, *above*, p. 80). In a business meeting of this kind the chairman gives explanations when necessary, and otherwise directs the proceedings. The secretary should keep a record of all the proceedings, and, as well as the chairman (*e*), initial the original resolutions when formally adopted, so that they may, at a future time, identify them. Frequently the original resolutions are pasted in the minute book, when written legibly; but the preferable course is for the secretary always to record each proceeding with his own hand.

The regulations, generally, empower the directors to appoint select committees of two or more members to consider special subjects. Such committees should have their quorum fixed, and be bound strictly by their order of reference (see *above*, p. 48).

The following *agenda*, or order of business, is given from the best authorities on such subjects as a suggestion, which will, of course, be varied according to circumstances :

1. First meeting for organization.—

> To elect chairman.
>
> To appoint a secretary.
>
> To approve and adopt a common seal.
>
> To appoint solicitor, banker, auditors and other necessary officers.
>
> To instruct a committee of two to frame regulations with aid of solicitor (*f*) and report at next meeting.

(*e*) In many companies in Canada, Mr. Richard White of Montreal informs me, the chairman generally initials such documents. From my experience of all classes of meetings, I think it is well if both chairman and secretary should do so. I have in this, as in every other part of this work, endeavoured to lay down sound rules of practice and not the varying and too often irregular methods that prevail generally in the Dominion.

(*f*) Palmer says (Legal Companion, p. 66) very properly : "Frequent questions of law arise in the management of a company, and as they have often to be answered at a moment's notice, the solicitor should be kept generally informed as

To consider and approve prospectus.

To consider renting of permanent premises.

To consider applications for shares.

And other business that may come up in connection with organizations.

2. Second meeting.—

Signing of attendance book by members present.

Reading and confirmation of minutes of previous meeting (*g*).

Report of committee on regulations and consideration thereof (*h*).

To consider and make final arrangements for permanent offices.

To authorize signing of cheques.

And such other business as the chairman and secretary may find it necessary to submit to the meeting.

3. Third meeting.—

Signing of attendance book by members present.

Reading and confirmation of minutes of last meeting.

To produce banker's book showing a balance of $——.

To report that since the last meeting the following cheques have been drawn, etc.

To sign cheques as follows, namely : to —— for legal expenses; to —— for books and stationery.

To pass transfers numbered 1 to 25 and to authorize the secretary to register the same, and to issue new certificates in respect of the shares transferred.

To read and consider letters from A. B.

To receive report of committee appointed at last meeting for the purposes of, etc.

To consider a proposal by C. D., as to, etc.

To give directions as to calls in arrears.

To consider and determine as to forfeitures of shares held by ——.

to the company's proceedings, and he will, of course be familiar with its regulations. In some companies the solicitor is required to be present at all general meetings to state the law, if necessary. He will also attend at meetings of the board, when required."

(*g*) See *above*, p. 11.

(*h*) For procedure on all reports of committees, see *above*, p. 50.

To authorize the affixing of seal to contract with ———, in terms
approved of at last meeting.

To appoint a committee to select new offices and to arrange, provisionally, terms for taking the same.

To receive report of solicitor, as to the company's claim against ——
and to give directions.

To receive auditor's report as to estimated profits of half year ending
the —— of ——, and to consider and declare *interim* dividend.

To consider and settle report to be made to the ordinary general
meeting, and to fix the day for holding the meeting, and to approve
notice convening the same, and to give directions for issue.

The following legal principles have been laid down by the
English courts and govern the proceedings of boards of public
companies generally in this country :—

Where there is a maximum and a minimum number fixed by
the law or regulation, the directors cannot act if the number falls
below the minimum (*i*), unless there is power expressly given to
act notwithstanding the vacancies (*j*).

Where there is no quorum fixed by Act and no power is given
to do so, the directors must act on the footing that to constitute a
valid meeting all the directors must be summoned, and a majority
must be present (*k*).

Commonly the directors determine to hold ordinary board
meetings on a special day or days in each week, or month, and at a
special place and hour, and, of course, notice of such determination
renders it unnecessary to give further notice of such meeting.
But notice must invariably be given of special meetings (*l*).

A director, who is disqualified, cannot be counted in a
quorum (*m*). But even when a quorum may, in fact, be present if
they have not been duly summoned according to the law or

(*i*) *Alma Spinning Co.*, 16 Ch. D. 681.

(*j*) *Scottish Petroleum Co.*, 23 Ch. D. 413, 431, 435 ; *Faure* v. *Phillipart*, 58
L. T. 527.

(*k*) *York Tramways Co.* v. *Willows*, 8 Q. B. D. 685.

(*l*) Palmer's Precedents, pp. 301-2. See regulations, *above*, p. 112.

(*m*) *York Tramways Co.* v. *Willows*, 8 Q. B. D. 697 ; Palmer citing other cases, 302.

regulations, they do not form a properly constituted meeting capable of transacting business (*n*).

If a director be excluded by his co-directors ·from a board, he has a personal right to compel them to admit him (*o*).

The directors are entitled at their meetings to take their business in such order as they deem proper (*p*).

A committee of the board need not consist of more than one person, when the directors have power to delegate their authority to committees consisting of such member or members as they think fit (*q*).

The phrase "whenever they think fit" in a statute or the regulations, applied to the action of the directors, means *prima facie* when, at a board meeting, they so determine (*r*).

4. SHAREHOLDERS' MEETINGS.

Meetings of shareholders are of two classes :

1. *Ordinary*, held at regular or stated periods, as established by the letters patent, or by-laws of the company.

2. *Extraordinary* or *special*, called by notice to consider matters not foreseen or provided for at the ordinary general meetings.

The Canadian Acts generally contain sections prescribing that the general meeting of shareholders shall be held within the limits of the jurisdiction from which the charter emanated, leaving it to the regulations of each company to prescribe the exact place at which they shall be held.

Directors have power under the law as a rule to pass regulations providing for both ordinary and extraordinary meetings (*s*). Great

(*n*) *Homer District Co.*, 39 Ch. D. 546.

(*o*) *Pullbrook* v. *Richmond Co.*, 9 Ch. D. 610; *Harben* v. *Phillips*, 23 Ch. D. 14 ; *Bainbridge* v. *Smith*, 41 Ch. D. 462.

(*p*) *Cawley & Co.*, 42 Ch. D. 209.

(*q*) *Taurine Co.*, 25 Ch. D. 118; Buckley, 510.

(*r*) *Browne* v. *La Trinidad Co.*, 37 Ch. D. 1; Palmer's Precedents, 282.

(*s*) See Warde, p. 38, and Canadian Statutes cited, *above*, p. 108 *n*.

care must be taken that the notice convening a meeting complies in form with the regulations, and that it is served on the members at the proper time in accordance with statute or regulations. If special business is to be or can be transacted at an ordinary meeting, the notice must state the exact nature of it, just as if the meeting were extraordinary and special; or an extraordinary meeting may be held on the same day as an ordinary one, and the notice must set forth the time and place.

The president, or in his absence the vice-president of a company, or the chairman of the board of directors, takes the chair as a rule, according to the regulations at the time fixed for the meeting. If the person entitled to preside is not present, a chairman will be elected by the meeting as at any public meeting (see *above*, p. 67).

If no quorum is present then the chairman should adjourn the meeting which is consequently dissolved.

If a quorum is present, in the opinion of the chairman, the chairman should read the notice convening the meeting, or the secretary may read it at the call of the chairman.

Minutes of the previous meeting are next read by the secretary, corrected when necessary and confirmed. The chairman may say "Shall I sign these minutes as correct?" This will be agreed to as a matter of course (see *above*, p. 11; *below;* p. 125, as to chairman's signature).

The business of the meeting should then be taken up in accordance with the notice, and with an agenda, prepared by the secretary, with the approval of the chairman of the board of directors.

This agenda will be read to the meeting by the chairman.

Every item of business will be taken up in due order, and discussed when duly submitted by the chair, on motions whenever necessary (see *above*, p. 11).

Amendments may be made to any proposed resolution, as in parliament, but great care must be taken in the case of amendments to a proposed resolution of which special notice has been given. Where the notice is framed in *general* terms, amendments can as a rule be moved, but where the proposed resolution of which notice has been given is *specific* and *definite*, no amendment can be submitted. In this latter case the meeting is bound strictly to the specific terms of the notice. The proposed resolution must be simply affirmed or negatived. This definite form is sometimes chosen to get a direct vote on an important question of policy or management; but in all other cases, it is more convenient to have the notice framed in some such general form as this :

For the purpose of considering, and if thought fit, passing the subjoined proposed resolution, either with or without any modifications (*t*).

Motions and amendments should be in writing except purely formal motions of business (see *above*, p. 12). The regulations should provide for motions, and the limitation of debate on each question (see *above*, p. 13). If the regulations do not require written amendments, it is a question whether a chairman can refuse to put an amendment submitted when unwritten. But members should as a rule write out all important motions.

When the chairman is satisfied the meeting is ready for a decision on a motion, he will first take the voices, or a show of hands (see *above*, pp. 69, 70), or a poll may be taken according to the regulations of the company (see *below*, p. 131).

When the business is concluded, it is usual for a vote of thanks to be passed to the officers of the previous year, should the meeting be one for the election of new officers ; and under all circumstances thanks should be given to the chairman for his conduct in the chair. The meeting is then formally adjourned.

From the foregoing necessarily imperfect summary of the ordinary procedure at a general meeting, it will be seen that the following matters are of signal importance in the proceedings of a company :

1. Notice.
2. Chairman.
3. Quorum.

(*t*) See Palmer's Leg. Comp. pp. 46, 47. All societies in proposing amendments to their charters or constitutions, of which notice is always given should carefully bear in mind the principles laid down in the text.

4. Minutes.
5. Resolutions.
6. Books.
7. Poll or voting.

All these matters are reviewed in their due order in the following pages.

5. NOTICE OF MEETINGS.

Every general meeting must be called by the directors in accordance with a notice issued in conformity with the law and the regulations passed by the company under the law. Under the Dominion Companies' Act, notice of the time and place for holding general meetings must be given at least twenty-one days previously thereto in some newspaper published at, or near as may be to, the office or chief place of business of the company. In Quebec the notice is ten days. In Ontario it is ten days, but it is added, "and also in the case of companies having a capital exceeding $3,000, either by publishing the same in the *Ontario Gazette*, or by mailing the same as a registered letter, duly addressed to each shareholder at least ten days previous to such meeting." In Nova Scotia, the notice is the same as in the Dominion. In the other provinces, it is a matter of by-law under the general power given companies by the provincial statutes incorporating them. In cases of special incorporation, it is also generally left to the regulations of the company.

The regulations should always state the mode in which notices are to be served on the members. Where the service is personal or by letter a record should be kept by some officer of the company so that, if the service should be subsequently disputed, he may be able to refer to the record and testify accordingly. A postal book should be kept, and envelopes numbered and entered according as despatched by registered post. By the Dominion Act notices may be served either personally or by sending them through the post in registered letters, addressed to the shareholders at their places of abode as they appear on the books of the company. Such notice served by post on a shareholder shall be held to be served at the time when the registered letter containing it would be delivered in the ordinary course of mail; and it is sufficient to prove that such letter was properly addressed and registered, and was put into the post office, and that adequate time had been given for its delivery in the ordinary course of things. Any notice may be signed by any director, manager or other authorized officer of the company and need not be under its seal.

The notice of an ordinary meeting need only state place, day and hour at which the meeting will be held "for the purpose of transacting the ordinary business of the company" unless the regulations provide expressly for a precise statement of business.

When no sufficient notice is given by charter, or statute, or by-law, each stockholder is entitled to express personal notice of each corporate meeting.

Notice is not required of an adjourned meeting (in the absence of an express rule to the contrary) as it is held to be the continuation of the original meeting, but it is not competent to transact any business save that which the original meeting left unfinished. New business, however, that is to say, business not entered upon at a general meeting can be entertained at an adjourned meeting, if due notice of the intention to propose such business be given, and the regulations do not provide to the contrary, and this practice is both expedient and convenient. Where the original meeting was duly convened, the stockholders are not entitled to any other notice of the adjourned meeting than that which is implied in the adjournment (*u*). It must be always borne in mind, however, that special business cannot be taken up in the absence of due notice of its general nature, and of any provision for the same in the regulations.

There is at common law a right of adjournment of a public meeting and it lies in the chairman *semble* (*v*).

But where notice of an adjourned meeting is necessary under the law or regulations, it has been held that, when business had

---

(*u*) *Wills* v. *Murray*, 4 Ex. 843.

(*v*) *Reg.* v. *D'Oyly*, 4 Perry & Davidson, 52; Buckley, 483.

been begun and not completed at the meeting, from which the adjournment took place, the notice of the adjourned meeting need not state the purpose for which it was summoned (w).

The days of notice required by the law or regulation, it is conceived, must be calculated from midnight to midnight (x). Neither the day of service nor the day of meeting will, therefore, form part of the twenty-one or ten days previously mentioned (see *above*, p. 119).

Where an extraordinary meeting is called for the transaction of business of which notice is necessary, the notice must give substantial information as to that which is proposed to be done ; for otherwise a resolution passed upon insufficient notice may be altogether invalid (y). And when a resolution passed at an extraordinary meeting is for the want of proper notice invalid, a confirmation at the annual general meeting will not render it valid (z).

Notice of a meeting summoned " on special business " is not sufficient notice of an extraordinary meeting (a).

Notices, however, are not to be construed with excessive strictness, or mere technicalities introduced into their construction, provided they give the shareholders proper notice of the substance of that which is proposed to be done (b).

If a meeting cannot be otherwise summoned at all, or if the object is a special one, the court might call a meeting (c). And so the court may control the directors as to the date at which a meeting shall be summoned, if it be shown they are executing their discretion improperly (d).

(w) *Scadding* v. *Lorant*, 3 H. L. C, 418.

(x) *Lawford* v. *Davies*, 4 P. D. 61 ; Buckley, 481.

(y) *Garden Gully Co.* v. *McLister*, 1 Ap. Cas. 39 ; Buckley, 481.

(z) *Lawes's Case*, 1 D. M. & G. 421.

(a) *Wills* v. *Murray*, 4 Ex. 843.

(b) *Wright's Case*. 12 Eq. 335 *n.*, 345 *n.*; Buckley, 185.

(c) *Atwool* v. *Merryweather*, 5 Eq. 464 *n.*; Buckley, 480, notes *d* and *e* for other cases.

(d) *Cannon* v. *Trask*, 20 Eq. 669.

But it must be a very strong case indeed which will justify the court in restraining a meeting of shareholders (e).

6. QUORUM.

It depends, as a rule, on the regulations or by-laws. In some cases a definite or fixed number of the shareholders constitutes the quorum, or it may be a specified number who hold a certain number of shares or a certain amount of capital. Under the Dominion, Ontario, Quebec and Nova Scotia Companies' Acts—and in the majority of special Acts of incorporation—powers are given to the directors to make by-laws for a quorum of all meetings. The register of members and stock book of a company should be always accessible to the chairman and secretary at a general meeting, ordinary, or special, in case a question arises as to a quorum.

7. MINUTES.

As a matter not merely of correct business, but of legal necessity also, it is incumbent upon every company to have minutes kept of all their proceedings and resolutions passed at general meetings (ordinary and extraordinary) of shareholders as well as at meetings of directors. These minutes must be written by the proper officer—the secretary of the meeting or company as a rule—in a book kept for that purpose. The regulations should so provide for the keeping of those minute books, and on this point reference is made to the judicious rules of the Presbyterian courts (see *Fourth Part*, III. of this work).

The secretary makes minutes of each proceeding as the meeting goes on. He must be guided by the directions of the chair in each case, and not by those of any member. When a resolution is passed, he should initial (f) and number it so that it may be easily identified at any future time. Every resolution accordingly should be in writing before put from the chair (see *above* p. 30).

(e) *Isle of Wight R. R. Co.* v. *Tahourdin*, 25 Ch. D. 320; *Harben v. Philips*, 23 Ch. D. 14; Buckley, 481.

(f) See *above*, p. 113, as to the chairman also initialling.

The secretary should write it out in full in his record of proceedings, when he comes to transcribe his notes in the proper book (g).

As a rule, separate books should be kept for shareholders' and directors' meetings. The books of directors being essentially private or confidential should be only open to the inspection of directors and secretary as a rule. The shareholders should, however, have always access to the books containing the minutes of their proceedings. In fact they are so open necessarily from the fact that the minutes must be confirmed at a general meeting, and may be called into question before confirmation (h).

The English authority from whom I have quoted so frequently gives the following excellent forms of minutes for companies' meetings, etc.

The fourth ordinary meeting of the　　　　　　　company, limited, held the
　　　　day of　　　　　, (at the registered office of the company) at
o'clock.

Mr.　　　　in the chair.

The notice convening the meeting was read by the secretary.

The minutes of the general meeting of the company, held the　　　th ultimo, were read by the secretary and signed by the chairman.

It was resolved unanimously that the report of the directors and the accounts annexed thereto be taken as read.

Upon motion of the chairman, seconded by Mr.　　　　, it was resolved unanimously (or nem. con. as the case may be).

That the report of the directors and the accounts annexed thereto be and the same are hereby adopted.

Upon, etc., it was resolved that a dividend, etc.

Upon the motion, etc., it was resolved that Mr.　　　　be and he is hereby elected a director in the place of Mr.　　　　.

Upon, etc. [vote of thanks].

A. B., Chairman.

If an amendment be moved the minutes will run thus :

It was moved by the chairman and seconded by Mr.　　　　, that, etc.

(g) The attention of secretaries and clerks of all municipal councils, assemblies and societies is directed to the foregoing rule for keeping minutes as practically embodying the usages of parliament.

(h) Palmer's Legal Companion, pp. 74, 75.

An amendment was thereupon moved by Mr.   , and seconded by Mr.   [here set it out, *e.g.*],

" That the report be received, but not adopted, and that a committee of five shareholders be appointed with power to add to their number, to inquire into the formation and past management of the company, and with power to call for books and documents, and to obtain such legal and professional assistance as may be necessary, such committee to report to a meeting to be called for day, the   th of   ."

The amendment was put to the meeting and negatived. The original question was then put to the meeting and declared by the chairman to be carried.

EXTRAORDINARY GENERAL MEETING OF THE   COMPANY
LIMITED, HELD THE   TH DAY OF   , AT, ETC.

Mr.   in the chair.

The notice convening the meeting was read by the secretary.

The minutes of, etc.

Upon the motion of the chairman, seconded by Mr.   ,

It was resolved unanimously that the capital of the company be increased to $, by the creation of   new shares of $ each.

A resolution moved by Mr.   , seconded by Mr.   ,

That, etc., was negatived.

Mr.   moved,

That, etc.

Mr.   seconded this motion.

A show of hands having been called for, the chairman declared that hands were held up in favour of, and   against the resolution, and that the motion was consequently carried [*or* lost, as the case may be].

A poll was then demanded and taken, the numbers being as follows : For the motion, 128 votes ; against the motion, 72 votes. [The minutes may distinguish the number of personal votes and of votes by proxy. The scrutineer's report (if any) will be entered].

The chairman then declared that the resolution was carried.

The minutes of a meeting of the directors will be as follows:

At a meeting of the directors held the   th day of   at, etc.
Present, Mr.   , chairman of the board ; Mr.   , and Mr.   .
The minutes of the meeting of the   th were read and signed.

Upon the motion, etc., it was resolved, etc.

A draft contract between, etc., having been read, the chairman was directed to affix the seal of the company to the engrossment thereof.

The secretary was directed to, etc.

A letter from, etc., addressed to the secretary having been read, and the board being of opinion, etc., the secretary was directed to reply, etc., and the manager was desired to, etc.

The minutes of a meeting should be read at the next meeting, when it is not possible to do so at the same,—and that can hardly often happen in the nature of things,—and when corrected and confirmed should be signed by the chairman.   Sir Reginald Palgrave (i) says that "the signature of a chairman to the minutes is only necessary when such minutes are under statute, *thereby* rendered legal evidence.   His signature is not otherwise essential to the confirmation of the minutes if an entry of the confirmation is duly minuted."

But it is advisable to have the chairman of a public company, exercising legal rights and responsibilities, sign the minutes, unless the regulations otherwise provide.   The original papers, like resolutions, reports of committees, directors' reports, etc., which have been considered and acted upon at a meeting, should be always accessible when the record of proceedings is read at a meeting, in case its correctness is doubted and verification is necessary.   Especially is this essential when neither the chairman of the meeting nor other member is present at that where the minutes are considered.

The remarks made elsewhere that no debate can be allowed on a proceeding or amendment proposed which is not a necessary correction of an inaccuracy, apply with full force to the minutes of public companies (see *above*, p. 11).

(i) Chairman's Hand-book, p. 24.

8. Chairman.

The chairman of a general meeting is, as a rule, the president, elected by the directors. The Dominion and Quebec Acts also expressly provide for the election of a vice-president, who may act in the absence of the regular chairman. It would be well if the regulations of all companies have a rule to provide:

If the president (*or* vice president), or the chairman of the board of directors is not present to take the chair at any general or other meeting of the company, it will be competent for the members present, within fifteen minutes after the time appointed for holding the meeting, to choose some one of their number to preside thereat.

The tenure of office of chairman of boards or other corporate boards is regulated by law and custom. He is specially charged with the duty of considering the legal effect of notice, when such is required by law or regulation, and the regularity of motions and amendments thereto. But both legislature and judiciary protect them while according them full responsibility in their position. Accordingly the decision of a majority of a duly constituted meeting will be upheld, although attended by technical informalities, provided that such irregularity has arisen through mistake or inadvertence, is unmarked by fraud, and causes no individual wrong.

The chairman has *prima facie* an authority to decide all questions which arise at a meeting and which necessarily require decision at the time, and the entry by the chairman in the minute book of the result of a poll, or of his decision on a matter of procedure, is *prima facie* evidence of that result, and of the correctness of that decision (*j*). Legal protection is afforded to the chairman of shareholders' meetings as regards the mode by which he obtained the decision of the meeting, establishing that, unless a poll is demanded, his declaration that a resolution has been carried shall be deemed conclusive evidence of the fact without proof of the number or proportion of the votes recorded in favour of or against such resolution. The principle thus established may be extended

(*j*) *Indian Zoedone Co.* 26 Ch. D. 70.

to that very customary usage under which a chairman, assured that the meeting comprehends the proceeding and consents thereto, declares that a motion springing from the ordinary course of business is agreed to without formally putting the question thereon to the vote (*k*).

It has been decided in the English courts that if a chairman improperly refuse to put an amendment, the resolution, if passed, is not binding (*l*).

9. RESOLUTIONS.

The regulations of a company generally provide that divers acts shall be done by the company in general meeting. The company expresses its will by its consent given by a resolution of the members present in person or by proxy, where proxies are allowed at a general meeting of the company. Whether the meeting should be an ordinary or an extraordinary one must depend on the nature of the business and the regulations. Notice must be given of special resolutions (see *above*, p. 120), and it must be duly submitted by the chairman to the decision of the meeting when debate thereon is closed as in the case of all motions in all public assemblies (see *above*, p. 12). A resolution which for want of sufficient notice is invalid cannot be ratified by a subsequent general meeting for the powers of the latter are limited to acts within the laws or regulations (*m*).

10. BOOKS.

Palmer gives the following books as necessary for the correct transaction of the business of every company :—

1. Register of members, p. 80.
2. The share ledger, App. Form 23.
3. Register of documents, containing particulars of all documents not recorded in other books.

(*k*) Palgrave, p. 47.

(*l*) *Henderson* v. *Bank of Australasia*, 62 L. T. 869, and on App. 6 Times L. R. 424, Buckley, 186.

(*m*) *Lawes's Case*, 1 D. M. & G. 421.

4. The certificate book containing forms of certificates of title, p. 5.

5. Transfer register.

6. Transfer certificate book, p. 13.

7. Minute books of general meetings [see *above*, p. 123].

8. Directors' minute book [see *above*, p. 123].

9. Directors' attendance book.

10. Seal book.

11. Postal book.

12. Register of mortgages, p. 34.

Full particulars of these several books will be found in the same authority.

The Dominion, Ontario and Quebec Companies' Acts provide that the books kept by the secretary or some other officer, specially charged with that duty, shall duly record :

"A copy of the letters patent incorporating the company, and of any supplementary letters patent issued to the company, and of all by-laws thereof; the names, alphabetically arranged, of all persons who are and have been shareholders ; the address and calling of every such person while such shareholder.

"The number of shares of stock held by each shareholder.

"The amounts paid in and remaining unpaid, respectively on the stock of each shareholder; all transfer of stock, in their order as presented to the company for entry, with the date and other particulars of each transfer, and the date of the entry thereof : and the names, addresses, and calling of all persons who are or have been directors of the company with the several dates at which each person became or ceased to be such director."

11. Voting.

The regulations of every company should contain provisions relative to the voting at shareholders' meetings. The general rule, laid down in the Companies' Acts of the Dominion and the Provinces, is that each shareholder is entitled to as many votes as he owns shares, but he must have paid all calls and not be in arrears thereon. Shareholders may also vote by proxy, according to the universal practice of joint stock companies, though no such right exists by common law. But should the law or the regulations fail to authorize voting by proxy, votes must be given personally. A lunatic or idiot, under the English law or articles, may vote by his guardian or trustee, and the same is the case with minors as a rule. But it has been laid down that if one or more persons are entitled to a share or shares the member whose name stands first on the register of members as one of the holders of such shares shall be entitled to vote in respect of same. A person is generally, by the Companies' Acts, entitled to vote on shares held by him in trust, and *semble* even where he is a trustee for the company itself, if his name appears on the register as the holder of such shares in trust (*n*).

The company have no right to enquire into the beneficial ownership or to reject votes on the ground that a member is by the regulations restricted to so many votes altogether, and that other registered shareholders who vote are really nominees of his, and that he is thus exceeding the limited number (*o*). A shareholder is entitled to increase his voting power by transfers to nominees (*p*).

Regulations generally provide for a show of hands, but if there is no such provision then the voices may be taken as in parliament. A vote by show of hands is obtained by challenging the chairman's opinion regarding the voices of the meeting. He will then direct that the vote be so taken. Tellers will be appointed, one for the yeas and one for the nays from the respective party or side on which each declared himself by his voice in the first instance. The vote is taken as in all such cases (see *above*, p. 69.)

By common right a chairman has no casting vote if the number of votes is equal. The law or the regulations, however, generally provide that the chairman of companies and boards is empowered to vote as an ordinary member, and then to give as chairman a second or casting vote in case of an equality of votes (*q*). The chairman must give his vote while the vote of the other members

(*n*) Warde, pp. 39, 40.

(*o*) *Pender* v. *Lushington*, 6 Ch. D. 70.

(*p*) *Stranton Iron Co.*, 16 Eq. 559. Palmer's Precedents, 287.

(*q*) This is generally done in union, labour and other organizations.

is being taken—first, generally, and before the tendency of the votes is visible. " It would therefore be a grave irregularity if a chairman reserved his votes and gave, if the number proved uneven, *i.e.*, 7 yeas to 6 nays, first to the noes his vote as member, and then his casting vote as chairman " (*r*).

It is best for the chairman always to declare the number of hands for or against a motion, though he is not bound to do so unless the regulations or rules so provide. In a show of hands a chairman will look to the number of hands only, and not take into account the votes which the owner of each represents in person or as proxy.

A shareholder is entitled to vote as he pleases and to consult his own interest provided his vote be *bona fide* and not contrary to public policy (*s*), and in the absence of anything in the articles or regulations to the contrary he is not debarred from voting on a question in which he is personally interested (*t*), and his vote, if not impeachable for fraud, may in fact determine the matter in his own favour by turning the scale (*u*).

It is observed by a high authority that "in the case of a meeting charged with a legal duty to pass a resolution or to perform an act, the members who abstain from voting are held, by their presence during the vote, to be acquiescent in the decision of the majority, and to impart validity to the proceeding if their votes, had they been given, were essential thereto. So also when to pass a valid resolution, a meeting required the votes of the majority of those present, or is subjected as regards its mode of voting to any special provision, members who abstain from voting when a question is put from the chair may, by their presence, render inoperative the transaction in which they refrained to join. And to prevent such misadventure, a rule (*v*) is in common use which

(*r*) Palgrave, p. 17.

(*s*) *Elliott* v. *Richardson*, L. R. 56 ; Buckley, 484.

(*t*) *London & Mercantile Discount Co.*, 1 Eq. 277; Buckley, 484, 485.

(*u*) *N. W. Transp. Co.* v. *Beatty*, 12 App. Cas. 589, 593.

(*v*) Palgrave, p. 40.

provides that every question shall be decided by a majority of the votes of the members present, 'and voting on that question.'"

As a general rule, however, no liability arises from the neutrality of members of a meeting, called for the purpose of discussion, or of shareholders' meetings, as the vote of a shareholder is not a trust, but a proprietary right, subordinate to the owner's freedom of will. A shareholder is entitled if he pleases, to execute his proprietary right in a manner entirely adverse to what others may think the interests of the company as a whole, and from motives or promptings of what he considers his own individual interest (*w*). But even the shareholder's freedom of vote is limited by this; that he must use his power consistently with the constitution of the corporation whose affairs he is entitled to control. So that if the majority affirm a proposition which is *ultra vires* the minority are not bound (*x*).

When a show of hands has been taken, or, at any time, according to the regulations, a poll may be taken.

By "poll" is meant that mode of voting by which each voter, by his personal act either orally or in writing, delivers his vote to an appointed officer. This method of voting is accordingly the regular and common law mode of taking the vote of a meeting, entrusted with legal responsibilities. A poll, therefore, unless forbidden by the clear words of a statute, or by the regulations, may be demanded on any question put to such meeting, as of right.

But the chairman (*y*) is not bound to grant a poll unless it is demanded in accordance with the regulations. Any qualified person under the common law may demand a poll (*z*). But a proxy authorizing a person to vote does not authorize him to demand a poll (*a*). When it is known that the persons demanding

(*w*) *Pender* v. *Lushington*, 6 Ch. D. 70.

(*x*) *Menier* v. *Hooper's Telegraph Co.*, 9 Ch. D. 350; Buckley, 485.

(*y*) " In the absence of regulations to the contrary the chairman is the person to grant a poll." *Reg.* v. *Hedges*, 12 A. & E. 159; Palmer's Precedents, 286.

(*z*) *Reg.* v. *Wimbledon Local Board*, 8 Q. B. D. 459; Buckley, 484, citing other cases.

(*a*) *Haven Gold Mining Company*, 20 Ch. D. 156, 157 ; Buckley, 483.

a poll are duly qualified, the chairman will read out the demand,
and state that he grants the same and fix the time where and
when the poll will be taken, and if necessary the meeting will be
adjourned. The question sometimes arises whether a poll can be
taken at once; that is, without an adjournment. This depends on
the regulations. If they give express authority, as well framed
regulations do, to take the poll "either at once or after an
adjournment," the poll can be taken accordingly, and even if there
is no such authority; that is, if it is to be taken "in such manner
as the chairman directs," it has been ruled in the English courts
that where voting by proxy is allowed the poll may be taken at
once (b).

Not unfrequently it is convenient, if the regulations allow, to
take the poll at once, but this is not always practicable in the case
of companies with a numerous list of voters. Indeed it should be
always borne in mind that a poll is an appeal to the whole constituency and is taken in order to ascertain the sense of the
general body of persons qualified to vote, and to give others besides
those who are present when the poll is demanded power to come in
and exercise their right of voting, and in order to ascertain
whether the voters have the qualification which is required in order
to entitle them to exercise the privilege of voting (c).

Unless the regulations otherwise require, a poll need not be
demanded publicly ; it is sufficient if the chairman acts on a private
demand (d). Where the regulations give power to adjourn "with
the consent of the meeting," the chairman cannot adjourn to take
even a poll without that consent.

When a poll has been granted, the chairman will fix it by
providing : "The poll on [state question] will be taken on
next, the   th inst. [or proximo] between the hours of   and
, at the regular office of the company," or "here as soon as
the other business of this meeting has been transacted."

(b) *Chillington Iron Co.* 29 Ch. D. 159; Buckley, 483, 484.

(c) *Per* Cotton, L.J., *Reg* v. *Wimbledon*, 46 L. T. 47.

(d) *Re Phœnix Co.*, 48 L. T. 260.

In case of a large company with many shareholders, one or more scrutineers may be appointed to compute the votes at a poll, and report to the chairman. The meeting can appoint scrutineers (e), even if the regulations do not provide for a scrutiny. Very commonly they are appointed by the chairman with the assent of the meeting (f). Sometimes in small companies the chairman acts as scrutineer (g).

The following tabular form is generally provided as a convenient way of recording the poll in accordance with the regulations :

NAMES OF MEMBERS.	NUMBER OF SHARES.	NUMBER OF VOTES.	OBSERVATIONS.	VOTES GIVEN.	
				FOR.	AGAINST.

At the time appointed for taking the poll, the members who vote personally will come up to the voting table and write their names on sheets of paper marked " for " or " against " the motion as the case may be. A member voting as proxy for another will write down his own name and also that of the person whose proxy he is, that is " John Smith, by W. Jones his proxy." The following is a form of proxy :

(e) *Wandsworth Co.* v. *Wright*, 22 L. T. 404.
(f) Palmer's Precedents, 286.
(g) *Ibid.*

PROXY.

THE TORONTO STEEL COMPANY, LIMITED.

I, John Smith, of the City of Halifax, in the province of Nova Scotia, in the Dominion of Canada, being a holder of two hundred shares of the said company, do hereby appoint and authorize Philip Thompson, of the city of Toronto, Esquire, to vote for me, and on my behalf at the ordinary [*or* extraordinary, as the case may be] general meeting of the said company, to be held on the 19th day of May next, in the year of our Lord one thousand eight hundred and ninety three, and at any adjournment of the said meeting that may be held within the present year.

Witness my hand and seal this fourteenth day of April, one thousand eight hundred and ninety-three.

Signed in presence of

JOHN SHARPE,
Halifax.
[Seal.]   JOHN SMITH.

Sometimes it is arranged that a member signing his own name shall be deemed to vote for himself and for all those whose proxy he is.

The question who is to vote upon a certain share of stock is, as a general rule, answered by reference to the corporate transfer book. In fact, all the books relating to the shares should be at hand in case of the right of members to vote being questioned.

Where a member proposes to vote on a poll as proxy, it should be ascertained :—

1. That the shareholder appointing him has a right to vote.

2. That the proxy himself is qualified to act.

3. That the instrument appointing him is in proper form, and deposited in due time.

4. That notice of revocation has not been given.

A shareholder may revoke the appointment of a proxy at any time, but a vote given by the proxy before the revocation reaches the company will be valid. In case of a revocation the shareholder ought before the meeting to write to the company, giving notice of the revocation. If in attendance he can hand a revocation to the chairman. If the proxy has the words, " in my absence to attend and vote," personal attendance revokes the instrument.

If a vote is found invalid by reason of arrears in calls and so forth, the chairman or scrutineer will reject the same and state the cause in the column of the form devoted to observations.

The chairman may also vote on his shares as any other member, though he may have the casting vote by law in case of a tie besides. A voter may vote at the poll even though not present when the poll was demanded (h).

The votes having all been taken, the chairman or scrutineers will enter them in the list of votes, in the column " for " or " against " as the case may be.

When the poll is finally closed, the scrutineers should make a report in writing of the result to the chairman. The latter will then state the result to the meeting, or adjourn the meeting as may be decided, and declare the motion has been carried or negatived.

When a poll has been demanded and taken the show of hands goes for nothing, and the decision of the meeting depends upon the result of the poll (i), and in contemplation of law the meeting continues until the poll has been fully taken (j). If the poll is not completed on the day on which it is commenced it must be continued subsequently for the chairman is not entitled to close the poll whilst votes are coming in (k); to shut out and exclude a voter may invalidate a poll (l); but the chairman is not bound to wait for hours to see if votes may come in (m). Nevertheless the chairman may direct the continuation of the poll at a subsequent period in order to give an opportunity to other voters to come in (n). To appoint a subsequent day for the taking or completion of the poll is not an adjournment of the meeting, although it in effect

(h) *Campbell* v. *Maund*, 5 A. & E. 865 ; Palmer's Precedents, 286.

(i) *Anthony* v. *Seger*, 1 Hag. Cas. Consis. 913 ; Palmer's Precedents, 286.

(j) *Reg.* v. *Wimbledon*, 30 W. R. 402, and 46 L. T. 47 ; Palmer's Precedents, 286.

(k) *Reg.* v. *St. Pancras*, 11 Ad. & E. 15; *Reg.* v. *Graham*, 9 W. R. 738 ; Palmer's Precedents, 286.

(l) *Reg.* v. *Lambeth*, 8 Ad. & E. 356.

(m) *Ibid.*

(n) Palmer's Precedents, 286.

continues the meeting (*o*), but it is usual to adjourn the meeting to hear the result. Sometimes there is no formal adjournment, but it is arranged that notice of the result shall be given, and to this the authorities say there would not seem to be any legal objection (*p*). If the meeting is adjourned to hear the result of a poll, the chairman will, at the adjourned meeting, state the result.

Unless some provision to the contrary is found in the charter or other instrument by which the company is incorporated, the resolution of a majority of the shareholders duly convened upon any question with which the company is legally competent to deal is binding upon the minority, and consequently upon the company (*q*).

A majority of the votes passed at a poll on an election or a particular question decides the result. This majority need not be an actual numerical majority of all the votes which all the stockholders have, but only the majority of the votes cast.

In the case of a ballot—as required by the Dominion, Ontario and Quebec Companies' Acts for the election of directors—the ballot papers should be prepared beforehand by the secretary, or chairman, or scrutineers, so that there will be one vote for every share of stock owned by a shareholder. The back of each paper should be initialled by the secretary or scrutineers or chairman, as it may be arranged, to prevent fraud, and the ballot taken as in all similar cases. (See *above*, pp. 76, 77). All the usual precautions should be taken, (as set forth *above*, pp. 134, 135,) that the voter has a right to vote. When he offers his vote, reference should be made to the proper list and his name duly checked against his shares. The ballots should be counted only when the vote is concluded; but no attempt should be made to record a member's vote when he deposits it as in the case of an ordinary poll (see *above*, p. 133), as the meaning and object of a ballot is secrecy.

(*o*) *Reg.* v. *Chester*, 1 Ad. & E. 342; *Reg.* v. *Wimbledon, ubi supra.*

(*p*) Palmer's Precedents, 286.

(*q*) *N. W. Transp. Co.* v. *Beatty*, 12 App. Cas. 589, 593: cf. *Farrar* v. *Farrars, Ltd.*, 40 Ch. D. 395; Buckley, 465.

FOURTH PART.

I.—SYNODS OF THE CHURCH OF ENGLAND IN CANADA.

II.—CONFERENCES OF THE METHODIST CHURCH.

III.—CHURCH COURTS OF THE PRESBYTERIAN CHURCH IN CANADA.

IV.—CONVENTIONS OF THE BAPTIST CHURCH, AND OTHER RELIGIOUS BODIES.

I.—SYNODS OF THE CHURCH OF ENGLAND IN CANADA.

1. PRELIMINARY OBSERVATIONS.

I come now to refer to the procedure of that very important class of meetings which are held at stated times to discuss matters affecting the interests of various religious denominations. These meetings are called synods, church courts, assemblies, or conferences, according to the phraseology sanctioned by the law and usage of the religious communities of Canada. These several bodies derive their authority to hold and sell property, enforce discipline in their churches, and manage their affairs generally by virtue of various Acts of the legislatures of Canada. These various Acts constitute the several synods and conferences of the provinces, so many bodies corporate, or in other words, so many corporate entities, having all the rights that the common or statutory law gives such associations. In the present treatise it is proposed to give a brief review of the procedure in the synods, assemblies and conferences of the three principal protestant denominations of Canada, viz., the Church of England, the Presbyterians, and the Methodists, as sufficient for all purposes.

2. Constitution of the General Synod.

The Church of England in Canada has established the following representative bodies for the management of its affairs within its several ecclesiastical divisions :

A General Synod.

Provincial Synods.

Diocesan Synods.

The general synod has the power " to deal with all matters affecting in any way the general interests and well-being of the church within its jurisdiction." It has no authority, however, " to withdraw from a provincial synod the right of passing upon any subject falling within its jurisdiction at the time of the formation of the general synod." (See " Basis of Constitution " for objects of general synod.)

The general synod, as constituted (a) in September, 1893, in the city of Toronto, consists of the bishops, and delegates chosen from

(a) The writer is indebted to the thoughtful consideration of Rev. Canon Spencer and J. A. Worrell, Esq., Q.C., clerical and lay secretaries of the lower house, for an advance copy of the constitution and rules of the general synod.

the clergy and laity of the twenty dioceses of the Dominion. It consists of two houses; the bishops composing the upper, and the clergy and laity together the lower house. The two houses sit separately, but when they decide to sit together, "each house shall vote separately." The president of the synod is named the primate of all Canada, the metropolitan of his own province, and the archbishop of the see over which he presides. He is elected by the members of the upper house from among the metropolitans or bishops not in any ecclesiastical province, holds office for life, or as long as he is bishop of any diocese of the general synod, but he can resign at any time. In this latter event a successor can be elected by the house of bishops.

The delegates are chosen by the several diocesan synods according to such rules as they may adopt, or, in a diocese which has no synodical organization, they may be appointed by the bishop. The representation is as follows : Dioceses having fewer than twenty-five licensed clergymen, one delegate from each order ; dioceses having twenty-five and fewer than fifty licensed clergymen, two of each order ; dioceses having fifty, and fewer than one hundred, three of each order ; dioceses having one hundred licensed clergymen and upwards, four of each order. Delegates must be resident in the diocese from which they are elected or appointed, "provided, that until circumstances permit of its being otherwise ordered by the general synod, the bishops of the dioceses of Moosonee, Selkirk, Caledonia, Mackenzie River, and Athabasca, and such other dioceses as may be formed out of them, be permitted to appoint non-resident delegates to the provincial synods, provided only that such delegates be resident within the bounds of the ecclesiastical province of Rupert's Land, or of the civil province of British Columbia respectively, and that until 1896 those dioceses may be represented by delegates from any dioceses whatsoever."

The chairman of the lower house is named prolocutor, who must be a clerical delegate, and elected *vivâ voce* by the two orders, and continues in office until the next meeting of the synod.

Each house appoints a secretary or secretaries (see *below*, p. 150), and " establishes its own order of proceedings and rules of order (see *below*, p. 149), and may publish such of its proceedings as it may deem advisable." Sittings are public or private, at the discretion of each house.

Clergy and laity vote by orders " if required." And " if the proposition be carried in the negative it shall be conclusive; but if in the affirmative, any six delegates (two from each of three different dioceses) may then demand a vote by dioceses, when, if the proposition be carried in the negative, it shall be conclusive; the vote of each diocese being determined by a majority of the delegates of that diocese. And in case of equality in the votes of the delegates from any diocese, such diocese shall not be counted."

A quorum of the synod shall consist of not less than a majority of the bishops and of not less than a majority of the members of each order of the lower house.

No alteration of the constitution or canons "shall come into operation until it has been confirmed at a second session of the general synod " (*a**).

The next meeting of the synod is to be held on the second Wednesday of September, 1896, in the city of Winnipeg.

The expenses of the synod, including the necessary travelling expenses of the members, "shall be provided for by an annual assessment of the several dioceses represented in the synod, proportioned to the number of licensed clergymen in them ; dioceses having less than ten clergymen being exempt. Provided, however, that the expense of any member of the synod not attending during the whole session of the synod shall only be paid *pro rata*, and such proportionate part thereof as his attendance bears to the whole time the synod is in session. And that a standing committee be

(*a**) Rev. Canon Spencer, clerical secretary, informs me that the constitution and rules of order and proceedings (except the "permanent order of proceedings," see s. 5, p. 145, *above*) of the general synod, have been " adopted *provisionally*, subject to amendment, by a majority vote at next session of the general synod." The constitution and rules of order of the provincial synod are given as they stood at close of the last session.

appointed who shall fix and determine the amount at any time to be paid hereunder : such committee, however, to have a discretionary power to allow a greater proportion in case of absence from illness or other good cause arising during the sitting of the synod."

3. THE PROVINCIAL SYNODS.

At the present time there are two ecclesiastical provinces in Canada, comprising two groups of dioceses under the jurisdiction of the two provincial synods. First, the ecclesiastical province of Canada comprises the dioceses of Nova Scotia, Fredericton, Quebec, Montreal, Ontario, Toronto, Niagara, Huron and Algoma (missionary). Secondly, the ecclesiastical province of Rupert's Land comprises the dioceses of Rupert's Land, Moosonee, Saskatchewan, Athabasca, Qu'Appelle, Calgary, Mackenzie River and Selkirk. In British Columbia there are the dioceses of Columbia, New Westminster and Caledonia, but they are not yet formally incorporated into an ecclesiastical province with a provincial synod, though they are included in the general synod of Canada.

A provincial synod is constituted of the bishops having sees, and of the delegates chosen by the clergy and laity within the ecclesiastical province. It is composed of two houses, an upper house of bishops, and a lower house of delegates. The presiding bishop of the upper house is the metropolitan of the ecclesiastical province, and is the archbishop of the diocese over which he presides. Consequently, at the present time, there are two archbishops of the Church of England, the archbishop of Rupert's Land, who is also primate of all Canada, as president of the general synod, and the archbishop of Ontario, who is the metropolitan of the ecclesiastical province of Canada. The chairman of the lower house is called prolocutor.

In each diocese of the ecclesiastical province there is also a diocesan synod, composed of the bishop and of clerical and lay delegates appointed by the several parishes of the diocese (see *below,* pp. 160 *et seq.*).

From the foregoing outlines of the constitutions of the several synods, it will be seen that the Church of England has practically a federal constitution.   That is to say, there is one federal or general synod in which all the separate ecclesiastical divisions or corporate entities are duly represented, and in which the affairs of the church common to all are considered; and there are so many local and diocesan synods called upon to deal with the special interests in the respective ecclesiastical divisions into which the whole Dominion is divided.

4. CONSTITUTION OF THE PROVINCIAL SYNOD OF CANADA.

This synod —the most important in the Dominion after the general synod—consists of the bishops of the sees already enumerated (see *above*, p. 143), and of delegates chosen from the clergy and laity respectively.

The bishops shall deliberate in one house, and the delegates from the clergy and laity in another ; and each house shall hold its sittings either in public or in private, at its own discretion.

The clerical and lay delegates shall consist of twelve of each order from each diocese. ˙

The synod shall meet on the second Wednesday in September in every third year, or oftener, at the discretion of the metropolitan ; or on the requisition of any two bishops, or of the bishop and half the delegates of each order in any diocese.   In a vacancy of the metropolitan see, a meeting may be called at the appointed period, or on either of the above requisitions, by the senior bishop of the ecclesiastical province of Canada.

A quorum of the synod shall consist of not less than a majority of the bishops, and of not less than one-fourth of the members of each order of the lower house.

The metropolitan (*b*), or some bishop appointed by him, shall be the president of the upper house ; and in the vacancy of the

---

(*b*) The bishop of Montreal was for many years, by virtue of his office, the metropolitan ; but at present the bishops elect the dignitary—generally the senior bishop.   In this election a majority of all the bishops of the ecclesiastical province

see, or in the event of the inability, from any cause, or on failure of the metropolitan to appoint a bishop as president, the house of bishops shall elect one of their own number to preside.

The lower house shall be presided over by their prolocutor, to be chosen *virâ voce* on motion of any member of the house. Each house shall appoint a secretary or secretaries (see *below*, p. 150), and "establish its own order of proceedings and rules of order (see *below*, p. 149), and may publish such of its proceedings as may appear advisable."

No alteration of the constitution or canons shall come into operation until it has been confirmed at a second session of the provincial synod.

The expenses of the synod shall be provided for, and its financial concerns managed by a committee of the lower house, after a manner to be approved by both houses.

5. Permanent Order of Proceedings of the General and Provincial Synods.

The rules governing the relations between the two houses and the rules of order and procedure of the general and provincial synods of Canada, are the same, with only a variation here and there of detail of little importance; and these differences will be noted in all cases hereafter in brackets.

The general [*or* provincial] synod shall meet at the time and place of which notice has been given by the primate, or, in the event of his inability to act, by the metropolitan next senior by consecration [*or* by the metropolitan or his deputy in the case of the provincial synod]. The bishops and clergy attend in their proper robes, and proceed to the cathedral or other place appointed by the primate [*or* metropolitan] for divine service; on which occasion the holy communion shall be always administered (*c*).

must concur, either by their vote at a meeting called for the purpose, or by writing under their hand and seal. The meeting for the purpose is held at the summons and under the presidency of the senior bishop (see Canon I. of Provincial Synod).

(*c*) In the provincial synod, "the litany shall be said by the junior bishop."

The preacher shall be appointed by the primate [*or* metropolitan], and special prayer shall be made for the synod. The collection shall be applied to the current expenses of the synod, unless otherwise ordered by the primate [*or* metropolitan].

At an appointed hour after divine service, the members of the synod shall assemble at the place of deliberation—the bishops being habited in their robes, and the clergy in gowns and hoods (*d*)—where the president, after he has taken his seat, shall inform the lower house with regard to their place of meeting, and direct them to elect their prolocuter.

When the prolocutor has been elected, he shall be conducted to the upper house [by the chairman, in the case of the provincial synod], accompanied at discretion by any members of the lower house, and his election duly announced to the president.

The president shall then inform the prolocutor of the business which the upper house desires to engage the attention of the lower house, and may, when necessary, specify the order in which the bishops desire it to be considered.

On every day of meeting after the first, the synod shall meet at 9.30 a.m. [and the provincial synod at 9 a.m.], and shall proceed at once, before any business is announced, to morning prayers at the cathedral or other appointed place.

The business of each day shall be commenced by prayer according to a form authorized by the house of bishops.

The relations between the two houses are governed by rules providing for messages, conferences and joint committees, as will be explained in the following section.

6. RELATIONS BETWEEN THE TWO HOUSES OF THE GENERAL AND PROVINCIAL SYNODS.

In the formation of two houses of the general and provincial synods, in the provisions for conferences, messages, joint committees, and in the rules of order generally of these bodies, we see a closer adherence to the law and practice of parliament,

---

(*d*) This last provision in parenthesis is not in the rules of the provincial synod, but the practice will necessarily be the same.

than in any other assembly in Canada. The following are the constitutional regulations that govern the relations between the two houses in the course of a session :—

15. [12 (*e*).] " The upper house may [shall] propose to the lower any business they may desire to have treated of or decided ; and it shall be incumbent on the lower house to take up and dispose of such business immediately after the subject under consideration shall have been disposed of for the time being, provided always that it shall be the duty of the prolocutor to read to the house the message immediately on its receipt, and the house may by its vote, without discussion, decide on proceeding to its consideration at once."

16. [13.] " The upper house may direct the lower to appoint a committee to report to the upper on any subject on which they may desire the judgment of the lower, or to appoint their portion of a joint committee ; or may summon the lower to a conference."

17. [14.] " Messages from the upper house shall be delivered by an officer of the upper to the secretary of the lower, by whom they shall be communicated to the prolocutor, who shall communicate them to the house."

18. [15.] "The lower house may present to the upper any matter which they conceive to be a grievance or to require amendment, even when they have no proposition to make on the same ; and the upper house shall thereupon place it in order for consideration, with a view of providing a remedy ; and shall, before the conclusion of the session, declare to the lower house the result."

19. [16.] " The prolocutor shall have the right of admission personally or by committee to the upper house, to communicate the desire or decisions of his house, and in such case, he shall ascertain by message when he or the committee can conveniently be received in the upper house, and act accordingly."

20. [17.] " It shall be competent to the lower house to request a joint committee or conference on any special object, beyond those submitted to it by the upper house, or to propose for discussion any specific measure ; to which request an answer shall be given, but it shall be at the option of the upper house to accede to their request or not."

21. [18.] "When either house shall desire a conference with the other, or a joint committee, the reason for either shall be agreed to by the house desiring it, and communicated in writing to the other, the prolocutor personally or by committee in either case proceeding to the upper house, either to deliver or to receive such reasons."

22. [19.] "When either house shall have come to a decision upon any subject in which the other house is concerned, it shall communicate its decision to the other."

(*e*) Figures in brackets here as elsewhere refer to number of regulations of the provincial synod.

23. [20.] "If the lower house should not concur in a decision of the upper, they shall, in stating their concurrence, state their reason, and may either propose an amendment or request the upper house to suggest an amendment to meet their reason, or request a conference."

24. [21.] "If the upper house should not concur in a resolution or decision of the lower, they may, in stating their non-concurrence, either state their reasons or not, and may either propose an amendment or request the lower house to prepare an amendment or appoint a conference, to which the lower house shall always give attention."

25. [22.] "The conference may be either by deputation from both houses, or by deputation from the lower house, or by open conference, as the upper house may think fit ; and the place shall be appointed by the president."

26. [23.] "No proposition shall be considered as sanctioned by the provincial synod until it has received the separate sanction of both houses, which shall be declared by the president in writing."

27. [24.] "Committees, whether of either house, or of the two houses, may hold their meetings either during recesses in the session, or during the prorogation of the synod."

The foregoing are special regulations based on the practice of parliament. For parliamentary rules regulating conferences, see *above*, p. 56 ; joint committees, *above*, p. 57. It will be seen that the modern parliamentary practice of " communicating reasons" in case of disagreement between the two houses—a practice which facilitates business—has been adopted to all intents and purposes (see *above*, p. 57). The regulation (24) allowing committees to meet during prorogation is necessary since no select committee of parliament can assemble after a prorogation (see Bourinot, p. 508).

A message from the upper house of the provincial synod is generally in such terms as these :

"The president of the upper house begs to inform the prolocutor that the upper house has adopted the report of the joint committee on the 'incorporation of the provincial synod and other matters,' and desires the concurrence of the lower house."

(Sgd.)   J. W. QUEBEC,
President.

Or :

"The upper house desires the lower house to take up the report of the committee on divinity degrees, and the canon submitted by that committee."

(Sgd.)   J. W. QUEBEC,
President.

7. Rules of Order and Procedure of the Lower Houses of the General and Provincial Synods.

The lower house meets on the first day of the session, at the time and place duly appointed by the primate [or metropolitan] or president. After the preliminary proceedings, set forth on a previous page (see *above*, p. 145) they reassemble and after prayer the clerical secretary calls the roll of the clerical delegates, and the same course is followed by the lay secretary in the case of the lay delegates.

The election of the clerical and lay delegates (*f*) must be certified under the hand and seal of the bishop of the diocese which they represent, or, in the absence of the bishop, by the chairman of the synod; and this certificate, which is final and conclusive, must be forwarded by the secretaries of the diocesan synod to the secretaries of the lower house of the general [or provincial] synod within fourteen days after the election in question. In case any of the delegates, duly certified as above, are unable to attend, the bishop, or, in his absence, the clerical secretary of the diocesan synod, shall certify under his hand and seal that the delegate in question, whether clerical or lay, cannot be present, and that another person, duly designated, is authorized by vote of the diocesan synod to fill the place of the former as delegate. This certificate is final and conclusive, whether it is presented before or during the session of the provincial synod (*g*).

The roll of delegates will be called according to dioceses, and each member must answer to his name. In the minutes signs will indicate those present and absent. In case members arrive subsequent to the calling of the roll, the secretaries will enter their names in the minutes and make an entry on the list, "arrived after session had commenced." Sometimes members who by some

(*f*) For delegates to general synod, see *above*, p. 141. Each diocesan synod sends twelve of each order to the provincial synod. For mode of latter election, in each diocese, see Nova Scotia, Const. s. 21 ; Fredericton, Canon IX.; Quebec, Canon IV.; Montreal, p. 37 of Const.; Ontario, Canons III. (7), XXVI.; Toronto, Const. ss. 44-49 ; Niagara, Const. 19, 20 ; Huron, Canon XXIX.

(*g*) Section 30 of Const. Gen. Synod ; s. 28 of Const. Prov. Synod.

inadvertence on their part had not reported themselves, though present, are allowed to have their statement entered in the proceedings of the following synod (*h*).

When it is announced that a full quorum of both orders is present, [a majority of each order in the general synod, one-fourth of the members of the clergy and laity respectively in the provincial synod], nominations will be made for a prolocutor, by motion formally moved and seconded. In case of several candidates being proposed, the procedure in case of the election of a speaker of the commons should be followed, and each name submitted in the order it is proposed, until a presiding officer is elected (see *above*, p. 27).

When a prolocutor has been chosen, he will express in suitable language his sense of the honour conferred upon him, and proceed to present himself to the bishops in the upper house (see *above*, p. 146).

Having returned to the house, the prolocutor will name a clerical member to act as his deputy in his absence, and introduce to the house the business which the upper house desire to have taken up.

The next proceedings in order are the elections of a clerical secretary, a lay secretary, a treasurer, and two auditors. These officers should be elected in the order here named. In case of several nominations to one office, the procedure for election of speaker should be followed. The clergy vote for their own secretary, the laity for theirs, in order. The treasurer and auditors hold their offices until their successors are appointed.

It is the duty of the secretaries to keep regular accounts of all proceedings in the house, to preserve memorials or other documents under the direction of the prolocutor, to attest all public acts of the synod, and deliver over all records and documents to their successors. The minutes of each day's proceedings are read, corrected and confirmed on the following day.

It is also the duty of the secretaries to arrange a list of business, and of all notices of motions sent to them by members,

(*h*) See Jour. of Prov. Synod, 14th sess., p. 19.

according to the order in which they are received, and under the
direction of the primate [or metropolitan] to cause a printed copy of
the same to be sent to every member of the synod twenty-one days
before its meeting. The business and motions, here provided for,
stand first on the order of the day of the synod when it meets.

The authentic record of the proceedings of each session is the
printed journal, "certified by the signatures of the prolocutor, and
the two secretaries of the lower house to a statement attached to
one or more copies, declaring the number of pages in the said
journal, and the number of words corrected, with the words so
corrected." The constitution of the general synod in each case
also requires they certify the same to be a true copy of the original
meetings and proceedings.

In case of a vacancy occurring in any of these offices when the
lower house is not in session, it shall be filled by the prolocutor,
and the person thus appointed shall hold office until the house
has duly elected his successor.

The house meets for business on each day after the first at 10
o'clock; adjourns, as a rule, from 1 o'clock to 2.30 p.m., and
concludes its sittings at 6 o'clock p.m., when the body proceeds to
the cathedral or other church for evensong. Committees may,
however, meet later if necessary (rule 1).

Business is preceded each day by prayer in an appointed form.

The daily order of business is regulated by the rules as
follows :—

(1) Reading, correcting and approving the minutes of the previous
meeting (see *above*, pp. 11, 125, as to the keeping and correction of minutes).

(2) Appointing committees (see *below*, p. 152).

(3) Presenting, reading and referring memorials or petitions.

(4) Presenting reports of committees, of treasurer, or auditors.

(5) Giving notices of motions.

(6) Taking up unfinished business.

(7) Consideration of motions.

(8) Orders of the day.

(9) Before the final adjournment of the synod, reading, correcting and
approving the minutes of the last day's proceedings.

It is not unusual to suspend the order of business for the moment in order to make purely formal motions, for the admission of distinguished visitors to the floor of the house, or other imperative business. Each visitor is admitted on special motion. It is only, however, by a two-thirds vote that any rule of order can be suspended in case of a division of opinion on the subject (see *below*, p. 155).

As soon as convenient after the calling of the rolls and the election of officers, the prolocutor (rule 3) names one clerical and one lay delegate from each diocese to constitute a committee for the purpose of submitting the names of the members of each of the following standing committees :—

(1) On the state of the church.

(2) On amendments to the constitution.

(3) On canons.

(4) On rules of order.

(5) On elections.

(6) On expenses.

(7) On memorials of deceased members.

(8) On unfinished business and printing.

These committees are appointed by the house on the recommendation of the nominating committee, but it is always competent for any member of the house to refer the report back, or to amend it by adding new names (see *above*, p. 51).

Any matter that may be appropriately considered by such committees may be referred, without debate, to the proper body for its consideration and report.   No committee can of course depart from its order of reference without an instruction from the house (see *above*, pp. 48-51, for parliamentary rules respecting special committees).

A standing committee (rule 32) of three clerical and three lay members of the provincial synod must be also appointed on the first day of meeting, to arrange for each day the order of precedence for the several motions of which notice has been given, and have them printed.   The appointment of this committee is generally left, by motion, with the prolocutor (see journal of 1889, pp. 7, 8). The committee on unfinished business and printing performs the foregoing duty for the general synod.

Whenever the upper house sends a message to the lower house, proposing any business, it is incumbent upon the latter body to take it up and dispose of it immediately after a subject under consideration has been disposed of for the time being. The prolocutor reads this message as soon as it is received, and the house may, by its vote, without discussion, proceed at once to its consideration.

The house may establish its own order of proceeding and rules of order (see *above*, pp. 142, 145). The following is the present code of rules relating to motions, debates, and proceedings generally, and it will be seen that they adhere closely to the procedure of parliament. In the case of each rule I give such references to the first part of this work, and such comments as will show where the rules of the two bodies are identical or different. This is necessary, since " in any unprovided case resort is had to the rules of order of the house of commons in Canada for guidance," in the general as well as provincial synod.

2 (*i*). " The prolocutor shall preserve order and decorum, and shall have power to appoint assessors in so doing, and he shall decide all questions of order, subject to an appeal to the house, to be decided without debate, and when called upon to decide a point of order, he shall state the rule applicable to the case without argument or comment."

See same parliamentary rules *above*, pp. 28, 40. For mode of appeal, *above*, p. 39.

Rule 3 provides for appointment of standing committees, as explained *above*, p. 152, though not always finally embodied in a rule.

4. " When any member wishes to speak he shall arise and address the chair."

See *above*. p. 37, for parliamentary rules.

(*i*) I retain the original numbering of the rules, which is the same in both synods, as most convenient for all purposes of reference. Rule 1 appears *above*, p. 151.

5. "When two or more members rise at the same time, the prolocutor shall name the party first to speak."

See *above*, p. 37, for parliamentary rule.

6. "A member called to order whilst speaking shall sit down, unless permitted to explain."

See *above*, pp. 39, 40, for parliamentary rules. The prolocutor should give such permission if the synod shows a desire for explanation, or it is necessary for a correct understanding of the question of order (see rule 9, *below*).

7. "No motion or amendment shall be considered as before the house unless seconded and reduced to writing."

See *above*, p. 30, for parliamentary rule. If not seconded and written the chairman cannot read or propose it to the house. For mode of proposing a question, see *above*, p. 31.

8. "No member, save the mover of a resolution, who, as mover, is entitled to reply, shall speak more than once, except by permission of the house."

See *above*, p. 38, for parliamentary rule. This permission is given, when necessary, by motion, and by a majority of the house.

9. "A member may rise to explain if permitted by the chair."

See *above*, p. 38, for parliamentary rule, and rule 6, *above*.

10. "No original motions, except motions of course, shall be received without notice, except by permission of the house."

The motions "of course" in parliament are for the adjournment of the house, or of the debate or the previous question, or relate to routine or purely formal business (see *above*, p. 30), which, being well understood by every one do not require to be written or placed on the notice paper. The synod may, however, give permission, *i.e.*, a majority can waive notice under exceptional circumstances.

11. "When a resolution has been moved and seconded, any member may require the previous question to be put, whether the motion so made be put or not, and that question shall be decided without debate."

This is a modification of the parliamentary rule respecting the previous question, "That the question be now put," and all debate must cease when the motion is made and a vote be taken at once. If the previous question is carried then a vote must next be taken at once on the main motion. If it is negatived, the main motion is superseded for the time (see *above*, p. 14).

12. "When a motion has been read to the house by the prolocutor, it cannot be withdrawn without the consent of the house."

In parliament the consent must be unanimous, since the rule does not permit a single negative voice (see *above*, p. 31). Every assembly expresses its consent to a motion or question by a majority vote, unless there is a rule to the contrary.

13. "When a question is under debate, no motion shall be received by the chair, unless to amend it, or to postpone it, or to lay it on the table, or for adjournment, or for the previous question, and no more than one amendment to a proposed amendment of a motion shall be in order."

Here we come to those dilatory or subsidiary motions on which I have commented at some length, *above*, pp. 21-26. These explanations are necessary here :

(a) Postponement, debatable since parliamentary rule prevails (see *above*, pp. 25, 26).

(b) Lay on the table, not debatable (see *below*, rule 15).

(c) Adjournment, not debatable (see *below*, rules 14, 15).

(d) Previous question, not debatable (see *above*, rule 11).

(e) Two amendments to a question are only admissible at one time. For full explanations, see *above*, p. 35. The four previous motions (*a-d*) are always in order, as they are not in the nature of amendments.

See also rule 16, *below*, which allows a motion to suspend a rule precedence even of the motions in this rule 13.

14. "A motion to adjourn shall always be in order."

See *above*, p. 33, for parliamentary form of motion. Here it is subject to following rule 15.

15. " Motions to adjourn or to lay on the table shall be decided without debate."

See *above*, rule 13.

16. "A motion to suspend a rule of order shall take precedence of all other motions, and shall be decided without debate, and no rule of order shall be suspended, except upon the vote of two-thirds of the members present."

This is a special rule not found in parliament. This motion to suspend a rule is privileged and has priority over all others.

17. " A member, if not interrupting a speaker, may require any motion in discussion to be read for his information at any time during the debate."

For the parliamentary rule, see *above*, p. 32.

18. "When amendments are made to any motion the amendment and the original motion shall be put in order, the reverse of that in which they were brought forward."

This is the Canadian parliamentary method of putting a question and amendments thereto (see *above*, pp. 33, 34).

19. "When a question is finally put by the prolocutor either on an original motion or on an amendment, no further debate shall be allowed ; the prolocutor first declaring that the question is finally put."

Intended to limit debate like the parliamentary rule forbidding debate when members have been called in preparatory to a division (see also *above*, p. 42).

But a point of order may be taken (see *above*, p. 44).

For mode of putting a question in parliament, see *above*, pp. 41, 42.

20. "When the prolocutor is putting a question no member shall rise from his seat, and every member present, when a question is put, shall be required to vote on the same unless excused by the house."

Every member in parliament must vote unless his vote is disallowed because he has a pecuniary and direct personal interest in a question (see *above*, pp. 42, 43 for parliamentary rule). The foregoing rule allows a member to be excused on motion, but the body will not excuse a member from voting except for reasons which it may consider sufficient. It is a duty to vote.

21. " In voting, those who vote in the affirmative shall first rise and then those who vote in the negative ; and in case of an equality of votes the question shall be decided by the casting vote of the prolocutor, who may also vote on the question."

The prolocutor has accordingly two votes. If he votes as a member on every question, he should rise at the same time with those with whom he votes, and not subsequently (see *above*, p. 78). It is questionable, however, whether he should not reserve his vote, as he can always do in his discretion under the rule, until there is an equality, and then give his decision in accordance with the principles that govern speakers of the commons house (see *above*, pp. 42, 69).

22. When required by two clerical and two lay delegates, the vote of the house upon any question may be taken by orders voting separately; and in that case a majority of both orders shall be necessary to an affirmative vote."

A special rule of the synod requiring no comment here. That is to say, the clergy first vote ; then the laity, as set forth in rule 21 *above*. See also constitutional rule of general synod, *above*, p. 142, as to voting by dioceses.

23. " On a division, the names of those who vote for or against a question shall be recorded in the minutes, if required by three members."

See parliamentary rule *above*, p. 41. All such votes are recorded in parliament.

24. " A question being once determined, shall not again be drawn into discussion in the same session, without the unanimous consent of the house."

Necessary to save time of session (see *above*, pp. 17, 32, for parliamentary rule). One member can prevent such a question being reconsidered. Here the consent must be "unanimous " and not of a majority.

25. " Committees shall not be appointed without notice, excepting standing committees, committees of the prolocutor to the upper house and committees of course, such as those which follow upon the adoption of a resolution, which requires a committee."

All committees in parliament are formed, as a rule, on notice duly made (see *above*, p. 48). The foregoing is a special rule of the synod.

26. " When a separate committee of this house has been named, whose function is deliberative, the prolocutor shall direct what number of its members do form a quorum, unless the quorum be fixed by the resolution under which the committee is appointed."

If there is no quorum so fixed, then there must be a majority of the whole committee present at a meeting before business can be transacted (see *above*, pp. 9, 48).

27. " When a committee is appointed, the mover of the resolution asking for the committee, shall be the chairman of the committee, or when a resolution is referred to a committee, the mover of the resolution shall be chairman, unless the committee has already been organized."

This rule goes further than the parliamentary usage which generally induces the committee, when it meets, to appoint as chairman the mover of the original resolution for the committee. Here the rule is mandatory, except in the case of a committee already organized (for parliamentary rules, see *above*, p. 48).

28. " Reports of committees shall be in writing, signed by the chairman, and shall be received in course, but a motion may be made for recommittal."

See *above*, pp. 50, 51, for parliamentary rule regulating reports. All reports can be recommitted if the house so order.

29. " Motions with reference to reports from committees shall take precedence of other motions on the paper."

A special rule of these synods.

30. " Whenever it shall happen that members appointed on committees are not re-elected to the general [or provincial] synod the prolocutor may appoint others from the same diocese, or dioceses, to fill their place ; and in order thereto a copy of the certified lists of clerical and lay delegates sent to the secretaries shall be sent by them to the prolocutor."

A special rule of these synods.

8. PROROGATION OF THE GENERAL SYNOD.

This synod, when assembled for business, shall be prorogued by the primate or president of the upper house, after a resolution fixing the time of prorogation has been agreed upon by both houses; and the president with the consent of the upper house, shall issue a schedule declaring the state in which each matter of business stands, which has been brought before the upper house, and shall promulgate the same to the lower house.

The prolocutor, on receiving this schedule, shall, at the first opportunity, communicate it to his house. The primate shall then, at the hour agreed upon, prorogue the synod.

A prorogation will supersede all business of that session under consideration at the time, and unless there are special resolutions to the contrary that unfinished business must be commenced anew at the next session (see Bourinot, p. 288).

9. Prorogation of the Provincial Synod.

The proceedings are practically the same as the foregoing. Before the conclusion of the session the president, with the consent of the upper house, and in accordance with the regulations, announces the list of measures—a schedule in official phrase—passed at that session of the synod, including the joint committees, and makes such comments on these and other subjects as he may deem expedient. This schedule " declaring the state in which each matter now stands which has been brought before the upper house " must be promulgated to the lower house. The prolocutor, on receiving this schedule, shall at the first opportunity, communicate it to his house, which shall not prolong its sittings beyond that day. All unfinished business is accordingly reserved until the next session, and the synod is practically prorogued after the doxology has been sung and the benediction pronounced by the president.

10. Enactment of Canons.

No canon shall be enacted, unless the same has been transmitted by the secretaries of the lower house to the members of the general [or provincial] synod at least three weeks [or a month for the provincial synod] before its meeting, or unless the same has been left over as unfinished business and accordingly printed in the journal of the previous session.

The constitution of the general synod *also* provides that "all canons shall be fairly transcribed in a book to be kept for that purpose, immediately after they are passed, and be attested by the primate or other presiding bishop, the prolocutor and the secretaries of both houses."

11. THE RULES OF ORDER AND PROCEDURE

OF THE

DIOCESAN SYNODS OF NOVA SCOTIA, FREDERICTON, QUEBEC, MONTREAL, ONTARIO, TORONTO, NIAGARA, AND HURON (*j*).

The synods of the several dioceses of the ecclesiastical provinces of Canada, are duly incorporated by law, and consist in each case of the bishop, of the clergy, and of a certain number of representatives of the laity (who must be communicants), of the diocese. The regulations providing for election of delegates are given in the constitution of the several synods to which reference must be made in all cases.

In the following summary I give only the rules of procedure of the diocesan synods of the province of Canada, with such references to their respective constitutions as are necessary to make the proceedings of their meetings intelligible. As many of their rules are the same, it is not necessary to give the code of each synod separately, but to group them together under a suitable heading of procedure, to which reference can be easily made.

I. **Time of Meeting.**—As a rule the bishop of the diocese, who is the head of a synod, appoints the place of meeting and adjourns or dissolves or prorogues the synod as he may deem advisable. The synod meets—

In Niagara.—On the second Tuesday in June, annually, or at such other date as may be deemed expedient by the bishop.

In Toronto.—On the first Tuesday in June, annually, or at such other date as may be fixed by the bishop.

In Huron.—On the third Tuesday in June, annually, or at such other time as may be fixed by the bishop.

In Ontario.—Annually or oftener at discretion of bishop.

(*j*) The author expresses his thanks to the bishops of Toronto, Niagara and Huron, and to the several clerical and lay secretaries of the diocesan synods for the aid they have given him in the preparation of this part of his work.

In Montreal.—Third Tuesday of January in every year in the city of Montreal or at any other time or place as the synod at its last previous meeting shall appoint. Special meetings may be held at discretion of bishop or on requisition of ten clerical and thirty lay members, and only such special business as the meeting has been called for shall be considered.

In Quebec.—At discretion of bishop, but a meeting must be held at least once in every two years.

In Fredericton.—Wednesday before the first Thursday in July of each year, at Fredericton and St. John alternately, unless the synod by resolution otherwise arranges time and place.

In Nova Scotia.—Biennial, and generally in Halifax. The bishop, or archdeacon in his absence, may summon additional meetings. The synod may accept invitations from other places in the diocese.

2. Presiding officer.—The bishop *ex officio* presides at every meeting of his diocesan synod. The constitutions of the several synods provide that in the absence of the bishop of the diocese, the following shall preside in the order of precedence given :—

Nova Scotia.—The bishop's commissary. In case of a vacancy the archdeacon of Nova Scotia, or the archdeacon of Prince Edward Island, or in the absence of both, the senior presbyter present presides at the synod where a bishop is elected.

Fredericton.—Bishop coadjutor, or the archdeacon, or the bishop's commissary ; and in the absence of the foregoing, the clergy and lay representatives present elect a presiding officer.

Quebec.—A deputy appointed by the bishop, who must be a clergyman of the diocese of not less than fifteen years' standing in priest's orders. In case of a vacancy in the see, the archdeacon, or rector of Quebec, or the senior clergyman in priest's orders, or in the absence of any one of these the senior clergyman present, shall act as president until one is elected. No election can take place unless there is present a quorum of three-fourths of all the clergy and lay representatives respectively. If there is no such quorum there must be an adjournment to any day within one week, and so on from time to time, if necessary, until such quorum be present.

Montreal.—The bishop's commissary. When the see is vacant the senior dignitary of the church next in rank to the bishop, shall summon a synod to be held in not less than thirty days, to elect a successor to the see, and he shall preside at this meeting at which no other business except the election of a bishop can be transacted.

D.M.P.—11

Ontario.—A coadjutor or assistant bishop, or another bishop appointed under one of the canons (XXVIII.) by the bishop to preside. When a bishop, at a session, leaves the chair temporarily, he may appoint one of the members of the synod to preside during his absence.

Toronto.—A deputy chairman appointed by the bishop, or if there is no such officer, then the senior dignitary or clergyman of the diocese present.

Niagara.—Same as Toronto, *above.*

Huron.—A chairman appointed by the bishop.

3. Quorum.—

Ontario.—One-fourth of the whole number of the clergy and one-fourth of the parishes on the synod list, each of which may be represented by one lay delegate.

Montreal.—Not less than twenty-five lay and fifteen clerical delegates.

Quebec.—Not less than one-fourth of the clerical and lay representatives respectively.

Nova Scotia.—Not less than one-fourth of the whole number of qualified clergy, and of lay representatives duly certified, but no vote of the synod shall take place unless in the presence of three-fourths of those forming a quorum, with the bishop or his commissary presiding.

Fredericton.—Not less than one-fourth of the whole number of qualified clergymen of the diocese, and not less than one-fourth of the lay representatives, whose election shall have been certified to the secretary of the synod, but any less number shall have power to adjourn from time to time until a quorum can be obtained.

Niagara.—At least one-fourth of the clergy of the diocese, and one-fourth of the congregations represented by at least one delegate.

Huron.—Of the chairman and not less than thirty of each order of the clergy and laity, except in the election of a bishop when seventy-five of each order must be present. If there is no quorum the synod is adjourned until next ordinary hour of meeting, and so on. Or the synod may be adjourned *sine die.*

Toronto.—Not less than one-fourth of the whole number of the licensed clergy of the diocese, and one-fourth of the lay representatives entitled to sit in the synod.

For parliamentary rules in absence of a quorum, see *above*, pp. 9, 29.

4. **Prayer.**—In all the synods when they have met at the appointed time and place, proceedings commence with prayer according to a form duly authorized by the bishop of the diocese.

5. Call of roll.—The roll must then be duly called as a rule in the synods of the clergy of the diocese and the qualified lay representatives of parishes by the clerical or lay secretaries respectively before any business can be transacted. The names of those in attendance shall be duly noted in a book kept for that purpose. In Toronto, however, the calling of the roll has been discontinued and each clergyman and lay representative signs his name in a book kept for that purpose.

6. Secretaries.—In all the synods, except that of Fredericton, the clergy and laity as orders respectively elect, by a majority vote in each case when necessary, a clerical and lay secretary at each annual meeting.

In Fredericton there is only one secretary who may be chosen at any meeting and remain in office during the pleasure of the synod.

In Nova Scotia there are two secretaries, but the appointment of the lay secretary shall be permanent and he need not be a member of the synod.

In Montreal they may be elected by ballot.

These secretaries keep regular minutes of all proceedings of their synods.

In Quebec provision is also made for an assistant clerical and an assistant lay secretary to act in the absence or incapacity of the regular officers.

In Niagara, Toronto, and Huron, there is also a secretary-treasurer; appointed in Niagara and Huron by vote of the synod, and in Toronto by the executive committee, subject to the confirmation of the synod. Their duties are defined by the respective constitutions. These officers attend to the synod business out of session.

The elective officers of the synods by the Ontario rules hold office until the appointment or election of their successors, and this is generally the case in all the synods.

*Reference must be made to the constitutions of the respective
synods for regulations respecting the foregoing and following officers,
the keeping of minutes and accounts, etc.*

7. Treasurer and auditors.—All the synods have an officer
called the treasurer (or as in some cases secretary-treasurer, see
above) to attend to financial matters. He is, generally speaking,
elected annually by votes of both orders in the synod.

In Fredericton, he must be a member of the synod chosen by
votes of both orders at any meeting, and remaining in office during
the pleasure of the synod.

In Montreal he may be elected by ballot and hold office until a
successor is appointed.

In Ontario and Quebec he is elected annually.

In Quebec provision is also made for an assistant treasurer in
case of the absence or incapacity of that officer.

Two auditors are as a rule appointed annually by all the synods
to inspect and report annually on the accounts.

In Montreal these and other officers may be elected by ballot
and shall hold office until their successors are appointed.

In Fredericton only one auditor is appointed. In Ontario,
there is an audit and accounts committee, composed of two laymen
and one clergyman, members of the synod, elected at each annual
meeting, after the introduction and consideration of the report of
the same outgoing committee for the previous year—the first proceeding in this synod after the calling of the roll (rule 4). Two
auditors, skilled accountants, are also appointed annually by the
executive committee at its first meeting after the meeting of synod,
to audit all accounts and submit their report to the chairman of
the audit committee (see Canon X.).

8. Order of Business.—Every synod, like other deliberative
bodies, has a rule providing for a regular order of business—that
of Huron (*below*, p. 167) being most complete.

In Nova Scotia—

1. Reading, correcting and approving the minutes of the previous meeting (see *above*, pp. 11, 122).

2. Appointing committees (see *below*, p. 181).

3. Presenting, reading and referring of memorials and petitions (see *above*, p. 52).

4. Presenting reports of committees (see *above*, p. 51).

5. Giving notice of motions (see *below*, p. 169).

6. Taking up unfinished business.

7. Consideration of motions (see *below*, p. 170).

This order can be changed or suspended at a meeting only by unanimous consent (see *below*, p. 192).

In Fredericton—

1. Calling of rolls.

2. Reading, correcting and approving of minutes of the previous meeting (see *above*, pp. 11, 122).

3. Presenting reports of committees (see *above*, p. 51).

4. Presenting, reading and receiving memorials and petitions (see *above*, p. 52).

5. Appointing standing committees (see *below*, p. 183).

6. Giving notice of motions (see *below*, p. 169).

7. Taking up unfinished business.

8. Consideration of motions (see *below*, p. 170) and appointing special committees see *below*, p. 183).

This order of business can be changed or suspended at a meeting only by unanimous consent (see *below* p. 192).

In Quebec—

1. Reading, correcting and approving minutes of the previous meeting (see *above*, pp. 11, 122).

2. Giving notice of motions (see *below*, p. 169).

3. Appointing committees (see *below*, p. 184).

4. Presenting, reading and referring memorials, petitions and correspondence (see *above*, p. 52).

5. Presenting reports of committees (see *above*, p. 51), and of the treasurer and auditors.

6. Taking up unfinished business.

7. Consideration of motions (see *below*, p. 170).

This order of business can be changed or suspended at a meeting only by consent of two-thirds of the members present (see *below*, p. 192).

In Montreal—

1. Reading, correcting and approving of the minutes of the previous meeting (see *above*, pp. 11, 122).

2. Appointing committees (see *below*, p. 185).

3. Presenting, reading and referring of memorials and petitions (see *above*, p. 52)

4. Presenting reports of committees (see *above*, p. 51), and of treasurer and auditors.

5. Giving notice of motions (see *below*. p. 169).

6. Taking up unfinished business.

7. Consideration of motions (see *below*, p. 170).

8. Orders of the day.

This order of proceedings can be changed or suspended at a meeting only by unanimous consent (see *below*, p. 192).

In Toronto—

1. Reading, correcting and approving the minutes of the previous meeting (see *above*, pp. 11, 122).

2. Appointing special committees (see *below*, p. 187).

3. Presenting, reading and referring to committees, all memorials, petitions and correspondence submitted to the synod.

4. Presenting reports, (see *above*, p. 51).

5. Reading, and consideration of reports in the order of their presentation.

6. Giving notice of motions (see *below*, p. 170).

7. Taking up unfinished business.

8. Consideration of motions in their order (see *below*, p. 170).

This order of proceeding can be changed or suspended at a meeting only by unanimous consent (see *below*, p. 192).

In Ontario—

1. Reading, correcting and approving of the minutes of the previous meeting (see *above*, pp. 11, 122).

2. Appointing committees (see *below*, p. 185).

3. Presenting, reading and referring memorials and correspondence (see *above*, p. 52).

4. Presenting, reading, discussing, and, if deemed advisable, adopting reports of committees in such order as the bishop determines (for parliamentary rules, see *above*, p. 51).

5. Giving notices of motions (see *below*, p. 169).

6. Taking up unfinished business.

7. Consideration of motions (see *below*, p. 170).

This order of proceeding can be changed or suspended at a meeting only by unanimous consent (see *below*, p. 192).

In Huron.—The order of business at the opening sitting shall be as follows :

(a) Election of secretaries and auditors, who shall hold office until their successors are appointed.

(b) Receiving report of committee on certificates and synod assessments, further reports of which committee may be made at any time.

(c) The bishop's charge.

(d) Receiving report of the executive committee.

(e) Receiving reports of other committees of the synod.

(f) Receiving petitions or memorials.

(g) Receiving notices of motion.

After disposing of the foregoing business the synod shall adjourn.

At the evening sitting, on the first day of meeting, the order of business shall be as follows :

(a) Receiving reports of committees.

(b) Receiving petitions or memorials.

(c) Receiving notices of motion.

(d) Consideration of the report of the executive committee, a motion for the adoption of which report shall be put by the chair.

(e) Consideration of reports of other committees of synod, in the order in which they have been received, a motion for the adoption of which shall be made by the chairman or other member of each committee.

(f) Business submitted by the bishop.

(g) Business submitted by the executive committee.

(h) Motions of which notice has been duly given, in the order of notice (see *below*, p. 170).

At all other sittings the order of business shall be as follows:—

(a) Confirmation of minutes of previous day's proceedings (see *above*, pp. 11, 122).

(b) Receiving reports of committees (see *above*, p. 51).

(e) Receiving petitions or memorials (see *above*, p. 52).

(d) Receiving notices of motions (see *below*, p. 170).

(e) Consideration of reports of committees (see *above*, p. 51).

(f) Business submitted by the bishop.

(g) Business submitted by the executive committee.

(h) Motions of which notice has been duly given, in the order of notice *(see below*, p. 170).

This order of business can be changed or suspended at a meeting only by unanimous consent (see *below*, p. 192).

In Niagara—

1. Reading, correcting and approving of the minutes of the previous meeting (see *above*, pp. 11, 122).

2. Presenting, reading and referring of memorials and petitions and correspondence (see *above*, p. 52).

3. Appointing committees (see *below*, p. 187).

4. Presenting reports (see *above*, p. 51).

5. Reading and consideration of reports (see *above*, p. 51).

6. Consideration of additions and alterations in constitution, canons, by-laws and rules of order (see *below*, pp. 191, 192).

7. Giving notice of motions (see *below*, p. 169).

8. Taking up unfinished business.

9. Consideration of motions (see *below*, p. 170).

This order of business can be changed or suspended at a meeting only by unanimous consent (see *below*, p. 192).

9. Bishop's address.—An address from the bishop is in order at any time in every synod, generally speaking by a special rule.

10. Notices of motions.—As in all well regulated assemblies (see *above*, p. 10), the diocesan synods have special rules providing for notices of motions, as follows:—

Nova Scotia—

6. " All notices of motion given by a presbyter or a representative of the laity for proceeding at a subsequent meeting, shall be read over at such meeting, and may be taken up by any member present at such meeting, in the same manner as if he had himself given the notice."

A later rule provides :—

3. " Every member giving notice of a motion may at the same time announce the name of the person by whom it shall be seconded."

Fredericton—

5. " Notices of motion to be submitted to the synod may be sent to the secretary at least one month previous to its annual meeting ; and the secretary shall cause such notices to be printed in the order in which they are received, and forward to the members of the synod with the usual notice of the synod meeting ; and motions of which notice has been given in such manner shall have priority of consideration, but shall not necessarily exclude other motions."

6. " Notices of motion, if any, given by a member of the synod for proceeding at a subsequent meeting shall be read over at such meeting, and may be taken up by any member present, in the same manner as if he had himself given the notice."

Quebec—

Special rules are wanting, though the order of proceedings (see *above*, p. 165) contemplates notice.

Montreal—

24. " All notices of motion intended to be brought before the next synod shall be sent to the clerical secretary at least six weeks before the day of meeting ; and it shall be the duty of the clerical secretary to keep a record of such notices, and to issue a circular statement of the business for the ensuing synod, with reports of committees, and the order in which the same shall be brought up. The circular to be forwarded to each clergyman and parish, one month before the meeting of the synod."

Ontario—

3. " To prevent surprise, no motion, except a motion in course (see *above*, pp. 30, 154) shall be considered until the succeeding day of meeting, notice thereof having been first given."

Niagara—

3. " To prevent surprise, no motions, except motions in course (see *above*, pp. 30, 154) shall be considered until all motions already before the synod shall be disposed of."

Toronto—By canon I. it is provided :—

(12) "No motion which is not of course (see *above*, pp. 30, 154), or which does not deal with some matter actually under the consideration of the house, shall be introduced to the synod, unless after one day's notice duly given at the time appointed in the order of proceedings, or after the rule of order to that effect be suspended by the synod."

(13) "Notice of motion must be in writing, and contain the name of the member who gives the notice, and shall be handed to one of the honorary secretaries, after having been read to the synod."

By rule 3, "To prevent surprise, no motion, except motions in course, shall be considered till the succeeding day of meeting." [This rule should have the addition as to notice given in the Ontario rule *above*, p. 169.]

Huron—

3. "All motions shall require one day's notice, except motions to adjourn, to suspend the standing orders, and relating to privilege, or any point of order arising during debate, all of which shall be in order at any time." [This rule far exceeds the parliamentary rule when it allows a suspension without notice; otherwise it expresses correct usage.]

11. **Motions.**—The rules of the synods generally provide that all motions shall be in writing and seconded, but in Ontario, Toronto, Niagara, Huron, Nova Scotia and Quebec, an exception is made in the case of those proposed by the bishop or a committee. Montreal rule 12 very properly rejects a motion prefaced by a preamble (see *above*, p. 31). Toronto Canon I. sec. 14, requires the writing to be legible, and the names of mover and seconder inserted.

When a motion has been read by the chair (*or* secretary, as in Nova Scotia, Toronto, Niagara and Ontario), it cannot be withdrawn—

Without consent of chair in Ontario, Niagara and Toronto.

Without consent of meeting in Quebec, Montreal, Nova Scotia, Huron and Fredericton.

All the synods have the parliamentary rule (see *above*, p. 32), that every member shall have the right to require at any period of the debate that a question in discussion be read for his information; but of course a member speaking cannot be interrupted except with his own consent or called to order (see *above*, p. 38).

See *above*, pp. 30-34, for parliamentary rules respecting motions.

12. Amendments.—The rules of the various synods, with respect to putting a question and amendments thereto vary, Those of Ontario, Fredericton, Quebec, Niagara and Huron follow the parliamentary usage (see *above*, p. 12), and an amendment must be considered before the main motion. If there are two amendments to a question before the synod, the amendment to the amendment must be first considered, then the amendment, and finally the main motion.

Nova Scotia rule 11 and Toronto rule 11, appear to depart from the general rule, since it is ordered that " all amendments shall be considered in the order in which they are moved." Later rules order that " all amendments to any question shall be decided on before the question or motion on which they arise is proposed for decision."

By Montreal rule 14, "all questions shall be put to the synod in the order in which they are moved "—which is, in words, a reversal of the ordinary practice in Canada.

While Montreal, Toronto, Niagara, Huron, Ontario and Fredericton allow only two amendments to a question at one time, as in parliament (see *above*, p. 35), on the other hand, Quebec and Nova Scotia limit the ordinary practice by providing that, when a proposed amendment is under consideration, no amendment to such amendment shall be in order until the former is disposed of.

Fredericton, Niagara, Toronto, Ontario and Nova Scotia permit, when there is a motion and amendment before the chair, "a substitute for the whole matter may be proposed, provided it deals directly with the subject in hand."

For parliamentary rules respecting amendments see *above*, pp. 33, 34.

13. A question once decided.—The parliamentary rule (see *above*, p. 32), that a question once determined shall not again be brought into discussion in the same session (see *above*, pp, 17, 32, for meaning of "the rule"), may be, in special cases, laid aside:

In Ontario, Toronto, Nova Scotia, Niagara and Fredericton by the special sanction of the presiding officer.   In Montreal, Huron and Quebec by the consent of the synod.

14. Division of a question.—The Niagara synod has the parliamentary rule as follows :

6. When any motion or amendment is under discussion which contains more than one distinct proposition, it shall be divided at the request of any member.

For same parliamentary rule, which should apply to all synods see *above*, pp. 35, 36.

15. Dilatory or subsidiary motions.— All the synods have special rules providing for amending or superseding or suppressing a question.

When a question is under consideration in the several synods no other motion shall be received

By *Nova Scotia rule 5 :*   unless—

To adjourn (not amendable or debatable under rule 6).

To lay it on the table (not debatable under rule 6).

To postpone it to a certain time (amendable, see *above*, pp. 25, 26).

To postpone it indefinitely (amendable, see *above*, pp. 25, 26).

To commit it (amendable, see *above*, p. 37).

To amend it (see *above*, p. 171).

Or to divide it (for parliamentary rule for divisions of a subject, see *above*, p. 35.)

And motions for any of these purposes shall have precedence in the order here named. (For meaning of precedence see *below*, p. 201).

By *Ontario rule 5 :*   unless—

To adjourn (not amendable or debatable by rule 6).

To move the previous question (not amendable but debatable under parliamentary usage here followed, see *above*, pp. 14, 15).

To lay it on the table (not amendable or debatable under rule 6).

To postpone it to a certain time (amendable, see *above*, pp. 25, 26).

To postpone it indefinitely (amendable, see *above*, pp. 25, 26).

To commit it (amendable, see *above*, p. 37).

To amend it (see *above*, p. 171).

Or to divide on it.

And motions for any of these purposes shall have precedence in the order here named. (For meaning of precedence see *below*, p. 201).

Fredericton, rule 5;—Same as Ontario rule 5, omitting the previous question.

By Montreal rule 16 :   unless—

To amend it (see *above*, p. 171).

To postpone it to a certain day (see *above*, pp. 25, 26).

To lay it upon the table (not amendable or debatable under rule 13).

To adjourn (not amendable or debatable under rule 13).

By Quebec rule 5 :   unless—

To amend (see *above*, p. 171).

To postpone (not amendable or debatable under rule 6).

To adjourn (not amendable or debatable under rule 6).

By Niagara rule 5 :   unless—

To adjourn (not amendable or debatable under rule 7).

To lay it on the table (not amendable or debatable under rule 7).

To postpone it to a certain time (amendable, see *above*, pp. 25, 26).

To postpone it indefinitely (amendable, see *above*, pp. 25, 26).

To commit it (see *above*, p. 37).

To amend it (see *above*, p. 171).

To divide upon it.

And motions for any of these purposes shall have precedence in the order here named. (For meaning of precedence, see *below*, p. 201).

By Toronto rule 5 :   unless—

To adjourn (not debatable or amendable under rule 6).

To lay it on the table (not debatable or amendable under rule 6).

To postpone it to a certain time (amendable, see *above*, pp. 25, 26).

To postpone it indefinitely (amendable, see *above*, pp. 25, 26).

To commit it (see *above*, p. 32).

To amend it (see *above*, p. 171).

Or, with the assent of the bishop, to move, " That the question be now put.

And motions for any of these purposes shall have precedence in the order here named. (For meaning of precedence, see *below*, p. 201).

The last motion must, in this synod, "be put to the vote forthwith" (practically the closure), and if decided in the affirmative, a vote must be taken at once on the motion before the synod, and without debate. If it be decided in the negative, the motion that "the question be now put" cannot be again proposed until a vote has been taken on the motion before the synod (see *above*, p. 14, as to the true effect of a negatived motion for the previous question). The effect, as understood in this synod, is at variance with the original intent of the previous question, and makes it meaningless.

Huron.—No such rule as other synods; simply provision (rule 5) that "motions to adjourn and suspend standing orders shall be put without debate."

16. **The previous question.**—The rules of diocesan synods do not, generally speaking, with the exception of Toronto (see *above*, p. 173), make any special provision with respect to the "previous question," as in the case of the provincial synod, which requires that that question shall be decided without debate, when proposed (see *above*, p. 154). Consequently the parliamentary rule must prevail in all unprovided cases, as set forth in the first part of this work, pp. 13-15. The Toronto rule, it will be seen from remarks on this page *above*, is peculiar to that synod. The Ontario rule (*above*, p. 172), simply gives the previous question a certain precedence, and does not alter the parliamentary rule.

17. **Debate.**—All the synods have the following rules, in accordance with parliamentary usage:

Every member must rise [his head uncovered of course] and address himself to the chair. When the bishop or other person presiding has taken the chair the meeting shall be called to order and no person shall continue standing.

The synods generally follow the general principles of debate as to times of speaking.

Ontario, rule 4, Nova Scotia, rule 4:

That no member shall speak more than twice on the same question without the permission of the chair.

Quebec, rule 4, Montreal, rule 7, Fredericton, rule 4 :

That no member, save the mover of the main motion who is entitled to reply shall speak more than once on the same question *without leave of the synod* (these words in italics are not in the Quebec rule), except in explanation of a material part of his speech, which may have been misunderstood, and then he is not to introduce new matter.

Niagara, rules 4 and 21 :

4. Not more than once on same question without the permission of the chair, except the mover and seconder.

22. Same as Toronto rule 22, *below.*

Toronto, rules 4 and 22 :

4. Not more than once on same question except the mover of a motion, who has the right of reply.

22. Every speaker, except in moving and seconding any motion, shall be limited to ten minutes ; and all speakers shall be timed by an assessor, or assessors, to be appointed by the bishop to aid in the maintenance of order and obedience to the rules of the synod (see *below*, rule 23).

Huron, rules 11 and 12 :

11. Not more than once to same question except by unanimous consent, or the mover of a motion or amendment who is entitled to reply. (This goes much further than the parliamentary rule, which allows only a reply to a mover of a substantive motion, see *above*, p. 38). Rule 12 limits speaking at one time to twenty minutes except by consent.

For parliamentary rules respecting debate see *above*, pp. 37, 39.

18. **Questions of order.**—In all synods, as in parliament (see *above*, p. 28), "all questions of order shall be decided by the chair," which seems to preclude an appeal to the synod.

A member called to order while speaking shall sit down, unless permitted to explain (see *above*, p. 39).

By Toronto rule 23 :

The bishop may appoint at each meeting of the synod two assessors, one clerical and one lay, whose duty it shall be to assist him in maintaining the the rules of order.

For parliamentary rules, so far as applicable, see *above*, pp. 38, 39.

19. Divisions on questions and recording of names.—All the synods have the following rule, which is practically the same as that of parliament (see *above*, p. 88) :—

While any question is being put from the chair the members shall continue in their seats and shall not hold any private discourse ; and when a motion is so put no member shall retire until such motion is disposed of.

As a rule the votes of the clergy and laity are taken separately in orders, but as the regulations vary in some respects it is necessary to cite them in each case in full :

Ontario, rule 14 ; Toronto, rule 15 ; Niagara, rule 16 :

When a division takes place, the votes of the clergy and laity shall be taken separately, if required by the bishop, or by [Toronto requires " in writing "] four members of each of the respective orders ; and the lay representatives shall in all such cases vote by parishes, and when so voting, the vote of the majority present shall be considered as the vote of the parish.

Montreal, section 15 of Const.:

The vote of each order shall be taken separately, when so required by any three members, each vote being determined by the majority of the members present in each order.

Quebec, section 13 of Const.:

At all meetings of the synod, when a division takes place, the votes of each order shall be taken separately.

Nova Scotia, section 13 of Const.:

The vote of each order shall be taken separately, such vote being determined by the majority of the members present and voting in each order.

Fredericton, rule 15 :

Whenever, on the occasion of any vote, the names shall be called for, such names shall be taken by call of the roll, of the clergy and lay representatives each of those answering yea or nay as his name shall be mentioned, and such names shall be entered in the minutes.

Huron, section 22 of Const.:

Ordinarily the votes of the whole synod shall be taken collectively ; but at the desire of the bishop, or at the request of not less than five members of the synod, the votes of the clergy and laity shall be taken separately.

Toronto rule 16 ; Ontario rule 15 ; Montreal rule 6 ; Nova Scotia rule 16 ; Fredericton rule 14 ; Quebec rule 14 require :

. That in voting, those who vote in the affirmative shall first rise, and then those who vote in the negative.   Quebec rule 14 adds: The vote of the clergy being first taken, unless it be otherwise ordered by the chair.

The following special rules of some of the synods provide that " no protest or dissent shall be entered upon the minutes of the proceedings ; " but

By Ontario rule 17 :

When required by any one member, the number of affirmative or negative votes shall be recorded ; and when required by three of either the clergy or lay representatives, the names of the clergy and parishes voting on either side of the question shall be also recorded.

By Fredericton rule 17 ; Montreal rule 17 ; Quebec rule 16 ; Niagara rule 18 :

When required by any three members, the names shall be recorded, but the Montreal rule has not the foregoing proviso with respect to a protest or dissent.

By Nova Scotia rule 18, and Toronto rule 18 :

When required by any one member, names are recorded.

By Niagara rule 15 :

On a question being put by the chair, it shall be determined by the voices as in parliament (see *above*, p. 41) ; or at the request of the chairman or three members, those who vote in the affirmative shall first rise, and then those who vote in the negative—unless a division is required as provided in rule 16 (see for this rule *above*, p. 176).

By Huron rule 8 :

On a vote being called for, the ayes and noes shall respectively rise at the call of the chair and remain standing while the count is taken.   Whenever a count is so taken, the numbers *pro* and *con* shall be entered on the minutes.

The Montreal rule (6) requires that every member present when a question is put shall vote on the same, and we must assume that the same parliamentary usage prevails in all synods unless a member is excused for the sufficient reason that he is pecuniarily or

personally interested (see *above*, pp. 42, 43). All the synods have
the rule that when a motion is put from the chair, " no member
shall retire until such motion is disposed of."

The constitutions of the several synods require that all
assessments and arrears shall be paid before the representatives
of a parish or mission can sit and vote in the synod.

For parliamentary rules respecting divisions, so far as they
may be applicable, see *above*, pp. 34, 41-43.

20. **Votes by ballot**.—In all the synods the constitution and
canons provide for a ballot in certain cases as follows :—

Nova Scotia.—Delegates to provincial synod, Const. s. 21;
election of bishop, Canon II. and Reg. of 1887; committees in
certain cases, rule 1 (see *below*, p. 181).

Fredericton.—Delegates to provincial synod, Canon IX.; election
of bishop or a coadjutor, Canons III., IV.; standing committee
(see *below*, p. 183).

Quebec.—Delegates to provincial synod, Canon IV.; election of
bishop (see journal of synod, 1892).

Montreal.—Delegates to provincial synod; election of bishop;
officers, "if demanded," rule 4; special committees when not
named under rule 21 (see *below*, p. 185). In 1894 a new rule of
taking votes by ballot for executive committee, diocesan court, and
provincial delegates was "acted" upon.

Ontario.—Delegates to provincial synod, Canon XXVI.; election
of bishop, Canon XXIV.

Toronto.—Delegates to provincial synod, Const. ss. 44-49;
election of bishop or a coadjutor, *ibid*. ss. 5-8.

Niagara.—Delegates to provincial synod, Const. XIX., XX.;
election of bishop, *ibid*. XXX.; standing committee, *ibid*. XXII.

Huron.—Delegates to provincial synod, Canon XXIX.; election
of bishop, Const. s. 23; executive committee, *ibid*. s. 16; other
committees, Canon XXIX.

It is competent for every synod to elect by ballot, whenever it
so resolves, unless there is a constitutional rule to the contrary.

This is done in the case of committees in several bodies. Whenever there is no special provision to meet such a proceeding—as in Huron—two scrutineers should be appointed from each order by the bishop, on motion duly made and adopted, to count the vote. In the case of delegates to the provincial synod, Niagara and Toronto require three scrutineers of each order, and Huron four. Huron provides also four scrutineers " of either order out of which members to be elected" for each committee that it may be necessary to elect in this way. Ballot boxes for each order and the proper papers should be always on hand for synods where the ballot is necessary. The Toronto rule seems the best adapted to meet all exigencies:

"47. Ballot boxes shall be provided to receive the ballot papers of the clergy and laity respectively. Upon each member of the synod depositing his vote, a mark shall be placed opposite his name on the certified roll given to the scrutineers by the honorary secretaries, and upon the requisition of any three members of the synod, the number of votes deposited shall be compared with the number of those who have voted upon the occasion. The scrutineers shall hand over the ballot papers to the honorary secretaries of the synod, whose duty it shall be to preserve them until the election of delegates shall be completed, and to destroy them at the end of the session of synod."

For ordinary method of taking the ballot, which does not differ from the foregoing, see *above*, p. 77.

21. Petitions and memorials.—The order of proceedings of each synod (see *above*, p. 165) has provisions for "presenting, reading and reference of petitions and memorials," but the synods have no special rules on the subject, except Montreal, Huron, Niagara and Toronto, as follows:—

Montreal, rule 19, and Niagara, rule 22. "Petitions, memorials and other papers addressed to the synod shall be presented by a member in his place, who shall be answerable to the synod that they do not contain improper or impertinent matter."

Toronto, rule 22. " Memorials and petitions must be dated and must be signed by the persons presenting the same, who shall be held responsible for the statements contained therein."

Huron rule 15 provides petitions and memorials shall be received without debate, except a question of order arises.

These rules practically embody the correct practice of all synods, and are based on that of parliament (see *above*, p. 52), except that the synods may accept all memorials and communications which are properly framed and signed, even when not in the strict form of petitions.

The following is the usual form of addressing a petition and memorial to a synod :—

To the Right Reverend the Bishop, the Reverend the Clergy, and the Laity of the Diocese of   , in Synod assembled :

The Petition (*or* Memorial), of (residence) (style, office, etc.)

Humbly sheweth, etc.

Here state subject-matter, in one or more paragraphs.

Then prayer.

And your petitioners (*or* memorialists) will ever pray.

                                                    Signatures.

22. Committees of the whole.—The synods, generally speaking, have no special rules providing for committees of the whole, and in the absence of such parliamentary usage should prevail (see *above*, pp. 44-46) when it might be deemed expedient to submit a canon or other matter of detail and special importance to this class of committee.

Huron is the only synod that has rules on the subject. Rule 14, like that of the house of commons, provides that the rules of order that obtain in the synod are applicable to proceedings in committee of the whole, except that the rule limiting members to one speech on a motion or amendment (see *above*, p. 175) shall not be in force, and speeches are limited to ten minutes (see *above*, p. 175).

The Huron constitution (s. 24) also makes the following provisions with respect to committees of the whole, which might advantageously be adopted by other synods :—

(*b*) " When a motion is made to enact a new canon, or to repeal or amend a canon, or to alter or amend the constitution of the synod, the principle of the proposed measure shall first be discussed on a motion 'that it be read a first time,' to which motion amendments shall be in order.

(*d*) " If the motion to read a first time be carried in the affirmative the synod shall forthwith resolve itself into committee of the whole for the discussion of the clause or clauses and details of the proposed measure.

- (*e*) "On the work of the committee being concluded, the synod shall resume its sittings and the chairman shall report the canon or motion to the synod with amendments or otherwise.

(*f*) "If any amendments have been made in committee of the whole, the form of motion shall be 'that the amendments be agreed to by the synod,' to which motion amendments cognate thereto shall be in order (see similar parliamentary rule, *above*, p. 46).

(*g*) "When the form of the proposed canon or motion has been finally determined on, or when the proposed canon or motion has been reported from committee of the whole, without amendment, the chairman shall put the motion that the canon, or motion, be read a second time,' and if agreed to it shall pass, or it may be referred back to the committee of the whole for specific amendment.

(*h*) " If the work of the committee of the whole be interrupted by a motion to report progress being carried, the chairman shall report to the synod accordingly, and the synod may, upon motion, direct the committee to sit again at such time as it may appoint (for same parliamentary rule, see *above*, p. 46).

(*i*) " Should the hour of adjournment arrive while the synod is in committee of the whole, the synod shall resume its sittings and may direct the committee to sit again after routine business at the next sitting.

(*j*) "A vote in committee of the whole shall be taken of the members collectively, or by orders if required.

(*k*) "In committee of the whole the quorum shall be the same as the quorum of the synod (see *above*, p. 162). If it shall be made to appear at any time there is not a quorum present, the committee shall rise, and the chairman having reported to the synod accordingly, the committee may be directed, on motion, to sit again in the same manner as when progress is reported.

(*l*) "Any motion may, by resolution, or by direction of the chairman, be referred to committee of the whole, in which case it will be subject to the same course of procedure as a new canon, or a motion to repeal or to amend a canon."

23. Standing and special committees.—The rules of the synod relating to standing and select committees are not very full in many cases, and vary considerably. I give all of them *in full* as most convenient for reference.

Nova Scotia :

1. "The names of members of committees shall be proposed by any member of the synod, and if no more than the number of members of such committee be proposed, then that shall be such committee, but if a greater number then a ballot shall be taken for such committee.

2. "The reports of committees shall be in writing and signed by the chairman, and shall be received in course.

3. "The chairman of the committee, or some member deputed by him, shall explain to the synod the bearing of any portion of the report, if requested by any member of the synod.

4. "All reports of committees recommending any action or expression of opinion shall be accompanied by a resolution for the action of the synod thereon.

5. "It shall be imperative for all committees appointed at any session of the synod to report at its next session, and not later, unless by consent of the synod a longer time to do so be granted.

6. "All vacancies in committees having charge of trust funds shall be filled by the synod and the synod shall have power to remove from such committee any members for cause deemed sufficient by the synod.

"A list of nomination of members to fill such vacancies shall be prepared by a committee of seven appointed by the synod, and laid on the table at the first meeting or opening day of the synod.

"All other committees shall be appointed at each meeting of the synod.

7. "The committee on education shall report at every meeting of the synod on the general condition of the educational establishment in connection with the church in this diocese, especially King's College and the Collegiate School at Windsor.

8. "Any committee appointed by the synod shall be considered a standing committee until discharged by the usual vote."

The constitution also provides that the treasurer and the lay and clerical secretaries shall be a standing committee on credentials to examine into the certificates of the representatives from parishes, etc. This committee must report to the bishop on the day before the meeting of the synod. The bishop must immediately lay the report before the synod, and in case of any question arising as to seats it shall be referred to a special committee on credentials of seven members, of which the foregoing committee shall be members *ex officio* together with four lay members whose right to a seat in the synod is unquestioned. No representative whose seat is in question can vote for members on the said special committee (see Const. s. 10).

The business committee of the synod is the executive committee, which shall have their report printed and circulated among the

clergy and lay representatives at least two weeks before the meeting
of the synod. At each ordinary meeting of the synod the clerical
and lay members of the committee whose names respectively shall
stand at the head of the list shall go out of office, also the clerical
and lay member whose attendance shall have been least frequent at
the meetings of the committee : but all such members shall be
eligible for re-election. If any vacancy shall occur between the
sessions of the synod it shall be filled up by the clerical or lay
members, as the case may be, such nomination to be subject to the
approval of the synod.

The following are the regular committees of this synod :

Executive, credentials, finance, investments, church endowment fund, board
home missions, widows and orphans of clergy, endowment of parishes, superannuation of clergy, Quebec scheme, foreign missions, temperance, board of
discipline, education, Sunday schools, organizations in parishes, S. P. C. K.
depository, parish property, vacancies in committees, printing report.

For parliamentary rules governing committees, see *above*, pp.
48-51.

Fredericton.—Standing and special committees.

18. " All committees shall be appointed by the chair, unless named by the
synod and the names shall be publicly announced while the synod is in session.

19. " The reports of the committees shall be in writing, signed by the
chairman of the committee or a majority of the members thereof."

At the annual meeting there shall be elected by ballot four
clerical and four lay members of the synod, who together with the
bishop coadjutor and archdeacon, if any, shall be the standing
committee for the ensuing year, to aid and advise with the bishop
in the administration of the temporal affairs of the diocese. The
bishop coadjutor or archdeacon, or if there are no such dignitaries,
the clergyman having the largest number of votes at the election
of the committee shall, in the absence of the bishop, be the chairman ; and in case of a vacancy in the see, this chairman, or any
three members of the standing committee, have authority to call
the committee together (see Const. s. 13).

The following are other important boards and committees of
this synod :

Sunday schools, corresponding committee in connection with the board of management of the domestic and foreign society, Bishop Medley divinity scholarship, board of discipline, finance ; governors of King's college (2), Windsor; girls' school (1), Windsor.

For parliamentary rules governing committees, see *above*, pp. 48, 51.

Quebec.—Standing and special committees.

Rule 20. "The reports of all committees shall be in writing, and shall be received of course, and without the motion for acceptance, unless recommitted by vote of the synod. All reports recommending or requiring any action or expression of opinion by the synod, shall be accompanied by a resolution for the action of the house thereon.

Rule 21. "Whenever a committee shall be appointed, a chairman shall be named ; and in case of no such nomination, the first person on the list shall be chairman."

Rule 23. "On the first day of each session of synod, the lord bishop shall appoint a committee, to consist of five clergymen and five lay delegates, to report on the morning of the second day, the names of those whom they recommend to serve on the various standing committees, boards of enquiry, members of board of management of the domestic and foreign missionary society, and diocesan board ; and a further committee of three clergymen and three lay delegates, to suggest the names of trustees and members of council of Bishop college, Lennoxville, and corporation of Compton ladies' college."

A committee composed of the clerical and lay secretaries and of two members appointed by the chair examine at beginning of synod the certificates of lay delegates.

The executive committee consists of a bishop, of six clerical members and six lay representatives chosen by each order of the synod, and of the secretaries and treasurer of the synod *ex officio*. Any vacancy is filled up by the bishop and five members form a quorum. It arranges the business of the synod so far as possible (see Canon V.).

The following are also standing or regular committees of the synod :

Dolittle scholarship advisory investment, assessments, corresponding committee in connection with the board of management of the domestic and foreign missionary society, religious needs and progress of the dioceses, statistics.

For parliamentary rules governing committees, see *above*, pp. 48-51.

Montreal.—Standing and special committees.

Rule 21. "All special committees shall be named by the chair, unless otherwise ordered, and in such cases the election shall be by ballot. They shall appoint their own chairman, and a majority of the number named or elected shall be a quorum competent to proceed to business.

Rule 22. "The reports of committees shall be in writing, signed by the chairman, who, or some member deputed by him, shall explain to the synod the bearing of any portion of the report, if requested by any member of the synod.

Rule 23. "Reports of the committees shall be received in course, unless ordered to be reconsidered, but the further action thereon shall be by motion, as in other business. And, in order to give effect to any recommendation or principle embodied in any report of a committee of the house, and intended to bind this synod, a specific resolution setting forth the rule or principle shall follow and be adopted by this synod."

The executive committee is composed of the bishop or his commissary, the secretaries, the registrar, the treasurer, and of fifteen clerical and fifteen lay members, elected annually by each order respectively, at the regular meeting of the synod, but vacancies may be filled by the bishop. The bishop or commissary, or a member elected in the absence of either, presides. A quorum consists of seven members, of whom three shall be laymen (see by-law for "administration of the property, missions and trusts of the synod"). It is elected by ballot (see *above*, p. 178).

The following are standing or regular committees of this synod :

Finance, canons, church provision for lumber districts, foreign missions, education, Sunday schools, works of mercy, printing, superannuation fund, diocesan library and on books and tracts, French work, deaconesses, statistics, Dunham ladies' college, church immigration and colonization.

For parliamentary rules governing committees, see *above*, pp. 48-51.

Ontario.—Standing and special committees.

Canon II. (4) "All committees of the synod shall be named by the bishop, unless their nomination be otherwise provided for."

Canon VIII. (1) "The following committees shall be the standing committees of the synod : — The executive committee, the audit and accounts committee, the finance committee, the board of diocesan missions, the committee on domestic and foreign missions, the episcopal fund committee, the clergy trust fund committee, the widows and orphans' fund committee, the clergy superannuation fund committee, the divinity students' fund committee, the rectory lands fund committee, the committee on the church book depository, the committee on the state of the church, and such additional committees as are designated by the synod from time to time.

(3) "The mover of the resolution with reference to which any provisional committee has been appointed shall be the chairman or convener of such committee unless and until other provisions be made either in the resolution itself, or by the bishop, or by the said committee.

(4) "The standing committees shall report to the executive committee at its half-yearly meetings, and to the synod at its annual session.

(5) "Each standing committee shall, at its first meeting, elect a chairman, and may make such rules and regulations as are requisite for the efficient performance of its duties.

(6) "When no other provision is made, one-third of the members of any committee shall be sufficient for the transaction of business. The clerical and lay secretaries and the treasurer shall, by virtue of their offices, be members of all standing committees."

Canon IX. (1) "The executive committee consists of twenty members, nominated by the bishop at the annual session of the synod, ten members being chosen from the clergy and ten members from the lay representatives. In addition to the twenty members so nominated, the chancellor, the registrar, the lay and clerical secretaries, the treasurer, and the chairmen of the several standing committees shall be members of the executive committee. The bishop shall preside, and in his absence from the diocese and in the absence of his commissary, the committee shall elect a committee for the time being. Seven members shall be sufficient for the transaction of business.

Canon IV. (18) "Every report of a committee shall be in writing, shall be signed by the chairman, and shall be received in course, unless a motion be made for its recommittal.

(19) "The chairman of the committee, or some member deputed by him, shall explain to the synod the bearing of any portion of the report, if requested by any member of the synod.

"Members of standing committees hold office until the appointment of their successors (Canon II.)."

For parliamentary rules governing committees, see *above*, pp. 48-51.

Niagara—Standing and special committees.

A standing (executive) committee, composed of eighteen clergymen and as many laymen, shall be elected annually on the second day of the synod, to manage all the funds under the control of that body. The clergy and laity respectively vote by orders and by ballot for twelve of each order, and six of each order shall be added by the bishop. The bishop is president while attending any meeting of the committee or its sub-committees, but shall have no veto power. A permanent chairman is appointed by the committee to preside in the absence of the bishop, and he shall have a deliberative vote only. This committee acts like executive committees of other synods, and prepares in due form the business that comes under the rules before a synod (see Const. sec. 22).

The following are other standing committees: church and parsonage building, discipline.

For parliamentary rules governing committees, see *above*, pp. 48-51.

Toronto—Standing and special committees.

By s. 4 (*b*) of the constitution, the synod "may appoint committees, with or without power to act, and such committees may appoint from among themselves sub-committees, with or without power to act.

The executive committee is appointed annually and consists of the bishop of the diocese and ten clerical and ten lay members of the synod (one half of each order of whom shall be appointed by the bishop, and the other half by the clerical and lay members of the synod). Seven members of this committee shall form a quorum thereof; and the committee shall continue in office until their successors are appointed, and shall be called together by the chairman, secretary-treasurer, or by any three members of the committee. The following are among its most important duties :

1. To prepare in due form all such matters as the bishop, or any member of the synod, may desire to bring forward; 2. to receive reports of all other committees, and to submit such reports to the synod ; 3. to prepare lists of all the standing committees for the approval of the synod.

To print the reports laid before them, or such parts of them as they may deem expedient, and to issue a convening circular under the bishop's direction, stating the time and place of meeting, the business for the ensuing synod, the order in which it shall be discussed, the names of members of synod, and of the members of the court on contested seats, which circular shall be forwarded to each clergyman and lay representative at least two weeks before the meeting of the synod ; also to pay out or cause to be paid out all moneys of the synod, except those which are placed under the control of other committees.

At its first meeting in November of each year, to appoint the following committees, viz. :

(*a*) On finance (including the audit of the several synod accounts).

(*b*) On general sub-committee work, including applications for leave to sell or mortgage church property).

And generally, to carry out all resolutions of the synod not devolved on other committees of synod ; and, in the interval between sessions of synod, to exercise the executive powers of the same.

Notices of motion and of other business to be submitted to the synod, and all reports of committees, in order to secure precedence in the order of proceedings, shall be sent to the executive committee at its meeting in May next before the meeting of synod.

The standing committees of the synod meet on the second Thursday, or following day in the months of February, May and November, or on such other days as may appear more desirable to the bishop, and at such other times as they may deem necessary.

(*a*) The said committees shall be as follows :

1. The clergy commutation trust committee.
2. The endowment of the see, rectory lands, and land investment committee.
3. The mission board.
4. The widows and orphans' fund and theological students' fund committee.
5. The general purposes, statistics and assessment committee.
6. The Sunday school, and book and tract committee.
7. The Toronto rectory endowment committee.
8. The investment committee.
9. The superannuation fund committee.

The bishop is *ex officio* a member of all committees.

This synod has also the following standing orders as to all committees :

All special committees, unless otherwise determined, shall be named by the chair.

(*a*) One-third of the members of any standing or special committee of synod shall be a quorum for the transaction of business.

(*b*) The secretary-treasurer shall convene the quarterly meetings of each committee of the synod. He shall also summon special committees at the request of the convener thereof ; and if there be no convener, then by direction of the bishop, or other officer of the synod.

(*c*) It is an instruction to the conveners of committees that, when practicable, no committee on which are country members, be called for any hour of the day earlier than twenty minutes after their trains are due in Toronto, nor later than two hours before the said trains leave the city, according to the railway time table.

(*d*) Each committee shall from time to time choose its own chairman.

(*e*) All reports of committees shall be in writing, signed by the chairman.

(*f*) The chairman of each committee, or any person on his behalf, shall explain, when requested by any member of the synod, any facts or other portions of the report not understood by such member.

(*g*) In the event of any vacancy occurring in a committee of synod during its recess, either by death, removal, or resignation of a member or members, or other cause, the bishop shall be notified thereof as early as possible by the chairman of the committee in which the vacancies occur, or by one of the honorary secretaries, and shall be requested to fill such vacancy.

(*h*) All reports of committees recommending any action or expression of opinion shall be accompanied by an appended resolution for the action of the synod thereon.

(*i*) The first meeting of each standing committee shall be held at 5.45 o'clock p.m., on the day after the appointment of such committee.

(*j*) Each standing committee having charge of any property or funds shall report to the synod annually whether any (and, if any, how many) of the securities held by them are over twelve months in arrear, and the amount of such arrears, but the committee shall not report the names of the defaulters.

Committees must report, in writing, to the body appointing them.

Reports of committees should primarily contain a clear and concise account of the business done, and of the condition of the fund, or of the work or affairs committed to them.

Every report must be dealt with by the body to which it is presented ; and on motion, may be :

1. Received or rejected.
2. Laid on the table.
3. Read, or taken as read.
4. Considered as a whole, or clause by clause.
5. Amended.
6. Referred back, or sent to another committee.
7. Ordered to be filed, entered among the proceedings, printed, etc.
8. Adopted.

When in a report some action is recommended there must, in order to give its propositions practical effect, be a distinct corresponding substantive motion appended to the report, of which motion due notice must be given.

Similarly, when any report which the synod is asked to adopt contains debatable opinions and sentiments, these should be proposed in separate and specific motions, which, if approved by the house, can then be incorporated in the report.

Huron.—Standing and special committees—

The executive committee (of which the bishop is chairman, or in his absence, a member of the committee appointed by himself in writing, or by the committee itself when no such officer has been appointed) consists of sixty members, or thirty from each order, who shall be elected annually by ballot from the two orders respectively. Ten form a quorum (see Const. ss. 16, 18, 19, and rules 1-3, p. 14 of Const.).

The following rules apply to committees generally :

(1) All committees, unless named by the synod, shall be appointed by the chairman, who, in that case, shall announce the names to the synod previous to entry upon the minutes. Unless otherwise directed, the mover of the resolution for the appointment of a committee shall be convener.

(2) The reports of committees (except reports of progress merely) shall be in writing and signed by the chairman.

(3) A quorum of a committee shall consist of a clear majority of its members, unless the synod otherwise directs.

(4) The executive committee shall have power to make such rules as may be necessary for the proper and orderly disposal of the duties assigned to it.

Another, rule 15, provides that the report of a committee shall
be "received" without debate, except a question of order arises.
Amendments (rule 10) to the adoption of a report must be cognate
to the subject-matter to which it refers.

For parliamentary rules respecting committees, see *above*, pp.
48-51.

24. Close of Proceedings.—All the synods observe the proper
rule that "when the synod is about to rise every member shall
keep his seat until the bishop, or other person presiding has left
the chair."

25. Unprovided cases.—The Toronto and Huron synods have
a special rule that "in all unprovided cases the synod shall be
governed by the rules and usages of the House of Commons of
Canada," so far as they are applicable.   In the absence of a similar
express provision the same practice should necessarily obtain in
this country, and United States practice has no standing in this
country unless there is a special rule adopting it (see *above*, p. 26
for full explanations on this point).

**26. Concurrence of bishop and the two orders in every act
and resolution.**—The rules of all the synods provide that no act or
resolution of a synod shall be valid without the concurrence of
the bishop and of a majority of the clergy and laity present.   As
in Toronto, Fredericton, and Huron, votes may be taken separately
by orders when asked for under the constitution.

27. Changes in the constitution.—All the synods have stringent provisions respecting any alterations in the constitution or
canons or rules of procedure.   See—

> Nova Scotia, Const. s. 17.
> Fredericton, Const. s. 14.
> Quebec, Const. s. 14
> Montreal, Const. s. 17.
> Ontario, Canon II. s. 7.
> Toronto, Canon I. ss. 2-11.
> Huron, Const. s. 24.
> Niagara, Const. s. 36.

28. Suspension of rules.—Quebec synod (rule 22) allows a suspension of rules by the consent of two-thirds of the members present.

Ontario synod (rule 20) gives precedence over all other motions to one to suspend the order of proceedings, which must be decided without debate. No such order of proceedings or other rule can be suspended except "upon the unanimous consent of the members present."

Toronto synod has a provision that "any motion to suspend the rules of order must clearly set forth the proposition which the mover thus asks leave to introduce," but has no specific rules as to suspension.

As the Toronto and other synods must be governed by the common law of parliament in the absence of special rules of their own on the subject, (as in the case of Quebec) no rules can be suspended except by unanimous consent of the members present, (see *above* p. 30).

II. CONFERENCES OF THE METHODIST CHURCH.

1, The general conference, p. 193.
2. The annual conferences, p. 194.
3. The annual district meeting, p. 196.

4. The quarterly official board, p. 197.
5. Rules of order, p. 197.

The Methodist Church of Canada (*a*) is under the jurisdiction of the following bodies :

A general conference.

Annual conference.

District meetings.

Quarterly meetings.

1. THE GENERAL CONFERENCE.

Is composed of an equal number of ministerial and lay delegates elected (see *below*, p. 195), by the annual conferences of the several territorial and ecclesiastical divisions of the church, and meets once every four years.   A general superintendent presides over all its sessions and its several standing committees, and in the case of his absence, a president *pro tem* is elected by ballot, without debate, by the general conference or by the committees of that body.

The general conference also elects by ballot, without debate, a secretary, whose duty it is to keep a correct record of its proceedings, and to publish the journal under the direction of the body. The secretary has authority to nominate, and the conference elect, one or more assistants.

(*a*) See Dom. Stat., 47 V. c. 106.

The conference shall elect from the ministers of the church by ballot, without debate, one or more itinerant general superintendents, who hold office for the term of eight years, and are eligible for re-election. The general superintendents are, *ex officio*, members of the general conference, sitting at the time their term of office expires. They are also members of all standing committees and boards appointed by the general conference, with the right to vote, but the one who presides shall have a casting vote only.

The general conference only shall have full power to make rules and regulations for the church, under certain limitations and restrictions set forth in the book of discipline (*b*).

Fifty members of the general conference form a quorum for the transaction of business (see *below*, p. 205).

An important body is the special committee of twelve ministers and twelve laymen, appointed by the general conference on the nomination of the general superintendent to watch over the rights and privileges of the church throughout the connection. This committee may at any time call a special session of the general conference, and elect a general superintendent in case of a vacancy, who holds office until the next general conference. The committee is called for this purpose by a general superintendent or the secretary of the general conference. See ss. 101-103, " The Discipline."

2. The Annual Conferences.

Meet in the following divisions : Toronto, London, Niagara, Guelph, Bay of Quinté, Montreal, Nova Scotia, New Brunswick and Prince Edward Island, Newfoundland, Manitoba and Northwest, British Columbia, and one Mission Conference, Japan. The boundaries of these conferences are determined by the general conference.

(*b*) " The Doctrine and Discipline of the Methodist Church," Toronto : William Briggs. It is on this authoritative work that this review of the procedure of the several conferences is necessarily based, and to which reference must be made in all cases of doubt.

Each conference consists of all the ministers within its jurisdiction who have been received into full connection, and an equal number of laymen elected by ballot without debate, by the lay members of the district in the proportion of one for each minister in full connection within the bounds of the division. The laymen must be at least twenty-five years of age and in good standing for the five years next preceding the election.

It meets not earlier than the first Wednesday in May, nor later than the last Wednesday in June of each year, and may determine its place of meeting.

It elects by ballot, without debate, a president from the ministerial members, and also a secretary, whose record of the proceedings must be signed by both of these officers.

The general superintendent, when present, opens the conference, and presides during the first day of its sessions, and afterwards alternately with the president elected by the body.

In the absence of a general superintendent, the president takes the chair and opens the conference.

Any questions of law arising in the conference are determined by the presiding officer, but any member of the body can appeal from his decision to the court of appeal. The president has the same authority as respects committees over which he presides, and any member may also appeal to the court just named.

The court of appeal consists of the general superintendents, six ministers and six laymen, elected by ballot by the general conference from twelve ministers and twelve laymen, nominated by the officers here first named. See s. 109, " The Discipline."

The general superintendents are members of the annual conferences to which they belonged at the time of their election to office. They cannot take part in the proceedings of these bodies any further than their duties as superintendents may require. They are responsible to the general conference for all their official acts.

The ministerial and lay members of the annual conference, at the session next preceding each quadrennial meeting of the general conference, respectively elect by ballot delegates to the general conference from within the jurisdiction of the annual conference electing them. Each body elects its own representatives. The ministerial delegates to the general conference consist of one member for every twelve ministerial members of each annual conference—a fraction of one-half entitling a conference to an additional representative. Each delegate must receive a majority of the votes of the members of the electoral conference who may be present and vote. No layman of less than twenty-five years of age, or who has not been a member of the church continuously during the five years next preceding his election can be chosen delegate. One reserve delegate, and in addition one for every ten members or fraction thereof of one-half, are also elected. The secretary of each electoral conference shall report to the annual conference the names of the delegates; and the president and secretary shall report as soon as practicable, their names and addresses to the secretary of the general conference. See ss. 123-130, " The Discipline."

3. The Annual District Meeting.

The annual district meeting consists of all ministers and probationers for the ministry within the bounds of one of the districts into which an annual conference is divided, and one lay delegate for each minister and probationer in active work from each circuit, mission or station in the district, who shall have been elected by ballot, without debate by the quarterly official board at its fourth meeting. The latter may elect by ballot a lay delegate who shall be a member of the annual district meeting in the case where a circuit or mission has no minister or probationer.

The chairman appoints the time and place of the first district meeting, but subsequently he fixes the time, and the district meeting, the place. When the chairman is absent a presiding officer for the time being will be elected by ballot, without debate, by the district meeting from its own ministerial members. A secretary is elected by ballot, and the minutes are signed by the two officers in question. The chairman keeps the book and brings it to the conference.

The president of the annual conference is, *ex officio*, chairman of the district in which he may be stationed during the year of his presidency.

A financial district meeting, composed of superintendents of circuits and a lay delegate from each circuit and mission in the district appointed by the quarterly official board, must be held in each district not later than the month of September of every year.

4. A QUARTERLY OFFICIAL BOARD.

A quarterly official board is provided for each circuit, mission or station, consisting of ministers, probationers for the ministry, local preachers, exhorters, etc.

The superintendent of the circuit is the chairman of the board. He is the minister on each circuit and mission who is appointed from time to time to take charge of the societies therein. When the chairman of the district is present he has the right to preside. See ss. 171-180, " The Discipline," p. 80.

5. RULES OF ORDER.

Rules of order as given in " The Discipline " are few in number, and generally based on the procedure of parliament with some special regulations derived from the practice of assemblies in the United States. I cite these rules in their order, with such comments as suggest themselves :

1. " The president shall take the chair at the hour to which the conference may stand adjourned, and cause the same to be opened by the reading of the Scriptures, singing and prayer."

As required by the regulations of the church (see *above*, p. 193) a general superintendent presides over the general conference, or a chairman *pro tem.* elected in his absence by the same conference, or by its committees. The general superintendent also presides on the first day of the sessions of the annual conference, and afterwards alternately with the president elected by the same (see *above*, p. 195).

In case of two or more candidates proposed for temporary chairman of the general conference, or for the presidency of an annual conference, the parliamentary practice should be followed (see *above*, pp. 8, 27).

2. " The following shall be the order of business :

(1) Reading of the minutes of preceding session.

(2) Communications.

(3) Memorials.

(4) Reports of standing committees.

(5) Reports of special committees.

(6) Motions of which notice has been previously given.

(7) Notices of motions.

(8) Questions of which notice has been given.

(9) Miscellaneous."

This order calls for no special comment, except that it is noteworthy as not including a call of the roll of ministerial and lay delegates. But as a matter of fact the roll of delegates is called at the beginning of the session of the conference—not of each sitting or sederunt. A call is made on a demand for a quorum. (Note from Dr. Carman to the author.) The regulations of the church provide for forwarding certificates of election of delegates to the secretary of the general conference, but the call should be placed on the order paper as a first proceeding to ensure a quorum (see *below*, p. 205) being present.

The minutes must be read and corrections made as in other assemblies (see *above* p. 11), and then confirmed on question put by chairman. The regulations of the general conference are silent as to signing these minutes or journal, though it is required that the president and secretary sign those of the annual conferences (see *above*, p. 195) ; we may assume the president of the meeting will sign them.

Communications and memorials should be submitted, read and endorsed on the back by the secretary, and appropriately disposed of by the president in accordance with usage.

Reports of committees should be brought up by the chairman of each committee. It is advisable for the president to call on each according to the order of its appointment and ask, " Is the committee appointed to consider [*subject*] ready to report ? " or, in accordance with parliamentary usage, he may simply call for reports of committees as given on the order paper, and the chairman of each will come forward, and either read his report or have it read by the secretary—the preferable course. (See for parliamentary rules of committees, *above*, pp. 48-51). Each report should be considered separately and, when necessary, paragraph by paragraph (see *above*, p. 21) according to the convenience of the conference. According to the following rule (3) all reports must be presented before one of them is even considered.

The proposing and debate of motions (6) are governed by special rules of the conferences, and in all undecided cases by the general parliamentary law see *above*, p. 30).

Questions (8) should be also framed as far as possible, in accordance with parliamentary law (see *above*, p. 31).

Miscellaneous (9) is for the disposal of general business which cannot well be summarized.

3. "On the call for reports of committees, all reports that are ready shall be called in before action is taken on any one of them."

See comments on foregoing rule.

4. "The president shall decide all questions of order, subject to an appeal to the conference; but in case of such appeal, the question shall be taken without debate. When a member rises to a point of order, or the president calls any member to order, in either case the point of order shall be distinctly stated."

For parliamentary usage in same case, see *above*, p. 39.

5. "No member shall remain standing during debate except the member addressing the president."

See parliamentary rule, *above*, p. 37.

6. "The president shall nominate all committees not otherwise specially ordered by the conference."

This is a special rule taken from the practice of congress, and not from that of parliament (see *above*, p. 48). In nominating committees the speaker of the house of representatives indicates the chairman by placing him first on the list. In parliament the mover of a motion for a committee is generally chosen chairman, if he is ready to serve, but he must be formally chosen by the committee itself.

7. "When a motion or a resolution is moved and seconded, or a report is presented and is read by the secretary or stated by the president, it shall be deemed to be in possession of the conference; nor shall any motion be withdrawn by the mover after being debated, without the consent of the conference."

For references to the parliamentary law on the several points embodied in this complicated rule, see :

(*a*) Moving and seconding of motions, *above*, p. 30.

(*b*) Presentation of reports, *above*, p. 51.

(*c*) Withdrawal of motions in the conference appears to depend on the consent of the majority. In parliament (see *above*, p. 31), the consent must be unanimous.

8. "All motions and resolutions shall be presented in writing by the proposer."

For the parliamentary rule, see *above*, p. 30. The reference to resolutions is hardly correct—a motion becomes a resolution, strictly speaking, when carried—"proposed resolution" is more accurate here as in preceding and other rules.

9. "The following motions are not debatable :—

(a) For the previous question.

(b) To lay on the table.

(c) For indefinite adjournment.

(d) For indefinite postponement."

All these several motions are derived from United States practice, and as they are not debatable they cannot be amended. But the rule is also subject to the following (No. 10) as respects order of precedence.

"Indefinite adjournment" means the ordinary motion, "That the house do now adjourn," which supersedes a question under consideration. See on this point, *above*, p. 33.

10. "No new motion or [proposed] resolution shall be entertained until the one under consideration has been disposed of, which may be done by adoption or rejection, unless one of the following motions shall intervene, which motions shall have the precedence in the order in which they are placed, viz.:

(a) Adjournment.

(b) Lay on the table.

(c) Indefinite postponement.

(d) Postponement to a given time.

(e) Reference to a committee.

(f) Amendment.

(g) Amendment to the amendment."

This rule is somewhat obscure, but reading the first part in accordance with well understood parliamentary principles it must mean that when a motion is proposed or stated from the chair, and thereby becomes a question for the consideration of the conference (see *above*, p. 199), it may be amended, postponed, superseded, adopted, or negatived ; and until such result is reached by the final determination of the conference, as announced by the chair, and the assembly is no longer in possession of the question, no other motion on a different subject-matter can intervene. Amendments proposed to the question must be relevant (see *above*, p. 33), but there are certain motions, known as dilatory, subsidiary or incidental to a motion, which may be moved, on every question, and these are mentioned as " motions which have the precedence in which they are placed." These motions are not necessarily given precedence in accordance with United States practice, since in this rule, "to postpone indefinitely" has the priority over "to postpone to a certain day"—the reverse of the American practice (see Neely, p. 76). The Rev. Dr. Carman, an authority on these questions. succinctly explains the meaning of " precedence " as follows : " It is our practice if a man move (d) and another wish to move (c) to give the latter (c) the floor, and test *indefinite* before *definite* postponement. So that if a man want (f) and another (b) or (a) or (c), we test in order of the letters, and when a majority is reached on any such motion we stop " (*c*).

The previous question is not mentioned in the rule as one of those motions which can intervene when a question is before the body, but in accordance with the practice of American assemblies, on which the rule is based, it can be moved and has precedence of " to postpone to a certain day," "to commit," or " recommit," " to postpone indefinitely," and "to amend," but it yields to the motion " to lie on the table." Roberts, pp. 47, 53, 54, 59.

The following motions cannot be amended :—

That the house do now adjourn. See *above*, p. 33, and rule 9.

To lay on the table. See *above*, rule 9.

That the question be now put. See *above*, rule 9, and *below*, rule 17.

An amendment to an amendment. See *above*, p. 35.

To postpone indefinitely. See *above*, rule 9.

(*c*) Dr. Neely (p. 74) has this clear explanation with respect to the precedence of one motion over another : " When a motion or motions may be pending, and yet another motion can be made, it is said *to take precedence*. When a motion is thus superseded by a superior motion, it is said that it *yields to it*. When a motion of higher rank is made direct action on the lower motion or motions is suspended, and the action is first on the superior motion. In consequence of this order of precedence, when a higher motion is pending, a lower one cannot be made, but a superior motion can be made when one inferior to it is pending."

11. " When any member is about to speak in debate or deliver any matter to the conference, he shall rise and address the president, and shall proceed only when the president announces his name and conference."

The first part of this rule is the parliamentary procedure (see *above*, p. 37), and the latter is only usual in parliament when the speaker has to choose between two or more who rise at the same moment to speak (see *above*, p. 37). If he cannot decide then a motion may be made and put, "that Mr. A. be heard" (see *above*, p. 37).

12. "No person shall speak more than once on the same question without leave of the conference, except the mover, who shall be entitled to a general reply."

This is wider than the parliamentary rule (see *above*, p. 38), since the conference may permit a second speech on a subject under particular circumstances, which would, in the opinion of the conference, justify the infringement of the common practice. The "leave of the conference" cannot mean "universal" or " unanimous assent," but must be gathered by the chairman from the meeting, or indicated by a motion duly made that "Mr. —— be heard," or "have leave to speak again on the question "—the most convenient course, as a rule.

13. " No person shall speak more than ten minutes at one time without leave of the conference which shall be granted or refused without debate."

No such rule exists in parliament, but it is desirable in assemblies whose sessions are limited. The leave for an extension of time may be granted when necessary, on motion ; but in any case it is given without debate.

14. " When any motion or resolution shall have passed [*strictly, a motion is a resolution when passed*] any member who voted in the majority may move a reconsideration."

This reconsideration may take place at the same, or at the next sitting of the same session of the conference, but not at the next session, since an adjournment —practically a prorogation—supersedes such a motion. For practice of reconsideration, see *above*, p. 17.

As to meaning of session, see *above*, p. 7.

15. " A motion to adjourn shall always be in order."

" That the house do now adjourn" is the usual form of the motion ; and it can be made on the previous question or when any of the dilatory or subsidiary motions, given in rule 10, *above*, are under consideration, since it is given precedence over all others. If the motion be qualified in any way, the qualification causes it to lose its special character, and it stands as any other principal motion to be amended. For parliamentary rules, see *above*, p. 33.

16. "**Motions relating to the rights and privileges of the conference, or to individual members and orders of the day, shall be considered questions of privilege.**"

This is a rule peculiar to all organized bodies, and necessary for its self-preservation, dignity and efficiency (see *above*, p. 40). When a matter is made an order of the day for a particular time, it becomes, under the rule, a principal question. That is to say, it has precedence over all other matters. The terms of the rule in this respect are wider than in the majority of assemblies. A motion for adjournment is, however, in order when a privileged question is under consideration.

See *above*, p. 33, and rule 15. For meaning of "privileged questions," *above*, p. 25*n*.

17. "**The previous question being moved, the president shall put it at once by asking, 'Shall the vote now be taken?' If the previous question is carried, all debate shall cease, and the president shall take the vote on the several motions before the conference.**"

This rule is, in some respects, practically an adaptation of the previous question as used in assemblies of the United States (see *above*, p. 15). The motion is undebatable, since the president must put it *at once*. (See also rule 9, *above*). If it carries, the motion to which the previous question is proposed must be immediately voted upon without debate. If it is negatived then the debate must cease under parliamentary rules (see *above*, p. 14). The practice of the Canadian commons precludes the previous question being moved on an amendment or after one is proposed (see *above*, p. 15); but the rule of the conference is much wider than that practice, since it is applied to "the several motions" before the conference. It is obvious that it can be moved, not only on the subsidiary or dilatory motions mentioned above (rule 10, p. 200), but also on a motion to amend. If it is proposed on a pending amendment, then the vote must be taken on the same at once, and if the amendment is negatived by the conference deciding that the amendment shall *not now* be put, then the vote must be taken on the main question.

If there is a question before the conference, and an amendment is proposed and subsequently the dilatory motion to postpone to a certain time, or to an indefinite time, or to commit, and if the previous question is last proposed and carried, the vote must be taken (1) on the dilatory motion, and if that is negatived then the vote must be taken on the amendment, and if the latter be rejected by the assembly declaring that it shall *not now* be put, then on the main question, without debate in each case. The rule, it would seem, is peremptory. In other words the effect of the previous question, when moved under these circumstances and carried, extends to the subsidiary motions as well as to the main motion. In fact it appears to be wider in its effects than even the same motion in American practice (see Roberts, sec. 20).

18. " No member shall absent himself from the sessions of the conference without leave, unless he be sick or unable to attend."

For the same parliamentary usage, see *above*, p. 28. If a member wishes to leave on urgent business, he should obtain permission from the conference.

19. " No member who is not within the bar when any question is put by the president, shall be allowed to vote on such question, except by leave of the conference."

No special comment is necessary on a rule obviously in the direction of order, when a question is being put, and of requiring every member to hear the question put. All members who vote in parliament must be in their seats— actually within the bar and folding doors.

20. " Before the president rises to put a motion to the conference, he shall ask, ' Is the conference ready for the question ? ' No member shall speak after the president has risen to put the question, and all members present shall vote unless excused by the conference."

The president shall put the question as soon as he has no doubt that the sense of the conference is in favour of coming to a final decison. All members must vote (see *above*, p. 43), as in parliament, unless their vote is excused or disallowed on motion duly made. Personal interest would of course be a reason for not voting (see *above*, p. 42).

21. " No member shall be interrupted when speaking except by the president to call him to order when he departs from the question, uses personalities, or disrespectful language ; but any member may call the attention of the president when he deems a speaker out of order, and any member may explain if he is misrepresented."

These are, very briefly, a statement of essential parliamentary rules of debate (see *above*, p. 38).

22. "No business shall pass from individuals to committees without reference through the conference."

All committees must have matters referred to them by motions or instructions (see *above*, p. 48), and duly made in accordance with rule and usage, in the conference itself. No individual member has authority to address or interfere in the proceedings of a committee unless he is a member of the same ; nor can he, when a member of a committee, bring any matter before it that is not within its order of reference. If he wishes to bring forward such a matter, he must first obtain authority from the conference, in the shape of a specia, instruction (see *above*, p. 48).

23. "Any member may call for the yeas and nays on any question before the conference, provided he be sustained by twenty members. Any member may require that the number of votes for and against a resolution be announced."

The sense of the meeting on any question may be first gathered by the voices or by a show of hands, but when a member wishes for the yeas and nays the chairman should under the rule ask, " Do twenty members ask for the yeas and nays?" and if he finds that number stand up he will call upon the secretary to call the roll alphabetically, and the members will respectively vote "yea" or "nay" (see *above*, p. 42), (*c*). In all cases the most correct practice is for the secretary, following the parliamentary procedure, to announce the numbers on each side, and the president should then declare the question carried in the affirmative or lost in the negative. Before the secretary announces the result he should read the roll of yeas and nays to enable members to correct mistakes, No member has a right to change his vote under parliamentary law (see *above*, p. 43). When a mistake in the votes appears in the minutes, it can be corrected the next occasion when the journal is read (see *above*, p. 43).

24. "In the general conference fifty members shall constitute a quorum."

It is the duty of the president to see that a quorum is present every day. For this reason the roll should be called as the preliminary proceeding of the conference when it assembles. If a member should call attention at any time that a quorum is not present, the president should deliberately count the members, in accordance with the parliamentary usage given *above*, p. 29. See also *above*, p. 29 for practice in case there is no quorum in a committee of the whole. If there is any business under consideration it is superseded (see *above*, p. 29).

(*e*) The Rev. Dr. Carman on this point writes the author : " When the president puts the question on any matter, we sometimes take the voices ; if doubtful, then, show of hands ; if still in doubt, rise to count. Taking ' yeas ' and ' nays ' is done by alphabetical roll call."

25. "The secretary shall provide a bulletin, upon which announcements of meetings of committees, and relating to the conference business may be made."

Always a procedure necessary for the intelligent consideration of all business. Such a bulletin should, like a parliamentary "order of the day," place all business before the conference in the order in which it is to be taken up. It ought to be printed and in the hands of every member, when that can be done ; or at all events copies should be type-written and placed in convenient places for members to see at any time.

In the foregoing comments the writer has attempted to state the correct practice under each rule according to the recognized authorities on the procedure of legislative bodies, even if, in doing so, he is sometimes at variance with the rulings of chairmen of the conference at different times. He must admit that these rules are neither satisfactorily arranged nor well framed, and that in interpreting them one must meet the difficulties that arise from a code which mingles indiscriminately the common law of parliament of this country with certain rules of procedure in operation in the neighbouring republic, and on which we have not in Canada any authoritative common usage. The difficulty is increased by the fact that there is no reference to a text book to be followed in unprovided cases. Following the usual practice, then, reference must be had to the common law of parliament as explained in the first part of this work.

III. CHURCH COURTS OF THE PRESBYTERIAN CHURCH IN CANADA.

The several courts of the Presbyterian Church in Canada consist of:—

The deacons' court.

The session.

The presbytery.

The synod.

The general assembly.

1. THE DEACONS' COURT.

The deacons' court is entrusted with the temporal affairs of a congregation and is composed of the minister or ministers of that body, the elders and the deacons. The chairman is the minister, and in case of there being several ministers, they arrange as to the chairmanship, and generally act alternately. In the absence of the minister any member of the court may be called to the chair. The chairman, like the speaker of legislative assemblies, has only a casting vote. The clerk and treasurer must be members of the court. The minute book is signed by chairman and clerk.

(a) In this compilation I use, as a rule, the indispensable Manual on " Rules and Procedure," by Rev. Dr. Reid, and W. B. McMurrich, Esq., Toronto, 1889, to which reference must be made in all doubtful cases. For Acts affecting Presbyterian Church, see Dom. Stat. 1882; Bourinot, p. 99.

Meetings should be held at least once every three months, but one may be called at any time on the authority of the chairman, or on requisition of at least three members of the court.

2. THE SESSION.

The session comprises the minister or ministers and·elders of a congregation, and its special function is to promote the spiritual interests of the body. The chairman is called moderator, and is the minister; or, if there are more than one, the ministers preside alternately, or as it may be arranged between them. When the moderator is absent, or does not deem it expedient for certain reasons to preside, he may appoint another to the position. The presbytery may appoint a temporary chairman when the moderator is dead or suspended. A clerk and treasurer are appointed by the session. The moderator and two other members constitute a quorum. The session appoints one of its members to represent it in presbytery or synod. Meetings are called by the moderator when he deems it necessary, or when enjoined by a superior court, or requested by one-third of the elders. The minutes, when read and confirmed (see *below*, p. 213), are duly signed by the moderator and clerk.

3. THE PRESBYTERY.

The presbytery comprises ordained ministers within the ecclesiastical bounds, theological and other church professors, missionaries, elders, and others engaged in the church's work, or placed on the roll by special authority of the assembly. Its duties are, in general, to superintend the congregations and sessions within the ecclesiastical bounds. It is presided over by a moderator, a minister, who holds office for six or twelve months, and generally directs, like all other chairmen of public bodies, the business of the court. He has only a casting vote, and like the speaker of the senate, he may address the body, or even propose a motion, but in doing so he must leave the chair, and call another for the time being to fill his place. In his absence from the chair, his predecessor in office, or any other minister chosen by the court, may preside over its deliberations. He cannot preside when he is personally concerned in any case before the court which in such an event must appoint another *pro tempore.* A clerk and treasurer are appointed by the body. The quorum consists of three members of whom two must be ministers. The regulations provide for the holding of meetings at stated intervals or such times as its business demands.

4. THE SYNOD.

The synod comprises all the ministers and elders on the rolls of the presbyteries within its bounds. It has general oversight of the presbyteries. The chairman must be a minister chosen at each ordinary meeting by an open vote, and is also called moderator. The synod appoints a clerk and treasurer. The quorum consists of fifteen members, of whom at least eight are ministers, " provided the members present belong to more than one presbytery." The ordinary meetings are annual and may be adjourned when necessary. Other meetings can be called by the moderator or by requisition of at least fifteen members.

5. THE GENERAL ASSEMBLY.

The general assembly, the highest court of the church, is called " the General Assembly of the Presbyterian Church in Canada," and consists : (1) Of one-fourth of the whole number of ministers whose names are on the rolls of the several presbyteries of the church, and an equal number of elders. (2) When the number of names on the roll of a presbytery is not divisible by four, the fourth shall be reckoned from the next higher multiple of four. (3) Each presbytery elects its own representatives at an ordinary meeting held at least twenty-one days before the meeting of the general assembly. If any one thus elected resigns his commission, the presbytery may, at any subsequent meeting, held not less than eight days before the meeting of the general assembly, appoint another in his stead. (4) A presbytery may appoint as its commissioner to the general assembly an elder belonging to any other presbytery of the church, provided always that the person so

B.M.P.—14

appointed is at the time an acting member of some session. (5) Ministers whose names are on the roll of a presbytery as ministers shall not be eligible to hold commissions as elders from their own or any other presbytery. (6) Each presbytery shall, through its clerk, transmit to the clerk of assembly, at least ten days before the assembly meets, a certified roll of the commissioners appointed at its ordinary meeting. A separate report of any commissions afterwards given to ministers or elders in place of such as may have resigned their commissions, shall be presented to the general assembly by the presbyteries as soon as convenient after the assembly has been constituted. (7) The roll to be called at the opening of the assembly shall be made up from the rolls of the several presbyteries, as transmitted to the clerk of the assembly, containing the names of commissioners appointed at least twenty-one days before. At its first session the assembly shall appoint a " committee on commissions," to which shall be referred reports of presbyteries regarding commissions issued at a later date and all matters affecting the roll. On the report of this committee the assembly shall order such changes to be made in the roll as may be required. This amended roll is the permanent roll of the assembly. (8) Forty commissioners, of whom twenty-one are ministers, shall constitute a quorum for the transaction of business. But twenty commissioners who were appointed twenty-one days before, being met at the time and place appointed, may constitute the court, and adjourn from time to time until a full quorum is present.

The general assembly meets once a year. As in other courts the moderator is always a minister (see *above*, pp. 208, 209). He must always open and close each meeting with prayer. His duties are to constitute the assembly in the first place. He maintains order, sees that the business is properly conducted, and that the minutes are correctly taken, announces decisions, signs all documents having the authority of the assembly, takes the vote, signs the minutes when confirmed, and exercises any other functions assigned to him by the court. If he wishes to take a part in debate, or submit a motion he leaves the chair, and calls another member of the court to take his place. Also, if he is a party in a call before the assembly, or if the presbytery or synod to which he belongs is a party, he leaves the chair, and with the approval of the court names another commissioner who takes his place, and for the time being has all the power and responsibilities of the office as moderator *pro tempore*. The moderator has only a casting vote in the case of a tie. The assembly has the services of two or more clerks appointed by itself.

A committee on bills and overtures arranges the order of business, and is constituted of the clerks of assemblies, clerks of synods and presbyteries, who are commissioners (see *above*, p. 210), together with one member nominated by each presbytery, and such other ministers and elders as the assembly may deem it expedient to appoint. It receives and reviews all papers intended for the assembly, and may refuse to transmit them if they are not regular (see Rules and Forms of Procedure, p. 31). It appoints its own convener and clerk. When the report of this committee, setting forth the order of business, has been approved by the assembly, it is at once printed like a parliamentary order of the day (see *above*, p. 29). It should be presented in all cases " not later than the fourth sederunt."

Besides the foregoing important committee, the assembly appoints the following sessional and standing committees :

On the records of synods and assembly.

On classifying returns to remits.

On the nomination of standing committees, of not less than two from each synod, and not more than four from any one synod.

On commissions.

On applications for the reception of ministers into the church.

On applications for leave to retire from the active duties of the ministry.

On special applications on behalf of students.

Standing, whose duties are to conduct the business of the several departments of the church during the year and report annually to the assembly.

The reports of standing committees must be printed and presented not later than the third sitting of the assembly.

Every other committee may report at any sitting after the confirmation of the minutes, and its final report must be made before the closing of the assembly. It appoints its own convener and clerk unless the assembly chooses to do so (see rule 142, *below*); keeps minutes of its proceedings, and reports in writing, as in parliament (see *above*, p. 51).

Committees, as in parliament, cannot sit while the assembly is sitting (see rule 143, *below*).

The standing orders provide for a committee to prepare the business of the first sitting of the assembly, consisting of the clerks of the general assembly, the clerks of synods and presbyteries, who may be commissioners (see *above*, p. 210). They convene at the call of the senior clerk of the assembly, before the hour fixed for the meeting of the assembly.

For standing orders regulating reports, papers, overtures, appeals, memorials, petitions, and committees, etc., see Rules and Forms of Procedure, pp. 30, 31.

6. General Rules of Procedure and Debate for Church Courts.

The following is the code of rules which govern the debates and proceedings of the courts generally, with such remarks as suggest themselves to the writer:

138. "The moderator takes the chair at the hour appointed, calls the members to order, and constitutes the court with prayer."

The duties of the moderator, who must be a minister, are stated briefly *above*, pp. 210, 211, where reference is made to the several courts. These duties are those of all chairmen, and in all unprovided cases he should be governed by the law of parliament (see *above*, p. 28).

139. "At the first assembling of the court the roll is called and the sederunt recorded. Members coming in afterwards have their names entered on reporting themselves to the clerk."

This is a proceeding absolutely necessary in such bodies to show that the court is properly constituted. See proceedings of Church of England Synod, *above*, p. 149. The roll should be alphabetically arranged in an attendance book, with a column for notice of attendance or absence, or other report necessary in each case. The several courts have rules respecting the rolls. The rolls called at the opening of the assembly are made up from the rolls of the several presbyteries, as transmitted to the clerk of the assembly. See rules 110 (6) (7) of Rules and Forms of Precedure.

140. " The minutes of last ordinary meeting and of all special meetings held in the interval are then read, and on being sustained are signed by the moderator. In the case of the general assembly and the synods the minutes of each sederunt are read at the beginning of the sederunt following."

When the minutes are read, then is the time to make corrections, but no general debate can be allowed (see *above*, p. 11).

For mode of keeping minutes, see *below*, p. 221.

141. "All reports and other papers intended to be brought before the court are called for and are received by the clerk. A docket of business is then prepared, consisting (1) of business arising out of the minutes ; (2) of new business ; and the order in which the several matters shall be taken up is determined. In the synods and general assembly the papers are given by the clerks to the committee on bills and overtures, who arrange the docket and prepare an order of business for the approval of the court."

All reports and papers should be endorsed by the clerk with a short note showing nature of each paper. The order of business should clearly indicate nature of each matter to be considered. For duties of commitees on bills and overtures, see *above*, p. 211.

142. " The moderator nominates all committees of the court, unless they have been appointed by special rule or resolution of the court. If the convener is not named, the first named member of the committee is convener, and, in his absence, the second named."

See for parliamentary law respecting committees, *above*, pp. 48-51. For standing orders of assembly appointing and regulating committees, *above*, p. 211.

143. " Committees may not meet nor continue in session while the court is sitting, unless leave has been granted by the court."

For same parliamentary rule, see *above*, p. 50.

144. "The courts of the church, except the sessions, are open courts; but on motion made any court may sit with closed doors. This is commonly done when matters affecting character, which should not be made public, are under consideration."

This is also a parliamentary practice. In the two houses it is usual to bring up matters of internal economy, or other questions of a distinctly private nature, after prayers and before the speaker gives orders to open the doors. On such occasions the rules of debate are not adhered to, but the house is practically in committee of the whole.

145. "A member of the court ought not to withdraw from attendance without leave. If he does so he cannot dissent from any decisions of the court arrived at in his absence."

See parliamentary rule, *above*, p. 28.

146. "The moderator is charged with seeing that the minutes record correctly the proceedings of the court."

As the moderator signs them, like the speaker, he is of course responsible for their correctness. As a matter of fact, everything depends on the fidelity and ability of the recording clerk. See *above*, pp. 11, 122, for rules governing a clerk in keeping minutes and records.

147. "The clerk of a superior court, on receipt of papers from a lower court, endorses on them the date of reception, numbers the papers, and authenticates them by his signature or initials."

Necessary as a matter of convenience and for the orderly discharge of public business. In the house of commons such is always done by the proper officer.

148. "Clerks of the courts are entitled to receive payment for extracts from the records and copies of papers furnished to individuals, at the rate of ten cents for every hundred words or fraction thereof."

A rule of internal economy. The disposition of such fees is a matter of internal arrangement.

7. RULES OF DEBATE.

149. "When any business has been introduced, and is before a court, it is desirable that no other business be taken up until that which is before the court has been issued."

A matter of necessity in all public bodies.

150. "No discussion is in order until a motion is before the court. Speakers should confine themselves to the matter referred to in the motion, and if they depart therefrom they may be called to order."

A motion is not before the court or assembly unless it is written, seconded, proposed or read by the chair, and in the hands of the clerk. See next rule, 151, and parliamentary rule *above*, p. 30.

Relevancy is always necessary, *above*, p. 37.

151. "Every motion or amendment shall be given in to the clerk in writing as soon as it has been made, and it cannot be discussed until it has been duly seconded."

Practically the parliamentary rule (*above*, p. 30); but the part referring to the writing of motions is not applied in practice to motions for the adjournment of house or debate, or for the previous question or such business motions as arise as a matter of ordinary routine and procedure in the course of proceedings (see *above*, p. 30).

152. "After a motion or amendment is in the clerk's hand and discussion has commenced, it cannot be withdrawn or altered without leave of the court."

This must mean a majority vote on a motion for withdrawal. The parliamentary rule requires a unanimous vote. See *above*, p. 31.

153. "When a question is under discussion, the motion before the court must be disposed of, and no other motion can be entertained unless to adjourn the court, to adjourn the debate, to lay on the table, to commit, to amend, or to take an immediate vote; and these several motions have precedence in the order in which they are herein arranged."

As to disposing of one question at a time, see *above*, p. 201.

To adjourn the court (or house), see *below*, rule 154.

To adjourn the debate, see *above*, p. 33.

To lay on the table, see *below*, rule 155.

To commit, see *above*, p. 37.

To amend, see *below*, rules 157 and 158.

To take an immediate vote, see *below*, rule 159.

As to precedence, the meaning is, a motion to adjourn the court has precedence over the others, and to adjourn the debate over next, and so on (see *above*, p. 201). A motion to adjourn is, however, regular at any time even when any of the motions mentioned are before the body. See *above*, p. 33, and rule 154, *below*.

154. "A motion to adjourn is always in order, and is voted on without debate."

This is the parliamentary rule (see *above*, p. 33), restrained by making the motion undebatable. It can be made whatever the question under consideration, whether an amendment or to lay on the table, etc., (see *above*, rule 153), and is not amendable (see *above*, p. 33, where proper form of motion is also given).

155. "A motion to lay on the table is voted on without debate. If carried in the affirmative the subject to which it refers, together with the motion and pending amendments, remain on the docket and may be taken up at a subsequent sederunt, but only by resolution adopted by a majority of the members of the court present."

The vote must be taken as soon as it is moved and proposed from the chair, "That the question [here stated at length by the moderator] do lie on the table." This is the American rule, removing with the original question all the subsidiary and incidental motions (see *above*, p. 23). Under the rule as above, however, there is a limitation to the effect of the motion : it removes the subject and accompanying motion from the consideration of the meeting only for the sitting at which the question was tabled. A resolution duly moved and adopted by a majority of the court present can reconsider the question. In effect, the motion is equivalent to the parliamentary proceeding which prevents a bill "being *now* read" a second or third time ; if not " now read " it can be taken up on a subsequent day, on a motion duly made and adopted, to place it again on the paper for consideration at precisely the same stage where it was interrupted in its progress.

156. "Any subject with the motion and pending amendments may be referred to a committee to be considered and reported on."

This is a parliamentary proceeding in principle, the effect being to withdraw a question from the consideration of the whole court until such time as the committee may report thereon. A committee should report in every case ; if it fails to do so, a member may move, "That the committee on [here state subject] do report forthwith to the court." See Bourinot, p. 743, and *above*, p. 50.

157. "A motion is amended by adding certain words or clauses thereto ; by striking out certain words or clauses ; by substituting

other words or clauses for those in the resolution ; or by striking out all after the word "resolved" and substituting another motion disposing of the matter in hand."

The parliamentary procedure (see *above*, p. 33). If it be proposed to substitute a motion in amendment to a proposed resolution, the procedure followed by the moderator ought to be strictly (see *above*, p. 34), speaking, as follows : Mr. A. moves, seconded by Mr. B. " That it be resolved, that in the opinion of this assembly or court, etc." To this proposed resolution, Mr. C. moves, to strike out all the words after " resolved," and substitute the following motion " That in the opinion of this assembly, etc." The parliamentary procedure which strikes out all the words after "That" seems preferable in practice (see *above*, p. 34). It is assumed by the writer that an amendment must in all cases be on the same subject-matter as the original motion (see *above*, p. 33), excepting, of course, the subsidiary or dilatory motions mentioned in rule 153 *above*, which are not amendments in the real sense of the term.

158. " It is in order to propose an amendment to the first amendment, but no other can be entertained until the amendment to the amendment has been disposed of; when this has been adopted or rejected, other amendments to the amendments may be considered and disposed of one by one ; when these have all been disposed of, the first amendment is voted on in answer to the question, ' Shall the motion be thus amended—yea or nay?' If this is decided in the affirmative, the main motion is amended accordingly, and the discussion proceeds. Other amendments to the main motion are then in order. When all amendments have been disposed of, the motion, as then before the court, is put in answer to the question, ' Shall this motion be adopted—yea or nay ?'"

This contains substantially the various parliamentary rules and usages, regulating motions and amendments, as explained *above*, pp. 33-35.

159. " A motion to take an immediate vote is put without debate. If carried in the affirmative, the amendment or amendments pending are put to the court without further discussion ; then the main motion is voted on, and the subject is disposed of. If the motion is lost, the debate continues, just as if no such motion had been made."

This is practically the "previous question " when undebatable, and brings a question and its subsidiary motions at once to a vote (see *above*, pp. 14, 15). It differs, however, from the parliamentary rule (see *above*, p. 14), since the debate goes on, if the motion for the previous question is negatived.

160. "A motion to reconsider a decision of the court cannot be entertained at the sederunt in which the decision was given ; nor at any subsequent time, unless notice of such motion has been given at a previous sederunt. A motion to reconsider can only be made and seconded by members who voted in the majority."

This embodies the principles that generally govern a motion for reconsideration in those assemblies where it is in use (see *above*, p. 17).

161. "A motion under discussion which consists of two or more distinct parts, shall, on the call of any two members, at any time before the final vote is taken, be divided and each part shall be voted on separately."

For same parliamentary rule, see *above*, p. 35.

162. "When a member rises to speak the moderator announces his name. If two or more rise at the same time the moderator decides who shall speak first."

This calling of a member's name is convenient in an assembly where the members cannot be well known to each other. The other part of the rule is a parliamentary proceeding (see *above*, p. 37).

163. "Every speaker addresses the moderator, and may not address any other member directly."

For same parliamentary rule, in the interest of decorum and order, see *above*, p. 38.

164. "A member when speaking should not be interrupted, unless upon a call to order, or when the time has come for a special order of the day, or for adjournment of the court. When business is resumed the speaker who was interrupted has possession of the floor."

This embodies, as respects a call to order, the parliamentary rule (see *above*, p. 38). In other respects it is a special rule of the courts, intended to facilitate the progress of business.

165. "Any member who is dissatisfied with the ruling of the moderator may appeal to the court. The question of sustaining

the ruling of the chair is then put by the clerk, and decided without debate."

The parliamentary rule (see *above*, p. 39), with the exception that the clerk here puts the question.

166. " When a member in speaking utters language which another member regards as offensive or censurable, the latter may require that the words be taken down by the clerk. After this is done, the speaker is allowed to proceed. The words so taken down may afterwards be considered by the court, and, if found censur-able, the speaker is dealt with as the offence may require. A party in a case, though not a member of the court, may claim this protection or incur this censure."

This contains the gist of the parliamentary rule, the conditions of which should be followed, as explained *above*, p. 41. It will be seen from the refer-ence to parliamentary proceedings the moderator should not order the words to be taken down hastily but should be guided by the sense of the meeting ; and if any one intervenes, or any debate ensues between the utterances of the objectionable words and the call to take them down, they cannot be entered.

167. " No member shall speak more than once to any motion, or amendment, unless by permission of the court, and in explana-tion or to correct mistakes. The right of reply, however, belongs to the mover before the final vote is taken on the main motion."

This is practically the parliamentary rule (see *above*, p. 38) ; it may be assumed that any " permission to speak more than once to any motion " will be granted only under the conditions stated in the rule—or under such very excep-tional circumstances as justify the suspension for a moment of a wise regulation.

168. " The vote is ordinarily taken by a show of hands, but the moderator may ask members to vote by rising to their feet. At the final vote on the main motion, the roll may be called, if required by two members of the court. Ordinarily the state of the vote is not recorded, but this may be done in regard to any vote, if required by two members of the court."

This is the ordinary procedure in all such bodies, to take the sense of the meeting. For voices, see *above*, p. 41 ; for show of hands, see *above*, p. 70 ; for calling of roll, see *above*, p. 42. The following rules regulate other matters connected with a division.

169. "Members should not, without good cause, decline to vote; and, unless excused by the court from voting, all who do not vote are held as acquiescing in the decision of the majority."

If a member for adequate reasons, declines to vote, it should be moved and agreed to, "That Mr. A. be excused from voting on this question." By the specific rule given above, members have a serious responsibility thrown upon them if they are not excused. It is practically the parliamentary rule which, in effect, requires that every member who has heard the question put from the chair should vote; the recognized exception being the vote of a member personally interested in a question. See *above*, p. 43n, for meaning of personal interest.

170. "When the vote is to be taken the doors are closed, and no further debate or remark is allowed, unless to correct a mistake in regard to the voting; when this happens, the vote is taken anew."

This is also practically the usage of parliament. Members can always ask to have the roll of votes called and mistakes corrected before the decision of the chair on the question under vote is finally given (see *above*, p. 43).

171. "In order to allow greater freedom in discussion, the court, when considering any particular matter, may, on motion duly seconded, resolve itself into a committee of the whole. On motion duly made, a chairman is appointed, and the moderator leaves the chair."

This and the following rule embody in express terms the parliamentary procedure of committee of the whole, of which the usages are explained *above*, pp. 44-46.

172. "While the court is in committee the motions considered are not recorded in the minutes, and members are at liberty to speak more than once on any motion. A separate minute of the proceeding is taken. When the committee rises its chairman presents a report to the committee embodying the result of the committee's deliberations, or he reports progress and asks leave to sit again."

These are practically parliamentary usages; see *above*, pp. 44-46 for proceedings in committee of the whole.

PETITIONS.

The right of every member to present petitions and memorials to any church court is distinctly affirmed by rules 173 to 178 inclusive in the Rules and Forms of Procedure, pp. 35, 36. All such documents should be in proper form and expressed in respectful language. See parliamentary rules governing petitions, *above*, pp. 52, 53.

OTHER PROCEEDINGS.

When the business of the assembly is ended, the minutes of the last sederunt are read and sustained [confirmed]. The moderator then addresses the court, and after praise and prayer declares the assembly to be dissolved, " indicts another assembly to meet at a time and place previously appointed by the court and closes the proceedings with the apostolic benediction (see p. 29, Rule and Forms of Procedure)."

Any business "emerging" during the interval between the annual meetings of assembly is referred to a commission, composed of the commissioners (see *above*, p. 209), appointed to the last assembly, with the addition of one minister appointed by the moderator. Thirty-one commissioners constitute a quorum. The commission elects its own moderator, and must submit its minutes to be confirmed at the next general assembly (see Rules and Forms of Procedure, p. 29).

RECORDS.

The rules of the courts (179 to 188 inclusive) also provide for the careful and correct keeping of their records. The number of each page must be written in words as well as figures, every page is signed by the clerk, and the record of each sitting or sederunt by the moderator and clerk. In case of the death or removal of the moderator or clerk, the record shall, when the minutes are confirmed, be signed in the presence of the court by the moderator or clerk acting at the time, with a note of the cause. The time and place of each meeting must be fully stated in the minutes and also shortly indicated at the top of each page on the margin. A suitable margin is left on every page, and contains an index of each item of business—a breviat to a statute in fact. All numbers shall be given in words as well as in figures. No inferior court may erase or alter any part of its record after it has been confirmed unless by order of a higher court. All erasures, cancellings, interlineations, or other changes shall be noted in the margin with the initials of the clerk's name. No unnecessary vacant space shall be left between the minutes of sittings of a court. All these special regulations governing the record of the courts show the legal caution which govern the proceedings of these well administered assemblies of the Presbyterian Church of Canada.

IV. CONVENTIONS OF THE BAPTISTS AND OTHER RELIGIOUS BODIES.

The following note from the Rev. D. M. Mihell, M.A., B. Th., Secretary-Treasurer of the Baptist Convention of Ontario and Quebec (a) explains itself: "I send you a copy of our 'Year Book' (Toronto, 1892-93) but I do not think it is exactly what you want. As a convention we have no formal established rules such as obtain in other bodies. In all our deliberations we follow a programme previously arranged by the executive committee for each session, and are governed by ordinary parliamentary usage." Therefore, as in all cases, not provided for in the foregoing sections relating to the Church of England, Methodists, and Presbyterians, reference must be had to the first part of this work on parliamentary law and usage.

(a) See for constitution of the Baptist Church in Ontario and Quebec, Dominion Statutes of 1889, chap. 105, and "Baptist Year Book," p. 30.

FIFTH PART.

—

MUNICIPAL COUNCILS.

—

I.—STATUTORY PROVISIONS IN ONTARIO RESPECTING COUNCILS AND THEIR MEETINGS.

II.—RULES OF ORDER AND PROCEDURE OF THE COUNCILS OF TORONTO, AND OTHER CITIES OF ONTARIO.

III.—PROPOSED CODE OF RULES FOR COUNCILS GENERALLY.

IV.—NOTE ON THE MUNICIPAL SYSTEMS OF THE OTHER PROVINCES OF CANADA.

I.—STATUTORY PROVISIONS IN ONTARIO RESPECTING COUNCILS AND THEIR MEETINGS.

1. GENERAL OBSERVATIONS.

Under the ninety-second section, s-s. 8, of the British North America Act of 1867, the legislature of each province of the Dominion of Canada has full legislative control over the municipal institutions of that province. It can amend, abridge, divide, restrain, and even abolish those institutions should it be necessary. Being the creation of a statute every municipal body is, as a legal consequence, strictly bound by the statute under which it acts and also by the general principles of the common law that may apply where the statutory law is silent. These municipal councils are the legislative and executive body by which the corporation exercises its powers. The jurisdiction of every council is confined to the municipality it represents, except where authority

beyond the same is expressly given by statute ; and the powers of
every such body are exercised by its by-laws, when not otherwise
provided for (see *below*, p. 254).   A by-law is, generally speaking, the
special law of the inhabitants of a corporate place or district, as
distinguished from the general law of the province in which the
municipality is situated and is consequently obligatory only over
that particular place or district (*a*).   While every province has a
general law regulating its municipal system, there are also special
statutes relating to the corporations of cities and towns.   All
councils, whether regulated by the general or a special statute,
can be restrained in all the provinces, by the courts when their
by-laws are in excess of their defined powers.   The courts may
also compel them to exercise their powers in special cases.   The
legislature grants the municipal authorities certain powers and at
the same time commits the proper exercise of those powers to the
controlling care of the courts.

It is in the province of Ontario that we find one of the most
complete systems in the world.   The municipal divisions of the
province are known as county, city, town, village, township, union
of counties, and union of townships, and the inhabitants of each
such division form a body corporate whose powers are exercised
by the council under the law (ss. 3-8) (*b*).   The name of every
such body corporate (except a provisional corporation) (*c*), is " The
corporation of the county, city, etc., of— as the case may be—
(s. 5) and cannot be changed except by the authority of the
legislature.   This legal name should be used on all occasions and
in all documents affecting the corporation (*d*).

In the following pages I cite in full those sections of the
Municipal Act which relate directly to the several councils after

(*a*) See *above*, p. 109, for a wider definition of such by-laws extending them
to the regulations of all corporate companies.

(*b*) See Consolidated Municipal Act, Ont. Stat. of 1892, 55 V. c. 42 ; amended
by 56 V. c. 35.   A useful work to consult is Harrison's Municipal Manual, 5th
ed. by F. J. Joseph, Toronto.   I give reference to sections of Act in all cases.

(*c*) To be styled " The Provisional Corporation of the County of ———, s. 6.

(*d*) See Harrison, p. 15, note *e*.

their election and are necessary to make their organization, and the procedure at their meetings, as intelligible as possible. In the majority of other cases, I give simply the subject and number of sections, in order to make this summary of the municipal law convenient for all purposes of reference. For instance :

For Formation of new Corporations see :

Villages, ss. 9-17.

Towns and cities, ss. 18-26.

Townships, ss. 27-34.

Counties, ss. 35-37.

Provisional County Corporations, ss. 38-52.

Matters Consequent upon the Formation of New Corporations :

By-laws to continue in force, ss. 53, 54.

Debts and liabilities how affected, ss. 55-59,

Officials and their sureties, how affected, ss. 60-63.

For Municipal Elections see :

Electors : Qualification of, ss. 79-87.

Elections :

Time and place of holding, ss. 88-96.

Returning officers and deputy-returning officers, ss. 97-101.

Oaths, ss. 102-106.

Proceedings preliminary to the poll, ss. 107-141.

The poll, ss. 142-161.

Miscellaneous provisions, ss. 162-176.

Vacancies in council, etc., ss. 177-186; see *below*, pp. 232, 233.

Controverted elections, ss. 187-208.

Prevention of corrupt practices, ss. 209-222.

For Qualifications of Members of Councils see :

In each municipality, s. 73.

Nature of estate to be possessed, s. 74.

In new township where there is no assessment roll, s. 75.

Where only one qualified person for each seat, s. 76.

Disqualifications of judges, etc., s. 77.

Exemptions of certain officials and other persons, s. 78.

Payment of members, ss. 231, 232.

2. Municipal Organization.

County.

The council of every county consists of the reeves and deputy-reeves of the townships and villages within that county, and of any towns which have not withdrawn from the jurisdiction of the same, and one of the reeves or deputy-reeves (by whom he is elected), is the head of the council, and called a warden (s. 64).

City.

The council of every city consists of a mayor who is the head of the same, and of three aldermen for every ward (s. 68). The mayor is elected by a general vote, and the aldermen by the electors of the respective wards.

Town.

The council of every town consists of the mayor or head of the same (elected by general vote), and of three councillors elected for every ward where there are less than five wards, and of two councillors for every ward where there are five or more wards, and if the town has not withdrawn from the jurisdiction of the council of the county in which it lies, then a reeve shall be added ; and if the town had the names of five hundred persons entitled to vote at municipal elections on the last revised voters' list then a deputy-reeve shall be added, and for every five hundred additional names of persons so entitled to vote on such list there shall be elected an additional deputy-reeve. It is provided, however, that the council of every town, where there are less than five wards may, upon a petition of not less than one hundred municipal electors, pass a by-law reducing the number of councillors for each ward to two ; but such by-law, before it is finally passed, must receive the assent of the electors of the municipality as provided (a) in the general municipal law (s. 69).

The law provides for the repeal of the by-law above-mentioned after two annual elections on the presentation of a petition to the council from not less than one hundred resident electors (s-s. 2, s. 69).

(a) See ss. 293, et seq.

Village.

The council of every incorporated village consists of one reeve, or head of the same, and of four councillors. If there are in this division five hundred voters then it can have a reeve, a deputy-reeve, and three councillors. For every additional five hundred names, an additional deputy-reeve takes the place of a councillor, s. 70. The election of reeve, deputy-reeve, and councillors is by general vote when the village is not divided into wards; when so divided the councillors elect the deputy-reeve or reeves (ss. 93, 94). The election is the same in the township.

Township.

The council of every township consists of a reeve, or head of the same, and of four councillors; but if there are five hundred electors within the division it receives a reeve, deputy-reeve, and three councillors. For every five hundred additional names an additional deputy-reeve takes the place of a councillor (s. 71). For election, see remarks *above* on the village, which apply also to the township.

Provisional Corporations.

The reeves and deputy-reeves of the municipalities within a junior county, for which a provisional council is established under the law, are, *ex officio*, the members of that body (s. 92).

The lieutenant-governor in council, after the formation of a provisional council under the law, appoints the time and place for the first meeting, and names a member to preside until a provisional warden is duly elected (ss. 38, 39).

A provisional warden is elected by the council from among the members for one year (s. 40).

The head of a Council.

As previously shown the head of every county or provisional corporation is named the warden; of every city and town, the mayor; of every township and incorporated village, the reeve (a).

(a) For meaning of words, Mayor, Reeve, see Bourinot's " Local Government in Canada," Roy. Soc. of Can. Trans., 1886.

These several heads are chief executive officers (*b*) of their respective corporations. Sections 38-40, and 225-227 provide for the election of warden (see *below*, pp. 238, 239); ss. 93, 107, *et seq.*, provide for the nomination and election of mayor and reeve.

3. VACANCIES IN A COUNCIL BY RESIGNATION, ETC.

Any mayor or other member of a council may, with the consent of the majority of the members present, to be entered on the minutes of the council, resign his seat in the council (s. 179).

In case the office of mayor of a city or town becomes vacant after the first day of December in any year, and an election to fill the vacancy has not been ordered by the court or a judge, the council may either direct that an election be held to fill the vacancy, or may elect one of their number to fill the office during the residue of the term (s. 182).

The warden of a county may resign his office by verbal intimation to the council while in session, or by letter to the county clerk if not in session, in which cases, and in case of vacancy by death or otherwise, the clerk shall notify all the members of the council, and shall, if required by a majority of the members of the county council, call a special meeting to fill such vacancy (s. 180).

If a warden resign by verbal intimation, the fact of such resignation should be duly entered on the minutes, as in analogous cases in the house of commons (see Bourinot, p. 181).   In case of resignation by letter, it would be also well to adopt the parliamentary form substantially as follows :—

" To   clerk of the county council of   :

" I   , warden of the county of   do hereby resign my office as warden for the county aforesaid.

Given under my hand and seal at   this   day of   , 18 ..

[L.S.]
Witness :

The person thereupon elected shall hold his seat for the residue of the term for which his predecessor was elected, or for which the office is to be filled (s. 183).

(*b*) See ss. 243, 244.

4. Vacancies in Council by Disqualification, etc.

If after the election of a person as member of a council he is convicted of felony or infamous crime or becomes insolvent within the meaning of the Insolvent Acts, or applies for relief as an indigent debtor, or remains in close custody, or assigns his property for the use of his creditors, or absents himself from the meetings of the council for three months without being authorized to do so by a resolution of the council entered in its minutes, his seat in the council shall thereby become vacant, and the council shall declare the seat vacant and order a new election (s. 177).

If a member should wish to absent himself for three months, he should ask formal leave from the council. This formal leave should be expressed in a resolution duly proposed and agreed to, "That Mr. A. have leave to absent himself from the service of the council for the space of three months from

," *(give date)*. If a member should be absent for three months, without leave, attention should be called to the fact by the clerk, or a member in his place. It would be well in this or other cases given in the section, if a committee of the council were chosen as in parliament to inquire into the alleged disqualifications and probable vacancy ; antecedent to any proceedings required by law. See Bourinot, pp. 141, 142, for case of senators absent for two consecutive sessions. When there is no question as to the facts, then the vacancy may be declared. As a rule, however, members who are disqualified will resign by letter. The next section provides a remedy in cases of members omitting to vacate their seats under the law.

In the event of a member of a municipal council forfeiting his seat at the council or his right thereto, or of his becoming disqualified to hold his seat, or of his seat becoming vacant by disqualification or otherwise, he shall forthwith vacate his seat, and in the event of his omitting to do so at any time after his election, proceedings by *quo warranto* to unseat such member, as provided by sections 187 to 208, both inclusive, of this Act, may be had and taken, and such sections shall, for the purposes of such proceedings, apply to any such forfeiture, disqualification or vacancy (s. 178).

Sections 181, 184 and 185, provide for holding new elections in cases of persons neglecting or refusing to accept office or to make the necessary declarations of office within the time required, etc.

5. PROCEEDINGS IN CASE OF FAILURE TO ELECT A NEW COUNCIL.

In case, at an annual or other election, the electors, from any cause not provided for by sections 158 or 159, neglect or decline to elect the members of council for a municipality on the day appointed, or to elect the requisite number of members, the new members of the council, if they equal or exceed the half of the council when complete, or a majority of such new members, or if a half of such members are not elected, then the members for the preceding year, or a majority of them, shall appoint as many qualified persons as will constitute or complete the number of members requisite; and the persons so appointed shall accept office and make the necessary declaration, under the same penalty, in case of refusal or neglect, as if elected (s. 186).

Sections 158 and 159 deal with cases of elections not commenced, or interrupted by reason of riot or other emergency, etc.

6. THE CLERK.

The law provides that every council shall appoint a clerk; and the clerk shall truly record in a book, without note or comment, all resolutions, decisions and other proceedings of the council and, if required by any member present, shall record the name and vote of every member voting on any matter submitted, and shall keep the books, records, and accounts of the council, and shall preserve and file all accounts acted upon by the council, and also the originals or certified copies of all by-laws, and of all minutes of the proceedings of the council, all of which he shall so keep in his office, or in the place appointed by by-law of the council (s. 245).

See *below*, p. 242, for declaration made by clerk on entering on duties of office.

The council may by resolution provide that, in case the clerk is absent, or incapable through illness of performing his duties of clerk, some other person to be named in the resolution, or to be appointed under the hand and seal of such clerk, shall act in his stead and the person so appointed shall while he so acts, have all the powers of the clerk (s. 246).

In other words there is to be a deputy-clerk.

Ss. 247, 248 and 265 provide regulations for the inspection of minutes, assessment rolls, returns of statistics and other information by clerk, and need not be given in this work of procedure. The various duties assigned to the clerk and other officers must be sought in the statute itself. Councils by by-law generally regulate the duties of the clerk and other officers. See next paragraph and *below*, p. 255. The clerk, while in office can only charge the council by acts within the scope of his general authority, or by such as the council beforehand directed or afterwards sanctioned ; *Ramsay* v. *Western District Council*, 4 U. C. Q. B. 374. While in office he may amend an erroneous record (see Harrison, p. 181, note *b*).

The law also provides for the appointment of a treasurer, asses-sors and collectors, auditors, valuators, on whose duties it is not necessary to dwell here.

For appointment and duties of

Treasurer, see ss. 249-253 ; also *below*, p. 252.

Assessors and collectors, see ss. 254-257; also *below*, p. 252.

Auditors and audit, see ss. 258-268 ; also *below*, p. 253.

Valuators, s. 269 ; also *below*, p. 254.

Duties of officers as to oaths, etc., ss. 270-277, see *below*, pp. 241-244, given in full.

Salaries, tenure of office, and security, see ss. 278-281.

All officers appointed by a council hold office until removed by that body—in effect, during pleasure; (*a*) and must, in addition to the duties assigned to them in the Act perform all other duties required by them by any statute or by any by-law of the council (s. 279). Every clerk, treasurer, assessor, auditor, and collector, etc., shall, before entering on the duties of his office, make a declaration as prescribed by law (see *below*, p. 242).

7. MEETINGS OF MUNICIPAL COUNCILS IN ONTARIO : ELECTION
OF WARDEN, ETC.

The members of every municipal council (except county councils) shall hold their first meeting at eleven o'clock in the forenoon, on

(*a*) See note on this subject in Harrison, p. 205, where an exception is made in the case of " an appointment at a yearly salary under the corporate seal or other appointment from which a yearly hiring is inferred."

the third Monday of the same January in which they are elected, or on some day thereafter ; and the members of every county council shall hold their first meeting at two o'clock in the afternoon, or some hour thereafter, on the fourth Tuesday of the same month, or on some day thereafter (s. 223).

Every member of the council is bound to know the day specially named for the first meeting (see *In re Slavin & Orillia*, 36 U. C. Q. B. 159, also Harrison, p. 169 *j*).

The members of every county council shall hold their first meeting at the county hall if there is one, or otherwise at the county court house (s. 228).

The law, it will be seen in designating the time (see *above*, p. 235) as well as the place of the first meeting, contemplates giving definite information and preventing any one from professing ignorance on these points. After organization the council has it in its power to make a by-law or regulations for all such matters (see s. 229, *below*, p. 241 on this point). Every established and well regulated council will have a permanent by-law, and leave as little as possible to mere resolutions of a temporary character.

No reeve or deputy-reeve can take his seat until he has filed with the clerk of the county council a certificate of the clerk of the township, village or town municipality, under his hand, and the seal of the municipal corporation, that such reeve or deputy-reeve was duly elected and has made and subscribed the declarations of office and qualification as such reeve or deputy-reeve ; nor, in case of a deputy-reeve, until he has also filed with the clerk of the county an affirmation or declaration of the clerk or other person having the legal custody of the last revised voters' list for the municipality which he represents, that there appear upon such voters' list the names of at least five hundred persons entitled to vote at municipal elections, for the first deputy-reeve elected for the municipality, and that no alteration reducing the limits of the municipality and the numbers of persons on said list entitled to vote at municipal elections below five hundred for each additional deputy-reeve, has taken place since the said voters' list was last revised (s. 65).

The certificate mentioned in section 65 may be in the following form :

I, A. B., of   , clerk of the corporation of the township (town *or* village *as the case may be*) of   , in the county of   , do hereby, under my hand and the seal of the said corporation, certify that C. D., of   , esquire, was duly elected reeve (*or* deputy-reeve *as the case may be*), of the said township (town or village *as the case may be*), and has made and subscribed the declaration of office and qualification of such reeve (or deputy-reeve, *as the case may be*).

Given under my hand and the seal of the said corporation of   at   , in the said township (town or village *as the case may be*), this   day of   A. D. 18   .

L. S.   A. B.

Township (town or village) clerk.

(s. 66).

The declaration mentioned in section 65 may be in the following form :

I, A. B., of   , gentleman, clerk of the township (town *or* village, *as the case may be*) of   , in the county of   do hereby declare and affirm as follows :

(1) That I am the person having the legal custody of the last revised voters' list for the said township (town *or* village, *as the case may be*).

(2) That there appears upon the said list the names of at least   hundred (*five hundred for each deputy reeve*) persons entitled to vote at municipal elections in the said township (town *or* village, *as the case may be*).

(3) That no alteration reducing the limits of the said municipality, and the number of persons entitled to vote at municipal elections, below   hundred (*five hundred for each deputy reeve*), has taken place since the said list was last revised.

(4) That in counting the names of the voters on the said list, the names of the voters thereon have not to the best of my information, knowledge or belief, been counted more than once, whether they appear upon the said list once or more than once.

A. B.

(s. 67).

For declarations of office and qualification mentioned in foregoing sections 65 and 66, see *below*, pp. 241-244.

No business shall be proceeded with at the first meeting of the council, until the declarations of office and qualification have been administered to all the members who present themselves to take the same (s. 224).

The election of a presiding officer would be business within the meaning of the law, as the next section in fact clearly shows that such election is the first proceeding after organization of the council.

For qualifications of mayor, alderman, reeve, deputy-reeve, or councillor, see ss. 73-77. Such persons must have certain property qualifications (or the wife must have) as proprietor or tenant, varying in the municipal divisions ; must be males of the full age of twenty-one years ; and subjects of the queen, natural-born or naturalized.

Every person elected or appointed under the Act to any office requiring a qualification of property must before he takes the declaration of office, or enters on his duties, make a declaration provided in sections 270-275 of the statute (see *below*, pp. 241-243 for oaths and declarations). The declarations of office and qualification can be and are generally made before the clerk of the municipality or before some court, judge, police-magistrate or other justice of the peace having jurisdiction in the municipality in question (see *below*, p. 243).

The members elect of every county council, being at least a majority of the whole number of the council when full, shall at their first meeting after the yearly elections, and after making the declarations of office and qualification when required to be taken, organize themselves as a council by electing one of themselves to be warden (s. 225).

See Harrison, 170 note *n.* The court will presume until the contrary be clearly shown that there was a quorum—that is to say, a majority of the whole number, of the council—present at the doing of a corporate act : *Citizens' Mutual Fire Insurance Co.* v. *Sortwell,* 8 Allan (Mass.) 217. Harrison is of opinion that a majority of the quorum suffice to elect a warden in case of divisions as the law simply makes the presence of a quorum at a meeting necessary. The previous section 65 (see *above*, p. 236) provides for certificates from the clerks of the several municipal divisions that the reeves and deputy-reeves have made the necessary declarations under the law, and such declarations are not made again before the clerk of the county council except "when required."

At every such election the clerk of the council shall preside, and if there is no clerk, the members present shall select one of themselves to preside, and the person selected may vote as a member (s. 226).

The following section 227 gives a member whether presiding or not on this occasion, a second or casting vote, if he happens to be reeve or deputy-reeve. But if the member who acts as presiding officer does not fall within conditions of the section, he has only one vote as a member. The clerk, while acting, cannot have a vote as he is not a member of the council.

(1) In case of an equality of votes on the election of the head of any county council, or provisional county council, then of those present, the reeve, or in his absence the deputy-reeve of the municipality which for the preceding year had the greatest equalized assessment shall have a second and casting vote, and in the event of no one municipality having the greatest equalized assessment, in consequence of two or more municipalities being equalized equally, then the reeve, or, in his absence, the deputy-reeve of the municipality having the greatest number of municipal voters entered on its last revised voters' list shall have such second or casting vote.

(2) In counting the names of voters referred to in this section the names of the same persons shall not be counted more than once, whether the name of such persons appears upon the voters' lists only once or more than once (s. 227).

See the remarks on the foregoing section as to the vote of a reeve or deputy-reeve.

From the foregoing sections of the law it will be seen a county council having been duly elected, meets at a fixed time and place as provided by law in the county court house or county hall, whenever such buildings have been provided, or elsewhere as it may have been arranged for the time being by the by-law until such permanent accommodation is provided. The clerk, or a reeve presides in his absence (see *above*, s. 226, p. 238), and commences the organization of the council by requiring the reading and filing of certificates from the several clerks of the municipal divisions of the election of reeves and deputy-reeves within their respective municipalities ; also of the affidavits required by law as to the number of names on last revised assessment rolls of the municipalities required to send deputy-reeves (see *above*, s. 65, p. 236).

The council having been thus far legally constituted, and a quorum being present, always a majority (see *above*, s. 225, p. 238) of the whole council, the clerk or presiding officer shall call for nominations for warden (see *above*, p. 238) according to the

by-law or regulation of the council for such elections. The
county of the county of Simcoe require a ballot on such occasions
as follows :

"At the first meeting of the council for the election of warden, the clerk, or,
in his absence, the person elected to take his place, shall, after calling the
members elect to order, and as soon as a sufficient number of the members to
elect a warden are within the bar, give fifteen minutes for nomination, and
after the expiry of the said time, the clerk, or other person elected in his place,
shall furnish to the members elect present slips of paper whereon the name of
the person (being one of those nominated) for whom the member votes shall be
written, the ballot papers shall be handed to the clerk, who shall (with two
members of the council to be elected by him, not being nominees) proceed to
count them, and if none of the candidates have a majority of the council, as
required by the statutes, then the one having the lowest number of votes shall
drop out, and the same vote shall take place again with the remaining nominees until the required majority is obtained, the lowest number always dropping
out.   And in case the whole number of names shall be voted on without any
of them obtaining the required majority, the clerk, or other person elected to
take his place, shall allow fifteen minutes more for nominations when the same
process is to be continued until some nominee obtains the required majority,
and the person who gets said majority shall be declared the warden elect for
the current year.   All persons who have been voted on shall be eligible to be
again nominated at any subsequent nomination."

No council can elect by ballot except it has legal authority to
that effect (a).   As a rule in councils the election is by open voting
by yeas and nays duly taken and recorded.   For instance, the fifth
rule of the council of Carleton county provides : " In the election
of the warden, the names of the candidates shall be put in the
order in which they are proposed—the yeas and nays to be recorded
when required by any member."   The clerk or presiding officer, in
such a case, will call for nominations, and two members will
respectively move and second, " That Mr. A. be warden for the
present year."   Then the presiding officer will put the question on
this motion.   If it is carried by the requisite majority—(see above,
p. 238)—he is declared duly elected by the presiding officer ; and
when he has signed the declaration of office (see above, p. 242)
required by law as the first legal proceeding after his election,

(a) See below, p. 382, where, in a note to proposed code of rules, the legality
of taking a ballot for warden, as in Simcoe, is questioned.

whatever may be the mode of election, he is conducted to the chair by the mover and seconder, and thanks the council for the honour conferred upon him (for same parliamentary usage see *above*, p. 28). If the first candidate is not chosen, then nominations are made and voted upon until there is an election under the law (*a*). If there is an equality of votes (including those of the reeve or deputy-reeve), and the clerk is presiding officer, there is no election, and another nomination must be put to the meeting. If in such a case the presiding officer is a reeve or deputy-reeve of the municipality, who comes under the conditions of section 227 (see *above*, p. 239), he has a second or casting vote. In a council where the election is by ballot, the same reeve or deputy-reeve would also be called upon to give a casting vote in case of an equality of votes (but see *below*, p. 382 *n*).

For proceedings at an inaugural meeting of a city council elect, see *below*, p. 264.

The subsequent meetings of the county council, and all the meetings of every other council shall be held at such place, either within or without the municipality, as the council, from time to time, by resolution on adjourning, to be entered on the minutes, or by by-law, appoints (s. 229).

The council of any county or township in which any city, town or incorporated village lies, may hold its sittings, keep its public offices, and transact all the business of the council and of its officers and servants within such city, town or incorporated village, and may purchase and hold such real property therein as may be convenient for such purposes (s. 230).

Ss. 231 and 232 provide for limited remuneration to councillors and committee; also for payment of heads of council as may be determined.

8. Duties of Officers Respecting Oaths and Declarations.

By section 270—(1) Every person elected or appointed under this Act to any office requiring a qualification of property in the incumbent shall, before he takes the declaration of office, or enters

(*a*) See new rule suggested *below*, p. 382, for such proceeding.

B.M.P.—16

on his duties, make and subscribe a solemn declaration to the effect following:

I, A. B., do solemnly declare that I am a natural born (*or* naturalized) subject of her majesty and have and had to my own use and benefit, in my own right (*or* have and had in the right of my wife, *as the case may be*), as proprietor (*or* tenant, *as the case may be*), at the time of my election (*or* appointment *as the case may require*) to the office of   hereinafter referred to, such an estate as does qualify me to act in the office of (*naming the office*) for (*naming the place for which such person has been elected or appointed*), and that such estate is (*the nature of the estate to be specified, as* an equitable estate of leasehold *or otherwise, as the case may require, and if land, the same to be designated by its local description, rents or otherwise*), and that such estate at the time of my election (*or* appointment, *as the case may require*) was of the value at least (*specifying the value*) over and above all charges, liens and incumbrances affecting the same.

Where any person has been elected as reeve, deputy-reeve, or councillor of any township council he may, instead of the foregoing declaration, make and subscribe a solemn declaration to the effect following :

I, A. B., do solemnly declare that I am a natural born (*or* naturalized) subject of her majesty ; and have and had to my own use and benefit, in my own right (*or* have and had in right of my wife, *as the case may be*) as proprietor at the time of my election to the office of   hereinafter referred to, such an estate as does qualify me to act in the office of (*naming the office*) for (*naming the place for which such person has been elected*), and that such estate is (*the nature of the estate to be specified and the land to be designated by its local description*) and that such estate at the time of my election was in my actual occupation, and was actually rated in the then last revised assessment roll of this township (*naming it*) at an amount not less than $2,000.

By section 271—Every member of a municipal council, every mayor and every clerk, treasurer, assessor and collector, engineer or clerk of works and street overseer or commissioner appointed by a council, shall also, before entering on the duties of his office, make and subscribe a solemn declaration to the effect following:

I, A. B., do solemnly promise and declare that I will truly, faithfully and impartially, to the best of my knowledge and ability, execute the office of (*inserting the name of the office*), to which I have been elected (*or* appointed) in this township (*or as the case may be*), and that I have not received, and will not receive, any payment or reward, or promise of such, for the exercise of any partiality or malversation or other undue execution of the said office, and that I have not by myself or partner, either directly or indirectly, any interest in any contract with or on behalf of the said corporation (*where declaration is made by the clerk, treasurer, assessor, collector, engineer, clerk of works or street overseer, the words following* : " save and except that arising out of my office or position of clerk (*or as the case may be*)."

Under section 272 the solemn declaration to be made by every auditor shall be as follows :

I, A. B., having been appointed to the office of auditor for the municipal corporation of   , do hereby promise and declare, that I will faithfully perform the duties of such office according to the best of my judgment and ability ; and I do solemnly declare, that I had not directly or indirectly any share or interest whatever in any contract or employment (except that of auditor, *if reappointed*) with, by, or on behalf of such municipal corporation, during the year preceding my appointment, and that I have not any such contract or employment except that of auditor, for the present year.

The head and other members of the council, and the subordinate officers of every municipality, shall take the declaration of office and qualification before some court, judge, police magistrate, or other justices of the peace having jurisdiction in the municipality for which such head, members or officers have been elected or appointed, or before the clerk of the municipality ; and the court, judge or other persons before whom such declarations are made, shall give the necessary certificate of the same having been duly made and subscribed (s. 273).

The head of any council, any alderman, reeve or deputy-reeve, any justice of the peace or clerk of a municipality, may, within the municipality, administer any oath, affirmation or declaration under this Act, relating to the business of the place in which he holds office, except where otherwise specially provided, and except where he is the party required to make the oath, affirmation or declaration (s. 274).

The deponent, affirmant or declarant shall subscribe every such oath, affirmation or declaration, and the person administering it shall duly certify and preserve the same, and within eight days deposit the same in the office of the clerk of the municipality to the affairs of which it relates (s. 275).

The head of every council, or in his absence the chairman thereof, may administer an oath or affirmation to any person concerning any account or other matter submitted to the council (s. 276).

Every qualified person duly elected or appointed to be a mayor, alderman, reeve or deputy-reeve, councillor, police trustee, assessor or collector, of, or in any municipality, who refuses such office, or does not within twenty days after knowing of his election or appointment, make the declarations of office and qualification where a property qualification is required, and every person authorized to administer such declaration, who, upon reasonable demand, refuses to administer the same, shall, on summary conviction thereof before two or more justices of the peace, forfeit not more than $80, nor less than $8, at the discretion of the justices, to the use of the municipality, together with the cost of prosecution (s. 277).

The following sections of the Municipal Law provide certain statutory regulations for the conduct of business in a council after it has met and been formally organized under the foregoing sections of the law :

9. CONDUCT OF BUSINESS IN ONTARIO COUNCILS : STATUTORY PROVISIONS.

Every council shall hold its ordinary meetings openly, and no person shall be excluded except for improper conduct, but the head or other chairman of the council may expel and exclude from any meeting, any person who has been guilty of improper conduct at such meeting (s. 233).

This principle of open meetings is essentially English, and all deliberative and legislative bodies must have power to exclude all persons whose conduct may interfere with the orderly and necessary transaction of business. It would not be competent for a council to have "closed doors" whenever it should think proper, like a legislative body, and there transact any business even if it should be a privileged question or other matter of internal arrangement such as is sometimes discussed with closed doors in parliament. But while the law thus limits the ordinary meetings of the council, it gives by a subsequent section (see *below*, p. 245) a discretionary power to hold a special meeting with closed doors.

A majority of the whole number of members required by law to constitute the council shall be necessary to form a quorum (s. 234).

See note to s. 225 *above*, p. 238.

When a council consists of only five members, the concurrent vote of at least three shall be necessary to carry any resolution or other measure (s. 235).

The court has refused to quash a by-law in a case where there are four councillors present at the passing of the law, two of the council having expressed themselves in favour of it, and the third having made no objection when the reeve put the question. *In re Mallough* v. *Ashfield*, 6 U. C. C. P. 415 ; Harrison, 176 note *d*.

(1) The head of every council shall preside at the meetings of council, and may at any time summon a special meeting thereof, and it shall be his duty to summon a special meeting whenever requested in writing by a majority of the members of the council.

(2) In the absence or death of the mayor or head of the council, a special meeting may be summoned at any time by the clerk upon a special requisition to him, signed by a majority of the members of the council (s. 236).

Harrison (p. 176), has a valuable note (*e*) as to the summoning of a special meeting under this section. When the special meeting is desired by a majority of the members of the council, it is not in the discretion of the head of the council but is obligatory upon him to call it. All the members entitled to be present at a special meeting should be notified to attend, and, if practicable, also of the purpose for which the meeting is called ; *Smyth* v. *Darley*, 2 H. L. Cas. 789 ; also, *ex parte Rogers*, 7 Cow. 526 ; *People* v. *Batchelor*, 22 N. Y. 128. The omission to notify a member entitled to be present may be held to invalidate all proceedings at such meetings, *Ib.* ; and where the purpose is specified in the notice, there is in general no power to transact business beside such purpose : *Rex* v. *Liverpool* 2 Burr. 735 ; *Rex* v. *Carlisle*, 1 Str 385 ; *Machell* v. *Nevinson*, 2 Ld. Rayd. 1355 ; *Bergen* v. *Clarkson*, 1 Halst. (N. J.) 352 ; (see also *below*, p. 119, as to legal notices for incorporated companies' meetings).

In case there is no by-law of a council fixing the place of meeting, any special meeting of the council shall be held at the place where the then last meeting of the council was held, and a special meeting may be opened or closed as in the opinion of the council, expressed by resolution in writing, the public interest requires (s. 237).

See *above*, p. 244. as to ordinary meetings which cannot be held "closed."

In case of the death or absence of the head of a town council the reeve, and in case of the absence or death of both of them, the deputy-reeve, and in case of the death or absence of the head of a village or township council, the deputy-reeve shall preside at the meetings of the council, and may at any time summon a special meeting thereof; but if there be more than one deputy-reeve, the council shall determine which of them shall preside at their meeting (s. 238).

In case of two deputy-reeves the council can only "determine" who shall preside by vote taken under the rules and usages that govern all such cases. A member can move, "That Mr. A., deputy-reeve, do take the chair." Though the section does not so provide, it is assumed that the clerk will, as in the house of commons, put the motion.

In the absence of the head of the council, and in the case of a town, village or township, in the absence also of the reeve, if there be one, and also of the deputy-reeve, or deputy-reeves, if there be one or more, by leave of the council or from illness, the council may, from among the members thereof, appoint a presiding officer, who, during such absence, shall have all the powers of the head of the council (s. 239).

This section is intended to meet cases where none of the persons mentioned in the preceding section 238 is present. When elected, the presiding officer may be designated as "Mr. Chairman" or "Mr. President," as it may be thought proper by the speaker. He will be appointed on motion duly made and put. In case of more than one nomination, the parliamentary rule should obtain in the absence of a special rule of a council (see *above*, p. 27). Sub-section 2 of the section provides that such presiding officer can also act as police commissioner in the place of the mayor.

If the person who ought to preside at any meeting does not attend within fifteen minutes after the hour appointed, the members present may appoint a chairman from amongst themselves, and such chairman shall have the same authority in presiding at the meeting as the absent person would have had if present (s. 240).

In the commons the deputy-speaker leaves the chair when the speaker returns. When the permanent chairman of committees is absent, but comes in before the committee to which a temporary chairman has been

APPOINTMENT OF COURT OF REVISION. 247

appointed has closed its business, the latter retires and the former assumes his proper place. It may be assumed a similar practice would in any case obtain in a council.

The head of the council, or the presiding officer or chairman of any meeting of any council, may vote with the other members on all questions, and any question on which there is an equality of votes shall be deemed to be negatived (s. 241).

This practice still exists in the house of lords and the senate of Canada as well as in the upper houses generally of the legislatures, and a question on which there is an equality of votes, *Semper præsumitur pro negante*, "it is deemed to be negatived " (see Bourinot, p. 453). The head of the council may or may not vote ; it is a right to be exercised within his own discretion. In a note (*m*) Harrison, p. 178, recalls the fact that the Act recognizes an exception to the rule with respect to an equality of voices ; and that is, in the case provided for by s. 227, *above*, p. 239 (election of head of a county council). See also ss. 515, 516 of the Municipal Act with reference to appropriations for improvements in a county of a union. Whenever any such measure is brought before the council of the united counties " none but the reeves and deputy-reeves of the county to be affected by the measure shall vote ; except in the case of an equality of votes, when the warden, whether a reeve or deputy-reeve of any portion of the county to be affected by the measure or not, shall have the casting vote" (s. 516).

Every council may adjourn its meetings from time to time (s. 242).

If a meeting is adjourned, either ordinary or special, the business for which it was originally convened can be considered without additional notice at the adjourned meeting. In fact, the latter meeting is simply a continuation of the first. The object of adjourning would necessarily be to finish the business which the meeting was called to transact in the first place (see as to legal rights of adjourning meetings, *Rex* v. *Harris*, 1 B & Ad. 936 ; *Scadding* v. *Lorant*, 3 H. L. Cas. 418 ; also *above*, p. 120, where shareholders' and companies' meetings are concerned).

10. APPOINTMENT OF COURT OF REVISION, HIGH SCHOOL TRUSTEES, REPRESENTATIVES ON FREE LIBRARY BOARD, LOCAL BOARD OF HEALTH, TREASURER, ASSESSORS, COLLECTORS, AUDITORS, VALUATORS.

1. Court of Revision.—The various Assessment Acts of the legislature of Ontario governing the municipalities of the province

were consolidated in 1890 (see 55 Vic. c. 48). By this Act (ss. 55, et seq.), every council has the right to appoint five of its members to be a court of revision. If the council consists of only five members, then these shall constitute the court. In any city having a population of 40,000 or over, the county may pass a by-law appointing in each year, as the court, three persons, none of whom shall be a member or in the employ of the council, and may provide for the remuneration of these officers. This court, on proper application, has the duty of revising the assessment rolls in each local municipality. Its functions are judicial, and limited by the statute which constitutes it. Appeal lies to the county judge not only against its decision but also against any omission, neglect or refusal to hear a complaint under the law.

2. **High School Trustees.**—By the High Schools Act (consolidated in 1891, c. 57, ss. 11, 12), the councils of the municipalities have the right to appoint at least six trustees, which form a high school corporation. In the case of high schools situated in any municipality within the jurisdiction of the county, the county council appoints three, and the municipalities composing the high school district appoint additional members as follows:—

(1) Where a high school district is composed of one municipality, the council thereof shall appoint three additional trustees ; where a high school district is composed of two municipalities, each municipality shall appoint two additional trustees; and where a district is composed of more than two municipalities, each municipality shall appoint one additional trustee. Any portion of a municipality assessed for $50,000, included in a high school district, shall be considered a municipality for the purposes of this section. In every case one of the trustees appointed by the county council and one trustee in each municipality composing the high school district shall retire each year ;

(2) Where a high school district is composed of a county, the county council shall appoint six trustees for such district, two of whom shall retire every year ;

(3) In cities and towns separated from the county, the council thereof shall appoint six trustees for each of the high schools of

such city or town; where the high schools in a city do not exceed three in number, the council shall appoint six trustees for each high school; and the trustees so appointed shall, with such additional trustees as are authorized by this Act, form one corporation. The council of every city and town shall, by by-law, provide for the annual retirement of so many of the trustees appointed by the council as shall secure a complete rotation every three years;

(4) Where the trustees of any high school situated in a city or in a town separated from the county, notify the county clerk that such high school is open to county pupils on the same terms as high schools in the municipalities not separated from the county, the county council may, from time to time, appoint three additional trustees of and for such high school as long as the school is open to county pupils on the terms aforesaid;

(5) The separate school board of the city, town, or incorporated village in which a high school is situated, may appoint one trustee of and for such high school board, who shall hold office for one year, provided always, in the case of a board of education, that such trustees shall not take part in any of the proceedings affecting the public school;

(6) Except in the case of a board of education, the public school trustees of every city, town, or incorporated village in which a high school is situated, may appoint annually one trustee of and for such high school board, who shall hold office for one year.

Vacancies arising from the annual retirement of trustees shall be filled at the first meeting thereof after being duly organized in each year by the municipal councils or by the boards of trustees empowered under this Act to make the appointments; and vacancies arising from death, resignation, or removal from the high school district or county, or otherwise, shall be filled forthwith by the municipal council or board of trustees having the right of appointment, and the person appointed to fill such vacancy shall hold office only for the unexpired term of the person whose place has become vacant (s. 12).

Any resident ratepayer 21 years of age who is not a member of the council of the municipality or county in which the high school is situated shall be qualified to serve as a high school trustee, or as a member of a board of education (s. 12).

3. **Representatives on free library board.**—In any city, town, or village where the electors thereof have established a free library under the Free Libraries Act (see Rev. Stat. of 1887, c. 189, s. 3), the council has the right to appoint certain persons on the board of management.   This board shall be composed of the mayor of the city or town, or the reeve of the village, and three other persons to be appointed by the council, three by the public school board, or the board of education, of the municipality, and two by the trustees of the separate school, if any.

2. No person who is a member of the body entitled to appoint shall be qualified to be a member of the board of management.

3. Of the representatives appointed by the council, and the public school board, or board of education, and separate school trustees, respectively, one shall retire annually, but may be reappointed.

4. Of the three members first appointed by the council, and public school board, or board of education, respectively, one shall hold office until the first day of February after his appointment, one until the first day of February in the following year, and one until the same day in the year next thereafter; and of the two members first appointed by the separate school trustees, one shall hold office until the first day of February after his appointment, and one until the first day of February of the following year; but every member of the board of management shall continue in office after the time named until his successor is appointed.

5. In case of a vacancy by death or resignation of a member, or from any cause other than the expiration of the time for which he was appointed, the member appointed in his place shall hold office for the remainder of his term.

6. Subject to these provisions, each of the members appointed by the council, or public school board, or board of education, shall

hold office for three years from the first day of February in the
year in which he is appointed ; and each of the members appointed
by separate school trustees, for two years from the first day of
February in the year in which he is appointed.

7. The first appointment of members of the board shall be
made at the first meeting of the appointing council or board, after
the final passing of the by-law.   The annual appointments thereafter shall be made at the first meeting of the appointing council
or board, after the first day of January in every year ; and any
vacancy arising from any cause, other than the expiration of the
time for which the member was appointed, shall be filled at the
first meeting thereafter of the appointing council or board.   But if
for any reason appointments are not made at the said dates, the
same shall be made as soon as may be thereafter.

4. **Local board of health.**—The Public Health Act (see Rev.
Stat. of 1887, c. 205, ss. 39-40) provides for the annual appointment by the municipal council of a local board of health composed :

In each township and incorporated village, of the reeve, clerk
and three ratepayers.

In each town of less than four thousand inhabitants, of the
mayor, clerk, and three ratepayers.

In each city and town of more than four thousand inhabitants,
of the mayor, and eight ratepayers.

These members of the board must be appointed at the first
meeting of a council after it has been duly organized.   In case of a
vacancy at any time, it shall be filled at the first meeting thereafter
of the council.   In case of the appointments not being made at the
proper dates for some sufficient reason they must be made thereafter as soon as possible.

Two or more councils may, by concurrent by-laws, form one
health district of their respective municipalities, and the members
of the district board shall consist of three members of each municipality included in the district, viz., the head of the council, the

clerk, and one other ratepayer, not a member of the council, to be
appointed by the council.

For powers and duties, see ss. 48 *et seq.*

5. **Treasurer.**—Every municipal council must appoint a treasurer, who receives either a fixed salary or a percentage, and gives
security (to be enquired into every year) before entering on the
duties of his office. It is his duty to receive and safely keep all
corporation moneys, and pay out the same as the law or the regulations of the council direct. In case of the death of a county treasurer the warden may, by warrant under his hand and seal, appoint
a treasurer *pro tempore* for such purpose or purposes as the warden
may deem necessary, and he shall hold office until the next meeting of the council. Security must also be given in this case.

For duties in full, etc., see ss. 249-253 of Municipal Act. For
declaration on assuming office, see *above*, p. 242. For salaries,
tenure of office and security, see ss. 278-281.

6. **Assessors and Collectors.**—The council of every city, town,
township and incorporated village shall, as soon as may be
convenient after the annual election, appoint as many assessors
and collectors as the assessment laws from time to time authorize
or require. No member of the council can act in this capacity. All
vacancies must be filled up as soon as possible. The council of a
city or town may, instead of assessors, appoint an assessment
commissioner, who, in conjunction with the mayor for the time
being, shall, from time to time, appoint such assessors and
valuators as may be necessary. These several officers, commissioner, assessors and valuators, constitute a board of assessors to
perform all the duties of assessors under the law. They hold
office at the pleasure of the council (see the Municipal Act, ss.
254-257).

By the Consolidated Assessment Act (55 Vic. c. 48, s. 12) the
council of every municipality, except counties, shall appoint such
number of assessors and collectors as may be deemed necessary, but
no such officer can also act as clerk or treasurer.

For duties of assessors in full see ss. 14 *et seq.* of Assessment Act.

For collectors and their duties, see ss. 122 *et seq.* of Assessment Act. For declaration on assuming duties of office, see *above*, p. 242. For salaries, tenure of office and security, see ss. 378-281.

7. **Auditors.**—Every council at its first meeting after organization, shall appoint two auditors, one of whom shall be such person as the head of the council nominates, but no one who, at such time, or during the preceding year, is or was a member, or clerk or treasurer of the council, or who has, or during the preceding year had, directly or indirectly, alone or in conjunction with any other person, a share or interest in any contract with or on behalf of the corporation, except as auditor, shall be appointed to the office. In case of an auditor appointed as above, being unable or refusing to act, the head of the council must nominate another person in his place, but he must not be in the employment of the head of the council. The council of any city may pass a by-law appointing its auditors in the month of December of each year, but the provisions of existing law as to the appointment, as stated above, shall also apply to the audit of the accounts of such city. In case of a vacancy at any time, the council of a city may proceed at once to fill such vacancy by by-law. The auditors shall examine and report upon all accounts affecting the corporation, or relating to any matter under its control or within its jurisdiction for the year ending on the 31st December preceding their appointment. In cities and towns the council may also appoint an auditor who shall, daily or otherwise as directed by the council, examine, report and audit the accounts of the corporation, in conformity with any regulation or by-law of the council; and in other municipalities the auditors shall also, monthly or quarterly, if directed by by-law, examine into and audit the accounts of the corporation. The law makes special provision for the city of Toronto (see *below* p. 357) and also enacts that auditors appointed in that city, and under the general provision allowing the appointment in cities in December (see *above*), shall every month, commencing at

the end of the first month in the year following the said month of December, and so on to the end of such year, examine and report upon all accounts affecting the corporation or relating to any matter under its control, or within its jurisdiction.

See for law in full respecting auditors, Municipal Act, ss. 258-268. For declaration of office, *above*, p. 243. For salaries, tenure of office and security, see ss. 278-281.

8. Valuators.—The council of every county may appoint two or more valuators for the purpose of valuing the real property within the county, and the valuation, as made under the direction of the council in every fifth year at furthest, shall be made the basis of equalization of the real property of the council for a period not exceeding five years. The valuators cannot exceed the powers possessed by assessors. The council may extend the said period, at or before its expiration, for a term not exceeding five years further.

See Municipal Act, s. 269. For appointment by by-law of valuators, pound keepers, fence viewers, overseers of highways, road surveyors, road commissioners, game inspectors and other officers necessary in the affairs of the corporation, and for regulating by by-law their remuneration, fees, charges and duties, see s. 479, s-s. 2, 3. For appointment in cities, s. 255, see *above*, p. 252, under head of "assessors and collectors." Also, for other provisions, Consolidated Assessment Act, s. 79, s-s. 8, and s. 81.

11. By-laws, Regulations and Powers of Ontario Councils.

The law expressly provides that the powers of every council "shall be exercised by by-law when not otherwise authorized or provided for" (s. 282). Every council may also make regulations not specifically provided for in this Act, and not contrary to law, for governing the proceedings of the council, the conduct of its members, the appointing or calling of special meetings, and generally such other regulations as the good of the inhabitants of the municipality requires, and may repeal, alter or amend its by-laws, save as by this Act restricted (s. 283.) Every such by-law to have legal validity must be under the seal of the corporation, signed by the head, or by the presiding officer of the meeting at which it was passed, and by the clerk of the corporation (s. 288). As the council of every municipality is a continuing body in law, it may on its election take up and carry on to completion any by-laws, reports and proceedings which had been under the consideration of the council previous to the meeting of the new body (s. 284). .

All those engaged in municipal legislation should bear well in mind the principles laid down so clearly in the notes to Harrison, from pp. 207-212, with respect to the effect of resolutions and by-laws. As it is well said, "nothing can be more erroneous" than the belief that "a municipal body can do by resolution whatever may be done by by-law." As set forth in the law "the powers of the council *shall* be exercised by by-law when *not otherwise* authorized or provided for." In fact, as Harrison clearly points out, "whenever a municipal council is in doubt whether it can or cannot do a particular thing by order or resolution, it would be much safer and wiser to use a by-law." Acting on this principle, in the absence of a legal authority to pass an order or resolution on a particular subject affecting the ratepayers and electors of a municipality, a council can hardly go astray.

12. General Provisions Applicable to all Municipalities.

The following references to other parts of the Municipal Act which do not necessarily fall within.the scope of this work may be useful :

General Jurisdiction of Councils.

    Nature and extent, ss. 282-287.

Respecting By-laws.

    Authentication of, ss. 288-290.

    Objections by ratepayers, ss. 291, 292.

    Voting on by electors, ss. 293-328.

    Confirmation of, ss. 229-331.

    Quashing, ss. 332-339.

By-laws creating debts, ss. 340-356.

By-laws respecting yearly rates, ss. 357-368.

Anticipatory appropriation, ss. 369-371.

Respecting Finance.

Accounts and investments, ss. 372-382.

Commission of enquiry into finances, ss. 283, 384.

Arbitrations.

Appointment of arbitrators, ss. 385-396.

Procedure, ss. 397-404.

Debentures and other Instruments, ss. 405-414

Administration of Justice and Judicial Proceedings.

Justices of the peace, ss. 415-419.

Penalties, ss. 420-423a.

Witnesses and jurors, ss. 424-426.

Convictions under by-laws, s. 427.

Execution against municipal corporations, ss. 428, 429.

Tender of amends, s. 430.

Contracts with members of council void, s. 431.

Police office and police magistrate, ss. 432 ; 433.

Board of commissioners of police and police force in cities and towns, ss. 434-451.

Court-houses, gaols, etc., ss. 452-476.

Investigation as to municipal officers and governments, s. 477.

When mayor may call out *posse comitatus*, s. 478.

POWERS OF MUNICIPAL COUNCILS.

Powers generally.

Counties, townships, cities, towns, and incorporated villages, ss. 479-488e.

Townships, cities, towns, and incorporated villages, ss. 489-492.

Townships, cities and towns, s. 493.

Counties and cities, s. 494.

Counties, cities, separated towns, s. 495.

Cities, towns and incorporated villages, ss. 496-503.

Cities and towns, ss. 504-508.

Townships, towns and villages, s. 509.

Towns and incorporated villages, s. 510.

Towns, s. 510*a*.

Counties, ss. 511-520.

Cities, ss. 520*a*-520*b*.

Townships, ss. 521-523.

Powers as to Highways and Bridges.

General provisions, ss. 524-549.

Counties, townships, cities, towns, and incorporated villages, ss. 550-554*a*.

Township, cities, towns and incorporated villages, ss. 555-565.

Counties and townships, s. 565.

Counties, s. 566.

Townships, ss. 567, 568.

Powers as to Drainage and other Improvements paid for by Local Rates.

Townships, cities, towns, and villages, ss. 568*a*-629.

Townships and villages, ss. 630-630*a*.

Counties, ss. 631-633.

Powers as to Railways, ss. 634-637.

Powers of Municipal Councils as to aiding Iron smelting Works in certain Districts, s. 637*a*.

POLICE VILLAGES.

Formation of, ss. 638, 639.

Trustees, and election thereof, ss. 640-660.

Duties of police trustees, ss. 661-670.

13. EXPLANATIONS OF THE RULES GIVEN IN THIS WORK.

As every council in the large province of Ontario with over 800 municipal divisions altogether has its own special rules for the conduct of its business as provided for in the section of the law just mentioned (see s. 283, *above*, p. 254), it is not possible within the limits of this work to do more than give examples of such rules as are in use in the councils of the several cities of the province— which rules are practically those in use in all municipal divisions— with such comments and references to the general parliamentary law in each case as seem necessary for an intelligent understanding of every question. In all instances, the general index at end of this treatise, as well as the tables of contents at heads of the first or parliamentary part, and of the rules of the councils, will enable one to obtain information on every point that is likely to arise in practice.

As a rule the respective councils have based their special codes of procedure on the rules of the house of commons of Canada, and the differences in practice are such as have necessarily arisen from the exigencies of business in bodies of a limited sphere and short sessions. Much stress has been laid on the previous question, reconsideration, laying on the table, postponement and such other questions of procedure, as letters to the writer from time to time show are not generally understood in the numerous public bodies of this country.

Further on I suggest a code of rules which are based on the practical experience of these and other important councils and seem adapted to the orderly discharge of public business, while giving at the same time that uniformity of procedure throughout the province which is always desirable, and which is very easily given since there is really no variance in principle in the numerous regulations now in force.

II.—RULES AND ORDER OF PROCEDURE

OF THE

COUNCILS OF TORONTO AND OTHER CITIES OF ONTARIO.

II.—RULES OF ORDER AND PRÒCEDURE OF THE COUNCILS OF TORONTO, HAMILTON, OTTAWA, KINGSTON, LONDON, ST. THOMAS, STRATFORD, BELLEVILLE, ST. CATHARINES, GUELPH, AND BRANTFORD.

REFERENCE TO DIVISIONS OF SUBJECTS.

In the following pages I give on the left the Toronto rules in full, with such comments as are necessary below. On the right hand page will be found the rules of all the other cities. When a rule is the same as that of Toronto, I refer simply to its number, and in other cases I give it in full or in abstract. Figures in black (or Toronto Rule) on left hand, correspond with similar figures on right hand and are thus given to make the reference easier.

TORONTO.

1. MEETINGS OF COUNCIL.

1. "In all the proceedings had or taken in the municipal council of the corporation of the city of Toronto, the following rules and regulations shall be observed, and shall be the rules and regulations for the order and despatch of business in the council, and in the committees thereof."

These rules and regulations are by-laws of the corporation, and as such have the weight of civic statutes, which can only be revoked or amended by other by-laws passed in due legal form by the council.

See by-law 2435, " to regulate the proceedings in the municipal council, etc.," amended by subsequent by-laws, mentioned where necessary hereafter. By-law 2434 has interpretation clauses ; by-law 2436 relates to duties of clerk, treasurer, city engineer and staff, street commissioner, firemen, city commissioner, collectors, and other officials (see Cons. By-laws, 1890, amended in subsequent years by by-laws 2534, 2854, 2925, 2985, 3119, etc.).

2. "After its inaugural meeting the council shall meet every alternate Monday in the year, at the hour of seven o'clock p.m., unless otherwise ordered by special motion, or unless such Monday shall be a public or civic holiday, in which case the council shall meet at the same hour the next day following, which is not a public or civic holiday.

" The inaugural meeting of the new council in each year shall be opened with prayer, the officiating clergyman to be chosen by the mayor elect."   [Continued on p. 264.

In the following pages I give on the left the Toronto rules in full, with such comments as are necessary below. On the right hand page will be found the rules of all the other cities. When a rule is the same as that of Toronto, I refer simply to its number, and in other cases I give it in full or in abstract. Figures in black (or Toronto Rule) on left hand, correspond with similar figures on right hand and are thus given to make the reference easier.

LONDON, HAMILTON, OTTAWA, KINGSTON, BELLEVILLE, ST. CATHARINES, GUELPH, BRANTFORD, AND ST. THOMAS.*

1. MEETINGS OF COUNCIL.

1. Similar enacting clause in by-laws of Ottawa and London, with the proviso in each case that " all rules existing and inconsistent with this by-law at the time of the passing thereof are hereby repealed." In the by-laws of other cities, generally speaking, such a clause necessarily obtains.

2. In London, Guelph and Ottawa meetings are held at half-past seven o'clock p.m., on the first and third Monday of every month, unless otherwise ordered by special motion.

* The clerk of the council of the city of St. Thomas informs me : " We are, and have been, since our incorporation as a city in 1881, guided by the rules regulating the proceedings of the council of the city of London." Consequently in the following *résumé* of the rules of the several cities, St. Thomas must be considered for all practical purposes as included in all references to the city of London, and will not be specifically mentioned except when necessary, as in case of standing committees.

[Continued on p. 255.

The "inaugural meeting," above referred to—*i.e.*, the first meeting of a new council—is held at 11 o'clock a.m. in the city hall, on the third Monday of the January in which the mayor and council were elected (see *above*, p. 235). It is usual for the mayor and members to subscribe to their declarations of qualification and office (see *above*, pp. 241, 243), previous to the meeting—the mayor before the county judge, and the members before the clerk, according to convenience. Unless this is done no member can take his seat (see *above*, p. 241). The fact of these legal preliminary requirements having been complied with is duly entered in the minutes of proceedings. A quorum being present (see *below*, rule 5) the mayor calls the meeting to order from his chair, and after prayers by an ordained minister, whom he has himself chosen, as provided in the rule, he delivers the inaugural address, which is always entered as an appendix to the minutes. On its conclusion he formally lays on the table the record of the legal declaration by the city clerk of the election of mayor and aldermen for the current year. Business is then taken up according to the orders of the day, which are printed (see *below*, p. 280, rules 27 and 28), petitions are presented (see *below*, p. 314, rules 62 and 63), notices given (see *below*, p. 286, rule 31), and a committee of six members appointed on motion duly made and adopted to strike the standing committees for the current year (see *below*, p. 318, rule 67). The council then adjourns until a later hour (generally 2 p.m.), to receive and consider the report of the committee, which is adopted with as little delay as possible, with amendments, when necessary. Other business is then transacted, and the council adjourns.[*]

See *below*, rule 3, as to the duty of clerk with respect to the giving of notice of all meetings.

Adjournment.

2a. "The council shall always adjourn at the hour of 11 o'clock p.m., if in session at that hour, unless otherwise determined by a vote of two-thirds of the members present."

See by-law 3060 (1892).

This determination should be, strictly speaking, signified by a vote on a motion "That the council do continue its sitting beyond 11 o'clock," but previous to the fixed hour for adjourning, If 11 o'clock arrives and no continuation is determined, the mayor should leave the chair without putting any question, and declare the council adjourned.

2. Special Meetings.

3. "The mayor may at any time summon a special meeting of the council; and it shall be his duty to summon a special

[*] I have to thank John Blevins, Esquire, the able and experienced clerk of the city council of Toronto, for the very complete information he has given me on these and all other matters relating to the rules and practice of that body. I am also under obligations to the clerks of the other city councils for the facilities they have given me for making this part of the work as accurate as possible to date.   [Continued on p. 266.

In Belleville, on every alternate Monday, at half-past seven o'clock, unless otherwise ordered, or Monday is a public holiday, when the council shall meet at the same hour on the next day following.

In Hamilton, from the 1st October until 31st March, at half-past seven o'clock, and from 1st April until 30th September, at eight o'clock p.m., on the second and last Monday of each month.

In Kingston and St. Catharines, every alternate Monday at 8 p.m., beginning with the first Monday after inauguration, unless otherwise ordered, or unless Monday be a holiday, when the council shall meet on following evening, at same hour.

In Brantford, on every Monday, at seven p.m., unless otherwise ordered.

In Stratford, upon the first and third Monday of each month, at half-past seven p.m., unless otherwise ordered, or Monday be a public holiday, when the council meet at the same hour on the following day.

London rule 79 and Stratford rule 81 (5) provide that the "clerk shall not be required to give notice of the meetings of the council unless the day of meeting shall be some other than the day hereinbefore appointed in this by-law" (see *above*).

No prayers are provided for in these cities by a special rule, as in Toronto.

Adjournment.

2a. London rule 5 ; Belleville rule 2.

Ottawa rule 6 requires a majority of the members present to order a sitting beyond eleven o'clock p.m.

Guelph rule 5 requires a two-thirds vote to sit after half-past ten p.m.

Stratford rule 5 fixes half-past ten, unless otherwise determined by a vote of two-thirds of members present.

No time fixed in the rules of the councils of the other cities.

2. SPECIAL MEETINGS.

3. Hamilton, rule 2. By the mayor, at such time as he may deem requisite; or, at the request of any twelve members of the council, by the clerk, and "it shall not be competent to consider or decide upon any matter at a special meeting unless such matter has been fully explained in the notice calling the meeting."

London, rule 3. By the mayor, at such time as he may deem requisite ; or at the request of a majority of the members of the council. The clerk "shall summon the meeting, and it shall not be competent to consider or decide upon any matter

[Continued on p. 267.

meeting whenever requested in writing to do so by a majority of the members of the council."

It is the duty of the clerk (by-law 2436, s. 15 (1)), to give notice to members of all meetings, at their residence or place of business, on the day previous to the meeting,

See also *above*, p. 245, for s. 236 of Municipal Act.

4. "In case of the absence or death of the mayor, or head of the council, a special meeting may be summoned at any time by the clerk upon a special requisition to him signed by a majority of the members of the council."

See *above*, p. 245, for s. 236 of Municipal Act.

3. Opening Proceedings.

5. "As soon after the hour of meeting as there shall be a quorum present, the mayor shall take the chair, and call the members to order."

[Continued on p. 268.

at a special meeting, unless such matter has been fully explained in the notice calling the meeting; and the deposit in her majesty's post office at London of the postal card or letter summoning the meeting, addressed to the respective members of the council, shall be deemed sufficient service."

See also *below*, p. 362, London, rule 72 (4), as to duty of clerk to give notice of all meetings other than regular ones. See Guelph, rules 7-9, *below*.

Kingston, rule 1. By mayor, or at request, in writing, of a majority of council —the latter obligatory on the mayor.

St. Catharines rule 3 is the same as Kingston rule, with provision for a special notice, stating object of meeting.

Belleville rule 3 is the same as Toronto rule, with the words added, "for the special purpose mentioned in the notice," as in St. Catharines rule *above*.

Brantford, rule 5. By mayor, or clerk in his absence, on the request of a majority of council.

Stratford, rule 7. The mayor instructs the clerk to give twenty-four hours notice (written), which shall specify business, and none other can be transacted at that meeting. Special meetings cannot be called for general business.

4. Ottawa, rules 3, 4 and 5—

3. By the mayor, or "whenever requested in writing so to do by a majority of the members of the council." In the latter case it is obligatory upon him.

4. In case of the absence or death of the mayor, or head of the council, "by the clerk, upon a special requisition to him, signed by a majority of the members of the council."

5. "Notices of special meetings shall be served by the messenger upon each alderman personally, or by leaving the same at his usual place of abode."

Ottawa rule 34 also provides that a special meeting may be closed to all persons except members and the clerk, whenever the council so declares by "a resolution in writing"—as all resolutions of a council should be.

See also *below*, rule 98, p. 344, as to serving of notices and papers for special meeting.

Guelph, rules 7-9. By the mayor, or on requisition of a majority of council; or in the absence of the mayor, by the clerk, on requisition of a majority of the same. All special meetings by a specific notice (as in the Hamilton rule) from the clerk to each member, and no other business can then be taken up.

All such notices must be carefully worded, and only the business therein set forth can be legally transacted. See *above*, p. 120, for analogous case.

3. Opening Proceedings.

5. Hamilton, rule 3 (at least twelve members). London, rule 7; Ottawa, rule 9; Kingston, rule 3; Belleville, rule 6; Guelph, rule 10; Brantford, rule 3; Stratford, rule 8. St. Catharines, rule 4 (ten members, including mayor or chairman).

[Continued on p. 269.

A quorum must in all cases be a majority of all the members of the council, including the mayor, or presiding officer (see *above*, p. 244, for s. 234 of Municipal Law).

The mayor should count the members, and if he finds a quorum, take the chair. He might always properly follow the practice of the English Commons— take temporarily the clerk's chair, and when he finds there is a quorum, rise and call the meeting formally to order from his own seat in the chamber.

6. "In case the mayor does not attend within fifteen minutes after the time appointed, the clerk shall call the members to order, and if a quorum be present, a chairman shall be chosen, who shall preside during the meeting, or until the arrival of the mayor."

See *above*, p. 246, for s. 240 of Municipal Law.

The clerk presides in his own seat, and a member will propose and another second a motion, "That alderman B. or C. do take the chair." If no other member be proposed the question is put by the clerk, and the member thus proposed is declared elected. In case of several candidates being proposed—very unlikely in such cases—they should be voted on in order (see *above*, p. 27, for parliamentary procedure in case of election of speaker).

4. Absence of Quorum.

7. "If there be no quorum present within half an hour after the time appointed for the meeting, the clerk shall call the roll and take down the names of the members then present, and the council shall stand adjourned until the next day of meeting, subject to the provisions of sections three and four of this by-law."

If members come in while the roll is being called, they can be counted in accordance with parliamentary practice (see *above*, p. 29). The councils of Toronto and other cities have no special rule which applies like that of Hamilton (4) to the case of an absence of quorum during a session, *i.e.*, after the business is in progress. For practice, both while house is sitting and in committee of the whole, see *above*, p. 29.

In the absence of a special rule like that of Guelph (39), or Brantford (37) p. 271, the business under consideration must disappear from the order paper and would have to be formally restored by motion duly made by a member.

[Continued on p. 270.

6. Hamilton, rule 6 (see rule 7, *below*) ; London, rules 8, 9 (see rule 9, *below*) ; Ottawa, rules 10 and 12; Belleville, rule 7; Brantford, rule 3.

Kingston rule 4 also makes provision for cases, "if the mayor should wish to leave the chair," or "if he is absent."

Guelph rule 10 provides for a similar proceeding since it sets forth that, in the absence of the mayor, a chairman must be "appointed by the council." The clerk will preside until this is duly done.

Hamilton rule 7, London rule 9, and Stratford rule 9, require an alderman to be chosen during the absence of the mayor, and for the meeting only for which he has been so chosen.

Rule 10 of Stratford council provides for an acting mayor to be elected by the council during the absence from the city, or illness of the mayor.

4. Absence of Quorum.

7. Hamilton, rule 4. "Whenever an adjournment takes place in consequence of there not being a quorum present, the names of the members present shall be inserted in the records of the council."

London, rule 4. "Unless there shall be a quorum present in half an hour after the time appointed for the meeting of the council, the council shall stand adjourned until the next day of meeting, and the clerk shall take down the names of the members present at the expiration of such half hour, and shall publish the names of the absent members in the city paper having the printing of the council."

Ottawa rule 11, and Stratford rule 4, are the same as that of Toronto.

Kingston rule 2 adjourns until next day of meeting, if no quorum present in ten minutes after time appointed for meeting of council.

Belleville rule 4 adjourns until next day of meeting, if no quorum present in half an hour after the time appointed; and the clerk takes down the names, "providing always that if all the members present remain until a quorum is made up they may proceed with the business."

St. Catharines rule 1 adjourns until next day of meeting, if in fifteen minutes no quorum (ten members).

Brantford rules 1 and 2 adjourn until next day of meeting, if at half-past seven p.m. (*i.e.*, in half an hour) no quorum; hour of adjournment and names must be recorded in all such cases.

[Continued on p. 271.

Minutes.

8. " Immediately after the mayor shall have taken his seat, the minutes of the preceding meeting shall be read by the clerk, if required by any alderman present, in order that any mistake therein may be corrected by the council."

It seems expedient to read the minutes of such bodies under all circumstances and make corrections when necessary. See *above,* pp. 11, 125, for remarks on corrections and limitations to debate at such time, and on the duty of clerk in keeping minutes. By s. 15 (2), by-law 2436, " it is the duty of the clerk to attend all meetings of the council, and read the minutes and proceedings thereof." See also *below,* p. 357, as to marginal references on minutes.

See *above,* p. 235, as to the right of clerk to correct an inaccurate minute.

5. DUTIES OF MAYOR OR OTHER PRESIDING OFFICER.

9. " The mayor shall preserve order and decorum, and decide questions of order, subject to an appeal to the council, and in the absence of the mayor, the chairman shall have the same authority while presiding at the meeting as the mayor would have had if present."

For same parliamentary rule, see *above,* p. 28.

This rule should be read in connection with rule 10 *below.*

See *above,* p. 39, for correct procedure in appealing from a decision of the chair on a question of order.

10. " When the mayor is called upon to decide a point of order or practice, the point shall be stated without unnecessary comment, and the mayor shall cite the rule or authority applicable to the case."

For same parliamentary rule, see *above,* p. 28. A presiding officer should never argue, but give his decision succinctly, and support it by a simple reference to authorities. [Continued on p. 272.

Guelph rule 4 adjourns in fifteen minutes, till next regular meeting, if no quorum present; names recorded.

Brantford rule 37 also provides for an absence of quorum at any stage of the proceedings of the council: " When any order, resolution or question shall be lost by the council or committee breaking up for want of a quorum, the order, resolution or question so lost shall be the first business to be proceeded with and disposed of at the next meeting of such committee or council, under that particular head."

See remarks p. 268, under Toronto, rule 7.

Guelph rule 39 is the same as the Brantford rule 37 above.

Minutes.

8. Ottawa rule 13, same as Toronto rule 8.   London rule 10, Kingston rule 8, St. Catharines rule 2, Brantford rule 4, Belleville rule 8, Guelph rule 10, Hamilton rule 3, and Stratford rule 11, make reading of minutes of all meetings, regular and special, imperative as soon as chair is taken, and not at request of an alderman, as in Ottawa and Toronto.

Guelph council require confirmation and signing by the mayor or chairman.

Brantford council require signing also by clerk. ·

For duties of clerk in connection with minutes, see Ottawa, *below*, p. 344.

5. Duties of Mayor or other Presiding Officer.

9. Hamilton, rule 5 ; London, rule 11; Ottawa, rule 14 ; Kingston, rule 5 ; Guelph, rule 13; Brantford, rule 7; Belleville, rule 9 ; St. Catharines, rule 5 ; Stratford, rule 12.

Kingston rule 5 also provides that the appeal shall be made on a motion duly made and seconded.   In the absence of such a special provision, any member can ask for an appeal as a matter of right under the law of parliament (see *above*, p. 39).

10. Hamilton, rule 5 ; London, rule 12 ; Ottawa, rule 19; St. Catharines, rule 5 ; Belleville, rule 9 ; Brantford, rule 7 ; Guelph, rule 13 ; Stratford, rule 13.

Kingston rule 7 requires the presiding officer to state his authority only when "requested by a member of the council." In all cases it is advisable to state authority for a decision.

[Continued on p. 273.

11. "The mayor may vote with the other members on all questions; and any question on which there is an equality of votes shall be deemed to be negatived."

The mayor may or may not vote in his discretion.

See *above*, p. 247, for s. 241 of Municipal Law.

The concluding part of this rule embodies the old common law rule, *semper præsumitur pro negante*, still in use in the senate of Canada (see Bourinot, p. 453). The mayor should vote first on the side on which he intends to vote. The clerk should look at him first when taking a vote and ascertain whether he wishes to vote. The rules of some councils provide that he may explain his vote (see opposite, Guelph, rule 15)—a parliamentary usage, in fact (see *above*, p. 42).

12. "If the mayor desires to leave the chair for the purpose of taking part in the debate or otherwise, he shall call on one of the aldermen to fill his place until he resumes the chair."

A very proper rule, as circumstances may arise when the mayor can, in the interests of the public, give valuable advice and information; but he should refrain from doing so in ordinary matters, and should in all cases treat a question in a judicial spirit, that he may not weaken his authority as chairman of the council. This rule assumes that he will not take part in debate while in the chair, except, of course, to give his decision on a point of order or business.

6. Rules of Conduct and Debate.

13. "Every member, previous to speaking to any question or motion, shall rise from his seat, uncovered, and shall address himself to the mayor."

For same parliamentary rule (see *above*, p. 37). He should say, " Mr. Mayor," or " Mr. Chairman," if there is another presiding officer for the time being in the chair, and not refer to either by name.

14. "When two or more members rise to speak, the mayor shall name the member who, in his opinion, first rose from his seat; but a motion may be made that any member who has risen ' be now heard,' or ' do now speak.' "

For same parliamentary rule, see *above*, p. 37.

15. "Every member who shall be present in the council chamber when a question is put shall vote thereon, unless the council shall excuse him, or unless he be personally interested in the question, provided such interest is resolvable into a personal pecuniary profit, or is peculiar to that member, and not in com-

[Continued on p. 274.

11. London, rule 13; Ottawa, rule 15; Belleville, rule 10; St. Catharines, rule 9.'

Hamilton council has no such rule, but it is assumed that the common law rule prevails, and the mayor being a member votes as a matter of course, and has no casting vote in the absence of a special regulation allowing him that vote.

The foregoing remark applies to Kingston and Brantford councils.

Guelph rule 15 simply provides that if the chairman "sees fit to exercise his right of voting on any question," he may explain his vote, but otherwise he shall take no part in any discussion, and "any question on which there is an equality of votes (in consequence of the mayor's or chairman's vote), shall be deemed to be negatived."

12. London, rule 14; Ottawa, rule 16; Stratford, rule 14.

Kingston rule 6, Belleville rule 10, Guelph rule 15 (see *above*), do not permit the mayor to take part in debate while presiding, but he may do so when the council is in committee of the whole.

Rules of St. Catharines, Hamilton and Brantford are silent on the point. Hence the parliamentary rule should prevail, and except in explaining a point of order or business, he should only speak in committee of the whole.

See opposite remarks.

6. Rules of Conduct and Debate.

13. Hamilton, rule 13; Guelph, rule 18; Brantford, rule 8; London, rule 15; Belleville, rule 11; Stratford, rule 15; St. Catharines, rule 10; Ottawa, rule 24.

Kingston rule 9 adds a curious exceptional proviso, "may read sitting." In all cases in parliament, he should stand up, except incapacitated by some infirmity.

14. Stratford, rule 16; London, rule 16; Ottawa, rule 17.

Guelph rule 19, Kingston rule 17, Brantford, rule 8, and Hamilton rule 13, all provide simply that, "should more than one member rise at once, the mayor or presiding officer shall determine who is entitled to the floor."

Belleville rule 12 allows an appeal to council after decision of presiding officer.

15. Stratford, rule 17; Hamilton, rule 16; London, rule 17; Ottawa, rule 32; Kingston, rule 19; St. Catharines, rule 8; Guelph, rule 26.

Belleville rule 13 is the same as that of Toronto and other cities given above, but adds this: "and if any member present persists in refusing to vote, he shall be recorded as voting in the negative, or against the motion or question before the council." This is intended to make voting compulsory.

B.M.P.—18   [Continued on p. 275.

˙mon with the interests of the citizens at large, and in such cases
he shall not vote." ·

For same parliamentary rule, see *above*, p. 42.   See also *above*, rule 11, as to
mayor's vote.

If a member is to be excused, a motion must be formally made to that effect.
If a member personally interested should vote, his name must be formally struck off
the list on motion duly made, "That the vote of ———— be disallowed," or "struck
off the vote on ————" (see *above*, p. 43, for explanations on personal interest).

16. "When the mayor is putting the question no member
shall walk across or out of the room, or make any noise or disturbance; nor when a member is speaking shall any other member
pass between him and the chair, or interrupt him, except to raise
a point of order."

For same parliamentary rule, see *above*, p. 38.

See Ottawa, rule 18, opposite, how the mayor should properly put the question,
by rising, and standing while reading a question and submitting it to a vote. A
point of order may be raised even when a question is put (see *above*, p. 44).

17. "A member called to order from the chair shall immediately sit down, but may afterwards explain; and the council, if
appealed to, shall decide the case, but without debate; if there be
no appeal the decision of the mayor shall be final."

For same parliamentary rule, see *above*, p. 39.   And for mode of putting
an appeal, *above*, p. 39.

18. "No member shall speak disrespectfully of her majesty
the queen, or of any of the royal family, or of the governor-
general, lieutenant-governor, or person administering the government of the dominion or of this province; nor shall he use offensive
words in or against the council or against any member thereof;
nor shall he speak beside the question in debate; and no member
shall reflect upon any vote of the council except for the purpose of
moving that such vote be rescinded; nor shall he resist the rules
of the council, or disobey the decision of the mayor or of the
council on questions of order or practice or upon the interpretation
of the rules of the council; and in case any member shall so resist

[Continued on p. 276.

Brantford rule 18 requires every member to vote unless excused, but has no provision with respect to personal interest. The same practice as in parliament, and set forth opposite, should obtain. A personal pecuniary interest is always a disqualification in such cases.

16. Hamilton, rule 17; London, rule 18; Stratford, rule 18.

Ottawa, rule 18 (which adds the correct parliamentary usage : " The mayor or chairman shall rise and stand when putting the question ").

Kingston, rule 20; Belleville, rule 14; St. Catharines, rule 11; Guelph, rules 23 and 24.

Brantford has no such rule, but the parliamentary practice, as stated in all the foregoing rules, must prevail.

17. Hamilton, rule 15; Stratford, rule 19; London, rule 19; Ottawa, rule 25 ; Kingston, rule 20 ; Belleville, rule 15 ; St. Catharines, rule 6.

Guelph rule 22 does not allow a member to explain when called to order, or to speak, unless to appeal from decision of the chair. But he should have under parliamentary law a right to explanation, which is itself in the interest of order.

Brantford rule 9 does not allow explanation or appeal to the council in the rule, but it is provided for by the previous rule 7 (see *above*, p. 271), in all cases.

18. Ottawa rule 28, London rule 20, and Belleville rule 16, do not provide, in express words, for removal of a troublesome member, but, as stated opposite, it is a power inherent in all such bodies, for the preservation of orderly proceedings and the transaction of business.

Ottawa rule 7 provides: " The chief constable shall have charge of the council chamber, and attend at all meetings of the council, and if ordered by the head or other chairman of the council, he shall expel and exclude from any meeting any person who has been guilty of improper conduct at such meeting."

See *above*, p. 244, for s. 233 of Municipal Act, giving the chairman power to exclude any person guilty of improper conduct.

In Hamilton there is no such special rule, but the council must be governed by the parliamentary usage set forth in the rules of the other cities.

The same remark applies to Kingston, Guelph and Brantford councils.

[Continued on p. 277.

or disobey, he may be ordered by the council to leave his seat for that meeting, and in case of his refusing to do so, he may, on the order of the mayor, be removed therefrom*by the police; but in case of ample apology being made by the offender, he may, by vote of the council, be permitted forthwith to take his seat."

For similar parliamentary rule, see *above*, p. 38.

Every parliamentary and deliberative body has the inherent right to enforce its own orders, and if a member proves recalcitrant and refuses to obey the orders of the body, and sets the chair at defiance, or interrupts the business by disorderly or improper conduct, he may be forcibly removed or otherwise punished. Every council has also the right, under the law (see *above*, p. 244), to issue regulations for its protection against persons, not members, interrupting its proceedings by riotous or unseemly conduct (see rule 23, *below*, p. 278, with respect to the admission of strangers).

19. "Any member may require the question or motion under discussion to be read at any time during the debate, but not so as to interrupt a member while speaking."

For same parliamentary rule, and remarks thereon, see *above*, p. 32.

20. "No member shall speak more than once to the same question, without leave of the council, except in explanation of a material part of his speech which may have been misconceived, and in doing so he is not to introduce new matter. A reply is allowed to a member who has made a substantive motion to the council, but not to any member who has moved an order of the day, an amendment, the previous question, or an instruction to a committee. No member, without leave of the council, shall speak to the same question, or in reply, for longer than a quarter of an hour."

For parliamentary rule, and remarks on the meaning of "substantive" motion, see *above*, p. 38.

The Toronto rule allows a member to speak again by leave, and has also the limitation that no member shall speak to one question more than a quarter of an hour, but the council can extend the time, on motion duly made, when necessary, and agreed to. This limitation of time is advisable in such business meetings. "Leave of the council" means a majority vote, if necessary, on motion duly made and put.

[Continued on p. 278.

The Guelph council (rule 3) provides a penalty, from $1 to $20, for first and subsequent offences, when any person has been convicted of disturbing or interrupting the proceedings, or behaving in a disorderly or riotous manner ; and in default of distress, a committal to gaol for not less than ten days.

St. Catharines rule 18 orders that all offending persons, not members, be taken into custody "to await the decision of the council."

Stratford rule 20 is the same as that of Toronto, as far as the end of the words, "such vote be rescinded."

19. Hamilton, rule 18, London, rule 21 ; Ottawa, rule 26; Kingston, rule 21 ; Belleville, rule 17 ; St. Catharines, rule 12; Guelph, rule 25 ; Brantford, rule 14 ; Stratford, rule 21.

20. Stratford, rule 22; London, rule 22 ; Ottawa, rule 27; Hamilton, rule 14, but without the limitation of time—a quarter of an hour—in the last sentence of the rules of the foregoing cities. Belleville, rule 18.

Kingston, rule 22. "No member shall speak more than once (and then not longer than ten minutes, unless permitted by the council), to the same questions except the mover, who shall have the right of replying, when all members choosing to speak shall have spoken, unless a member wishes to explain a material part of his speech, which may have been misconceived or misunderstood, but then he is not to introduce new matter."

The reply, it will be seen, is only permissible after debate is closed. The rule respecting explanations is the parliamentary usage (see *above*, p. 38).

St. Catharines, rule 27. "No member shall speak longer than fifteen minutes nor more than twice on the same question, without leave from the council."

Guelph, rule 21. "No member shall, without leave of the council, speak longer than ten minutes, nor more than once on any question, unless in explanation of a material part of his remarks which may have been misunderstood, and then he shall not introduce new matter. The member proposing a question or motion may be permitted to reply."

It would be exceptional, of course, for a member to speak after a mover is understood to have closed a debate, but unless the rule or usage so closes the debate, a member who has not already spoken may speak even then to the question.

[Continued on p. 279.

7. Divisions.

21. "Upon a division of the council, the names of those who vote for and those who vote against the question shall be entered upon the minutes, not only in the cases required by law, but whenever any member shall call for the yeas and nays."

For similar parliamentary rule, and mode of taking a division, see *above*, p. 41.

All bodies of a deliberative or legislative character have a similar regulation.

8. Enquiries.

22. "All enquiries shall be in writing, and shall be handed to the clerk of the council at least two clear days before the day of the meeting at which such enquiry is to be made; and the answer to such enquiry shall also be put in writing and handed to the mayor or other presiding officer at least one hour before the meeting, and shall be read by him from the chair."

For similar parliamentary rules, see *above*, p. 44.

These enquiries should be, strictly speaking, answered in the order in which they are handed to and entered by the clerk.

9. Admission of Strangers.

23. "No person except members and officers of the council shall be allowed to come within the bar during the sittings of the council without the permission of the mayor."

A rule necessary for the preservation of order and the control of the members of every deliberative body.

[Continued on p. 280.

Brantford rules 10 and 15 limit each member to five minutes in speaking, and a reply to the mover of a substantive motion only as in other cases. A member may, however, speak again in explanation or by special leave of the council.

7. Divisions.

21. London, rule 23; Ottawa, rule 36; Stratford, rules 23 and 74 (7) (see *Lelow*, p. 335).

Hamilton rule 19 makes the recording of names imperative, and not at the demand of a single member, as in other cases cited.

Kingston, rule 16. " Yeas may be called for by any member."

St. Catharines, rule 17. " Yeas and nays shall be taken upon a division."

Brantford, rule 17. Names entered if demanded by one alderman.

Belleville rule 19 adds to Toronto rule, "immediately after the result of the vote is declared "—which seems unnecessary.

Guelph, rule 27. " Previous to any question being finally put, any member may require that the names of the members voting for or against be taken down by the clerk and entered in the minutes."

8. Enquiries.

22. Ottawa, rule 31.

Ottawa rule 30, Belleville rule 20, Stratford rule 24, and London rule 24, also state parliamentary rule in these words : " Questions may be put to the mayor or other presiding officer, or through him to any member of the council relating to any by-law, motion, or other matter connected with the business of the council, or the affairs of the city, but no argument or opinion is to be offered or facts to be stated except so far as may be necessary to explain the same, and in answering any such question a member is not to debate the matter to which the same refers."

In Hamilton, Guelph, Brantford, Kingston and St. Catharines there is no such special rule, but parliamentary usage should prevail, as stated above.

9. Admission of Strangers.

23. Guelph, rule 2; Belleville, rule 19; London, rule 26; Ottawa, rule 19; London, rule 26; Ottawa, rule 33.

In other cities none, but parliamentary usage prevails necessarily.

See Guelph rule 3, p. 277, *above*, and St. Catharines rule 18, *above*, p. 277, with respect to disorderly conduct at a meeting.

See *below*, p. 329, for Belleville rule 60, with respect to the admission of the public to committee meetings.

Stratford rule 25 adds to Toronto rule the words : "or other presiding officer, and when the doors shall be directed to be closed, all persons except the members and the clerk shall retire."

[Continued on p. 281.

10. Conduct at Adjournment.

24. "The members of the council shall not leave their places, on adjournment, until the mayor leaves the chair."

A special rule, necessary for the maintenance of the order and the dignity of an assembly.

11. Suspension of Rules.

25. "No standing rule or order of council shall be suspended, except by a vote of two-thirds of the members present."

A very necessary rule, if regulations are to have any value. It is better to have such a fixed rule than to allow unanimous consent to be asked; that is too often granted in the Canadian parliament.

12. Unprovided Cases.

26. "In all unprovided cases in the proceedings of council or in committee, the law of parliament shall be followed."

A necessary rule for all deliberative and legislative bodies in Canada (see *above*, p. 6).

It is with the view of meeting such cases that a digest of the principal rules and usages of parliament have been given in the FIRST PART (pp. 27-57), of this Manual.

13. Orders of the Day.

27. "The clerk shall have prepared and printed for the use of members at the regular meetings of the council 'The General Orders of the Day,' as follows:—1st, reading of minutes; 2nd, original communications; 3rd, presenting petitions; 4th, enquiries

[Continued on p. 282.

10. Conduct at Adjournment.

24. London, rule 6; Ottawa, rule 23; Stratford, rule 6; Kingston, rule 43; Belleville, rule 5; Guelph, rule 30; St. Catharines, rule 3.

In Hamilton and Brantford, none, but the same practice should prevail.

11. Suspension of Rules.

25. Belleville, rule 80; Stratford, rule 78; and London, rule 81, same as Toronto rule.

Ottawa, rule 101, as follows :—" Any one or more of these rules and orders may be temporarily suspended by a vote of two-thirds of the *whole* council, but they shall not be repealed, altered or amended without one week's previous notice being given of the intended motion."

Hamilton, rule 31, as follows :—" Any one or more of these rules may be at any time temporarily suspended, with the consent of two-thirds of the members present, with exception of rule 28 " respecting money votes (which see *below*, p. 374).

Kingston, rule 41, same as Ottawa rule, with the addition that no rule can be suspended after the week's notice, except with the consent of a majority of the *whole* council.

In St. Catharines, Guelph, and Brantford, no special rule; consequently no rule can be suspended, except by unanimous consent.

12. Unprovided Cases.

26. Ottawa, rule 102.

London rule 82, Guelph rule 17, Stratford rule 79, and Belleville rule 81, are the same, with the addition, " in such cases the decision of the mayor or other presiding officer shall be final and acquiesced in without debate." In other words, no appeal is allowed in such a case.

The other cities have no such rule, but the common law of parliament must be necessarily followed. An appeal, however, will be allowed in the absence of a special rule like those of London and Belleville.

18. Orders of the Day.

27. Hamilton, rule 8. " The business of the council shall be taken up in the following order :—1. Presentation of petitions and memorials. 2. Reading of the same by the clerk. 3. Presentation of reports from the standing committees, according to seniority, or special committees, according to date of appointment. 4. Third reading of by-laws. 5. Reference of memorials, or petitions by the mayor or

[Continued on p. 283.

and answers thereto; 5th, giving notice; 6th, introduction and consideration of bills; 7th, presentation and consideration of reports of the executive and other committees; 8th, motions; 9th, unfinished business."

Every assembly must have some such order of proceeding, if business is to be done intelligently. I give the orders of the day in all the other cities on the opposite page.

[Continued on p. 284.

presiding officers to their appropriate committees, without motion. 6. Consideration of the reports of the standing and special committees in the order in which they were presented, unless with the unanimous consent of the members present. 7. First reading of by-laws. 8. Consideration of any business of which notice has been given on a previous evening. 9. Second reading of by-laws, and their consideration in committee of the whole. 10. Notices, in writing, of intention to introduce any measure or resolution may be given at any time during the evening, and shall always be entered on the order of the day." Rule 9 also adds: " No business of moment shall be determined upon until it has been reported upon by the appropriate committee, unless it may appear that the committee has neglected to fulfil its duty."

London, rule 27. " The clerk shall prepare for the use of the members 'The General Orders of the Day,' for each meeting of the council, containing—1. Confirming minutes of the last meeting. 2. Original petitions and communications. 3. Referring petitions and communications. 4. Reports of committees and consideration thereof. 5. Unfinished business. 6. Enquiries. 7. Motions. 8. Giving notice. 9. Introduction and consideration of bills and by-laws."

Ottawa, rule 37. " The clerk shall cause to be prepared and printed for the use of members at the ordinary meetings of the council, ' The General Orders of the Day,' containing—1. Reading of minutes. 2. Original communications. 3. Petitions. 4. Referring petitions and communications. 5. Reports of committees and consideration thereof. 6. Reports of officers. 7. Unfinished business. 8. Introduction and consideration of by-laws. 9. Enquiries. 10. Answers to questions. 11. Giving notice. 12. Motions."

Kingston, rule 31 :—" 1. Calling roll by clerk. 2. Reading minutes. 3. Reading communications. 4. Reading petitions. 5. Reports. 6. Unfinished business. 7. Consideration of by-laws. 8. Motions."

Belleville, rule 22. " 1. Reading of minutes. 2. Communications and petitions. 3. Referring petitions and communications. 4. Reports of committees. 5. Consideration of reports. 6. Enquiries. 7. Introduction of by-laws. 8. Consideration of by-laws. 9. Motions. 10. Unfinished business. 11. Giving Notices. 12. Orders of the day."

Guelph, rule 11. " 1. Communications from the mayor or clerk. 2. Presentation of petitions and memorials, and reading of same by members or by the clerk. 3. Reference of the same by the mayor or chairman to the appropriate committee, or to the council for consideration. 4. Third reading of by-laws. 5. Presentation of reports from standing and select committees, and board of health, in the following order :—Finance and assessment—Water works—Board of works—Markets and public buildings—Fire, gas and water—Relief—Parks and shade trees—By-laws and licenses—Police—Railways—Cemetery—Hospital —Special or other committees—Board of health. 6. The consideration of the reports of standing and special committees, and board of health in the order in which they were presented, unless otherwise agreed to by the vote of two-thirds of the members present. 7. First and second reading of by-laws. 8. Consideration

[Continued on p. 285.

28. "At all special meetings of the council, 'The General Orders of the Day' shall be prepared and printed when and as the mayor may direct; and in default of such direction, then as provided in the last preceding section."

In the Canadian houses of parliament there is a daily order of business issued with the journal of the previous day's proceedings.

29. " The business shall in all cases be taken up in the order in which it stands upon 'The General Orders of the Day.' "

For same parliamentary rule, see *above*, p. 30.

If a single member objects to a departure from the order of procedure, the mayor or presiding officer must rule the objection well taken, and ask for a vote of two-thirds of the members present, under rule 25 (*above*, p. 280), which allows a suspension of the rules by such a majority.

[Continued on p. 286.

of by-laws in committee of the whole. 9. Consideration of any business of which notice has been previously given. 10. Consideration of any business introduced by members on motion."

St. Catharines, rule 15. "All petitions, remonstrances, or other written applications to the council, shall be read by the clerk immediately after the reading and confirmation of minutes [see *above*, p. 270] ; then shall follow here, in order, reports of committees, motions and bills."

Brantford, rules 4 and 6. "1. Calling of roll, 2. Reading of minutes. 3. Reception and disposal of communications. 4. Presenting, referring and disposing of petitions. 5. Presenting, referring or passing accounts. 6. Reception of reports of committees and action thereon. 7. Notices of motions. 8. First, second and third reading of by-laws. 9. Motions of which notice has been given. 10. Motions and questions."

Stratford, rule 26. "1. Reading of minutes. 2. Business left unfinished at previous meetings. 3. Original communications. 4. Introduction of bills. 5. Consideration of bills. 6. Petitions. 7. Referring petitions and communications. 8. Reports of committees and consideration thereof. 9. Enquiries. 10. Giving notice. 11. Motions."

28. Ottawa, rule 38.

See *above*, p. 267, with respect to Guelph, rule 9, Hamilton, rule 2, p. 265 ; St. Catharines, rule 3, p. 267 ; Stratford, rule 7, p. 267 ; Belleville, rule 3, p. 267 ; London, rule 3, p. 265—all requiring a special notice of business to be taken up at such special meetings.

29. Ottawa, rule 39, and Belleville, rule 23, as follows :—" The business shall in all cases be taken up in the order in which it stands upon ' The General Orders of the Day,' unless otherwise determined by a vote of two-thirds of the members present."

Stratford rule 27 adds to foregoing rule, " and without debate thereon."

London, rule 28. " The business shall in all cases be taken up in the order in which it stands upon ' The General Orders of the Day,' unless otherwise determined upon by a vote of two-thirds of the members present, and all questions relating to the priority of business shall be decided without debate." Practically the closure on such a motion to alter order of proceedings for the session.

Hamilton rule 8 (see *above*, p. 281) requires the business of the council to be taken up in the order therein indicated.

In the councils of the other cities there is no such special rule, but, as in Hamilton, each rule simply provides that the business "shall be taken up" in a certain order. Consequently it can only be changed when the rules provide for a suspension of rules. See *above*, p. 281, for rules so providing.

Guelph rule 39 provides : "The order of the day shall always have the preference to any motion before the council, except that when any resolution or

[Continued on p. 297.

30. " All motions called in pursuance of ' The General Orders of the Day,' and not disposed of, shall be placed at the foot of the list, unless otherwise decided by the council."

For same parliamentary rule, see Bourinot, p. 301.

It is intended to prevent business being dropped from the order paper after having been duly called. See *above*, p. 271, for rule of some councils providing for priority of business temporarily suspended by an absence of quorum.

14. MOTIONS IN GENERAL.

31. " One day's notice shall be given of all motions for introducing new matter other than matters of privilege and bringing up petitions; and no motion shall be discussed unless such notice has been given, or unless the council dispense with such notice by a two-thirds vote of the members present, without debate."

For parliamentary rule, see *above*, p. 30.

If it be proposed to dispense with the rule, a member must formally so move, '• That rule 31 be dispensed with in case of (*state question*) " ; and the mayor or chairman will call upon members in favour of suspending the rule to stand up and the clerk will count the votes, and the chairman will declare the result.

32. " All motions shall be in writing and seconded before being debated or put from the chair. When a motion is seconded, it shall be read by the mayor, before debate."

For same fundamental parliamentary rule, see *above*, p. 30.

[Continued on p. 288.

motion shall be lost by the council breaking up for want of a quorum, such resolution or motion shall be the first business to be proceeded with at the next regular
meeting of the council." Consequently, in making up orders of a day, such
business must be given priority.

30. Ottawa has similar rule, 41; other cities none, but the same practice should
obtain, as in parliament.

14. Motions in General.

31. For Hamilton rule 8 (10), see *above*, p. 282.

Ottawa rule 42 is the same as Toronto rule 31, with the addition that the
required notice " shall be printed in the ' general orders of the day' "—a very proper regulation.

London, rule 27. " Notice shall be given of all motions for introducing new
matter other than matters of privilege and bringing up petitions, and no motion
shall be discussed unless such notice has been given at the last regular meeting of
the council."

Belleville rule 24 is the same as Toronto rule 31.

Guelph, rule 12. " Notice in writing of an intention to introduce a measure
may be given in writing ' at any time during the meeting,' and shall always be
entered by the clerk in the minutes."

This rule is vague, but it must mean a notice of a measure to be introduced at
a subsequent meeting. Otherwise the notice is useless, since members not present
will be surprised by a motion, and the true object of a notice is to give every
member information of a subject to be brought before the council.

St. Catharines, rule 29. " No resolution or by-law affecting important measures or changes, shall be introduced without notice thereof having been first
given, in writing, at a previous meeting of the council, except with the consent
of two-thirds of the entire council."

Kingston, Stratford and Brantford have no such proper rule, but as notice is
a usage of parliament it should obtain in the practice of all councils.

32. Hamilton, rule 10; London, rules 30, 31 ; Ottawa, rules 43, 44; Kingston,
rule 13 ; Belleville, rule 25 ; St. Catharines, rule 13.

Stratford rule 28 requires the motion in writing when requested by the
chair.

Brantford rule 15 and Guelph rule 31 require a motion to be written in ink
and read—that should be always done—by a member in his place.

[Continued on p. 289.

A motion is not in possession of the council, to be debated, etc., until it is read by the chair, or, in parliamentary phrase, " proposed " (see next rule 33). The clerk cannot enter any motion in his minutes until it is so proposed by the chair (see *above*, pp. 11, 12).

33. " After a motion is read by the mayor, it shall be deemed to be in possession of the council, but may, with permission of the council, be withdrawn at any time before decision or amendment."

For form of motions, see *above*, p. 31 ; for method of proposing motions, *above*, p. 31 ; for amendment of motions, *above*, p. 33.

The parliamentary rule requires unanimous consent (see *above*, p. 31), before a motion can be withdrawn ; but here a majority on a motion duly made can order withdrawal. A motion withdrawn can be again proposed (see *above*, p. 31).

34. " A motion for commitment, until it is decided, shall preclude all amendment of the main question."

For meaning of the rule, see *above*, p. 37.

35. " A motion to adjourn the council or to adjourn the debate shall always be in order, but no second motion to the same effect shall be made until after some intermediate proceeding shall have been had."

For same parliamentary rule, see *above*, p. 33.

The motions must be simply, " That the council do now adjourn," or " That the debate be adjourned " (see *above*, p. 33). Such motions are not amendable (see *above*, p. 33), and cannot be made in a committee (see *above*, p. 46). Such motions, being well understood, need not be written in parliament, nor in any assemblies, generally speaking. Some councils have special rules on the subject (see preceding rule, p. 287).

[Continued on p. 2 0.

But motions to adjourn and go into committee of the whole (Guelph rule 32) may be made *vivâ voce*. Same practice obtains in parliament with respect to all such purely formal motions.

Guelph rule 32 also allows a motion to extend time of sitting (see *above*, p. 265) to be made *vivâ voce*.

Guelph rule 33 forbids a preamble prefacing a motion — a salutary rule in accordance with correct parliamentary usage, see *above*, p. 31.

Brantford rule 11 allows motions to adjourn and receive petitions and reports to be made in any way without a seconder.

33. Hamilton, rule 11; London, rule 32; Ottawa, rule 45; Kingston, rule 11; Belleville, rule 26; St. Catharines, rule 14; Guelph, rule 35; Brantford, rule 12.

Stratford rule 29 allows withdrawal "before decision at the request of the mover and seconder."

Brantford rule 13 only states the usual practice of allowing a member to propose a motion and speak before it is put from the chair. "That no member shall speak to any motion until it is put by the mayor or chairman, except the introducer. When this motion is read by the chair, it can be discussed by others."

34. London, rule 33; Ottawa, rule 50; St. Catharines, rule 31; Belleville, rule 27; Brantford, rule 21; Stratford, rule 30.

In other cities, none, but the parliamentary usage should obtain.

35. Hamilton, rule 20; Belleville, rule 28; London, rule 34; Stratford, rule 31; Ottawa, rule 57. The Ottawa council has also following rule:

56. "A motion to adjourn the council or to adjourn the debate shall be always in order, except—1. When a member is in possession of the floor. 2. When the yeas and nays have been called. 3. When the members are voting. 4. When it has been decided that the previous question shall be taken."

This is practically the parliamentary usage.

Kingston rule 12 and St. Catharines rule 30 are practically same as that of Ottawa, but "it must be decided by the council without debate."

Guelph, rule 37. "A motion for adjournment shall always be in order," but not debatable, see *below*, p. 291.

It must be understood that the parliamentary rule governing such cases prevails in the absence of more distinct provisions.

Brantford, rule 24. "A motion for adjournment shall always be in order *except in committee of the whole.*"

The words in italics should be unnecessary in view of the correct parliamentary usage which would forbid a committee of the whole—which is a body with merely delegated and defined powers—from adjourning the whole assembly; yet I am informed that was actually done in a Cobourg council in 1893.

Motions equivalent to adjournment can, however, be made in committee of the whole, see *above*, p. 46.

B.M.P.—19 [Continued on p. 291.

15. Dilatory Motions.

36. "When a question is under debate, no motion shall be received, unless to commit it; to amend it; to lay it on the table; to postpone it; to adjourn it; to move the previous question."

A similar rule exists in the majority of assemblies, outside of legislative bodies, in Canada.

For comments on these proceedings see :

1. To commit (not amendable under certain conditions) p. 37.
2. To amend, p. 33.
3. To lay on the table, p. 25.
4. To postpone (to a certain time), p. 25.
5. To postpone (indefinitely), p. 25.
6. To adjourn (not amendable but debatable), p. 33.
7. To adjourn to a certain day (amendable and debatable, p. 33).
8. To move the previous question (not amendable or debatable), see next rule 37, *below*.

As all these proceedings are governed by ordinary parliamentary usages, *in the absence of express regulations to the contrary* (see *above*, p. 26), it is necessary here to add, that " to lay on the table," " to postpone," " to refer," and " to amend," are amendable and debatable in the Toronto Council like other motions (see *above*, p. 26), since we are not in Canada governed by the law of congress and United States assemblies.

Ottawa council (see opposite) has recognized the necessity of adopting a special rule, with reference to the motion " to lay on the table."

See *below*, p. 386, where a new rule is suggested for these dilatory and not very easily understood motions.

[Continued on p. 292.

15. DILATORY MOTIONS.

36. Ottawa rule 48 is the same except that it adds, " To adjourn to a certain day." Ottawa has also following special rules with respect to lay on the table and to postpone indefinitely :

54. " A motion to lay a question on the table simply, is not debatable, but a motion to ' lay on the table and publish,' or any other condition is subject to amendment and debate."

55. " When a motion is postponed indefinitely it shall not be taken up again during the same evening."

It will be noticed that the Ottawa rule does not expressly except a motion " to postpone " from amendment.

Kingston, rule 14 ; Belleville, rule 29 ; London, rule 35 ; St. Catharines, rule 32 ; Brantford, rule 19 ; Stratford, rule 32 ; all same as Toronto rule 36.

Guelph, rule 36. " When a resolution is under consideration no motion shall be received unless to adjourn, to suspend rule 5 (should the time be after ten o'clock), the previous question, to lay on the table, to postpone, to refer, or to amend, which shall have precedence in the order in which they are named, and the first four of which several motions shall be decided without debate."

From the foregoing rule we gather these points :

1. To adjourn (not amendable or debatable).

2. To suspend rule 5, which limits time of a sitting to half-past ten p.m. (not amendable or debatable).

3. To move the previous question (not amendable or debatable).

4. To lay on the table (not amendable or debatable).

All the foregoing motions must be taken in order as well as these following :

5. To postpone.

6. To refer.

7. To amend.

For explanation of what is meant by order of precedence, see *above*, p. 201.

Hamilton rule 12 is as follows: " When any resolution is under consideration no motion shall be received unless

" To adjourn (not amendable or debatable).

" To lay on the table (amendable and debatable).

" To move previous question (not debatable).

" To postpone (amendable and debatable).

" To refer (which means ' to commit,' see *above*, p. 37).

" To amend (see *above*, p. 33).

" Which shall have precedence in the order in which they are arranged (for precedence see *above*, p. 201) ; the first and third of which shall be decided without debate."

[Continued on p. 293.

16. THE PREVIOUS QUESTION.

37. "The previous question until it is decided, shall preclude all amendment of the main question, and shall be put, without debate, in the following words : "That this question be now put"; if this motion be resolved in the affirmative, the original question is to be put forthwith, without any amendment or debate; but if the previous question be resolved in the negative, the main question may then be debated and amended."

This is not the parliamentary rule (see for full explanation on this perplexing question, *above*, pp. 13-16), which allows debate to continue on the motion until a vote is taken thereon, but it is practically the closure on a question; since the council can force a vote at once on the main motion by giving a vote in favour of the previous question. If the previous question is adopted then a vote must be taken at once on the main motion. If the majority vote against the previous question, then debate and amendments are in order on the original question— another variation from the parliamentary rule which prevents a vote or further consideration of the main motion if the previous question is negatived (see *above*, p. 14).

It is well to observe here that under the Toronto rule the previous question, having been once negatived, cannot be again proposed while the same main question is under the consideration of the council. It can, however, be moved on any new question at the same session or sitting (see *below*, p. 387, where a new rule is suggested for all councils).

In this council the previous question has been permitted on even two amendments to a question. This is at variance with the parliamentary law which governs where the special rule above is silent (see *above*, p. 280). If an amendment is withdrawn or negatived, the previous question can be proposed.

[Continued on p. 294.

16. The Previous Question.

37. The Hamilton rule 12 (see *above*, p. 291) makes the previous question undebatable ; consequently it must be put at once to the vote without amendment or debate ; when decided, the council follow parliamentary usage (as *above*, p. 13).

The Ottawa rule 59 is that of parliament (see *above*, p. 36) so far as it allows debate but no amendment on the main motion when the previous question has been proposed from the chair. If the previous question is voted, then the vote is taken at once on the main motion ; if it is negatived, then the Ottawa rule departs from the practice of parliament, for debate and amendment are allowable as under the Toronto rule opposite (see remarks on this point).

The London rule 36 is that of parliament, and foregoing remarks apply.

Kingston rule 15 and Brantford rule 20. " The previous question, until it is decided, shall preclude all amendments and debate of the main question, and shall be in this form ' Shall the main question be now put ? ' "

Many councils have a similar rule, which is somewhat vague since it would seem to allow a debate to follow, not on the main question, but on the advisability of agreeing to the previous question. The Toronto rule is clearer in this respect, and should be adopted by all assemblies that would adopt the closure. It must be assumed that the intention of the rule cited above is the same to stop all amendment and debate and come to a vote at once on the main question, otherwise much delay might take place on a desultory debate as to adopting the previous question.

In this vague rule the parliamentary usage would obtain, after a vote on the previous question. A vote would at once be taken on the main question if the previous question is carried ; if not, there could be no such vote (see *above*, p. 14), for there would be no question to be put.

Stratford rule 33 is the parliamentary rule, and debate continues on the main question until the previous question is decided.

Belleville rule 30 and St. Catharines rule 33 are in same terms as Toronto rule, without the last condition that the main question is open to debate and amendment if the previous question is negatived. In such a case the parliamentary rule should prevail, and there could be *no* question to debate or amend (see *above*, p. 14).

Guelph, rule 28. " On call of any member a majority of the members present may demand that the previous question be put, which shall always be in this form, ' Shall the main question be now put ? ' and until it is decided shall preclude all amendments to the main question and all further debate."

Here the previous question is initiated in a way different from that generally followed. A member rises and calls—does not move in the usual mode—for the previous question. It is for the chairman to learn whether a majority are in favour of putting the main question by immediately submitting the question, " Shall the main question be now put ? " If a majority vote " yea," the main

[Continued on p. 295.

17. AMENDMENTS IN GENERAL.

38. " Amendments shall be put in the reverse order to that in which they are moved, except in filling up blanks, when the longest time and largest sum shall be put first. Every amendment submitted shall be reduced to writing, and shall be decided or withdrawn before the main question is put to the vote. Only one amendment shall be allowed to an amendment, and any amendment more than one must be to the main question."

Amendments are here put as in Canadian parliament (see *above*, p. 34, where the practice is stated with some fulness). All motions in amendment must be in writing and disposed of before the main question is submitted. Only one amendment is allowed to an amendment to a main motion ; or, in other words, at one time only three motions can be before the council. But a motion to adjourn or to adjourn the debate (or to lay on the table and to postpone in some councils, see *above*, rule 36), is always in order as these are not actually amending but practically *dilatory* motions.

It will be seen that the several councils generally have the provision that in filling up blanks the longest time and largest sum shall be put first. The old parliamentary rule, in the direction of lessening as far as possible the burdens of the people, was to put first the longest time and the smallest sum (see *above,* p. 47). Why now follow a United States practice and place the largest sum in these rules ?

This rule of the council is inconsistent not only with the old parliamentary usage, but also with the ordinary rule of putting questions without any sufficient reason being shown for the distinction. The Simcoe county council has embodied the correct procedure in its rule.

[Continued on p. 296.

question must be put at once; if "nay," the main question, as in parliament, should really disappear, since the council has *actually* declared it shall *not now* be put. See last paragraph of remarks on Toronto, rule 37, p. 292.

The following are the rules of other councils on the previous question.

Peterborough town council, 26, same as Belleville rule 30, *above*.

Mt. Forest	"	"	28	"	"	Guelph	"	28	"
Pembroke	"	"	22	"	"	Kingston	"	15	"
Cobourg	"	"	13	"	"	"	"	15	"

17. Amendments in General.

38. The Ottawa rules 20, 51-53, which embody similar principles, are as follows:

20. " All questions shall be put in the order in which they are made."

51. " An amendment modifying the intention of a motion shall be in order, but an amendment relating to a different subject shall not be in order. Only one amendment shall be allowed to an amendment, and any amendment more than one, must be to the main question."

52. " The paragraph to be amended shall first be read as it stands, then the words proposed to be struck out, and those to be inserted; and finally the paragraph as it would stand if so amended."

53. " Amendments shall be put in the reverse order to that in which they are moved, except in filling up blanks, when the longest time and the largest sum shall be put first. Every amendment submitted shall be reduced to writing, and it shall be decided or withdrawn before the main question is put to the vote."

The London rule 37 and St. Catharines rule 34 are same as Toronto rule, with this addition: "all motions for the appointment of any member of the council or of any other person to any office in the gift of the council shall preclude all amendments." This is a special rule of these councils.

Hamilton has no special rule on subject, but is governed by common law of parliament respecting amendments, as explained under the Toronto rule, and on pp. 33, 34, *above*.

Hamilton rule 29 provides like the rules of other councils, that "when a blank is to be filled in any by-law, report or resolution, the question shall be first taken on the highest sum or number, and on the longest time proposed."

Guelph rule 40 and Kingston rule 10 follow the practice of other councils with respect to motions and amendments, and the largest sum and longest time.

Brantford rule 22 is simply confined to a statement of the usual practice in putting motions and amendments.

Stratford rule 34 and Belleville rule 31 are the same as that of Toronto, opposite.

[Continued on p. 297.

18. Voting on Appointments.

39. " In all motions for the appointment of any person to any office in the gift of the council the candidates shall be voted on separately in the order in which they are proposed [see *Ottawa rule, opposite*]; but no member of the council, while retaining his seat therein, shall be eligible for any office to which there is attached any salary, remuneration or emolument payable by the council."

This rule requires a vote to be taken on several candidates in the order of nomination, as in the case of speakership of commons' house (see *above*, p. 27).

In some councils all the nominations are given, and then a ballot taken until an appointment is made (see Guelph rule 41, opposite).

The second part of the foregoing rule requires a member to resign his seat in the council if he is to be eligible for an appointment to a remunerative office in its gift; it is an independence of council clause, in effect. A member should resign by a formal letter of resignation, witnessed by one or two members of the council, and addressed to the mayor, who should lay it before the council forthwith, or the member may, if he have the opportunity, resign from his place in the chamber. His resignation in either case should be formally entered in the minutes of the council.

For analogous parliamentary forms of resignations see Bourinot, p. 879, and *above*, p. 232.

[Continued on p. 298.

18. Voting on Appointments.

39. Ottawa rules 60 and 61 are the same as the Toronto rule 39, with the addition after word " proposed " of this provision : " and when there are more than two applicants the motion shall be put so that each shall be voted for until a majority is obtained for some one of them, the candidate receiving the lowest number of votes at the end of each series of votes falling out before the next series is taken, and so on until a majority is obtained for some one candidate, or the matter is postponed or otherwise disposed of."

London rule 80 is as follows : " In making appointments to office where there are more than two applicants, the motion shall be put so that each shall be voted for ; the persons receiving the lowest number of votes falling out in succession." A previous rule (see *above*, p. 295, rule 37) precludes all amendments to motions for appointment.

In Hamilton, Kingston and Brantford no such rule, but the parliamentary rule must obtain, and each candidate be voted on separately (see *above*, p. 29).

Belleville, rule 32. " In all motions for the appointment of any person to any office in the gift of the council, the names of all candidates shall be submitted before any vote is taken, and if required by any member this vote shall be by ballot."

In this case each candidate should be voted on separately as in parliament, if open voting is preferred (see *above*, p. 37). But if a ballot is to be taken the procedure explained below in Guelph rule 41 can be followed (or as *above*, p. 77).

St. Catharines rules 20 and 34, require a written notice of any motion for an appointment to office, and do not allow amendments to such motions.

Stratford rule 35 provides that " all motions for the appointment of any member of the council, or of any other person, to any office in the gift of the council, shall preclude any amendments, and in making appointments to office when there are more than two applicants the motion shall be put so that each shall be voted for, the person receiving the lowest number of votes falling out in succession."

Guelph, rule 41. " All appointments to office by the council shall be by ballot : the clerk shall prepare one ballot marked with his initials for each member of the council, having written thereon the names of all the applicants ; each member shall mark his ballot in the usual manner, by placing an X opposite the name of the person for whom he desires to vote ; and the candidate receiving a majority vote of the members then present shall be declared elected ; [the balloting shall then proceed as before, until the requisite number shall have been elected.] The mayor or chairman and the clerk shall act as scrutineers in all such cases."

The words I have placed in brackets are a little vague. They should read as follows and form a distinct sentence, for I suppose the reference is to the case where there are two or more appointments to be filled at one session : " In case of other appointments to be made, the balloting shall proceed in each case as at first until the requisite number shall have been elected."

[Continued on p. 299.

19. DIVISION OF A QUESTION.

40. " When the question under consideration contains distinct propositions, upon the request of any member, the vote upon each proposition will be taken separately."

For the parliamentary rule governing such questions, see *above*, p. 35.

20. FINAL DECISION ON QUESTIONS.

41. " After the question is finally put by the mayor, no member shall speak to the question, nor shall any other motion be made until after the result of the vote has been declared ; and the decision of the mayor, as to whether the question has been finally put, shall be conclusive."   •

This is substantially the parliamentary usage which requires the determination of one question before another is submitted. When the chairman has declared a motion passed or negatived or withdrawn, then another or new question can be proposed. For method of putting questions in parliament, first by voices and then by division if necessary (see *above*, pp. 41-44). A question of order may, however, be raised (see *above*, p. 44).

21. MOTIONS RULED OUT OF ORDER.

42. " Whenever a mayor is of opinion that a motion is contrary to the rules and privileges of the council, he shall apprise the members thereof immediately, before putting the question, and shall cite the rule or authority applicable to the case without argument or comment."

For same parliamentary rule, see *above*, p. 28.

It is essentially the duty of the chairman to maintain the rules of the council, and call attention to any breach thereof, when necessary, without waiting for a member to raise a point of order (see Bourinot, p. 214). An appeal is always allowed against a chairman's decision (see *above*, p. 39).

22. PRIVILEGE.

43. " Whenever any matter of privilege arises, it shall be immediately taken into consideration."

It must be a matter directly affecting the privileges of the council or of its members, under the law—a matter which has suddenly arisen and demands the immediate interposition of the council (see for same parliamentary rule, *above*, p. 40).

[Continued on p. 300.

19. Division of a Question.

40. London, rule 38; Belleville, rule 33; St. Catharines, rule 35; Stratford, rule 36.

Ottawa rule 46 is the same, more extended.

In Hamilton, Guelph, Kingston, Brantford, no such rule, but the parliamentary rule should obtain as a matter of usage.

20. Final Decision on Questions.

41. London, rule 39; Guelph, rule 29; Belleville, rule 34; Ottawa, rule 22; Stratford, rule 37; St. Catharines, rule 36; Brantford, rule 16.

In Hamilton and Kingston none, and parliamentary rule must obtain (see opposite).

21. Motions Ruled Out of Order.

42. Hamilton, rule 5; London, rule 40; Ottawa, rule 21; Belleville, rule 35; St. Catharines, rule 37; Guelph, rule 16; Brantford, rule 23; Stratford, rule 38.

In Kingston none, but the parliamentary usage as set forth in the rule should obtain.

22. Privilege.

43. London rule 29 dispenses with notice simply.

Ottawa, rule 49.

Rule 24 of Belleville dispenses with notice in such cases of privilege, only a difference in form of the rule opposite.

In Hamilton, Kingston, Guelph, St. Catharines, Brantford, no such special rule. But in all councils and assemblies the parliamentary usage, as stated in opposite rule, obtains *ex necessitate rerum.*

[Continued on p. 301.

23. Conduct of Members on Divisions.

44. "Members, having been previously summoned, shall immediately take their places when any division is called for."

The usual parliamentary rule (see *above*, p. 41), necessary for the orderly taking of a division. And the rule might add "shall remain in their places until the mayor or chairman has declared the result on the question." The mode of putting a question and then taking a division in the house of commons, is explained at some length, *above*, p. 41.

24. Reconsideration.

The Toronto council has no special rule like the councils of the other cities to provide for the reconsideration of a question that has been decided. Under these circumstances it is governed by the parliamentary law, and after due notice a member may move to rescind a motion passed in the affirmative, or bring up the question passed in the negative in another shape or, in other words, practically bring about a reconsideration. All that the parliamentary rule forbids is the bringing up of the same question in the one session ; but one sitting of a council is a session (see *above*, p. 7) and all that would be irregular would be to reconsider the same question at that one sitting where it was decided. But a member could give notice that at the next meeting he would move to rescind a motion passed at the one he gives such notice. Or he could give notice as provided for by rule 31 (see *above*, p. 286). In all cases the rules and usages of parliament would have to be followed in the Toronto council. In the councils of the other cities their special rules respecting reconsideration must govern ; but where these rules are defective, the law of parliament must obtain (see *above*, pp. 25, 26, where this question is reviewed at some length). It is desirable in all cases to have special rules carefully framed for reconsideration. That of the Ottawa council, opposite, appears sufficient for general purposes.

[Continued on p. 302.

23. Conduct of Members on Divisions.

44. Brantford, rule 17 ; Belleville, rule 36 ; Stratford, rule 39 ; London, rule 46 ; Ottawa, rule 35 ; St. Catharines, rule 38 ; Guelph, rule 26.

In Hamilton and Kingston the parliamentary usage should obtain in the absence of a special rule.

24. Reconsideration.

Hamilton, rule 30. " After any question, except one of indefinite postponement has been decided, any member who voted in the majority may, at the same or at a subsequent meeting, move for a reconsideration thereof, but no discussion of the main question shall be allowed unless reconsidered ; nor shall any question be reconsidered more than once " (see opposite).

London, rule 25. " After any question, except one of indefinite postponement, has been decided, any member who voted in the majority may, at the same session or at a subsequent session if he has given notice thereof in writing for such subsequent session, move for a reconsideration thereof, but no discussion of the main question shall be allowed unless reconsidered ; nor shall any question be reconsidered more than once, and then only by two-thirds of the members present voting in favour of such reconsideration."

Ottawa council also have these rules : 62. " After any question, except one of indefinite postponement, has been decided, any member may, at the same or at the first meeting held thereafter, move for a reconsideration thereof, but no discussion of the main question shall be allowed unless reconsidered, and there shall be no reconsideration unless notice of such reconsideration be given at the meeting at which the main motion is carried, and after such notice is given no action shall be taken by the council on the main motion until such reconsideration is disposed of."

63. " If the motion for reconsideration be not made until the next meeting the question shall not be reconsidered unless a majority of the whole council vote therefor. No question shall be reconsidered more than once, nor shall a vote to reconsider be reconsidered."

Guelph, rule 42. " No motion to rescind a resolution entered upon the minutes shall be received or put unless a notice of intention to introduce such motion to rescind shall have been made in writing at a previous meeting."

As Brantford, Stratford, St. Catharines, and Belleville, have no special rule providing for reconsideration, the remarks in the Toronto column opposite apply to their cases.

Kingston, rule 23. " When a motion has once been made and carried in the affirmative or negative, it shall be in order for any member to move for a reconsid-

[Continued on p. 303.

25. Proceedings in Committee of The Whole.

45. " Whenever it shall be moved and carried that the council go into committee of the whole the mayor shall leave the chair, but he shall first appoint a chairman of the committee of the whole, who shall maintain order in the committee, and who shall report the proceedings thereof."

For the parliamentary rules which govern committees of the whole except where there are special rules of the council, see *above*, pp. 44-46.

A motion " That the council do now resolve itself into committee of the whole to consider (here state question) "; having been carried, the mayor or presiding officer says, " Mr. A. or B. will please take the chair of the committee "; Mr. A., or B., having taken the chair, calls the committee to order and reads the question before the committee.

46. " No bill or report of a committee shall be discussed in committee of the whole, unless such bill or report has been previously printed and placed in the hands of the members, except it shall be otherwise decided by a vote of two-thirds of the members present, without debate."

A special rule but in accordance with parliamentary usages and rules, which require all bills and resolutions to be printed and in the hands of members before considered in committee. It is a rule which should be suspended only in a case of urgency.

47. " The rules of the council shall be observed in committee of the whole, so far as may be applicable, except that no motion shall require to be seconded, nor shall a motion for the previous question, or for an adjournment be allowed ; and in taking the yeas and nays the names of members shall not be recorded, nor shall the number of times of speaking on any question be limited."

This is substantially the parliamentary rule as given fully *above*, p. 45.

[Continued on p. 304.

eration ; and if such motion is seconded, it shall be open to debate and be disposed of by the council, and in case the motion be made at the same meeting, it shall be competent for a majority of the members present to pass a vote of reconsideration ; but if it be not made until next meeting, the subject shall not be reconsidered, unless a majority of the whole council shall vote therefor ; but no more than one motion for reconsideration of any vote shall be permitted."

25. Proceedings in Committee of the Whole.

45. Hamilton, rule 25 ; London, rule 42 ; Stratford, rule 40 ; Ottawa, rule 64 ; Kingston, rule 24 ; Belleville, rule 37 ; St. Catharines, rule 39 ; Brantford, rule 38.

Guelph rule 44 is the same, with the proviso that "each member" of the council shall serve as chairman of the committee "in alphabetical order of his name." This is intended, or it must have that effect, to give each member in his turn experience of the working of a committee of the whole.

But the Guelph rule 45 also provides for a special case where the chairman is interested : " When a report or by-law is under discussion in committee of the whole, the chairman of a committee whose report is under consideration, or the introducer of the by-law, shall not be required to take the chair, but the member who is next in turn liable to serve as chairman of committee, shall be called to the chair."

This appears to be a wise rule, which might well be generally adopted.

46. Ottawa, rule 65 ; St. Catharines, rule 40.

London, Hamilton, and other cities have none, but they should adopt it in the interest of the intelligent consideration of every question before a committee.

47. Hamilton, rule 25 ; London, rule 43 ; Stratford, rule 41 ; Ottawa, rule 66 ; Belleville, rule 38 ; St. Catharines, rule 41.

Guelph rule 43 is the same as the Toronto rule, except that there is this limitation, " no member shall speak for a longer time than ten minutes on any clause of a report or resolution." By-laws do not appear to fall within this limitation of debate.

Kingston, rule 24 (in part). " The rules of proceedings in council shall be observed in committee of the whole, so far as they may be applicable, except the rule limiting the number of times of speaking, and the taking of the yeas and nays, but no member shall speak more than once to any question until every other member choosing to speak shall have spoken."

[Continued on p. 305.

48. " Questions of order arising in committee of the whole shall be decided by the chairman, subject to an appeal to the council ; and if any disorder should arise in the committee the mayor shall resume the chair, without any question being put."

For same parliamentary rule, see *above*, p. 45.

A member who objects to a ruling may say, "I appeal to the council against the ruling." The chairman will then leave the chair and state the question to the mayor or presiding officer, who will again state it to the council, and ask "Shall the decision [or ruling] of Mr. A., chairman of the committee on   , be sustained?" The vote will then be taken in the usual way (see *above*, p. 39, for similar proceeding).

When the question in dispute has been decided by the council, the committee may be resumed by order of the mayor or other presiding officer, with the words " The committee on   may resume."

49. " On motion in committee of the whole to rise and report, the question shall be decided without debate."

This is a limitation of Canadian parliamentary usage (see *above*, p. 46), which allows debate to continue on the question under consideration even when it is moved to rise and report. It is a wise limitation, which should be adopted by all councils to save time and prevent " obstruction." When the committee has agreed to report the chairman leaves the chair forthwith and makes his report.

50. " A motion in the committee of the whole to rise without reporting, or that the chairman leave the chair, shall always be in order, and shall take precedence of any other motion. On such motion debate shall be allowed, and on an affirmative vote the subject referred to the committee shall be considered as disposed of in the negative, and the mayor shall resume the chair, and proceed with the next order of business."

This is substantially the parliamentary rule which is explained *above*, p. 46, since the question before the committee is superseded for that sitting or session if the chairman rises without reporting. The proper form of this motion is, " That the chairman do leave the chair." It is equivalent to a motion for adjournment in the council. It is competent at another sitting to revive the same question by a motion " That the by-law [or state the question whatever it may be]

[Continued on p. 306.

Brantford, rule 40. " The rules of this council shall be observed in committee of the whole, so far as they may be applicable, except the rules limiting the number of times of speaking, and the names of members on a division being entered on the minutes."

48. Stratford, rule 42; St. Catharines, rule 42; London, rule 44; Ottawa, rule 67.

In Hamilton and other cities the same parliamentary usage should obtain as explained in opposite column.

Belleville rule 39 allows an appeal to the committee from a chairman's ruling. The chairman " may ask the mayor to decide the question, which he may do, subject to like appeal." The mayor may resume in case of disorder.

49. London, rule 45; Ottawa, rule 68; Kingston, rule 25; Belleville, rule 40; Brantford, rule 39; Guelph, rule 47; St. Catharines, rule 43; Stratford, rule 43.

Hamilton, rule 26 adds, " need not be in writing," but this is the parliamentary usage with respect to such well-known motions.

London rule 46, Ottawa rule 69 and Stratford rule 44, have also the following provision which simply enunciates the convenient usage: " In the committee of the whole all motions relating to the matter under consideration shall be put in the order in which they are proposed."

50. Stratford, rule 45; St. Catharines, rule 44; Belleville, rule 41; London, rule 47; Ottawa, rule 70.

In Hamilton, Kingston, and Brantford, none, but parliamentary usage should obtain.

Guelph rule 48 is the same as that of other cities with the limitation that " no member shall speak more than once " on motions to rise without reporting, or " that the chairman leave the chair."

[Continued on p. 307.

be placed on the order of the day for further consideration," after notice duly given under rule 31 (see *above*, p. 286); and if the council so vote, the question is renewed at the exact point where it was superseded or "disposed of " in committee.

Money appropriations to be first considered in committee of the whole in certain councils. Ottawa rule 99 (*below*, p. 344); London rule 77 (*below*, p. 363); Belleville rule 64 (*below*, p. 368); and Stratford rule 76 (*below*, p. 380), all provide to the foregoing effect. The same practice should obtain in all other councils.

26. BILLS AND PROCEEDINGS THEREON.

51. "Every bill shall be introduced upon motion for leave, specifying the title of the bill, or upon motion to appoint a committee to prepare and bring in the bill."

For parliamentary rules on bills and mode of introduction, second reading, etc., see *above*, p. 53.

Such a motion for introduction of a bill must be moved and seconded like any other motion. When leave is given by the council to introduce the bill, then the first reading takes place without debate (see rule 53).

52. "No bill shall be introduced either in blank, or in an imperfect shape."

For same parliamentary rule, see *above*, p. 53.

And when a bill has been formally introduced, it cannot be altered except by the council itself. The clerk cannot permit it to be otherwise altered or amended (see *above*, pp. 53-56).

53. "The question, 'That this bill be now read a first time,' shall be decided without amendment or debate; and every bill shall be printed immediately after the first reading thereof, and shall be read a second time, and then considered in committee of the whole, and shall be read a third time before it is signed by the mayor."

For same parliamentary rule in full, see *above*, pp. 53, 54.

It would be well if all councils adopted the same rule, which includes a consideration in committee of the whole; that stage when a bill is most conveniently discussed in detail.

[Continued on p. 308

26. Bills and Proceedings Thereon.

51. Ottawa rule 71, Hamilton rule 21, Brantford rule 25, and Belleville rule 42, add to Toronto rule, " or by order of the council on the report of a committee." Guelph rule 49 adds, " or by a report of by-law committee."

In other cities there is no such rule, but the parliamentary usage which should govern these councils, allows a bill to be introduced by the various methods set forth in the rules herein mentioned.

52. Ottawa, rule 72.

In Hamilton and other cities the same correct parliamentary usage should obtain.

53. London rule 49. Ottawa rule 73 differs from the Toronto rule, since it leaves the council to determine whether the bill shall be considered in committee.

Hamilton rule 22 requires that " every proposed by-law shall receive three several readings, but not more than two on the same evening, unless with the unanimous consent of the members present. The clerk shall certify the reading and the time on the back of the by-law."

Kingston, rule 29. " Every act or by-law shall be read twice before it is committed and engrossed, and read a third time before it is signed by the mayor. The second reading shall be always in committee of the whole and clause by clause."

This provision is not consistent with correct parliamentary usage, or that of councils generally. A committee stage should be separate from the second reading.

Belleville, rule 45. " Every by-law shall be read twice and approved before it is engrossed and read a third time before it is signed by the mayor." Rule 43 (see *below*, p. 311), provides for reference to a committee of the whole.

[Continued on p. 309.

54. " Every bill (unless previously reported upon by a committee, or otherwise determined by the council) shall be referred, after the second reading thereof, to a standing or select committee of the council to report upon the leading features of the same."

A special and useful rule, quite in accordance with parliamentary usage; see *above* p. 54.

55. " Every bill shall receive three several readings, and on different days previous to its being passed, except on urgent and extraordinary occasions, and upon a vote of two-thirds of the

[Continued on p. 310.

St. Catharines, rules 21 and 22. " Every bill (or by-law) shall be introduced upon motion for leave, specifying the title of the bill (or by-law) ; and the first reading shall take place without amendment or debate, and each bill or by-law shall receive three separate readings, and on different days, previous to its being passed, except upon receiving the votes of two-thirds of the entire council, when it may be read twice or thrice or advanced two or more stages in one day."

22. " No bill (or by-law) shall be passed, amended or repealed except by the votes of a majority of the *whole* council elect." An important limitation—a majority of the *whole* council, and not of the members present.

Guelph, rule 50. " No by-law shall be referred to committee of the whole for adoption or amendment until it shall have been read twice."

[Compare this correct practice with that of Kingston, *above*, p. 307].

51. " Every by-law shall be read and passed in committee of the whole before being read a third time."

53. " No by-law shall receive more than two readings at any one meeting, except upon a vote representing at least two-thirds of the members constituting the city council, and on such a vote it may be passed through all its several stages, and finally passed."

56. " Every proposed by-law shall receive three several readings before it is finally passed."

Stratford rule 47 is the same as that of Toronto, with the omission of part requiring an immediate printing. The practice, however, should be to print.

Brantford, rule 26. " Every by-law shall receive three separate readings previous to its being finally passed, but no by-law shall be read three times on the same day, except on urgent occasions, and this rule suspended by resolution for the single occasion ; and no by-law shall be committed or amended until it shall have been twice read, provided always that no resolution to suspend this rule shall be carried unless on a call of the yeas and nays two-thirds of the members of the council then present vote in favour of the same."

27. " Every by-law shall be read and passed in committee of the whole between its second and third readings."

54. Ottawa, rule 74 ; Belleville rule 43 (see *below*, p. 311). In Hamilton and other cities no such rule, but it is always competent for the council to refer any bill to a select committee on motion duly made and agreed to.

55. Ottawa, rule 76 ; Hamilton, rule 22, see *above*, p. 307 ; London, rule 50 and Stratford, rule 48 (excepting the two-thirds vote).

Kingston rule 30. " No Act or by-law brought into the council shall have more than one reading on the same day."

[Continued on p. 311.

members present, when it may be read twice or thrice, or advanced two or more stages in one day."

This is substantially the parliamentary usage (see *above*, p. 56), with the proviso in this case that a two-thirds vote of the members present may advance a measure several stages at one sitting. As a matter of fact there is no special parliamentary usage to prevent several stages being taken on one day should the house believe the case to be urgent and extraordinary (see Bourinot, p. 637, and also *above*, p. 56).

56. " The clerk shall endorse on all bills read in the council the dates of the several readings thereof, and shall be responsible for their correctness, should they have been amended."

For same parliamentary rule, see *above*, p. 56.

57. " In proceedings in committee of the whole upon bills, each clause shall be considered in its proper order, then the preamble, and then the title."

For same parliamentary rule, see *above*, p. 55. If a clause is considered, it should be amended in the order of its lines ; if a particular line is amended, and the council has taken up another, it is not regular to go back to the previous part of the clause, but this is often done by unanimous consent as a matter of convenience and necessity.

58. " All amendments made in committee of the whole shall be reported by the chairman to the council, which shall receive the

[Continued on p. 312.

Belleville, rule 46.   Practically the same as that of Toronto.

For St. Catharines rule 21 to same effect, see *above*, p. 309.

For Guelph rules 53 and 56 to same effect, see *above*, p. 309.

For Brantford rule 26 to same effect, see *above*, p. 309.

56. Hamilton, rule 22 (see *above*, p. 307) ; Stratford, rule 46 ; London, rule 48 ; Ottawa, rule 79 ; Belleville, rule 44 ; St. Catharines, rule 24 ; Guelph, rule 52 ; Kingston, rule 28 (in part) ; Brantford, rule 30 (the clerk must also sign a bill when it passes, and put the date thereto, rule 31).

57. Stratford, rule 50 ; London, rule 52 ; Ottawa, rule 77.

No such rule in Hamilton or Kingston, but the parliamentary usage must prevail—that is to say, each clause or question must be taken in its order.

Belleville, rule 43. " By-laws shall be committed to a committee of the whole council, after having been first read throughout by the clerk in council, and there debated by clauses, leaving the preamble and title to be last considered, and then referred to the committee on by-laws, except when otherwise ordered. The council may refer any by-law to a special committee for consideration and report."

In all these rules a " proposed by-law" would be more correct ; it is really a bill which becomes a by-law when it passes through all the forms required by law.

Brantford rule 28 is the same as that of Toronto, except it requires all by-laws to be read by the chairman. He should do that always when required, as in parliament.

Guelph rule 54 is the same as the last, except the reading is by the clerk.

St. Catharines rule 46 is the same as Toronto rule 57. This council have also this special rule :

23. "On an amendment to 'strike out and insert,' the paragraph to be amended shall first be read as it stands, then the words proposed to be struck out and those to be inserted, and finally the paragraph as it would stand if so amended."

This rule is clearly intended to give the council information which will enable them to vote intelligently on a complicated question, and it is consequently a practice that should be followed by the chairman of all committees in all councils.

58. Ottawa rule 78, St. Catharines rule 47, and London rule 53 give the same rule with the following proper addition, which is also in the Canadian commons

[Continued on p. 313.

same forthwith.   After the report has been received the bill shall be open to debate and amendment before it is ordered for a third reading."

This is practically the parliamentary rule in England; but in Canada bills are never amended when reported and considered as amended, but probably the more convenient course is followed of referring the bill back to committee where the limitations of debate are not observed (see Bourinot, p. 624, for parliamentary rule).

59. "All by-laws adopted by the council, shall be printed, paged and bound up in a separate volume for the year in which they are passed, and shall have a separate index."

A rule which is necessary to ensure easy reference to every by-law.   The same practice is necessarily followed in the house of commons' offices.

60. "Every by-law which has passed the council shall immediately after being sealed with the seal of the corporation, and signed by the mayor, be deposited by the clerk for security in the safe connected with his office."

In parliamentary bodies, there is an officer—the clerk of parliament, who is always the clerk of the upper house—assigned the duty of keeping their original records and giving certified copies thereof (see Bourinot, p. 662).

27. PETITIONS AND COMMUNICATIONS.

61. "Every petition, remonstrance, or other written application intended to be presented to the council must be fairly written or printed on paper or parchments, and signed by at least one person, and no letters, affidavits, or other documents shall be attached to it."

For parliamentary rules respecting petitions, see *above*, pp. 52, 53.

The signature of at least one person should be on the sheet containing the petition or its prayer, for otherwise fraud might be practised.   A signature might

[Continued on p. 314.

rule (see *above*, p. 56): "When a bill is reported without amendment it shall be forthwith ordered to be read a third time at such time as may be appointed by the council."

- Guelph, rule 55; Stratford, rule 51; Belleville, rule 47; same as that of Toronto.

Brantford rule 29 is the same practically: "That all amendments made in committee shall be reported by the council, and by it adopted, before the question to engross shall be put." "Engross" practically means "pass."

Kingston has no such special rule, but the parliamentary usage, as set forth in Toronto rule, should obtain.

59. St. Catharines, rule 48.

London, rule 54. "All by-laws after having been finally passed shall be numbered and shall be forthwith filed by the city clerk, and shall remain in his custody."

Ottawa, rule 80. "Every by-law which has passed the council shall be numbered, and shall be forthwith entered and copied at full length in a book to be kept for that purpose, and after being sealed with the seal of the corporation and signed by the mayor shall be deposited with the clerk for security in the safe connected with his office."

Stratford rule 52 is practically same as that of Ottawa.

Hamilton and other councils, it is assumed, follow the same convenient and necessary practice in the absence of a special regulation of their own.

60. Belleville, rule 48. See for similar London and Ottawa rules, *above.* Also Ottawa rule 96, *below*, p. 344.

In Brantford rule 31 requires the clerk to sign all by-laws. In these and other cities the Toronto rule should be adopted formally.

27. Petitions and Communications.

61. Ottawa, rule 81; St. Catharines, rule 49.

In London and Hamilton and other councils the same parliamentary usage must prevail in the absence of special rules.

[Continued on p. 315.

be obtained for another object, and attached to the petition. For this reason three signatures must be on the sheet containing the prayer of a petition presented to parliament with a number of signatures.

62. "Every petition, remonstrance, or other written application may be presented to the council by any member thereof, not signing or being a party to the same, on any day, but not later than the hour at which the council meets, except on extraordinary occasions; and every member presenting any petition, remonstrance, or other written application to the council, shall examine the same and be answerable that it does not contain any impertinent or improper matter, and that the same is respectful and temperate in its language; he shall also endorse thereon the name of the applicant and the substance of such application, and sign his name thereto, which endorsement only shall be read by the mayor, unless a member shall require the reading of the document, in which case the whole shall be read."

This is substantially the parliamentary rule (see *above*, p. 52), with the exception that the mayor in the council, and not the clerk or clerk's assistant, as in the commons, reads the endorsation. In presenting a petition a member reads the endorsation thereon, which he must make under the rule, and which should be the prayer in substance. If a member asks for the reading of a petition, the clerk must read it immediately.

63. "All petitions or written communications on any subject within the cognizance of any standing committee shall, on presentation, be considered as referred to the proper committee without any motion unless otherwise ordered; and no member shall speak upon, nor shall a debate be allowed upon, the presentation of a petition or other communication to the council; but a member may move that in referring a petition or other communication

[Continued on p. 316.

62. London, rule 55 ; Ottawa, rule 82 ; Stratford, rule 53.

Hamilton rule 23 but only in part since there is no reference to the reading of petitions. In this case, then, the parliamentary rule may prevail and the clerk read the petition ; but this will be probably regulated by usage—it is not a necessary rule of the common law of parliament. Hamilton rule 23 is as follows :

" First, any member presenting memorials or other papers addressed to the council shall be accountable that they do not contain improper or impertinent matter, and no memorial or other paper shall be read unless endorsed by the member presenting it.

" Second, any member who shall present any petition, or make any application, or offer any scheme to or for consideration by the council, in writing, with his name endorsed thereon, shall be at liberty to press and urge the same before any committee to which the same may be referred.

" Third, when any petition, application or scheme, with the name of any member endorsed thereon, shall be referred to any committee, such member shall be duly notified of the meeting or meetings of the committee at which the same is to be held, considered or resolved upon, in the same manner as if he were a member thereof."

Belleville rule 49 is to all intents the same as the Toronto rule.

Guelph, rule 20. " All petitions, memorials and communications addressed to the council shall be presented by a member from his place in the council chamber, and every such document shall have endorsed thereon the object thereof, the date of presentation, and the name of the member making the same, and such member shall be answerable to the council that the document does not contain improper or impertinent matter.

Brantford rule 32 simply requires endorsation by an alderman, and proper and pertinent matter therein. The parliamentary usage should also prevail in other respects.

St. Catharines and Kingston have no special rules and parliamentary usage should obtain in such unprovided cases.

63. London, rule 56 ; Ottawa, rule 83 ; St. Catharines, rule 50 ; Stratford, rule 54.

Belleville rule 50 same with the addition that a petition " may be laid upon the table "—which is always open to any council to order and does not require a special mention in a rule.

Brantford rule 33 simply orders a reference to the proper committee, when necessary, by resolution of the council.

[Continued on p. 317.

certain instructions may be given by the council, or that the petition or communication shall be referred to a select committee, and if the petition or communication complain of some present personal grievance, requiring immediate remedy, the matter contained therein may be brought into immediate discussion and disposed of forthwith."

This is substantially a special rule, based on parliamentary usage, especially that portion allowing a matter of present personal grievance to be immediately disposed of (see *above*, p. 53).

The mayor may decide that the matter is one to be immediately taken up, or he may gather the general sense of the council on the subject if he is not certain.

64. " Any member may move to take up or refer a communication or petition made or presented to the council during the year in which such motion is made, or during the year next preceding such year, and whether such communication or petition has been referred to a committee and reported upon or not ; but no motion shall be in order to take up or refer a communication or petition made or presented at any time before the commencement of the year next preceding such motion."

A special rule explaining itself.

28. Appointment of Special and Standing Committees.

65. " All standing and select committees shall be appointed on motion of a member by consent of a majority of the members present at any meeting of the council, and any member of the council may be placed on a committee, notwithstanding the absence of such member at the time of his being named upon such committee."

A special rule, quite in accordance with parliamentary practice. No committee could, however, be appointed without the consent of a majority of all the members present, and that part of the rule seems practically superfluous. For parliamentary rule governing committees, see *above*, pp. 48-51.

[Continued on p. 318.

Hamilton and Guelph have no such rule, but every council under their own or the parliamentary rule has the right of referring any document, on a vote if necessary, to a select or other committee.

Kingston rule 28 only to end of " unless otherwise ordered " in Toronto rule.

The Kingston rules also provide that " in future all communications addressed to the council be briefly summarized by the clerk—such summary to be read to the council in lieu of the whole communication, provided that any member may request that the communication be read at length."

64. Ottawa, rule 84 ; Stratford, rule 55 ; Belleville, rule 51 ; St. Catharines, rule 51.

In Hamilton and other cities, none; they should adopt the Toronto rule.

28. Appointment of Special and Standing Committees.

65. St. Catharines, rule 16, and Kingston, rule 32 [in part]. "Committees shall be appointed on motion of a member, by consent of a majority of the council."

Belleville rule 52 same as that of Toronto with the addition : " The mayor shall be, *ex officio*, a member of all committees, standing and special."

St. Catharines rule 52 same as that of Belleville with the addition: " no committee shall consist of more than six members without the consent of the council."

Stratford rule 56 provides that "any member of the council may be placed on a committee notwithstanding the absence of such member at the time of his being named upon such committee, and the mayor shall be *ex officio* a member of all committees."

London rule 57 contains that latter part of Toronto rule which allows any member to be placed on a committee.

Ottawa rule 88 allows a member to be placed on a committee in his absence.

Other cities have no such special rule, which embodies the parliamentary usage which should obtain in all such unprovided cases. [Continued on p. 319

66. "Every member who shall introduce a bill, petition, or motion upon any subject which may be referred to a select committee shall be one of the committee without being named by the council, and shall, unless the committee otherwise determines, be the chairman of such committee."

This is substantially the parliamentary practice (see *above*, p. 49).

67. "There shall be annually appointed at the first meeting of each newly elected council the following committees which shall compose the standing committees of the council : 1st, the executive committee ; 2nd, the committee on works; 3rd, the committee on fire and light ; 4th, the committee on property; 5th, the committee on parks and gardens; and the council shall also at the same meeting appoint from among the members of the council the persons who shall compose the court of revision, and shall also appoint the local board of health, the members necessary to be selected for the free library board, the city's representative on the harbour commission, and the trustees necessary to be selected for the high school and other boards."

In parliament also, at commencement of session select standing committees are appointed (see Bourinot, p. 493 ; also *above*, p. 48).

For number on each committee, see *below*, pp. 322, 324 ; for quorum, see *below*, p. 322.

In 1892 the reception and legislation committees were incorporated (by-law 2985) with the executive committee (see *below*, pp. 350, 351).

In 1893 the committees on water-works and markets were incorporated (by-law 3119) with those of works and property (see *below*, p. 349).

The practice in this council is to appoint a committee of six members, one from each ward, at the inaugural meeting to strike the standing committees. This committee reports at the same session, which is adjourned until a later hour for that purpose (see *above*, p. 264). The report is referred at once to a committee of the whole, where it is considered and amended if necessary. The report is considered forthwith, and may be amended by the council on motion duly made to strike out certain names and insert others (see parliamentary rule in such cases, *above*, p. 51). The report is then adopted, with or without amendments as the case may be (see Toronto minutes for January 17th, 1893).

The court of revision, composed of five persons, is appointed by the council in accordance with the municipal law (see *above*, p. 247, for general law on subject). By by-law 2438 the city clerk regulates all notices of appeal and the sittings of the court of revision, and for hearing of appeals by the county judge.

[Continued on p. 320.

66. Hamilton, rule 24 ; London, rule 58; Ottawa, rule 90 ; Kingston, rule 27 ; Belleville, rule 53; Brantford, rule 34.

St. Catharines rule 16 and Stratford rule 57 leave the mover to determine whether he shall be chairman or not.

Guelph, rule 46. "The mover of a special committee shall be a member, and the convener thereof, and the introducer of a measure shall be a member of the committee if a special committee is instructed to consider it."

67. Ottawa, rule 85. "There shall be appointed annually at the first or second meeting of each newly elected council or as soon thereafter as convenience will permit, the following committees which shall compose the standing committees of the council :

"1. Finance committee. 2. Board of works committee. 3. By-law committee. 4. Water-works committee. 5. Market committee. 6. License committee. 7. Printing committee. 8. Fire committee. 9. Board of health committee. 10. Property and parks committee. 11. Court of revision."

See *below*, p. 325, for number on each committee.

For quorum, see *below*, p. 323.

Ottawa, rule 78 also provides : "The council may dispense with the appointment of any one or more of the said standing committees, or may assign the duties of any one or more of them to any other or others of the said standing committees, or may amalgamate any two or more of the said standing committees as may be thought expedient."

London, rule 60. "There shall be appointed annually at the first or second meeting of each newly elected council the following committees, which shall compose the standing committees of the council :

"(a) Committee number one ; (b) committee number two ; (c) committee number three."

See *below*, p. 325, for number on each committee ; *below*, p. 323, for quorum.

Kingston, rule 42. "1. Finance and accounts, seven members ; this committee shall do the work of the late committee on licenses and schools. 2. Board of works, seven members ; this committee shall do the work of the late committee on streets and improvements and of the late committee on wharfs and harbours. 3. Water-works, seven members. 4. Court of revision, five members. 5. Fire, water and light, five members. 6. City property and markets, seven members. 7. Parks, seven members. 8. Printing, five members. 9. House of industry, four members. 10. Board of health, consisting of the mayor and eight ratepayers to be appointed by the council, three of the members to be members of the council. The duties of the reception committee now abolished, and the duties of the committee on railways and improvements now also abolished, shall be performed by a special committee of the council, to be appointed by the council, for the purpose when necessary.

For quorum, see *below*, p. 323.

[Continued on p. 321.

By-law 2477 provides that the local board of health shall comprise the mayor and eight aldermen, appointed annually by the council (see *above*, p. 251, for general law on subject).

By Free Libraries Act (Rev. Stat. of Ont. of 1887, c. 189), the city is represented on the board of management by the mayor and three other persons, one of whom retires annually, but may be reappointed (see *above*, p. 250, for general Act on subject).

By High School Act, 1891, the city can appoint six trustees for each of the three high schools therein ; six retire, or two for each school, on the 31st of January, and their successors must be appointed by by-law (see No. 3114 at end of minutes of council for January 17th, 1893; also, *above*, p. 248, for general Act on subject).

By 13-14 Vic. c. 80 (Stat. of the old province of Canada), " An Act to provide for the management of the Toronto harbour," the Toronto council appoint two commissioners, the Toronto Board of Trade two others, and the majority of such commissioners recommend another, who shall be appointed by the governor of the province, and in case a majority cannot make such a recommendation then the governor appoints.   All hold office during pleasure, and are a body corporate for the purposes of the Act.

The city has representatives on other local boards not necessary to mention here.

[Continued on p. 322.

St. Catharines, rule 54. " There shall be annually appointed, at the first or second meeting of each newly elected council, the following committees, which shall compose the standing committees of the council :

"1. Finance and assessment. 2. Board of works. 3. Fire, water and gas. 4. By-laws and licenses. 5. Market and public buildings. 6. Printing. 7. Board of health. 8. Relief. 9. Cemetery. 10, Park and shade trees."

For number on each committee. see *below*, p. 325 ; for quorum, see *below*, p. 323.

St. Thomas. "1. Finance, railway and printing. 2. Public works, sewer, and market. 3. Fire and gas. 4. Police, license, relief and sanitary. 5. Board of health."

Belleville, rule 55. " At the first meeting of each newly elected council, the following committees, which shall compose the standing committees for the year, shall be appointed by the council:

"1. Executive committee. 2. Public works. 3. Fire. 4. Water and gas. 5. Harbour and ferry. 6. Market and city property. 7. Court of revision and committee on by-laws. 8. Industries and railways."

For number on each committee, see *below*, p. 325 ; for quorum, see *below*, p. 323.

Stratford, rule 59. " Appointed annually at first or second meeting of each newly elected council :

"1. Finance, assessment, license and printing. 2. Board of works. 3. Market and police. 4. Board of health and relief. 5. Park and cemetery. 6. Court of revision."

For number on each committee, see *below*, p. 325; for quorum, see *below*, p. 323.

Guelph, rule 57. " The council shall at its first evening meeting, on the third Monday in January in each and every year, appoint a board of health, and the following standing committees :

"1. Finance and assessment. 2. Water-works. 3. Board of works. 4. Market and public buildings. 5. Fire, water and gas. 6. Relief. 7. Parks and shade trees. 8. By-laws and licenses. 9. Police. 10. Railways. 11. Cemetery. 12. Hospital and any other standing committee hereafter constituted."

For number on each committee, see *below*, p. 327 ; for quorum, see *below*, p. 325.

The printed copy of the Brantford rules do not give specifically the designations or number of the standing committees of the council of that city, but the clerk, Mr. Woodyatt, informs me they are as follows :

1. Finance, printing and license. 2. Board of works. 3. Fire, light and sewers. 4. Building and grounds. 5. Court of revision. 6. Manufactures. 7. Board of health.

For quorum, see *below*, p. 323.

Hamilton, rule 27. "1. Board of Works. 2. Markets, fire, police and license. 3. Hospital and house of refuge. 4. Gaol and court house. 5. Water works. 6. Health. 7. Parks, crystal palace, and cemetery. 8. Sewers. 9. Claims. 10. Finance, printing, assessment, railway and legislation.

For number on each committee, see *below*, p. 325 ; for quorum, see *below*, p. 323.

                                              [Continued on p. 323.

68. "No special or select committee shall be appointed unless and until notice thereof specifying the matters to be dealt with by such committee, and the names of the members thereof shall have been given at a previous meeting of the council, and the same shall have been printed in the orders of the day and distributed to members at least twenty-four hours before the meeting at which such committee is to be appointed."

See by-law 2985, s. 5 (1892).

A rule based on parliamentary usage (see *above*, p. 48), and in the interest of business.

29. Number of Members on Standing and Select Committees.

68a. "Of the number of members appointed to compose any committee, five shall be a quorum, but if a committee consists of less than nine members, a majority shall be a quorum, and the mayor (if present) shall be counted in making up such quorum."

See by-law 2985, s. 4 (1892).

A special rule. For parliamentary rule respecting quorum, see *above*, p. 48. No business can be transacted in absence of a quorum.

[Continued on p. 324.

68. All councils having a general rule providing for a notice of all special motions would require such a notice in the case of the proposed appointment of a select committee.

The Toronto rule as a whole, should be formally adopted by all similar bodies.

Ottawa rule 89 provides simply, " The council may from time to time appoint special committees."

29. Number of Members on Standing and Select Committees.

68a. Ottawa, rule 92, and Stratford, rule 58, provide: " Of the number of members appointed to compose any standing or special committee, such number thereof as shall be equal to a majority of the whole number chosen ; exclusive of any *ex officio* member, shall be a quorum competent to proceed to business."

London rule 59 is the same as Ottawa rule.

Both Ottawa and London rules make the mayor a member of all standing committees *ex officio*, and consequently he does not count in a quorum.

In Hamilton there is no such rule, and parliamentary usage must obtain ; see opposite.

Belleville rule 54 same as Ottawa rule, with the addition (unnecessary since the council have always the power so to order), " unless otherwise ordered by the council when such committee be struck."

As rule 56 of Belleville (see *below*, p. 325), makes all the committees to consist of seven members, except the three hereinafter stated, a quorum must be four, as the mayor does not count, under the rule, when present. The quorum of the three excepted committees will be : of the executive committee, four or five accord-ing as it is composed of seven or nine members ; of the court of revision and com-mittee on by-laws, three members.

Brantford rule 35 is the same as that of Kingston (26) *below*, but there is no special number fixed as in Kingston for a committee (see rule 33, *below*, p. 325, which is very vague, and may or may not refer to a select or standing committee).

Kingston, rule 26. " Of the number of members appointed to compose a committee, such number thereof as shall be equal to a majority of the whole number chosen, shall be a quorum competent to proceed to business."

By rule 33 (see *below*, p. 325), committees cannot be less than five nor more than seven ; hence the quorum must be three and four in all cases.

St. Catharines, rule 53. A majority of the whole number, exclusive of *ex officio* members, constitute a quorum.

[Continued on p. 325.

68b. "The executive committee of the council, the committee on property and the committee on works, shall each consist of two members from each ward, and each of the other standing committees shall consist of one member from each ward."

For duties of executive committee, see *below*, pp. 344-348; committee on works, *below*, pp. 348, 349; committee on fire and light, *below*, p. 349 ; committee on property, *below*, pp. 349, 350; committee on parks and gardens, *below*, p. 350.

69. " [Each standing committee of the council shall consist of one member from each ward, and] the mayor shall be *ex officio* a member of all standing and special committees."

The words in brackets have been repealed by by-laws 2985 and 3119, under which rule 68 (*b*), *above*, has become a regulation of the council.

[Continued on p. 325.

Rule 52 makes the mayor an *ex officio* member, consequently he is not counted on a quorum. For number of a committee, see *below*.

Guelph, rule 58. " A quorum of each standing committee shall consist of one-half the members of the committee including the mayor as a member of the committee."

The mayor here counts. For number of members composing a committee of this council see *below*, p. 327.

69. Ottawa, rule 86. " Each standing committee shall consist of one member from each ward, and all vacancies shall be filled up from time to time as they occur so that each standing committee shall always consist of one member from each ward. Provided nothing herein shall apply to the court of revision, which shall be appointed by the council as the law directs."

Ottawa rule 88 also makes the mayor *ex officio* a member of all committees.

London rules 57 and 61 are the same as Toronto rule as originally, *i.e.*, retaining words in brackets.

Hamilton rule 27 limits the number of members to one for each of the seven wards, except the claims' committee, the number of which " shall be determined by the council."

Kingston, rule 33 (in part), has : " No committee of the council shall consist of less than five members nor more than seven."

Belleville rule 56 gives one member from each ward, " excepting the executive committee, which shall consist of not less than seven nor more than nine members and the court of revision and committee on by-laws, which shall consist of five members, and in case of vacancy through death or otherwise, such vacancy may be filled by the council at any subsequent meeting.''

By rule 52 (*above*, p. 317) the mayor is *ex officio* a member of all committees of this council."

St. Catharines, rule 52. " The mayor shall be *ex officio* a member of all committees, and no committee shall consist of more than six members without the consent of the council."

For quorum, see *above*, p. 323.

Stratford, rule 60. " Each standing committee shall be composed of not less than five, nor more than seven members.''

For quorum, see *above*, p. 323.

[Continued on p. 327.

30. Meetings of Standing and Select Committees.

70. " The members of each standing committee of the council shall meet at the city hall for the purpose of organization immediately after the adjournment of the first meeting of the council."

A special and necessary rule, fixing a definite time and place of committee meetings.

By s. 15 (3), by-law 2436, it is the duty of the clerk " to notify each member of the standing committees, as soon as the appointment has been made, of the time and place at which the first meeting of the committee will be held."

Also (4), to furnish each member of the committees with a copy of the by-law 2435 [and its amendments to date], at or before the first meeting of the committees.

See also *below*, rule 76 (1).

71. " The members of each standing committee of the council shall at their first meeting proceed to elect from among themselves a chairman; and immediately after such chairman has been elected, the days of the future regular meetings of the executive committee, the committee on works, the committee on fire and light, the committee on property, and the committee on parks and gardens, shall be determined by the members thereof, and also the hour at which each of such meetings shall be held."

For parliamentary rules generally regulating committees, see *above*, pp. 48, 51.

[Continued on p. 328.

Guelph, rule 58.   "Each of the aforesaid (see *above*, p. 321, rule 57) commit-tees shall consist of five members, except the board of works which shall have an additional member, and the hereinafter named shall be composed as follows : cemetery, the mayor and one member ; police, the mayor and two members ; hospital, the mayor and one member.   The mayor shall be a member *ex officio* of each and every committee, whether standing or special, except the cemetery and hospital committees."

For quorum, see *above*, p. 325.

30. Meetings of Standing and Select Committees.

70. Belleville, rule 57 [in part].   At the city hall, "on Wednesday evening following the first meeting of the newly elected council, at half-past seven, p.m."

St. Catharines, rule 55.   At the city buildings, "within three days after that on which they are appointed, at such hour as the mayor may direct, or in default of the mayor naming such hour. the city clerk shall appoint the hour of such meeting."

Guelph, rule 59 [in part].   "At their convenience [at the city hall, it may be assumed], within at least one week of their appointment."

Stratford rule 61 requires the organization "within ten days after that on which they are appointed."

All other councils should have a similar rule.

71. Belleville, rule 57 [in part], with the addition that "no member of the council shall hold the chairmanship of more than one standing committee."

St. Catharines rule 56 with the proviso, "the interval between the meetings not to exceed one month "—a very proper regulation.

Guelph rule 59 provides that each committee shall at its first meeting elect a member thereof as chairman, and he shall forthwith notify the clerk of the council of such election."

Stratford rule 62 is the same as that of Toronto with respect to election of chairman and days of regular meetings of standing committees.

Hamilton has only following rules with respect to meetings :—

34. "Each committee shall, at its first meeting, fix the day and hour for its regular meetings during the year.

35. "Meetings of committee shall be called by the clerk on request of the chairman, or, in his absence, on request of the mayor."

Kingston, rule 34.   "No meeting of any committee shall be called upon less than six hours' notice."

London rule 67 (1) provides that every committee shall elect its own chair-man.   For rest of rule, see *below*, p. 333.

[Continued on p. 329.

72. " The regular meetings of the executive committee, the committee on works, and the committee on property, determined as aforesaid, shall be held in each alternate week, except when otherwise ordered by the council; and the other standing committees shall meet as often as may be determined upon, at the call of the chairman."

A special rule, but it is a common parliamentary practice to adjourn committees subject to call of chairman. See *above*, p. 50.

73. " Special meetings of standing committees may be called by the chairman whenever he shall consider it necessary to do so, and it shall be the duty of the chairman, or, in case of his illness or absence from the city, it shall be the duty of the clerk of the council, or the clerk of the standing committee (if a special clerk shall have been appointed in that behalf) to summon a special meeting of the committee whenever requested in writing to do so by a majority of the members composing it."

Such a rule is necessary to ensure regular meetings of committees composed of a very small number of members. Under parliamentary usage, in case a committee neglect to meet and consider the question before it, the house will intervene, if their attention is called to it, and deal with the difficulty as may be deemed most advisable (see Bourinot, p. 744).

The Guelph rules (see *below*, p. 331), provide specially for such cases.

74. " Members of the council may attend the meetings of any of its committees, but shall not be allowed to vote ; nor shall they be allowed to take part in any discussion or debate, except by the permission of the majority of the members of the committee."

This is the parliamentary rule, except as respects the permission to take part in debate (see Bourinot, p. 509).

If a member should desire to take part in the debate, the chairman should formally obtain permission from the committee by asking, " Shall Mr. A. be allowed to address the committee? "

The Toronto council has not adopted the rules (see opposite) of the London and Guelph councils, which are intended to ensure regular meetings of a committee. No committee can be allowed to evade its responsibility to report on every question regularly submitted to it. The council can intervene at any moment, under general parliamentary usage (see Bourinot, p. 744). The Guelph and London rules practically embody parliamentary usage in such cases.

[Continued on p. 330.

72. Stratford rule 63 provides that "the regular meetings of the standing committees on finance, assessment, license and printing, and of the board of works so determined (see rule 62, *above*, p. 327), shall be held once in each week preceding the regular meeting of the council, and by each of the other standing committees as often as may then be determined upon."

73. Belleville rule 58 is the same as Toronto rule 73, without the condition that the clerk of the standing committee may also call a meeting thereof. In parliament, it is the special duty of that clerk to call a meeting on the order of the committee or its chairman.

St. Catharines rule 57 same as Belleville rule 58 except the clerk can summon a special meeting only at request of a majority of two members of the committee.

Guelph, rule 61. "Each committee shall meet at the written summons of the clerk by order of the chairman, and in case of his absence, on requisition to the clerk signed by the majority of the committee, reasonable notice being given in each case."

See *below* for rule (63) of this council, providing for cases of a committee not meeting.

Stratford rule 64 is the same as that of Toronto, omitting the reference to a clerk of the standing committee.

74. Stratford, rule 65; Kingston, rule 35; Belleville, rule 59; St. Catharines, rule 58.

In the absence of an express rule, the parliamentary usage, as explained opposite, should obtain in other councils.

Belleville rule 60 allows "meetings of the standing committees" to be open to the public "in the same manner and subject to the same conditions as meetings of council."

London rules 67 (9), 68 and 69 provide as follows :

67. (9) " A chairman of committee may at any time be removed from the office of chairman at a special meeting called for the purpose, and another elected chairman in his stead.

68. " Whenever any member of a special or standing committee is about to leave the city for any period so as to interfere with or prevent his attendance at any meeting of such committee, it shall be his duty to give notice in writing of his intention to the clerk, in which notice he shall state the period during which his absence is to continue, and it shall be the duty of the clerk to cause such notice to be laid before the council at its next meeting.

[Continued on p. 331.

74*a.* "The chairmen of the standing committees of the council shall constitute a committee whose duty it shall be to allocate to each of the several aldermen a seat in the council chamber which he shall be entitled to occupy in council assembled for the current year.

(2) "It shall be the duty of the city clerk to notify the members of the said committee to meet at some time and place within ten days after the first meeting of the new council in each year.

(3) "The said committee shall, at their first meeting, elect by ballot from amongst these, a chairman, who shall preside at all meetings of the committee during the current year.

(4) "The said committee shall allocate, by ballot, or otherwise, to each alderman a seat in the council chamber and report to council, and the seats of members shall, during the current year, be those allotted to them in the said report when adopted in council.

[Continued on p. 332.

69. "The council may appoint a member thereof to act on any special or standing committee in lieu and during the absence of any member thereof who is absent from the city or unable from illness to attend the meetings of such committee, and the member so appointed shall be a member for the ward to which the absent member belongs, and shall be deemed a member of the committee, and entitled to act thereon only during such absence or illness."

Guelph, rules 63 and 64. 63. "Should a chairman of any of the aforesaid [standing or special] neglect or refuse to call a meeting of his committee at such times, or with such frequency as the proper despatch of the business entrusted to them requires, or do the business of the committee without the knowledge or consent of its members, or contrary to their wishes or sanction, the committee may report such neglect, refusal or action to the council, who may, if they deem it advisable, remove the said chairman from the committee, and appoint another in his place, and every such reconstructed committee shall have a right to appoint a chairman, who shall report such appointment to the clerk of the council."

64. "Should any member or members of any of the aforesaid committees neglect or refuse to attend the properly summoned meetings of their committees, the chairman may report such neglect or refusal to the council, who may remove the said member or members from the committee and appoint another member or other members in his or their places : or should any committee neglect or refuse to give due attention to all business or matters before them, the council may by resolution discharge such committee and appoint another in their stead."

[Continued on p. 333.

(5) " In case the seat of any alderman becomes vacant by reason of death, resignation or otherwise, the seat rendered vacant shall be allocated as aforesaid by the said committee."

The foregoing rule, added in 1890, is a special provision of this council requiring no comment. For usage in parliament, see Bourinot, p. 201.

Ottawa rule 8 and Hamilton rule 32, also provide for sitting of members in order.

31. General Regulations for Conducting Business in Select and Standing Committees.

75. " The business of the respective standing and select committees shall be conducted under the following regulations :

(1) " The chairman shall preside at every meeting, and shall vote on all questions submitted, and in case of an equal division the question shall be passed in the negative ;"

That is to say, the same practice obtains necessarily in committees as in the council with respect to divisions. The statute (see *above*, p. 247) practically regulates such matters. For parliamentary rule see *above*, p. 49.

(2) " The chairman shall sign all orders and documents which the committee may legally adopt ;"

A parliamentary usage.

(3) " In the absence of the chairman one of the other members shall be elected to preside, who shall discharge the duties of the chairman during the meeting or until the arrival of the chairman ;"

A chairman *pro tempore* can always be appointed under the parliamentary law, he leaves the chair when the regular chairman arrives.

(4) " The minutes of the transactions of every committee shall be accurately entered in a book to be provided for that purpose, and at each meeting the minutes of the preceding meeting shall be submitted for confirmation or amendment, and after they have received the approval of a majority of the members present, shall be signed by the chairman ;"

[Continued on p. 334.

31. General Regulations for Conducting Business in Select and Standing Committees.

75. The councils of Hamilton, Kingston, Brantford, Guelph, St. Catharines and Ottawa, it will be seen hereafter, have not so complete regulations as those of Toronto, Belleville, and London for the guidance of select committees. These regulations should be generally adopted :

(1) London, rule 67 (1); Belleville, rule 61 (1) ; Guelph, rule 59; Stratford, rule 74 (1).

(2) Stratford, rule 74 (2).

London, rule 67 (2) ; Belleville, rule 61 (2). See p. 335, rule 60, for duty of chairman in Guelph council as respects minutes.

(3) London, rule 67 (3); Guelph, rule 59 ; Stratford, rule 3.

Belleville, rule 61 (3) ; adds "or the adjournment," which is as a matter of course.

Kingston, rule 32. " In the absence of the chairman of any committee the committee shall have power to appoint a chairman, *pro tempore.*" Stratford rule 74 (9) is the same as foregoing.

(4) Belleville rule 61 (4). London rule 67 (4) is the same as Toronto rule opposite, but the next rules 67 (5 and 6) make this additional provision : " There shall be entered in the minute book of each committee all reports ordered to be submitted to the council, all orders passed, and all accounts audited with a reference to the by-law or resolution under which such audit is made, together with such other matters as the committee shall consider essential to a record of its proceedings. Each minute so recorded shall have attached to it a progressive number for reference, and an analytical index shall be kept for each minute book."

[Continued on p. 335.

(5) " Each minute shall have attached to it a progressive number for reference, and an analytical index shall be kept for each minute book;"

This is a parliamentary usage, in effect; see *below*, p. 357, for rule 134 with respect to minutes of the council in general.

(6) " When a division takes place on any question the votes of the members shall be recorded, if required by one of the members."

The Belleville rule opposite is more stringent.

(7) " No order or authority to do any matter or thing shall be recognized as emanating from any committee unless it is in writing,

[Continued on p. 336.

Stratford rule 74 (4) is the same as Toronto rule opposite, but a later rule 66 requires the book always kept in the custody of the clerk of the council.

Hamilton, rule 33. "All chairmen of standing committees shall keep minutes of their proceedings in a book to be furnished for that purpose by the clerk, and such book will be left with the clerk at the expiration of office."

Guelph, rule 60. "Each committee, standing or special, shall keep a proper record of its proceedings in a book for that purpose, and shall confirm the minutes of the meeting. All motions shall be moved and seconded and entered on the minutes. All reports before presentation to the council must be entered in the minute book, signed by the chairman and members of the committee either for or against as each member voted, and must be presented to the council in such book."

Other cities have no such special rules, but similar books should be provided and kept as set forth in the Toronto rule.

(5) Stratford, rule 74 (6); London, rule 67 (6), (see *above*, p 333).

Belleville, rule 61 (5, 6). "There shall be entered on the minute of each standing committee, all reports ordered to be submitted to the executive committee or to the council, all orders that may be passed, and such other matters as the committee shall consider essential to a correct exhibition of its proceedings and each minute recorded shall have attached to it a progressive number for reference."

"The minute books of all special committees together with the reports and documents to be laid before the council, shall be placed in the possession of the executive committee at each regular meeting to be referred by said executive committee to the council, with or without any report thereon as may be deemed advisable and all reports of special committees shall be submitted to the executive committee before being received by the council, unless the council otherwise determines.

Other councils should have this convenient practice.

Stratford rule 74 (6) is the same as that of Toronto. The same council has also additional rule 74 (5): "There shall be entered in the minute book of each committee all reports ordered to be submitted to the council, all orders passed, and all accounts audited with a reference to the by-law or resolution under which such audit is made, together with such other matters as the committee shall consider essential to a record of its proceedings."

(6) London rule 67 (7); Belleville rule 61 (8). "Where a decision takes place on any question all the members of the committee present shall vote unless excused by the committee, and the votes shall be recorded if required by one of the members, and in the event of any member refusing to vote without being excused, his vote shall be counted in the negative."

See a similar rule as to votes in the council itself, *above*, p. 273, rule 13.

Stratford rule 74 (7) same as that of Toronto.

(7) London, rule 67 (8); Belleville, rule 61 (7); Stratford, rule 74 (8).

[Continued on p. 337.

nor unless it is signed by the chairman, or acting chairman, or secretary thereof and refers to the minute of the board or committee under which it is issued."

The council and its officers have no cognizance of the action of a committee until it makes a report in writing signed by the chairman, on any subject properly under its purview.

76. "It shall be the duty of the secretary of every standing and select committee :"

By by-law 2436, s. 15 (5) it is the duty of the clerk of the council "to attend or cause an assistant to attend, all meetings of the standing and special committees of the council, except the executive committee, the committee on works, [and the committee on water works]." The latter committee is now incorporated with the committee on works ; see *below*, p. 349, s. 88 (7).

Also (6) "To keep or cause to be kept full and accurate minutes of the meetings of all committees, which minutes shall have a progressive marginal number for each minute, and to index the minute book within one week after any meeting."

Also (7) "To communicate or convey to committees petitions or other documents referred to them by the council."

Also (8) "To furnish the solicitor, the treasurer, the secretary of the committee on works and the chairman of the other committees, with certified copies of all resolutions, enactments, and orders of the council, relative to the matters over which the said officers and committees may respectively have jurisdiction, on the day next succeeding that upon which the action of the council in respect thereof takes place."

(1) "To cause a notice of each regular and special meeting of such committee to be served on each of the members thereof, at their residence or ordinary place of business, and also upon the mayor, [city solicitor, city treasurer, city engineer, and city commissioner] on the day previous to such meeting being held ;"

The brackets are mine, see opposite.

The parliamentary usage as respects duty of a clerk of a committee is herein set forth.

See previous note and *above*, rule 70.

(2) "To attend all meetings of the committee [when required so to do by the chairman or acting chairman thereof], and to record the minutes, orders, and requests of all such meetings."

[Continued on p. 338.

76. In the Belleville council rule 84 requires the clerk of the council " to act as secretary of all standing committees, keep their minutes and prepare their reports for the council." In some large councils there is another clerk (the assistant) who generally acts for committees.

For duties of Stratford clerk, see *below*, p. 378.

(1) London rule 75 (2) except that, of course, all the officers mentioned and bracketed by me after " mayor " in Toronto rule are not specified.

Brantford rule 36 requires the "clerk of the council as soon as the standing committees are appointed, to post the names of the members of each in some conspicuous place in the council chamber and keep them so posted throughout the year."

This is a parliamentary usage, and should obtain in all councils.

London, rule 75 (1). The words in brackets are not in this rule, but they are not necessary since the secretary always acts under the orders of the chairman.

The London rule 75 (3) has also the following duty of the secretary:

" To prepare all reports from the committees in presentation to council or otherwise."

A necessary duty of the secretary of every such committee.

[Continued on p. 339.

The brackets are mine, see opposite.

The parliamentary usage as respects the duties of a clerk of a committee as here set forth.

77. "The general duties of all the standing and select committees of the council shall be as follows :—

(1) " To report to the council from time to time, whenever desired by the council, and as often as the interests of the city may require, on all matters connected with the duties imposed on them respectively, and to recommend such action by the council in relation thereto as may be deemed necessary ;"   ·

If they do not report as instructed, the council may intervene (see *above*, p. 328).

[Continued on p. 341.

77.

(1) London, rule 70 (1) ; Belleville, rule 62 (1) ; Stratford, rule 75 (1).

Ottawa council has the following special rules as to reports :

93. " Standing and special committees to whom references are made, shall in all cases report in writing the state of facts with their opinions thereon, which report shall be signed by a majority of the committee, and no such report shall be received unless so signed.

94. " All reports of committees shall be addressed to " the corporation of the city of Ottawa. They shall briefly describe the matters referred to and the conclusion shall be summed up in the form of an order, resolution or recommendation."

95. " All members of a committee approving of a report or proceeding of a committee, shall sign the same and those members not signing shall be deemed to have dissented therefrom."

Ottawa rule 91 also provides : " On the acceptance of a final report, from a special committee the said committee shall be considered discharged."

This does not apply to standing committees which meet and report during the whole term of their legal existence on the subjects that come under their purview, but only to committees appointed for a special purpose. A similar practice obtains in parliament.

Kingston, rules 32, 33. " Committees appointed to report on any subject referred to them by the council shall report a statement of facts, and also their opinion thereon in writing, and no report shall be received unless the same be signed by a majority of the committee."

St. Catharines rule 16 is the same as the foregoing.

Kingston rule 33 also adds : " And no report shall be received from any committee unless agreed to in committee actually assembled for the transaction of business."

Guelph, rule 62. " Each of the aforesaid committees [standing or special] shall report on every matter and question referred to them, at the first regular meeting of the council next after the time of reference, unless otherwise instructed in the order or resolution of reference, and each committee shall properly number and endorse their reports in the order of their presentation."

See *above*, p. 333, for signing of reports by chairman and members of a Guelph committee ; also (*above*, p. 331) for proceedings in case of the committees not meeting through neglect of chairman or for other reasons ; also (*below*, p. 363) for reports of standing committees on financial and special matters referred to them.

[Continued on p. 341.

(2) " To prepare and introduce into the council all by-laws as may be necessary to give effect to such of their reports or recommendations as are adopted by the council ;"

Their report will include drafts of any by-laws which they have a right to consider under the regulations of the council.

(3) " To give effect through the proper officer to all by-laws and resolutions of the council that relate to their duties ;"

(4) " To examine all accounts connected with the discharge of their duties, or with the performance of any works, or the purchase of any material or goods, under their supervision ;"

The rules *below* (pp. 344 *et seq.*), show how very onerous are the duties of the standing committees of large cities like Toronto.

(5) " To consider, and report on, any and all matters referred to them by the council or the mayor ; and every such report shall be signed by the chairman bringing up the same ;"

The first part of this rule is practically embraced in No. (1) 77, but the latter part is uecessary in all cases.

See *below*, p. 357, rule 133, as to sending reports of committees to members of council at their residence or place of business.

(6) " To adhere strictly, in the transaction of all business to the rules prescribed by the by-laws of the council ;"

Such a rule is seemingly unnecessary—the by-laws must govern in all cases.

(7) " To present to the council on or before the last regular meeting of the council, in each and every year, for the information of the council, and of the citizens generally, as well as for the guidance of the committees of the following year, a general report of the state of the various matters referred to them respectively during the year, the work or business done through or by each committee, and the expenditure made under their authority or superintendence. Such report shall also state the number of meetings called by each committee during the year ; the number of the meetings at which a quorum was present ; the number of times each member was absent ; and such report shall contain

[Continued on p. 342.

(2) London, rule 70 (2) ; Stratford, rule 75 (2) ; Belleville, rule 62 (2). All committees appointed to consider a special subject would, in the absence of an express rule or instruction to the contrary, have authority to report a by-law in reference to that subject.

(3) London, rule 70 (3) ; Belleville, rule 62 (3) ; Stratford, rule 75 (3).

(4) London rule 70 (4), except it uses "audit" instead of "examine" the result is the same.

Stratford rule 75 (4) and Belleville rule 62 (4) same as London rule.

(5) London, rule 70 (5) ; Belleville, rule 62 (5) ; Stratford, rule 75 (5).

(6) London, rule 70 (6); Belleville, rule 62 (6) ; Stratford, rule 75 (6).

(7) London, rule 70 (7) ; Belleville, rule 62 (7) ; Stratford, rule 75 (7).

[Continued on p. 343.

such suggestions in regard to the future action of the succeeding committees as experience may enable the reporting committee to make in respect of the matters embraced in their report;"

A special rule in the interest of sound legislation.

(8) "To see that the persons in office, or appointed to office, connected with the department of each respective committee, have given, or do give, the necessary security for the performance of their duties, and in the case of any new appointment, that the security is given before any such person enters upon his duties."

(3) London, rule 70 (8) ; Stratford, rule 75 (8) ; Belleville, rule 62 (8).

Sub-committees.

Belleville has also this additional rule :—62 (9). "Any committee may appoint one or more sub-committees from amongst its own members to perform such duties as it may from time to time assign to them and to report to such committee."

Such sub-committees are found very convenient in parliamentary usage (see Bourinot, p. 513) but as set forth in the foregoing rule, each must report to the committee of which it forms a part, and its report can only appear as the report of that committee or as an appendix to the same.

In the absence of any express rule to the contrary, the committees of all councils can properly make use of this convenient practice of parliament.

----

32. SPECIAL RULES

OF

TORONTO, LONDON, GUELPH, BELLEVILLE, KINGSTON, ST. CATHARINES, STRATFORD, HAMILTON, AND OTTAWA, RELATING TO MONEY APPROPRIATIONS, CIVIC OFFICERS AND COMMITTEES.

So far we have been able to make comparisons on opposite pages between the rules of all the cities of Toronto, London (which includes St. Thomas), Stratford, Kingston, Belleville, Hamilton, St. Catharines, Guelph, Brantford, and Ottawa. It is now necessary to complete this review of procedure by giving the special rules of a number of the councils with respect to money appropriations and the duties of their officers and committees, those of Toronto, it will be seen, being notably elaborate in the case of the committees. No comments are necessary in respect to such special rules, which are not, generally speaking, governed by the rules and usages common to parliament. Each council must work out such rules in accordance with their own regular practice and legal interpretation.

33. OTTAWA.

1. Duties of clerk—

96. The clerk shall duly record in a book without note or comment, all resolutions, decisions and other proceedings of the council, and if required by any member present shall record the name and vote of every member voting on any matter submitted, and shall keep the books, records and accounts of the council, and shall preserve and file all accounts acted upon by the council, and also the originals or certified copies of all by-laws, and of all minutes of the proceedings of the council, in the safe in his office or other place appointed by by-law of the council.

97. The clerk shall cause the minutes of the council to be printed after each meeting, and a copy of said minutes to be delivered to or left at the residence of each member of the council one day at least before the next ordinary meeting thereof.

98. The clerk shall cause to be duly served all notices for special meetings and all reports, enquiries or other papers necessary to be served on the members of the council or any of them.

2. Money appropriations—

99. All appropriations of money shall be submitted to a committee of the whole before being taken up in full council.

100. No money appropriation shall be finally acted upon by the council until it shall have been first referred to the standing committee on finance, and no money shall be paid by the treasurer, nor shall any expenditure be authorized by any member of the council, without a resolution of the council ordering the same and specifying the amount, or unless authorized in that behalf by some law or by-law of the said corporation.

34. TORONTO RULES.

1. Executive committee—

78. No by-law, resolution, report, contract, order, engagement, nomination, or other proceeding of the council, or of any standing or special committee (other than the executive committee), or of any officer or agent of the corporation :—

(1) Involving an expenditure of money (except as in this by-law is provided) or

(2) For the appropriation of any part of the city revenue to any purpose, or

(3) For the remission or refunding of any taxes, rentals, licenses, fees, or other moneys whereby the revenue of the city may be affected or diminished, shall have any legal effect or operation until the same shall have been laid before the executive committee for the then present year, and supervised, recommended, and reported on by them, and until such report shall have been adopted by the council; and in case the executive committee disapproves of any such expenditure, appropriation, remuneration, or refund (wholly or in part), then such expenditure, appropriation, remuneration, or refund shall not be made except upon a vote of two-thirds of the members of the council then present and voting.

79. The executive committee shall have the right to object to any claim or account, or to any by-law, resolution, report, contract, order, engagement, nomination, or other proceeding relating to expenditure or revenue as in the preceding section mentioned :—

(1) Where the law or by-laws of the council have not been complied with ;

(2) Where the appropriation made to any standing or special committee would be exceeded ;

(3) Where the appropriation to any special work or service would be exceeded ; or

(4) Where for any work or service an expenditure would be required beyond the estimates for the then current year, and in all cases where objection is taken by the said committee on any of the grounds aforesaid, the report of the committee shall be final, unless upon an appeal to the council such report shall be varied or rejected by a vote of two-thirds of the members of the council then present and voting.

80. Notwithstanding anything in the last two preceding sections contained in all cases where the expenditure of money is contemplated, and a by-law or resolution of the council is, at any time, adopted by a vote of two-thirds of the members of the council then present and voting, that the executive committee shall report and provide funds to meet any expenditure mentioned in such by-law or resolution, the executive committee shall, as soon as may be, report as the council shall have ordered, as aforesaid ; and when a by-law or resolution is adopted by the council ordering the executive committee to report and provide funds, the yeas and nays shall be recorded ; and further, in all cases where a report originates in the executive committee, whether it relates either to an expenditure of money or to the revenue of the city, or to any other matter, such report of the executive committee may be amended or rejected by a vote of a majority of the members of the council then present and voting ; and such majority of the council may reject or reduce the amount of any expenditure contained in any report whatever, either of the executive committee or other standing or special committee of the council.

81. The executive committee shall supervise all accounts, claims, expenditure, and outlay exceeding the sum of $10, either of the council or of any standing or select committee, or of any officer or agent of the corporation, and also all claims under any contract with the corporation, and shall require the law and all

by-laws and resolutions of the council with respect thereto to be complied with
before any payments are made for or on account thereof; and no such account,
claim, expenditure, outlay, or claim under any contract with the corporation not
expressly authorized to be paid by law or by a by-law or resolution of the council
shall be paid, nor shall any payment be made on account thereof, by the treasurer
or other officer of the corporation, until the same shall have been first laid before
the executive committee and shall have been supervised, recommended, and
reported on by them, and the report shall have been adopted by the council.

[It is the duty of the city treasurer to act as secretary to the executive committee, and keep a record of all minutes, orders, and reports, but the committee may,
from time to time, allow the assistant treasurer or one of the clerks in the office
of the treasurer to act as such secretary. For his important duties in connection
with this committee, see especially by-laws 2436 and 3119].

82. Notwithstanding anything in this by-law contained, the treasurer of the
city may pay :—

(1) All sums not exceeding $10, on the order of the mayor, or, in his absence,
on the order of the alderman acting for him, or the chairman of the executive
committee ; the account therefor having been first certified by the superior officer,
under whose supervision the expenditure was incurred ;

(2) All daily and weekly wages appearing by any pay-sheet to be due any
person in the employ of the corporation, all accounts for freight charges, customs
duties, telegrams, insurance premiums on city property, or for gas or light supplied
to city buildings, and when the council does not hold fortnightly meetings, between
the 20th July and the 20th September in any year, all progress certificates (but
not final certificates), given for any contract bearing the city seal which may accrue
due to any person ; and every such pay-sheet, account, or progress certificate shall
be duly certified and signed by the superior officer of the department in which such
payments are due, or under whose supervision such contract is being performed,
and also by the chairman of the committee of the council having control of the
same, and countersigned by the mayor, or, in his absence, by the chairman of the
executive committee. The particulars of all such payments shall be included in
the next report to the council of the committee having charge of the service,
matter, or work in respect of which such payments are respectively made.

83. The treasurer shall carry the unexpended balances at the credit of any of
the committees or other services on the 31st December in any year to the credit of
the several committees or services [by-law 3110], after making due provision for
all ascertained liabilities on account of such services.

84. It shall further be the duty of the executive committee :—

(1) To present to the council, on or before the last Monday in April in each
year, a full and particular exhibit of the financial affairs of the city at the termination of the preceding financial year, and the estimates of the amount required to
be raised by assessment during the current year ;

(2) To recommend for appointment by the council, at an early day in each
year, after the adoption of the estimates, the names of such number of fit and

proper persons to be collectors of taxes as may be necessary for the performance of that duty ;

(3) To introduce a by-law after the adoption of estimates in each year to regulate the manner in which the revenue required for the current year shall be raised ;

(4) To consider and report as often as may be necessary, on the management of all matters connected with the railway stock, bonds, or other securities held by the corporation ;

(5) To have the supervision of the books of account, and of all documents and vouchers, moneys, debentures, and securities, in the treasurer's office ;

(7) To advise the treasurer when called upon to do so, in all matters pertaining to his office ;

(7) To see that all duties which ought to be performed by the treasurer and the officers in his department are properly executed ;

(8) To forbid the signing or delivery of any chequés, or of any security, or the payment of any money by the treasurer, if they shall think it expedient so to do, until the matter can be further considered, or can be referred to the council ;

(9) To regulate all matters connected with the receipt and payment of money, and to order the adoption of such regulations in connection therewith, as may be deemed necessary for the prevention of any payment being made in contravention of the by-laws and resolutions of the council, and generally to manage the financial affairs of the city [including the rating and collecting of water rates].

[The words in brackets were added by by-law 3119.]

(10) To direct the purchase of books and stationery for the several departments of the corporation, the advertisement of the city notices, and the performance of the corporation printing, and from time to time report thereon to the council ;

(11) To cause to be furnished to the council, not later than the second meeting of the council in every month, after the passing of the annual estimates and from month to month, a statement of all amounts expended during the previous month by every committee, and the balance remaining at the credit of such committee, which statement shall be according to the form " A " in the schedule to this by-law.

[By sec. 2, by-law 2985 it is also provided that the executive committee shall, in addition to its other duties, perform those heretofore performed by the committee on legislation and the reception committee].

(12) To consider and report on all matters for which it may be necessary for the city to seek legislation.

(13) To attend to all matters in connection with receptions and entertainments of a public character under the direction of the council.

[By by-law 3119 (s. 12) the financial portion of the water-works department, including the officers, rating and collection of water rates, is under the executive committee. The works and property of the water-works under the direction of the committee on works (see *below*, s. 88, sub-s. 7)].

85. The minutes of proceedings of all other committees shall be furnished to the executive committee from time to time, when required by the executive committee.

86. In cases of emergency or necessity, and on a report in writing from the superior officer or assistant officer of the department in which the emergency or necessity arises, stating generally the locality and nature of the service required, and probable cost of the work to be done, and upon the chairman of the committee to which the same appertains, endorsing thereon his approval and the date of his signing the same, a sum not exceeding $200 in all for any one service or work, may be expended by the committee in charge of such work or service; and it shall be the duty of the officer reporting thereon to forward a copy of such report forthwith, or at latest within twenty-four hours after the same has been signed by the chairman of the committee, to the chairman of the executive committee: and the executive committee shall have power to order the work to cease, if they deem it prudent so to do, and the said work or service shall be reported by the chairman of the committee in whose department the work or service is required, at the next meeting of the council thereafter, and on his default, the chairman of the executive committee at such meeting, or at latest at the next subsequent meeting of the council, shall make a report of the work or service ordered to be done or countermanded by the executive committee.

87. No committee or officer of the council shall exceed the appropriation made to any committee for the purpose, nor shall any committee, without the approval of the executive committee and of the council, expend money appropriated to any particular purpose on any other purpose, work, or service. ·

2. Committee on works—

88. In addition to the duties prescribed by law or by section 77 of this by-law, or by any other by-law of the city, the duties of the committee on works shall be as follows:—

(1) To consider and report on all matters relating to sewers, drains, streets, lanes, alleys, and public thoroughfares, except such as specially pertain to other boards or committees;

(2) To report and recommend to the council such regulations for the control of drains and fences as may be requisite for the public safety and welfare;

(3) To recommend to the council, at the end of each year, such works of permanent improvement under their control which they consider essential for the welfare and convenience of the citizens to be carried out during the ensuing year, together with the estimated cost of the works so recommended;

(4) To see that the duties of the city engineer and his staff are properly executed:

(5) To give effect to all orders of the council in relation to the performance of works under other committees;

(6) To confer from time to time with any other committee, commission, or company having any special or statutory right in the streets, so as to provide a

uniform system of opening up streets, or breaking in upon the macadamized or paved portions thereof, with the least possible damage thereto.

(7) To manage and report on all matters relating to the water-works of the city and property of the city connected therewith, except as to the financial portion of the water-works department, including the offices, rating and collecting of the water rates, which are to be placed under the direction of the city treasurer, and under the control of the executive committee.

[Sec. 89 repealed by by-law 3119 and the duties of committees on markets and licenses added to those of the committee on property. See *below*, sec. 92, sub-s. 7-11].

[Sec. 90 with respect to committee on water-works repealed by by-law 3119 and the duties of that committee added to those of the committee on works. See *above*, sec. 88. subs. 7].

3. Committee on fire and light—

91. In addition to the duties prescribed by law or by section 77 of this by-law, or by any other by-law of the city, the duties of the standing committee on fire and light shall be as follows :—

(1) To manage the fire department of the city, and the buildings and property connected therewith, and report on the organization, strength, and efficiency of the fire department ;

(2) To report on the lighting of the city, on the erection of lamps and electric lights, and the inspection of gas meters ;

(3) To consider and report on all matters connected with the establishment of fire limits, the inspection of buildings with reference thereto, and the prosecution of offenders against such regulations as may be enacted ;

(4) To confer with the committee on works, so as to provide a uniform system of opening up streets or breaking in upon the macadamized or paved portions thereof with the least possible damage thereto.

4. Committee on property—

92. In addition to the duties prescribed by-law, or by section 77 of this by-law, or by any other by-law of the city, the duties of the committee on property shall be as follows :—

(1) To manage and report on all matters connected with wharfs and other property of the city abutting on the waters of the bay;

(2) To manage and report, in conjunction with the executive committee, on all matters relating to the filling in of water lots, the adjustment of the amount to be charged to the respective owners of water lots in respect of said work, and the assessment therefor, in accordance with the legislative enactments in relation -hereto;

(3) To manage and control, subject to the approval of the council, all city property except the lands in actual use for park purposes, and such lands, buildings and property as by this by-law or any other by-law is placed under the control or management of any other committee or authority ;

(4) To consider and report (in conjunction with the executive committee) on all matters connected with the sale or disposal of the lands deeded to the city of Toronto by the trustees named in a certain patent from the crown, dated one thousand eight hundred and eighteen, and which lands are commonly known as public walks and gardens, and to manage and direct the disposal of the funds accruing from such sales, in such manner as may be consistent with the acts of the legislature in that behalf, and most conducive to the interests of the city ;

(5) To consider and report on all matters connected with the leasing or selling of city property ;

(6) To manage and report on all matters in connection with the purchase of sites for public buildings, and the erection and maintenance of all buildings erected thereon, where the same are under their management or control.

(7) To manage, and report on, all affairs relating to the regulations of the public markets and weigh-houses, the inspection of weights and measures, the prevention of forestalling or regrating, the regulation of the assize of bread, the dealings of hucksters, the cleaning of markets, and the prevention of the sale of tainted or unwholesome food ;

(8) To report on the levying and collecting of market dues or tolls and weigh-house fees, and the rental of market stalls ;

(9) To attend to all matters pertaining to cleaning and watering the public streets and lanes, and the scavenger work of the city ;

(10) To regulate all matters connected with the gaol ;

(11) To regulate all matters connected with licenses issued by the corporation,

[By sec. 2 of by-law 2985 it is provided that :—

" The committee on property shall, in addition to its other duties, perform those heretofore performed by the court house committee]."

5. Committee on parks and gardens—

93. In addition to the duties prescribed by law or by section 77 of this by-law, or by any other by-law of the city, the duties of the committee on parks and gardens shall be as follows :—

(1) To manage and report on all matters connected with the preservation of grounds set apart for public parks, squares, gardens, walks and avenues, and the buildings erected therein, and to prevent encroachments on such properties ;   ·

(2) To report on all matters connected with fencing, ornamenting and preserving of parks, squares, gardens, walks or avenues, as aforesaid, and to carry out all works connected therewith, as the council may authorize.

94. [By by-law 2985 the duties of the committee on legislation are now performed by the executive committee, see *above*, p. 347].

95. [See *above*, p. 347. The duties of the reception committee are now performed by the executive committee under by-law 2985].

6. Matters not specially appertaining to any committee—

96. All matters not designated as belonging or appertaining to any of the foregoing committees shall belong to and be under the control of the executive committee, unless the council shall refer the same to some other committee.

7. Money appropriations, accounts, expenditures, contracts and improvements—

97. Except as herein otherwise provided no committee or member of the council, and no officer of the corporation, shall on behalf of the corporation enter into any contract, or incur or authorize any expenditure, without having obtained, by by-law or resolution, the sanction of the council; and no contract shall be entered into until the necessary appropriation shall have been made, either from the public funds or by the passing of a local improvement by-law.

98. No contract or expenditure shall be authorized or permitted in contemplation of a loan, whereby a debt is incurred requiring the approval of the ratepayers, until after the by-law for such a loan or debt has been approved of by the ratepayers, according to law, and passed by the council.

99. No work or improvement shall be authorized by the council, without either having an estimate of the probable cost thereof (or in the absence of an estimate) limiting an amount therefor ; and no contract shall be entered into for any work or improvement at a larger sum, or involving a larger expenditure, than the amount so estimated or limited. Whenever such amount is found insufficient, the fact shall be immediately reported to the council.

100. When money is duly authorized to be expended for any purpose, the amount to be expended is not to be credited by the treasurer to any committee, but he is to credit the same to an account to be opened for the object for which the money is voted, and he shall at the same time charge the amount against the fund out of which the same is to be paid, so as to show how much of such fund is from time to time appropriated ; and he shall afterwards charge against the account which is to receive the credit, the sums from time to time paid of the amount so voted.

101. In case money appropriated to any particular purpose exceeds the amount which such purpose is afterwards found to require, the treasurer shall carry the surplus to the credit of an account to be opened in his books for unappropriated money, or carry it to the general credit of the city on resolution of the council authorizing the same.

102. No money voted or raised for any purpose shall be applied to any other purpose, without expressly rescinding or repealing the resolution or by-law under which the same was voted or raised, so far as such resolution or by-law stated the purpose.

103. Every report recommending the expenditure of money shall state the grounds on which the recommendation is made, with sufficient fulness to enable the council to judge of the propriety of the proposed expenditure.

104. In case the expenditure is for any work or improvement the superintendence of which, if authorized, would fall within the duty of the city engineer or some other superior officer of the corporation, the committee shall first procure a report from such engineer or other officer on the subject of the proposed expenditure, and showing how far the same is, in his opinion, necessary or expedient for the general interests or requirements of the city.

105. No report of a committee recommending any expenditure for any work or improvement, shall be received by the council, unless accompanied by the report of the proper officer, as is in the last preceding section provided, except in cases of emergency, to be fully shown in the report of the committee, and assented to by a vote of two-thirds of the members of the council then present and voting.

106. When a committee in a report recommends, or any member of the council by resolution proposes the construction of any improvement, or the expenditure of money, for or in respect of property of any kind, it shall be the duty of such committee, or member, as the case may be, to ascertain, as far as practicable, whether such improvement passes through or along any property in which any member of the council or officer of the corporation is interested, or whether any member or officer is interested in the property for or in respect of which the money is proposed to be expended, and to report or state the facts to the council. When a committee reports that a member or officer of the corporation is interested in the property so benefited as aforesaid, no action shall be taken or permitted upon such report until the information in the possession of the committee is laid before the council, except in cases of emergency, and with the sanction of two-thirds of the members of the council then present and voting.

107. With the view of preventing members and officers of the corporation from being interested in contracts, it is hereby expressly declared that no member of the council, and no officer of the corporation, shall be interested in a private capacity, directly or indirectly, in any contract or agreement for labour, or for any materials, goods, wares or merchandise furnished to the city, wherein the city is a party interested.

108. Any violation of the provisions of the last preceding section of this by-law on the part of any officer of the corporation, shall subject him to forfeiture of his office and immediate removal therefrom.

109. No account or claim against the city, arising out of or connected with any contract, agreement, purchase or sale, made contrary to section 107 of this by-law, shall be certified by any engineer or other officer of the corporation, or approved by any committee, or the chairman thereof, or paid by the treasurer.

110. Every contract shall contain a clause declaring that the contract is entered into on the part of the corporation in full faith that no member of the council or officer of the corporation has any interest whatever therein, and further declaring that the persons contracting, and their representatives, are to forfeit all

claims under the contract, and for all work done, or materials, goods, wares, or merchandise furnished under it, if it shall appear that any member of the council or officer of the corporation is at the time interested therein, or if any interest therein is afterwards given or agreed to be given to any such member or officer, and providing that no payment shall be required unless a declaration, as required by the next succeeding section of this by-law, is made at the time of requiring payment.

111. Every account for work done, or materials, goods, wares, or merchandise furnished for the corporation shall, before the same is paid, be accompanied by a written or printed declaration by the person claiming the same, and signed by him, to the effect that no member of the council, or officer of the corporation, is, in a private capacity, directly or indirectly interested in such account, or in any part of the work or materials mentioned therein, or of the money thereby claimed, and that the said account attached thereto amounts to the sum of $——. If in consequence of the absence, or for other sufficient cause, the person, or one or more of the persons claiming such payment, cannot make the required declaration, the executive committee may in lieu thereof receive such other evidence of the facts, and may take such other declaration as they may consider satisfactory, and shall in such case report what they do to the council. The committee to whose department the account relates, or the executive committee, may, if they see fit, require the declaration in any case to be taken before the mayor.

112. No property or material belonging to the corporation shall be delivered to, or used by any person, nor shall any person, other than the superior officer of a department, take, on account of the corporation, any such property or material, unless he shall first have made a requisition in writing for the said property or material so required, designating particularly the kind, quality and quantity of the said property or material, and the work for which the same is required ; and should the property or material so required be on hand, or contracted for delivery, and the person applying therefor be entitled thereto for the work in question, it shall be the duty of such superior officer, or person in charge of the department, to deliver such property or material to such person, or give him an order therefor, as the case may be, and take his receipt therefor.

113. No contractor or other person engaged on any work for the city shall be paid the compensation allowed him by his contract, or any part thereof (unless otherwise provided for by his contract), unless at the time of paying the same he shall present to the treasurer a certificate from the superior officer, or person in charge of the department having control of the work, stating that he has examined, measured, and computed the work, and that the same was completed, or that the payment commanded was due on such work; and also stating the nature of the work on which such money is due.

[The following section was added to by-law 2435 by by-law 2854 in 1891].

114. (1) Every account for work done, for material, goods, wares or merchandise furnished for the corporation of the city of Toronto, shall, before the same is considered or recommended for payment by any committee, be examined, checked

and certified by the superior officer under whose superintendence the work was done, or material, goods, wares or merchandise provided ;

(2) After being so certified, the account shall be forwarded to the city treasurer for further examination and for entry in the " appropriation ledger, " and the accountant of the city treasurer's department shall, after entering the same in the said ledger, endorse his initials thereon, if there is a sufficient appropriation to meet the required expenditure, or, if otherwise, shall so certify on the back of the account ;

(3) The account shall then be forwarded by the city treasurer to the committee under whose authority the expenditure was made, and (if so initialled) shall be examined by said committee, and, if approved, shall be recommended for payment before being presented to the executive committee for presentation to the council, and such certificate shall also refer in some distinct manner to the by-law or resolution of the council by or under which the expenditure was authorized ;

(4) After payment of the account has been ordered by the council, the city auditors shall examine and audit the same before payment thereof, and no account shall be paid by the city treasurer until the city auditors have first certified that the same has passed through the stages required by this by-law, and may be legally paid by the corporation of the city of Toronto ;

(5) Forthwith after the certificate of the said auditor has been endorsed thereon, the city treasurer shall pay the same out of the funds of the corporation in his hands or under his control, and if the funds of the corporation are in a bank, the city treasurer shall have the proper cheque prepared and signed by himself and the mayor, or acting mayor, so that prompt payment of the said account may be thereupon made.

115. Whenever work is done or material supplied under a written contract, no account or estimate for such work or material, or any part thereof, shall be certified by the chief officer of the department, or paid by the treasurer until the complete execution of the contract and bond (if any) shall first have been certified by the city solicitor.

116. In case a committee has reason to believe that any member of the council or officer of the corporation is interested in any account presented for the approval of such committee, it shall be the duty of such committee to withhold any certificate, and to give the parties interested or supposed to be interested in the account an opportunity of disproving the supposed interest; and if they fail to do so to the satisfaction of such committee, it shall be the duty of the committee to report the same forthwith to the council,

117. The treasurer, for the convenience of parties, shall provide printed forms for the necessary certificates and declaration, such forms being subject to the approval of the executive committee.

118. No money shall be paid to any member of the council, or to any officer of the corporation, as agent or attorney, or in any manner for or on behalf of a contractor.

119. No member of the council shall direct or interfere with the performance of any work for the corporation; and the officer in charge shall be subject only to his superior officer (if any) and to the council, or to the committee to which the council may in any case give authority in that behalf.

8. Tenders—

120. All work and material exceeding in value $200 shall be done and provided by contract, and after tenders have been advertised for at least ten days, or called for in any other manner which the extent and importance of the work may in the discretion of the committee having charge of the matter consider necessary. In case of an emergency rendering it necessary to dispense with this rule, such dispensation shall require the sanction of a majority, and in no case less than five of the members of the committee having charge of the matter; and every such case is to be entered in the minutes of the committee and to be reported to the council at its next meeting, with the reason which rendered it necessary to dispense with this rule.

121. Every tender for work or for the supply of material shall be accompanied at the time of its delivery to the proper officer of the corporation with a cheque marked good or a cash deposit equal to five per cent. of the whole amount of the contract for which such tender shall be made or put in when the amount of the contract does not exceed $1,000, and for all contracts over $1,000, the amount of such cash deposit shall be two and one-half per cent. of the whole amount of the contract: and every such cheque or cash deposit shall be forwarded to and remain in the custody of the city treasurer, and by him be placed to the credit of a special account, entitled "contractors' deposits" until the contract for which such tender shall have been put in has been awarded by the committee, when all cheques or cash deposits except those of the two lowest tenderers shall be forthwith returned to them unless the committee otherwise orders, and when the contract has been awarded by the council, all such cheques and deposits, except those of the successful tenderers shall be forthwith returned, but the cheques or deposits of the successful tenderers shall remain on deposit until after the execution of the contract, and bond (if any required) for the work or material, as the case may be, has been certified by the city solicitor ; and in all cases where a tender has been accepted and the party tendering fails to execute his contract and furnish the requisite bonds and sureties, the sum deposited shall be forfeited to the use of the city.

9. Contracts by day labour—

122. Notwithstanding anything in the two last preceding sections contained, the council may, by resolution to be passed by two-thirds of the members then present, and voting, direct that any particular work or undertaking may be done by day labour instead of by contract.

123. Upon a resolution being passed, as in the last preceding section mentioned, the city engineer, with such assistants, inspectors, mechanics, workmen and labourers as he may require, shall be authorized to perform such work as such resolution may authorize.

124. For the purposes mentioned in the last preceding section, and under the authority of the resolution as aforesaid, the city engineer may engage and employ such assistants, inspectors, mechanics, workmen, labourers and other persons, together with such horses, carts, and other means for the removal or supply of material as he thinks necessary and from time to time may require; and may purchase all tools, implements, and material as may be necessary for the proper carrying on of the work referred to in the resolution, subject, however, to the approval of the committee on works.

125. The city engineer shall have complete control over all persons employed upon such work, and shall have the right to dismiss and discharge any person so employed whenever he thinks fit.

126. Such work shall be carried on according to plans and specifications to be prepared in the office of the city engineer before such work is undertaken ; and all persons so employed by the city engineer upon or in connection with such work shall be paid weekly according to the pay sheets which shall be furnished to the city treasurer, and certified by the city engineer.

127. All accounts for material, implements, tools, and other supplies for the work referred to in the resolution shall be paid monthly upon the certificate of the city engineer.

128. The city engineer shall at each regular meeting of the committee on works during the time such work or undertaking may be in progress, lay before the said committee a statement of account showing the total amount of money expended to date, and the amount of money expended since his last preceding statement, distinguishing the amounts paid for—(1) material and supplies, (2) engineering, assistants and inspection, (3) work and labour ; and the statement shall show the progress made and the amount of work done.

129. The city engineer shall report at least monthly, so far as he is able, how the cost of the work done and the material supplied for the work authorized by such resolution, compares with the cost of the said work and materials, as shown by him in his estimates to the committee on works before such work was authorized to be undertaken.

130. Notwithstanding anything in the preceding sections contained, any resolutions passed under the provisions of section 122 of this by-law, may at any time be repealed by a majority of the council then present and voting, and the said work shall thereupon cease, and shall only be carried out thereafter under the provisions of sections 120 and 121 of this by-law.

10. Frauds by contractors—

131. No contractor or other person found by the chief officer, or person in charge of any department, or by any committee of the council, or declared by a resolution of the council, or ascertained by a judicial decision to have been guilty of defrauding, or attempting to defraud, the city, shall again be employed in any capacity on behalf of or receive any contract from the city without the express sanction of the council.

132. It shall be the duty of the various officers of the corporation to forthwith report all frauds or attempted frauds, of which they may become cognizant, to their superior officer, and for such superior officer to report the same to the committee having control of the department in which the fraud has been committed.

11. Reports of committees—

133. Copies of all reports of committees for the current two weeks shall be sent to every member of the council at their residence or usual place of business on or before the last day of such two weeks.

12. Minutes of the council—

134. There shall be attached to every minute of the proceedings of the council a progressive marginal number in each year, and every document or certified copy of a minute communicated to any committee of the council, as hereinbefore required, shall bear the number of the minute to which it refers.

[The duties of treasurer, city engineer, and other officers of the corporation are regulated by by-law 2436, and other Acts. See consolidated by-laws of the city of Toronto, by-laws 2534, 2925, 3119, etc., 1890. These several Acts do not fall within the scope of this work].

13. Auditors—

The Municipal Act (ss. 258-268) provides for the appointment and duties of two auditors at the first meeting of every council after being duly organized. In the case of cities, however, it is provided that the council may pass a by-law appointing its auditors in the month of December in each year (s. 200). Special provision as follows is made for the city of Toronto:

259. (1) The council of the corporation of the city of Toronto shall appoint two auditors, who shall hold office during pleasure;

(2) The treasurer shall prepare in duplicate, not later than the first day of April in each year, an abstract of the receipts and expenditures of the city for the year ending on the 31st of December preceding, and of the assets and liabilities thereof at that date, and shall submit the same to the auditors for examination. The auditors shall audit his abstract with the treasurer's books, and shall make a report on all accounts audited by them, and a special report as to any expenditure made contrary to law; and on or before the first day of May shall transmit one copy of the said abstract with their report thereon, to the secretary of the bureau of industries, Toronto, and file the other in the office of the clerk of the council; and thereafter any individual or ratepayer of the municipality may inspect the same, at all reasonable hours, and may, by himself or his agent, at his own expense take a copy thereof or extracts therefrom.

35. London Committees, etc.

1. London committee No. 1—

63. The following shall be the duties of committee No. 1 ;—

(1) To present to the council on or before the first Monday in March in each year a full and particular exhibit of the financial affairs of the city at the termination of the preceding year ;

(2) To report to the council on or before the first Monday in July in each year as to the manner in which the revenue required for the current year shall be raised ;

(3) To consider and report as often as may be necessary on the management of all matters connected with railway stocks, bonds or other securities held by or belonging to the corporation ;

(4) To consider and report on all matters connected with the leasing or selling of city property ;

(5) To have the special supervision of the books of account, documents and vouchers, and of all moneys, debentures and securities in the treasurer's office, and the supervision of the treasurer and all officers in his department under him ;

(6) To advise with the treasurer when called upon to do so, on all matters pertaining to his office ;

(7) To see that an account is kept in the corporation's bank in the name of the corporation, and that all moneys paid to the treasurer are deposited to the credit of that account ;

(8) To see that all duties and services which ought to be performed by the treasurer and the officers in his department are fully executed ;

(9) To forbid the signing or delivery of any cheque or security for the payment of any money by the treasurer if they shall think it expedient so to do until the matter can be further considered or can be referred to the council ;

(10) To regulate all matters connected with the receipt and payment of money and to order the adoption of such regulations in connection therewith as may be deemed necessary for the prevention of any payment being made in contravention of the by-laws and generally to manage the financial affairs of the corporation ;

(11) To direct the purchase of stationery and the advertisements of city notices and to report thereon to the council ;

(12) To consider and report from time to time as may be necessary as to the duties to be performed by all officers, servants, and employees of the corporation, and from time to time as may be necessary, to consider and report as to the salary or remuneration of such officer, servant or employee ;

(13) To consider and report upon all matters relating to the printing required to be done for the corporation ;

(14) To consider and report upon all matters relating to railways in which the city may be interested ;

(15) To consider and report upon all matters relating to expenditures on account of criminal justice, the payment of jurors, maintenance of prisoners, use of court-house and gaol, the payment of crown witnesses and all matters required to be adjusted between the corporation of the county of Middlesex and the corporation of the city of London with reference to such matters or any of them, or to matters of a cognate character.

2. London committee No. 2—

64. The following shall be the duties of committee No. 2 :—

(1) To consider and report on all matters relating to sewers, drains, streets and thoroughfares ;

(2) To report and recommend to the council such regulations with regard to private buildings, drains and fences as may be requisite for the public safety and welfare ;

(3) To report to the council in their final report for each year on all such works of permanent improvement in connection with the sewers, drains, streets and thoroughfares as it may be considered essential to the welfare and convenience of the citizens to be carried out during the ensuing year, together with the estimated cost of the works so recommended ;

(4) To direct and control the city engineer and his staff in the discharge of their duties and to report to the council from time to time on all matters connected with the duties of his department ;

(5) To give effect to the orders of the council in relation to the performance of works under other committees ;

(6) To see to the keeping in repair of all buildings belonging to the corporation ;

(7) To see that the streets are cleaned and kept cleaned in accordance with the by-laws of the municipality;

(8) To expend in such manner as shall be most advantageous and beneficial to the citizens such moneys as shall be appropriated by the council for general improvements within the city ;

(9) To have the supervision of the street commissioner and to see that his duties are properly performed ;

(10) To consider and report upon all matters relating to the holding of industrial, agricultural or other exhibitions ;

(11) To manage and report upon all matters relating to the preservation of Victoria Park and all other public parks, squares, gardens or boulevards within the city or belonging to the corporation ;

(12) To report on all matters connected with the fencing, planting and ornamenting Victoria Park and all other public parks, squares, gardens or boulevards within the city or belonging to the corporation, and to carry out all such works connected therewith as the council may authorize ;

(13) To consider and report all matters concerning work on bridges, buildings, etc., carried on jointly by the city and county of Middlesex.

65. No sum shall be paid in respect of any expenditure incurred by committee No. 2 until the account therefor has been certified by the engineer, or ordered to be paid by the committee.

3. London committee No. 3—

66. The following shall be the duties of committee No. 3 :—

(1) To manage and report on the organization, equipment and maintenance of the fire brigade, and the supply and maintenance of the hose reels, wagons, horses and apparatus of the fire department and to see that the same are kept in good order, repair and efficiency ;

(2) To see that proper books of account are kept and statements furnished to the council of all purchases and expenditures of the fire department, and of all property from time to time belonging to the fire department or used in connection therewith ;

(3) To recommend the appointment and promotion of the members of the fire brigade ;

(4) To report on the lighting of the city, the erection of gas or electric lamps, and the inspection thereof and of gas meters ;

(5) To enquire into and report on the supply of water and the erection and maintenance of hydrants ;

(6) To consider and report on all matters connected with the watering of the public streets or squares, and the mode in which the cost thereof should be defrayed ;

(7) To consider and report on all matters connected with the establishment of fire limits, the inspection of buildings with reference thereto, and the prosecution of offenders against such regulations as may be enacted for the prevention of fires ;

(8) To consider and report on the manner of heating and lighting the city hall and other public buildings belonging to the corporation, and to advertise for tenders for the supply of coal and fuel for the use of the corporation, to receive and examine the tenders received and to report thereon to the council ;

(9) To see that all supplies required for the use of the fire department are obtained by tender so far as practicable, unless otherwise authorized by the council ;

(10) To manage and report on all matters relating to the regulation of the public markets and weighing houses, the inspection of weights and measures, the assize of bread, the prevention of the sale of tainted and unwholesome food, and all other matters with reference to markets as to which the council has power to pass by-laws ;

(11) To report on the levying and collecting of fees for weighing and rental of stalls or spaces upon the market ;

(12) To report on all works that may be required for the maintenance and keeping in repair of the market houses and the cleaning of the market grounds, and to carry out all such works in connection therewith as the council may authorize ;

(13) To have the control and direction of the clerk of the market, and all officers and servants employed in or about the public markets of the city ;

(14) To call for tenders for the position of weigh clerk in the month of March in each year, or as may be directed by the council, to examine and report upon the tenders received, and to see to the giving of security by the successful applicant therefor, for the payment of the sum agreed to and the performance of his duties ;

(15) To consider and report upon all matters relating to the issue of licenses in regard to matters within the control of the council, and the regulation and government of persons to whom licenses shall be issued, and the premises in respect of which licenses may be issued, and the license fees to be paid ;

(16) To have the control and direction of the city electrician ;

(17) No sum shall be paid in respect of any expenditure incurred by committee No. 3, until the account therefor has been certified by the engineer, and ordered to be paid by the committee.

4. London treasurer—

91. The duties of the treasurer in addition to those prescribed by law shall be:—

(1) To keep correct and proper books of account of all transactions relating to or occurring in his department ;

(2) To deposit all moneys which shall come to his hands belonging to the corporation to the credit of an account to be kept in the corporation's bank in its name, when such moneys amount to one hundred dollars ;

(3) To supply all information relative to the finances of the city, and to all other matters connected with his office, as committee No. 1 may require ;

(4) To conform to all directions of the said committee consistent with law and the by-laws of the city ;

(5) To perform such other duties as may be assigned to him by the council.

5. London clerk—

72. The duties of the clerk of the council in addition to those prescribed by law shall be :—

(1) To furnish the treasurer and the chairman of each of the committees with certified copies of all resolutions, enactments and orders of the council relative to the matters over which such committees may respectively have jurisdiction on the day next succeeding that upon which the action of the council in respect thereof takes place ;

(2) To communicate or convey to the committees all petitions or other documents referred by the council ;

(3) To have control over all officers employed in his office, subject to such orders as he may from time receive from the mayor or council ;

(4) To give notice to the members of the council of all meetings of the council when held on any other day than the day appointed by this by-law, on the day previous to that on which such meeting is to be held ;

(5) To have charge of the city seal and to attach the same to any document connected with the council on the order of the mayor, of the council, or any of the committees thereof ;

(6) To cause to be mailed to each member of the council, not later than the Saturday preceding each regular meeting thereof, a copy of the minutes of the last regular (and special, if any,) meeting or meetings of same ;

(7) To perform such other duties as may be assigned to him by the council.

6. London engineer—

73.   The following shall be the duties of the engineer :—

(1) To examine all work done for the corporation and to certify as to the completion thereof to his satisfaction, and the amount to be paid in respect of such work ;

(2) When required by committee No. 2, to prepare plans and estimates for all works required to be done by or on behalf of the corporation ;

(3) To direct the doing of the work and to prepare contracts in connection therewith, and that the work be done only upon his order ;

(4) To submit a weekly pay sheet of all workmen employed by the corporation on repairs and improvements, the time employed and wages paid, to committee No. 2, and when passed by them to deliver same to the treasurer ;

(5) To render such professional service as may be necessary to the board of education, the water commissioners and the hospital trust, and to perform such other duties as may be required of him by the council.

7. London street commissioner—

74.   The following shall be the duties of the street commissioner :—

(1) To examine into the state of repairs of all streets and highways within the city and to report any want of repairs that may be found therein to the city engineer who shall report the same to committee No. 2;

(2) If any repairs require to be promptly done to cause the same to be done forthwith and immediately to report the same to the city engineer who shall report the same to committee No. 2 ;

(3) To see that the streets and thoroughfares of the city are kept clean, and to have the same cleaned whenever directed to do so by the city engineer or committee No. 2 ;

(4) To superintend, under the direction of the city engineer, the doing of all work which is being done for the corporation on any of the streets or thoroughfares within the city, and to have the charge and supervision of the men employed when the work is not done by contract ;

(5) To keep a correct record of the men employed by the corporation on street repairs, and of the time they are employed, and the wages paid to them, and to make a return thereof to the city engineer once in each week ;

(6) To perform such other duties as may be assigned to him by the council, or No. 2 committee or the city engineer.

8. London cheques—

76. All cheques upon the corporation's bank for any sum of money whatever to be paid on account of the city shall be signed by the treasurer and counter-signed by the mayor, or, in case of his absence or illness, by one of the aldermen.

9. London money appropriations—

51. Any bill for the appropriation of money brought in on the report of a committee of the whole shall pass through all its stages without being again referred to a committee of the whole unless upon special motion.

77. All appropriations of money shall be submitted to a committee of the whole before being taken up in full council.

78. No money appropriation shall be finally acted upon by the council until it has been first referred to the finance and assessment committee, and no money shall be paid by the treasurer or any expenditure be authorized by any member of the council without a resolution of the council ordering the same and specifying the amount.

36. Guelph Committees, etc.

1. Duties of standing committees—

65. Each standing committee shall report to the council at the second regular meeting in each month a correct statement of all moneys expended, the amount for which the funds of the committee are liable, including contracts, the balance at the credit of said committee after making provision for aforesaid payments and liabilities—such statement shall be made up to the end of each preceding month.

66. It shall be the duty of the finance committee to examine and report on all accounts referred to them, to examine and report on all annual estimates of expenditure, proposals for purchase of debentures or other municipal securities, to prepare estimates of the revenue, expenditures and assessment of each year, to have in charge everything relating to printing and stationery and generally all matters connected with the finances of the city.

66. The water works committee shall have the supervision and charge of the water works of the city of Guelph, and the persons employed thereon and in connection therewith, and of all contracts for supply of water and of the supply of materials and of the laying of mains and services, and of all work in

connection therewith, and of the making of assessments and charges for the use or supply of water, and of the keeping of books of account and other books used in connection therewith.

67. The board of works shall have in charge all matters connected with the construction, repairs and improvements of the streets, highways, bridges, sidewalks, sewers and drains of the city and encroachments on and obstructions and injuries to the same.

68. The market and public buildings committee shall have charge of the public markets, the market square, the drill shed, the city hall buildings, and all stalls and other erections connected with the said markets.

69. The committee on fire, water and gas shall have charge of the engine house, steam fire engine, all fire apparatus, tanks and wells, and all other matters and improvements connected with the suppression of fires and the lighting of the street lamps of the city.

70. It shall be the duty of the relief committee to expend in a proper and judicious manner the appropriation made by the council for the relief of the poor or infirm of the city.

71. The committee on parks and shade trees shall have in charge the exhibition and other parks and buildings and fences therein and all matters connected with planting trees, shrubs and flowers, whether in parks or on streets, and the protection of the same.

72. It shall be the duty of the by-law and license committee to examine and report on the true interpretation, efficiency or otherwise of existing by-laws or any of them, to revise and consolidate them if required, to prepare and introduce new by-laws, and to report on all matters respecting licenses referred to them by the council.

73. The police committee shall have in charge the police office and cells, and the disposition and management of the police force, and all matters relating thereto.

74. The railway committee shall have in charge all matters connected with railways in which the city is directly or indirectly interested.

75. Nevertheless each of the aforesaid committees in the exercise of their several functions when the same are not expressly prescribed by statute or by-law shall be under the control and direction of the council.

76. It shall be the duty of each of the aforesaid committees to report to the council on or before its second regular meeting in April of each and every year, a general statement of its proposed improvements, repairs and expenditure, together with an estimate of revenue, if any, which may fairly be expected from the department under its supervision for the current year, the council shall then refer these several reports with or without amendment to the finance committee who shall prepare and report to the council on or before its first regular meeting in May, an estimate of the total revenue, expenditure and assessment for the said year, based on the aforesaid reports as data.

77. The council shall then on the receipt of the report of the finance committee amend or not the aforesaid reports of the standing committees, reducing, increasing, or confirming the several estimates of each or any of them as they deem necessary and advisable, and such several reports thus amended or confirmed shall then be adopted and the several sums set down in each shall constitute the appropriations for the several committees for the said year.

78. No expenditure of the appropriations granted under the seventy-seventh section of this by-law shall be made by any committee until a detailed report of every such expenditure shall have been submitted by each committee and approved by the council (a). In case, however, of emergency, or sudden injury or damage to municipal property, requiring immediate repairs, the appropriate committee may, without the sanction of the council, expend a sum not exceeding fifty dollars on such repairs.

79. The council may at any time during the year make a different application of the appropriations made under the seventy-seventh section of this by-law, or such unexpended portions of them as remain in the treasurer's hands, but no moneys hereafter voted or raised for any purpose, shall be applied to any other purpose, without expressly rescinding or repealing the resolution, report or by-law, by or under which the same was voted or raised, so far as such resolution, report or by-law stated the purpose.

80. Any committee or chairman of any committee expending more than the said appropriation of money, for which no provision has been made, shall be personally liable for every such excess or expenditure over and above the appropriations of the aforesaid report. The council, may, however, pass a by-law to indemnify him or them for each such breach of this by-law, and make provision for the payment of such excessive expenditure.

81. On the third Monday in November in each year, the clerk shall advertise for all accounts due by the corporation to be sent in, and at the second regular meeting in December, of the council thereafter each committee shall present to the council a full report of the receipts and expenditures in their several departments under their control for the current year.

2. Guelph—Payments, moneys, accounts, etc.—

82. All accounts shall be rendered to the clerk, and presented by him to the council ; they shall then be referred to the appropriate committees, which shall report to the council, and if correct recommend their payment, and when such report is passed by the council the chairman shall give his order for the same, stating the name of the committee to whose account it is to be charged, the number of the report recommending payment, and date on which such report was passed in council, when the treasurer may on receipt of such order countersigned by the mayor, or in his absence by the chairman of the finance committee, pay the same out of such moneys as have been appropriated for that purpose, and

(a) Rule 38 provides that "no specific appropriation shall be made or determined on until it has been reported on by the appropriation committee."

shall file in his office all such accounts duly receipted and numbered to correspond with voucher in his receipt book, but no such order will be necessary for the payment of debentures, interest coupons, county rates, bills discounted, gas accounts, water rates, fixed salaries, school moneys, hay and oats, relief orders not exceeding five dollars, pay list of board of works, when certified by the chairman and foreman, and the treasurer shall pay no moneys otherwise than provided in this clause.

83. After the introduction and passing of the estimates for the year, and by-law, reports and resolutions proposing an expenditure of money shall receive a two-thirds vote of the members present, and shall then be referred to the finance committee to report the ways and means, and in no case shall any committee or officer of the corporation act upon any such by-law, report or resolution, till a report of said committee certifying the mode of providing the necessary funds has been adopted by the council.

84. No contract shall be authorized or permitted in contemplation of a loan whereby a debt is incurred requiring the approval of the ratepayers until after such loan or debt has been duly passed and has been approved by the ratepayers, according to law, nor shall any contract be valid or binding on the corporation provided the same exceeds the value of fifty dollars, unless the same shall have been submitted to and approved by the council and signed by the mayor and the clerk, and having the corporation seal attached.

37. BELLEVILLE—COMMITTEES AND OFFICERS.

1. Special duties of standing committees—

63. In addition to the general duties prescribed, the special duties imposed on the executive committee shall be as follows :

(1) To supervise all the contracts, orders, engagements, reports, recommendations, and proceedings involving the expenditure of money, of all or any of the other committees of the council, or of any officer of the corporation ; and no contract, order, engagement, report, recommendation, or proceeding involving the expenditure of money of any of the said committees other than the executive committee, or of any officer of the corporation, shall have any legal effect or operation until the same shall have been laid before the said executive committee, and reported therefrom to the council and passed in the usual manner;

(2) To supervise all accounts, expenditure and outlay, and all sums payable under contract, of all the other committees, before any moneys are paid therefor, and shall require the law, and by-laws and resolutions of the council with respect thereto, to be complied with before claims or accounts are paid ; and no account, claim, demand, or request for money whatever, not expressly authorized to be paid by statute, by-law, or resolution of the council shall be paid by the treasurer until the same shall have been first laid before the said executive committee and reported therefrom to the council and passed in the usual manner ;

(3) The executive committee shall have the right to object to any contract, order, engagement, report, recommendation, claim, account, or proceeding involving the expenditure of money, should the same either (1) not comply with the law, or with the by-laws of the council, or (2) exceed the appropriation made to the committee reporting, or (3) exceed the appropriation to the special work or service reported on, or (4) require the expenditure of money beyond the estimates for the year for any work or service. In case any contract, order, engagement, report, recommendation, claim, account, or proceeding of any other committee shall be objected to by the executive committee, on any of the grounds aforesaid, and the objection appealed against by any member of the council, the appeal shall not be sustained, nor the matter in question adopted or passed by the council except by a two-thirds vote ;

(4) To cause all contracts, orders and expenditure authorized or ordered to be paid, by the executive committee, to be entered by the secretary in a book to be kept for that purpose (to be called the appropriation book) distinguishing therein the liability authorized, and the expenditure made, in separate accounts against the committee to whose department they belong and against the appropriations for the committee, contract, order, work or service, respectively ; and it shall also be the duty of the executive committee to cause to be kept in such book an entry of all appropriations made, or allowed to every committee and every service, and all entries shall bear the respective numbers of the minutes authorizing them. No account or other claim authorized by the executive committee shall be passed for payment unless it bear the particular number of the minute referring to it ;

(5) To present to the council, on or before the last Monday in April in each year, a full and particular exhibit of the financial affairs of the city, and the estimates of the amount required to be raised by assessment during the current year ;

(6) To introduce a by-law after the adoption of the estimates in each year to regulate the manner in which the revenue required for the current year should be raised ;

(7) To consider and report as often as may be necessary, on the management of all matters connected with any securities held by the corporation ;

(8) To have the special supervision of the books of accounts, documents and vouchers, and all moneys, debentures and securities, in the treasurer's office, and shall also have the supervision and direction of the treasurer, and of all other officers in his department ;

(9) To advise the treasurer, when called upon to do so, in all matters pertaining to his office ;

(10) To see that all duties and services which ought to be performed by the treasurer and the other officers in his department are fully executed;

(11) To forbid the signing or delivery of any cheques, or of any security, or the payment of any money by the treasurer, if they shall think it expedient to do so, until the matter can be further considered, or can be referred to the council ;

(12) To regulate all matters connected with the receipt and payment of money, and to order the adoption of such regulations in connection therewith, as may be deemed necessary for the prevention of any payment being made in contravention of the by-laws, and generally to manage the financial affairs of the city ;

(13) To direct the purchase of books and stationery, and the printing of the city ;

(14) To cause to be furnished to the council as often as required a report of all amounts expended by every committee, and also totals of all estimates or ascertained liabilities of the city ;

(15) Each other standing committee of the council shall have and possess all the powers and authority and observe and perform all the duties heretofore conferred or enjoyed on, or performed by it, except as herein or hereby limited or modified ;

(16) All matters not specially belonging or appertaining to any committee of the council shall belong to, and be under the control of the executive committee, which shall have power to deal with the same, unless otherwise ordered by the council ;

(17) Any other committee which has had referred to it by the council for consideration, any account, proposed expenditure or items which require consideration, by the executive committee may report over to such executive committee for consideration and report.

2. Money appropriations, accounts, expenditures, contracts and improvements in Belleville—

64. All appropriations of money shall be submitted to a committee of the whole before being taken up in full council.

65. No committee, or member of the council, and no officer of the corporation shall on behalf of the corporation enter into a contract, or incur or authorize any expenditure, without having obtained by by-law or resolution, the previous authority or sanction of the council, except in the case of great emergency, and then only to no greater extent than $25, and in such case a report shall be made immediately to the chairman of the executive committee, and the executive committee shall have power, if deemed prudent, to order the work to cease until it be laid before the council.

66. No committee or officer of the council shall exceed the appropriation made to such committee or officer for any purpose. Nor shall any committee, without the consent of the executive committee and of the council, expend money appropriated to any specified purpose, work or service on any other than that for which it was appropriated.

67. No contract or expenditure shall be authorized or permitted in contemplation of a loan, whereby a debt is incurred requiring the approval of the ratepayers, until after the by-law for such loan or debt has been duly passed, and has been approved of by the ratepayers according to law.

68. Prior to the introduction and passing of the annual estimates of receipts and expenditures, all resolutions of the council or by-laws professing to authorize the expenditure of money shall only be passed subject to a reference to the executive committee to estimate for the same, and after the introduction of the estimates, such by-laws or resolutions shall only be passed subject to a two-thirds vote of the council for such reference, in order that the said committee may consider the means of providing funds for the same, and in neither case shall any committee or officer of the corporation act upon any such by-law or resolution until a report of the executive committee certifying the mode of providing funds, has been adopted by the council.

69. In all cases where a resolution of council or by-law provides for the issuing of debentures for the purpose of raising the ways and means of meeting the expenditure thereby contemplated, the same may be passed by the council without the reference in the preceding clause mentioned.

70. No work or improvements shall hereafter be authorized by the council, without either having an estimate of the probable cost thereof, or (in the absence of an estimate), limiting an amount therefor ; and no contract shall be entered into for such work or improvement, at a larger sum or involving a larger expenditure than the amount so estimated or limited ; and if such amount is found insufficient, the fact is to be reported to the council before the work is commenced or contracted for.

71. For the purpose of better securing to the council full and accurate information before being called upon to authorize the expenditure of city money, every report recommending an expenditure of money shall state the reasons and grounds on which the recommendation is made, and shall as far as practicable, state the same with sufficient fulness to enable others to judge of the propriety of the proposed expenditure.

72. With the view of preventing members and officers of the corporation from being interested in the corporation contracts, it is hereby expressly declared that no member of the council, and no officer of the corporation shall be interested in a private capacity, directly or indirectly, in any contract or agreement for labour, or for materials, goods, wares, or merchandise, furnished to the city, wherein the city is a party interested.

73. Any breach of the duty imposed by the preceding section of this by-law, on the part of any officer of the corporation shall subject him to the forfeiture of his office, and an immediate removal therefrom.

74. No account or claim against the city, arising out of or connected with any contract, agreement, purchase or sale made contrary to this by-law, shall be certified by any officer of the corporation, or approved by any committee, or the chairman thereof, or paid by the treasurer.

75. Every contract shall contain a clause declaring that the contract is entered into on the part of the corporation in full faith that no member of the council, or officer, or servant of the corporation has any interest therein, and further, all claims thereunder for payment or recompense shall be forfeited absolutely if it be

found that any such member, officer or servant is interested in the subject matter of the contract, or is to receive or has received any reward or remuneration in connection therewith.

76. Every account for work done or materials, goods, wares, or merchandise furnished for the corporation shall be accompanied by a written or printed declaration by the person claiming the same, and over his signature to the effect that no member of the council or officer of the corporation is in a private capacity, directly or indirectly, interested in such account, or in any part of the work or material mentioned therein or of the money thereby claimed, and that the said account amounts to $　. But if from any sufficient cause a declaration cannot be made, the executive committee may receive other evidence and report what they do for the information of the council.

77. With a view of further carrying out the various objects embraced in this by-law, every account before being paid shall be certified firstly by the officer, under whose superintendence the work was done, or material was provided, and secondly by the committee (if any) under whose authority the contract or expenditure was made, this latter certificate being given by or by order of such committee, or a majority thereof, and signed by the members or by the chairman in their presence; and such certificate shall also refer in some distinct manner to the by-law or resolution of the council by or under which the expenditure was authorized.

78. In case the committee has reason to believe that any member of the council, or officer of the corporation is interested in any account presented for the approval of such committee, it shall be the duty of such committee to withhold a certificate, and to give the parties interested and supposed to be interested in the account, an opportunity of disproving the supposed interest, and if they fail to do so to the satisfaction of the committee, it shall be the duty of the committee to report the same forthwith to the council.

3. Duties of Belleville clerk—

82. The city clerk shall perform all duties ordinarily belonging to his office, as well as all of the duties imposed upon him, as such officer, by any Act of parliament, or by-law of this corporation, and made incidental to the office of corporation clerk.

83. He shall be required to attend at his office in the city building, from 9 a.m. until 4 p.m., and as much longer as the duties of the office may from time to time require, except on Saturdays, when 3 p.m. shall be the hour at which he may leave his office.

84. He shall act as secretary to all the standing committees of the council, keep their minutes and prepare their reports for the council.

85. He shall be the custodian of the corporate seal.

86. He shall prepare the collector's rolls with accuracy and despatch, after the estimates have been passed and rates struck.

87. The caretaker shall be under his direction.

88. The council may from time to time, by resolution, define or explain any particular duty or work imposed upon his office, or to be done by him.

89. The clerk of the police court shall furnish to the treasurer monthly, a statement of all moneys received by him and due, such as fines and costs imposed but not collected, and the treasurer shall submit a copy of the same to the executive committee at its next meeting.

90. The clerk of the police court shall submit each month a detailed statement of all moneys received by him for the city, and all moneys due and payable but not paid over.

91. It shall be the duty of the clerk of the council to communicate to the treasurer forthwith, a statement of all moneys authorized to be paid.

92. All moneys due or payable to the city from fees, licenses, or any other source whatsoever shall be paid to the treasurer and be deposited to the credit of the city's bank account, and no license, permission or authority, for which fees should be paid to the city, shall be issued by the clerk, except upon certificate from the treasurer that such fees have been so paid.

4. Belleville treasurer—

93. The treasurer shall, whenever required, attend the meetings of the executive committee.

94. He shall receive all moneys belonging to the city and shall deposit the same to the credit of the corporation in such bank or place as the council may from time to time select as its banker.

95. He shall give such security for faithful performance of his duties and accounting for the corporation moneys and documents and property entrusted to his charge as may from time to time be required of him.

96. It shall be his duty to report by letter to each successive council, at its first meeting after election, the names, nature and amount of his sureties and the particulars of his bonds, and the names, amount and particulars of all bonds in his possession, belonging to the city.

97. He shall be the custodian of all titles, deeds, leases, bonds and securities of fidelity other than his own, and shall only allow the same to be taken from his office on the order of the council, or requisition and receipt of the city solicitor.

98. He shall draw and sign all cheques properly authorized (to be counter-signed by the chairman of the executive committee) for payment of moneys.

99. He shall supervise the collection of taxes and report from time to time in writing to the chairman of the executive committee in reference thereto, particularly when any collector is not performing his duties properly.

100. He shall keep or cause to be kept, according to the most approved system of book-keeping, such books of account as may be necessary to show distinctly and continuously from day to day the receipts and disbursements, and all other reckonings and accountings of what nature or kind soever connected with the monetary transactions of the corporation.

101. He shall keep a duplicate receipt book and shall give a receipt for every item of money received by him for or on account of the corporation and keep a duplicate stub thereof, which shall, along with all his other books and papers, be constantly open to the inspection of the chairman or acting chairman of the executive committee, and shall be submitted to the city auditors and to the executive committee and council when required.

102. He shall furnish to the chairman of the executive committee a monthly statement of all receipts and expenditures of the city, and he shall supply all information to the executive committee as relate to the finances of the city and his office as said committee or the chairman thereof may require.

103. He shall attend in his office at the city hall from 9 o'clock a.m. until 4 o'clock p.m. and as much longer as may be necessary from time to time for the performance of all the duties appertaining to his office, except Saturdays, when he may close his office at 3 p.m.

104. It shall be his duty to assist the clerk in the preparation of the collector's rolls in such particulars as come more immediately within his department, and he shall keep an accurate and proper record of overdue taxes, and see they are properly placed upon the rolls for collection, and attend to and be responsible for the collection, by sale or otherwise, of " back taxes."

105. He shall report to the executive committee as often as, and whenever an appropriation of the council, for any particular purpose, is about expended; and he shall keep an account in his books for each appropriation in the estimates, and for every special appropriation.

106. It shall be his duty to look after all moneys due to the city, see they are collected, and paid over.

107. The executive committee subject to the approval of the council at its next regular meeting, may from time to time by resolution, declare or define his duties as to any particular matter.

5. Belleville city solicitor—

108. The city solicitor shall be the legal adviser of the corporation.

109. He shall draft all petitions and memorials as may be presented by the council, engross and forward the same to their proper destination, and attend upon any committees or persons required, and superintend, and when necessary, personally attend to the passage through parliament of any Act promoted by the city, or oppose any resisted by the city.

110. He shall draft and settle all by-laws of the corporation.

111. He shall prepare and revise the conveyancing of the corporation, including advertisements, such as for tenders.

112. He shall attend meetings of the council and of the committees thereof, when required.

113. He shall attend before the police magistrate's court when required, upon any case for the infringement of any of the city by-laws.

114. He shall advise the court of revision upon all questions coming before it, upon which it wants advice.

115. He shall conduct all the legal business of the city.

116. He shall advise the clerk and treasurer upon legal questions arising in their office, and in particular to the preparation of the collector's rolls, and he shall see that the assessors and collectors make all proper and necessary entries and returns, and it shall be his duty to report, without delay, to the executive committee, any assessor or collector who is performing his duty negligently or slothfully, so as to guard the city from possible loss.

117. And generally he shall attend and perform the duties appertaining to the usual business of the law department of the city of Belleville, and usually performed by a regular standing solicitor and legal adviser.

118. The council may from time to time define or explain his duties in any particular.

6. Belleville street surveyor—

119. The street surveyor, in addition to the duties heretofore performed shall keep in a book, to be furnished him for the purpose, a memorandum of all the work performed by all the city employees whose names appear upon the street pay rolls. Said surveyor's book shall show the work upon which each individual or team of horses has been employed each day, and the street or locality where the work has been done.

120. He shall also keep in the same book a memorandum in detail of all purchases made by him for the corporation, on contract or otherwise, giving the names of the parties from whom the purchases are made ; the dates of such purchases; the quantities, prices, and all other proper items of information connected therewith.

121. He shall also enter in said book the quantities of all materials delivered for use in the department of public works, and the quantities of all materials so used ; and any information connected therewith that may be necessary. Said book to accompany the pay rolls when they are laid before the executive committee.

122. He shall make a yearly estimate of all work to be done by the 1st of May in each year.

122a. He shall be responsible to the council except in urgent cases when he may act on his own responsibility.

88. KINGSTON.

Payments and expenditures –

36. No committee shall enter into any contract with or authorize the purchase of any article from any of its members.

37. The chairman of the finance committee shall not audit or approve of any bill or account against the city, or any supplies for services, which shall not have been regularly ordered or authorized by the council, or a committee properly authorized.

38. No payments shall be made by the treasurer (except salaries) on account of the city, unless first passed upon and reported by the finance committee to the council, and sanctioned by the council.

39. No motion for the expenditure of money shall be in order before the finance committee reports that there are funds on hand for the purpose or arrangements made for the payment of the same.

39. St. Catharines, Rules 25, 26, and 28.

1. Salaries —

25. The salaries of the officers of the corporation shall only be paid on a resolution passed by the council.

2. Accounts—

26. All accounts shall be regularly certified by the proper authorities before being passed by the council.

3. Elections —

28. All officers of the corporation are forbidden hereafter to take an active part in the election of members thereof, otherwise than by simply casting their votes, under penalty of dismissal.

4. Money appropriations —

45. Any bill for the appropriation of money brought in on the report of the committee of the whole shall pass through all its stages without being again referred to a committee of the whole, unless upon special motion in writing. [See also rule 20 *above*].

40. Hamilton.

Money appropriations—

28. No money appropriations shall be finally acted upon by the council until it shall have been referred to the standing committee on finance, except by a vote of two-thirds of the council; and no money shall be paid by the treasurer until ordered by the council, such order being signed by the mayor, or, in case of his absence, by the chairman of the finance committee, except coupons for interest on debentures, coroners' orders for inquests, and pay.lists, which he is hereby authorized to pay on presentation; the latter being first signed by the chairman of the respective committees by which such are usually audited.

41. STRATFORD COMMITTEES AND OFFICERS.

1. Finance, assessment, license and printing committee—

67. The following and such other duties as may herein, or by any other by-law hereinafter be assigned to them, shall be the duties of the finance, assessment, license and printing committee :—

(1) To present to the council on or before the first Monday in March in each year a full and particular exhibit of the financial affairs of the city at the termination of the preceding financial year ;

(2) To report to the council on or before the first Monday in September in each year as to the manner in which the revenue required for the current year is to be raised ;

(3) To have the special supervision of the books of accounts, documents and vouchers, and of all moneys, debentures and securities in the treasurer's office, and the supervision of the treasurer ;

(4) To advise with the treasurer when called upon to do so on all matters pertaining to his office ;

(5) To see that all duties and services which ought to be performed by the treasurer are fully executed ;

(6) To forbid the signing or delivery of any cheque or security, or the payment of any money by the treasurer if they shall think it expedient so to do until the matter can be further considered, or can be referred to the council ;

(7) To regulate all matters connected with the receipt or payment of money, and to order the adoption of such regulations in connection therewith, as may be deemed necessary for the prevention of any payment being made in contravention of the by-laws, and generally to manage the financial affairs of the corporation.

(8) To direct the purchase of stationery, the advertisement of corporation notices, and all matters relating to the printing required to be done for the corporation, and to report thereon to the council ;

(9) To consider and report on all matters relating to the issue of licenses, in regard to matters within the control of the council, and the regulations and government of persons to whom licenses shall be issued, and the provisions in respect to which the licenses may be issued, and the license fee to be paid.

2. Stratford board of works—

68. The following, and such other duties as may herein or by any other by-law hereinafter be assigned to them, shall be the duties of the board of works :

(1) To consider and report on all matters relating to sewers, drains, and thoroughfares ;

(2) To report and recommend to the council such regulations with regard to private buildings, drains and fences, as may be requisite for the public safety and welfare ;

(3) To report to the council in their final report for each year on all such works of permanent improvements in connection with the sewers, drains, streets and thoroughfares as it may be essential to the welfare and convenience of the citizens, to be carried out during the ensuing year, together with the estimated cost of the works so recommended ;

(4) To give effect to the orders of the council in relation to the performance of works under other committees ;

(5) To see that the streets are cleaned and kept cleaned in accordance with the by-laws of the municipality ;

(6) To expend in such manner as will be most advantageous and beneficial to the citizens such moneys as shall be appropriated by the council for general improvements within the municipality.

3. Stratford fire, water and gas committee—

69. The following, and such other duties as may herein or by any other by-law hereinafter be assigned to them, shall be the duties of the fire, water and gas committee :—

(1) To manage and report on the organization, equipment and maintenance of the fire brigade, and the supply and maintenance of the apparatus of the fire department, and to see that the same are kept in good order, repair and efficiency ;

(2) To appoint the members of the fire brigade subject to ratification by the council ;

(3) To manage and report on the lighting of the city, the erection of street lamps and the inspection thereof ;

(4) To report on the supply of water and the erection and maintenance of tanks and hydrants ;

(5) To consider and report on all matters connected with the watering of the public streets and squares ;

(6) To consider and report on all matters connected with the establishment of fire limits, the inspection of buildings with reference thereto, and the prosecution of offenders against such regulations as may be enacted, for the prevention of fires.

4. Stratford market and police committee—

70. The following, and such other duties as may herein or by any other by-law hereafter be assigned to them, shall be the duties of the market and police committee :—

(1) To manage and report on all matters relating to the regulations of the public market and weighing houses, the inspection of weights and measures, the

assize of bread, the prevention of the sale of tainted and unwholesome food, and all other matters with reference to markets as to which the council has power to pass by-laws ;

(2) To report on the rental of stores, cellars and stalls, and leasing of the weigh scales ;

(3) To report on all works that may be required for the maintenance and keeping in repair of the city hall building, market houses and grounds, and to carry out all such works in connection therewith as the council may authorize ;

(4) To have control and direction of the weigh clerk, janitor of the city hall and market building, and all officers and servants employed in or about the public markets ;

(5) To cause the fees of market scales to be advertised for sale in the month of December in each year by public auction, or as may be directed by the council, and to see to the giving of security by the purchaser thereof for the payment of the purchase money and the performance of his duties ;

(6) To cause the stores, stalls and cellars in the city hall and market building to be advertized to let at the same time as the sale of market scale fees in each year and to let the same by public auction, or as may be directed by the council ;

(7) To control and report upon the general management of the police court and lock-up, and to have the control and direction of all officers connected therewith.

5. Stratford board of health and relief—

71. The following, and such other duties as may herein or by any other by-law hereafter be assigned them, shall be the duties of the board of health and relief :—

(1) The board of health and relief shall have all the powers and authorities conferred upon or vested in the members of the municipal council of the city by the Act respecting the public health or any other Act for the like purpose, so far as same remain, if at all, in the said council, and so far as said council can delegate same to such committee ;

(2) The said board of health and relief shall immediately on their organization select and report a suitable committee to be appointed a local board of health under the Public Health Act of 1884, and any Acts amending same ;

(3) The said board of health and relief shall also supervise the distribution of relief.

6. Stratford park and cemetery committee—

72. The following, and such other duties as may herein, or by any other by-law hereafter be assigned them, shall be the duties of the park and cemetery committee :—

(1) To manage and report upon all matters connected with the preservation of all grounds set apart for public parks, squares, walks or cemeteries, and all buildings erected thereon, and the prevention of encroachments on such properties ;

(2) To report on all matters connected with fencing, ornamenting and preserving the parks, squares, gardens, walks or cemeteries as aforesaid, and to carry out all such works connected therewith as the council may authorize.

7. Stratford court of revision —

73. The court of revision shall be constituted, and its duties shall be as defined by statute.

8. Duties of Stratford treasurer—

80. The duties of the treasurer, in addition to those prescribed by law and assigned to him by this or any subsequent by-law or direction of the council, shall be :—

(1) To keep correct and proper books of account of all transactions relating to or occurring in his department ;

(2) To supply all information relating to the finances of the city, and to all other matters connected with his office as the finance, assessment, license, and printing committee may require ;

(3) To conform to all directions of the said committee consistent with law and the by-laws of the city ;

(4) To receive all license fees and give such certificate as required by this or any other by-law.

9. Duties of Stratford clerk—

81. The duties of the clerk of the council, in addition to those prescribed by law and assigned to him by this or any subsequent by-law or direction of the council, shall be :—

(1) To notify each member of the respective committees appointed by the council so soon as the appointment has been made of the time and place at which the first meeting of the committee will be held ;

(2) To furnish the chairman of each of the committees with certified copies of all resolutions, enactments and orders of the council relative to the matters over which such committees may respectively have jurisdiction on the day next succeeding that upon which the action of the council in respect thereof takes place ;

(3) To communicate or convey to the committees and officers of the corporation all petitions or other documents referred to them respectively by the council ;

(4) To attend to all meetings of the committees when required so to do by the chairman or acting chairman thereof, and to record the minutes, orders and reports, of all such meetings in the manner hereinbefore provided ;

(5) To give notice to the members of the council of all meetings of the council when held on any other day than the regular meeting day of the council, on the day previous to that on which such meeting is to be held ;

(6) To have charge of the corporate seal and to attach the same to any document connected with the council or any of the committees thereof so authorized by the council ;

(7) To collect all fines and costs payable into the police court, and all fees payable to him as clerk thereof, and pay over same to the city treasurer on or before the day of the first regular meeting of the council in each month ;

(8) To make a certified return to the council at the first regular meeting in each month, showing for the preceding month the number of cases tried at the police court, the names of the complainants and defendants, the amount received for fines and fees respectively, how each case was disposed of, and how much in each case remains uncollected, and the reasons for non-collection :

(9) To keep a book wherein he shall enter a record of the cases disposed of in the police court, and how disposed of, and what fines and fees paid, and when paid and payable ;

(10) To return, with his monthly report, the receipt of the city treasurer for monthly payment ;

(11) To report to the council at each of its first regular meetings in each month all licenses issued by him during each next preceding month ;

(12) To furnish city auditors the books and returns hereinbefore mentioned when auditing the police court accounts ;

(13) To furnish the chief of police receipts for all payments made by him on account of fines and fees received by him in the clerk's absence.

10. Duties of Stratford officers and servants as to fees—

82   No officer or servant of the corporation shall directly or indirectly take or receive for his own use, in addition to the salary or wages from to time assigned to him by the council, any fee, emolument or reward for any service performed by him in his capacity of such officer or servant, or by reason of his occupying or holding that position, whether the same is payable by the corporation or by the crown, or by any other person ; but all such fees shall be forthwith, after the same shall be received, accounted for, and paid over to the city treasurer for the use of the municipality ; and if any such fee, emolument or reward shall be received by such officer or servant, and shall be applied to his own use, or shall not be forthwith accounted for and paid over to the treasurer, such officer or servant shall incur the penalty of instant dismissal from his office or employment, and, the corporation may at its option deduct the amount of any such fee, emolument or reward so received from any moneys which such officer or servant is entitled to receive from the corporation, provided always that nothing herein contained shall extend or apply to the fees or emoluments to which the treasurer is, or may be, entitled by law or to any officer or servant whose salary or remuneration is paid by fees wholly or in part.

11. Stratford money appropriations—

49. Any bill for the appropriation of money belonging to the report of a committee of the whole shall pass through all its stages without being again referred to a committee of the whole unless upon special motion.

76. All appropriations of money to committees shall be submitted to a committee of the whole before being finally passed by the council.

77. No money appropriation shall be finally acted upon by the council until it has been first referred to the finance, assessment, license and printing committee, and no money shall be paid by the treasurer, or any expenditure be authorized by any member of the council without a resolution of the council ordering the same and specifying the amount.

III.—PROPOSED CODE OF RULES OF ORDER AND PROCEDURE FOR COUNTY AND OTHER COUNCILS (a).

The foregoing rules of the councils of the cities of Ontario embody, generally, the rules that also govern the councils of county and other municipalities, since all are copied from the rules of the House of Commons of Canada. In suggesting the following uniform code for all councils, the writer has not considered it necessary to repeat, but has simply referred by their number to those rules of the city councils that can be adopted in their entirety, or with a few verbal changes by councils generally, and has then added such other rules as seem well adapted to all municipal divisions. *As a matter of fact, the code is, as far as practicable, simply an adaptation and a more convenient arrangement of existing rules.* Before giving a summary of those rules that can be conveniently and advantageously adopted it is necessary to provide for the first meetings of municipal bodies.

First Meeting of a Newly Elected County Council.

Rule 1.—" The first meeting of the council, after its election, shall be held at the hour of two o'clock in the afternoon of the fourth Tuesday of the month of January in which the said council has been elected, or if the said Tuesday be a statutory or other public holiday, then the council shall meet at the same hour on the next day following which is not ;a statutory or other public holiday.

" The members elect, being [at least a majority of the whole number of the council when full, shall at this first meeting, after

(a) See note (c) on p. 383, *below.*

filing with the clerk of the council such certificates and declarations as are required by section 65 of 'The Municipal Act,' organize themselves as a council by electing a warden (b).

" At the election of such warden, the clerk of the council, or, in his absence, the member elected to take his place, shall first call the members to order, and as soon as there is present a majority of the whole number of the council when full, shall allow fifteen minutes for nominations for candidates to the said office by a motion duly made and seconded in the case of each candidate. At the expiration of the said fifteen minutes the clerk, or the person elected to take his place, shall proceed to put the name or names of the candidate or candidates in the order in which they were proposed, and the candidate who receives the required majority in accordance with the law shall be declared duly elected. If the first list of names nominated is exhausted without an election, then another fifteen minutes shall be allowed for new nominations, and the procedure as in the first case of nominations shall be followed, and so on

(b) In proposing a rule for the election of warden, as above, I may here again refer to the fact that so important a body as the Simcoe county council (see *above*, p. 240) has passed a by-law for the ballot, and that other bodies have followed its example. Doubts, however, may be raised as to the legality of such a by-law in the absence of express statutory authority from the legislature to which the municipality owes its existence as a distinct corporate entity. It is a well known and admitted principle that a municipal body has no other powers than those expressly conferred upon it, or which are necessary incidents of its statutory powers. It cannot invest itself with any powers which are beyond those so conferred, or in conflict with the common law. Open voting, by poll or by show of hands, is only recognized by the common law (see Palmer's " Company Precedents," p. 285, and *Faulkener v. Elger*, 4 B. and C. 454, showing that the common law right of open vote is not to be restricted by imposing the ballot). Open voting is also only recognized by parliament in the election of speaker, and in the votes of representatives generally.

The municipal law of Ontario is so specific in all cases, that it is obvious if the legislature had intended that the ballot be used in the election of warden, it would have been so expressly set forth. On the contrary, the undoubted inference from the 227th section (see *above*, p. 239), which gives a reeve or deputy-reeve a casting vote when there is an equality of votes at the election in question, is that the ballot was never in the mind of the legislature in passing the three sections (225-227, see *above*, pp. 238-239), providing for such election. The reeve or deputy-reeve must in such a case necessarily vote openly. Under the Simcoe rule, then, we would have

until an election is made. In every vote taken on a name, the yeas and nays shall be recorded in the minutes when required by any one member. Any person who has not received the necessary number of votes at one nomination shall be eligible as a candidate at a subsequent nomination."

Rule 2.—"The warden shall make the declaration of office required by law, immediately after his election."

RULES OF ORDER AND PROCEDURE FOR COUNCILS IN GENERAL (c).

I shall now proceed to refer to those rules which may be generally adopted by all councils at subsequent meetings. In referring to the rules of the city councils, the word " mayor " will read " warden" or " reeve " when the application has to be made to county, township and village councils, and such hours and days of meeting must be chosen as councils may deem most convenient.

two systems, open voting and the ballot or secrecy. The ballot is an innovation on the common law mode of election, and has not been specifically introduced into our municipal or representative system. Indeed it is incompatible with the representative form of government, the distinguishing feature of which is publicity and responsibility, whereas that of the ballot is secrecy and irresponsibility. A representative's constituents have the right to know how their reeve in a council, or member in the legislature, votes on every question. A by-law cannot help in any way to validate that which the statute has not prescribed in express terms. A council has undoubtedly under the law the right to make regulations for its own proceedings (see *above*, p. 254) ; but such regulations can apply only to the council after its organization, and hardly to a body which is not a council in the legal sense until it is formally organized by the election of warden under section 225 (see *above*, p. 238). In any case, no council has authority to alter the common law by any by-law of its own, without express statutory power to that effect.

The writer feels bound to throw out these doubts which are also entertained by so eminent an authority as the Honourable J. R. Gowan, C. M. G., whose large experience as county judge, and of the municipal law of Ontario, entitles his opinions to every respect. It is also understood that Judge Ardagh, senior judge of Simcoe, and Judge Mosgrove, of Carleton county, besides other lawyers, have doubts on this subject. It is clearly a question deserving of serious consideration before other councils or public bodies follow the course of the Simcoe county council.

(c) *This summary of rules can be consulted as a short guide to the leading rules of order and procedure already in force in councils generally throughout the province.*

Subject of Rules.	Rules to be Adopted.

1. Meetings of councils—

Ordinary meetings.

Toronto rule 2, p. 262.

Special meetings.

Called by mayor or when requested by majority of council.

"   3, " 264.

In absence or death of mayor, by clerk on requisition from majority of council.

"   4, " 266.

2. Opening proceedings—

Mayor takes chair when quorum present.

"   5, " 2C6.

Chairman chosen in absence of mayor.

"   6, " 268.

Minutes read and corrected.

"   8, " 270.

Omitting " if requested by any alderman "—the reading consequently imperative.

3. Order of proceeding—

Order of each day's business.

Each city can conveniently keep its present order of proceedings, except St. Catharines, where it is defective. Ottawa rule 37, p. 283, is sug-gested for that city, and all councils in general as adapted to all exigencies.

Business taken up in order.

Toronto rule 29, p. 284.

Motions called and undisposed of placed at foot of list.

"   30, " 286.

Priority given to business superseded by want of quorum.

Brantford rule 37, p. 271.

4. Quorum—

Proceedings in absence of quorum.

London rule 4, p. 269.

Subject of Rules.	*Rules to be Adopted.*

5. Duties of mayor, or head of council, or other chairman—

Maintains order and decorum.	Toronto rule 9, p. 270.
States practice or rule without comment.	" 10, " 270.
Votes as other members.	" 11, " 272.
Leaves chair when taking part in debate.	" 12, " 272.

6. Rules of conduct of debate—

Members rise to speak uncovered and address mayor or chairman.	" 13, " 272.
Procedure if one or more rise to speak.	" 14, " 272.
All vote unless personally interested or excused.	" 15, " 272.
Must create no disturbance.	" 16. " 274.
Called to order, explain and council decide on appeal.	" 17, " 274.
Must not speak disrespectfully of queen, governor-general, etc., or resist rules of council ; may be removed in case of disobedience of orders or improper conduct.	" 18, " 274.
May require question read again.	" 19, " 276.
Must speak only once on a question and reply only allowed to mover of a substantive motion.	" 20, " 276.
Keep seats until mayor leaves chair at adjournment.	" 24, " 280.

7. Motions in general—

Notice of special motions required.	" 31, " 286.
Must be written and seconded when proposed from chair.	" 32, " 286.
When proposed from chair in possession of council.	" 33, " 288.

Subject of Rules.	*Rules to be Adopted.*

Motion for commitment precludes amendment of main question or bill.

Toronto, rule 34, p. 288.

Motion to adjourn always in order within certain limitations.

"   35, " 288.

8. Dilatory motions—

Following rule suggested :

Toronto, rule 36, with additions as given opposite.

"When a question is under consideration, no motion shall be received unless

    (1) To commit,

    (2) To amend,

    (3) To lay on the table,

    (4) To postpone indefinitely,

    (5) To postpone to a certain time,

    (6) To adjourn,

    (7) To move the previous question.

" These several motions shall have precedence in the order in which they are named, and the last five shall be neither amendable nor debatable.

"A motion to adjourn shall be always in order, but it must be simply in the form, 'That the council do now adjourn,' or 'That the debate be adjourned,' and a motion to adjourn the council or the debate to a certain day or adding any expression of opinion or qualification thereto, shall not come within the terms of this rule.

"Only a motion simply to lay a question on the table is not debatable under this rule, and consequently a motion ' to lay on

Subject of Rules.

the table to publish,' or adding some condition or opinion or qualification, is subject to amendment and debate."

9. The previous question—

If it is proposed to adopt the rule of the Canadian house of commons, which allows debate but not amendment on the previous question, then—

But if it be proposed to stop all amendment and debate on moving of previous question then the following rule is suggested as fuller and clearer than that generally adopted in councils :

Rules to be Adopted.

Parliamentary rule *above* p. 36, with the addition to state parliamentary usage clearly : "But if the previous question be resolved in the negative then the council shall proceed to other business." This means, as elsewhere stated (*above*, p. 14) there is no question before the council, since it has been decided no question shall now be put.

"The previous question, until it is decided, shall preclude all amendment and debate of the main motion, and shall be put forthwith without debate in the form, ' That the main question be now put,' and if this motion is resolved in the affirmative then the main motion is put immediately without amendment or debate ; but if the aforesaid motion for the previous question is resolved in the negative, then the main motion is superseded and a new subject or motion must be submitted to the council."

For closure, see opposite.

10. Privileges—

Privileged motions or questions have precedence always.

Toronto rule 43, p. 298.

388   PROPOSED CODE OF RULES

Subject of Rules.   *Rules to be Adopted.*

11. Amendments in general—

Motions and amendments thereto put in reverse order to that in which they are moved.

Ottawa rules 51, 52 and 53 combined, p. 295, but the "largest" sum changed to "lowest" or "smallest sum" (d).

12. Motions ruled out of order—

Chairman calls attention to irregular motions.

Toronto, rule 42, p. 298.

13. Division of a question—

Complicated question may be divided.

"   40, "   298.

14. Divisions—

Question finally put, no member to speak again.

"   41, "   298.

Members take their places.

"   44, "   300.

Yeas and nays entered.

"   21, "   278.

15. Reconsideration—

Question once decided may be reconsidered within certain limitations.

Ottawa rules 62 and 63, p. 301.

16. Voting on appointments—

Separately on each candidate in order, by ballot.

Belleville rule 32, p. 297, with ballot taken as in Guelph rule 41, p. 297.

17. Enquiries—

Questions put to members relating to by-laws, or other matters.

Ottawa rule 30, p. 279, and Toronto rule 22, p. 278, combined.

(d) See reasons given on p. 294, for this change. The rules of the Simcoe county council adopt the correct procedure.

Subject of Rules.   *Rules to be Adopted.*

18. Proceedings in committee of the whole.

Chairman appointed by mayor.

Toronto rule 45, p. 302, with addition of Guelph rule 45, p. 303, with reference to chairman interested in question before committee.

No bill or report considered in committee until printed.

Toronto rule 46, p. 302.

Rules of debate therein.

" 47, " 302, with limitation that no member shall speak longer than 10 minutes on any one question.

Questions of order decided by chairman, subject to appeal to council.

Toronto rule 48, p. 304.

Motion to rise and report decided without debate.

" 49, " 304.

Motion " That the chairman do leave the chair," *i.e.*, without a report, always in order and debatable.

" 50, " 304, with limitation of Guelph rule 48, that " No member shall speak more than once to such a motion."

19. Bills and proceedings thereon—

Introduction on motion for leave, etc.

Toronto rule 51, p. 306, with additions given in rules of other cities on opposite page.

Must not be in blank or imperfect.

Toronto rule 52, p. 306.

" That the bill be now read a first time," neither amendable nor debatable; and every bill read three times and committed.

" 53, " 306.

Referred as a rule to a select or standing committee.

" 54, " 308.

Cannot pass all its stages on same day except in cases of urgency.

" 55, " 308.

Subject of Rules.	*Rules to be Adopted.*

Considered in order of clauses, then preamble, then title.
> Toronto, rule 57, p. 310, with addition of St. Catharines rule 23, p. 311.

All amendments thereto reported and received forthwith by council.
> Toronto rule 58, p. 310.

Endorsed by clerk.
> "   56,   " 310.

All by-laws printed and bound up with index.
> "   59,   " 312.

Every by-law signed by mayor and kept by clerk.
> "   60,   " 312.

20. Petitions and communications—

Petitions fairly written or printed.
> "   61,   " 312.

Endorsed and presented to council by any member.
> "   62,   " 314.

Referred to committees.
> "   63,   " 314.

Referred during the year, etc.
> "   64,   " 316.

21. Appointment of select and standing committees—

Appointment on motion.
> "   65,   " 316, with the proviso the mayor, warden or reeve shall be *ex officio* a member of all committees.

Members introducing bill, petition, or other matter referred, always member of committee.
> Toronto rule 66, p. 318.

Select committees only appointed after notice of matters to be considered.
> "   68,   " 322.

Certain standing committees appointed by each council.

All cities to retain present standing committees as most convenient in practice.
> Cities to retain present committees. See opposite.

Each other municipal division to retain

Subject of Rules.

present committees if found practically adapted to all their business exigencies. Otherwise counties might advantageously adopt the following rule of the Simcoe county council:

47. "In the first session of the council, in each and every year, standing committees to consist of not less than three members each, be appointed for the following purposes, viz.: 1. Finance and assessment; 2. Education; 3. Roads and bridges; 4. County property; 5. Printing; 6. Gaol; 7. Railways; 8. Canals; 9. Contingencies. To whom all matters relating to those objects shall severally be referred."

Towns might adopt following rules of Peterborough council:

42. "The standing committees of this council shall be composed of: 1. Finance committee; 2. Appointment to office and supervision of police; 3. Licenses; 4. Streets and bridges; 5. Charity; 6. Fire, water and light; 7. Market; 8. Printing; 9. Health and sanitary; 10. Property and building; 11. Joint with county; 12. Court of revision. The first named member of each committee shall be chairman thereof."

36. "No standing committee of the council, except on charity, shall consist of less than five nor more than seven members."

Number of members on standing committees.

Rules to be Adopted.

Counties to adopt Simcoe rule 47, if necessary. See opposite.

Towns to adopt Peterborough rule 42, if necessary. See opposite.

Each city to retain present number or generally adopt Toronto rule 69, p. 324. Other

Subject of Rules.

Rules to be Adopted.

municipal divisions to retain
present rules or adopt generally rule 36, Peterborough
council, p. 391, *above.*

22. Meetings of committees—

When and where to meet.

In cities.

St. Catharines rule 55, p. 327.

Rule for counties, etc.

In counties, etc.

"The members of each standing com- See opposite.
mittee of the council shall meet at the
county hall [or court house, or town hall,
or at whatever place may be legally designated by law or resolution] for the purpose
of organization on such day and at such
hour as the warden [or mayor or reeve]
may direct, or in default of the warden
[or mayor or reeve] naming the day and
hour the clerk of the municipal division
shall appoint the day and hour for such
meetings of committees."

Election of chairman.

Times of future meetings.

Toronto rule 71, p. 326,
substituting special names of
standing committees of other
cities and municipal divisions,
as set forth in their special
rules retained (see *above*, p.
390), and adding St. Catharines rule 56, p. 327.

Certain standing committees to meet at
fixed periods or at call of chairman.

Toronto rule 72, p. 328,
with names of such com-
mittees as city and county
and other councils may substitute.

Special meetings of standing committees called by chairman.

Toronto rule 73, p. 328.

Subject of Rules.	Rules to be Adopted.
Members of council attend, but do not vote.	Toronto rule 74, p. 328.
Chairman removed when unable to attend.	London rule 67 (9), p. 329.
Or neglecting to call meetings.	Guelph rule 63, p. 331.
Other members appointed to take place of members who cannot attend.	London rule 69, p. 331.
Committee or its members neglecting or refusing to attend to duties discharged and others appointed.	Guelph rule 64, p. 331.

23. General regulations for conduct of business—

Chairman presides.	Toronto rule 75 (1), p. 332.
Signs orders, etc.	" " (2), " 332.
In his absence another appointed.	" " (3), " 332.
All orders in writing and authorized by committee.	" " (7), " 334.
Keeping of minutes.	" " (4, 5)," 332.
Divisions.	Belleville rule 61 (8), p. 335.

24. Duties of secretary or clerk—

To serve notices for each meeting.	Toronto rule 76 (1), p. 336. Brantford rule 36, p. 337.
To attend all meetings.	Toronto rule 76 (2), p. 336.

25. Duties of committees—

To report on every subject referred.	" 77 (1), " 336.
To prepare and introduce by-laws when necessary, etc.	" " (2), " 338.
To give effect to by-laws and resolutions.	" " (3), " 338.

Subject of Rules.	Rules to be Adopted.
To examine certain accouuts.	Toronto rule 77 (4), p. 338.
Chairman to sign all reports.	" " (5), " 338.
To adhere strictly to rules.	" " (6), " 338.
To present annual general reports of matters referred during year.	" " (7), " 336.
To see that certain officers give proper security.	" " (8), " 340.

26. Suspension of rules—

Rules suspended only by a two-third vote, and repealed or amended only after week's notice.

Ottawa rule 101, p. 281.

27. Unprovided cases—

Law of parliament followed.

Toronto rule 26, p. 280.

28. Admission of strangers—

No stranger allowed within bar except by permission.

"   23, " 278.

Disorderly persons may be expelled (e).

Ottawa, rule 7, p. 275.

29. Hour of adjournment—

Council to adjourn at hour of 11 o'clock p.m., unless determined otherwise by a vote.

Toronto rule 2 (a), p. 264, for councils in cities and towns that meet at night. County councils need no such rule.

30. Money appropriations—

We now leave those rules which are practically those of parliament, and come to the special regulations that relate to the duties of municipal or civic officers and the payment of appropriations of the public

---

(e) See above p. 244, for statute in this behalf.

Subject of Rules.	Rules to be Adopted.

moneys. The rules of Toronto and London are very elaborate in this regard, and no doubt those of smaller municipalities like Belleville and Guelph have been found, by experience, to afford all the checks necessary to guard their expenditures when rigidly carried out. The rules of Kingston, Ottawa, Hamilton and St. Catharines are, however, very defective, as well as those of the great majority of county and town corporations I have studied. It is, therefore, recommended that all cities and towns, which require an amended code of rules, should adopt a combination of those of Guelph and Belleville which, without being as elaborate as those of Toronto and London, appear framed with sufficient care to meet all emergencies that are likely to arise. The same remarks apply to populous and important counties; but whether such rules be adopted in their entirety or not, the following should be found in the code of every county municipality as absolutely essential to the careful appropriation of municipal funds :

See Toronto rules, p. 344, *et seq.*

See London rules, p. 358, *et seq.*

See Belleville rules, p. 366, *et seq.*

See Guelph rules, p. 363, *et seq.*

" All petitions or applications for money grants by members and others shall be presented to the council during the first three days of a session of a council held under the law."

Simcoe county rule 55.

" All appropriations of money shall be submitted to a committee of the whole before being considered in full council."

London rule 77, p. 363.

No bill relating to the expenditure or appropriation of public money shall pass

New rule, based on parliamentary practice.

all its stages on the same day, but a day
must invariably intervene between the
committee of the whole stage and the third
reading or passage of said bill.

"It shall be the duty of the finance   Guelph rule 66, p. 363.
committee [*or* finance and assessment com-
mittee, *or* whatever may be the name of
the financial committee of a council, *as the
case may be*] to examine and report on all
accounts referred to them on all annual
and other estimates of expenditure, on all
proposals for purchase of debentures or
other municipal securities; to prepare
estimates of the revenue, expenditure and
assessment of each year ; to consider and
report on all reports of other committees
that involve expenditure, and in short to
have supervision generally of all matters
relating to the finances of the municipality."

"It shall be the duty of all the standing   "   76, " 364.
or other committees of the council to con-
sider and report to the council on or before
[*give date*] of every year, a general statement of its proposed improvements, repairs
and expenditures, together with the probable cost of the same, together with an
estimate of revenue when any is derived
or may be expected from the department
or service under their supervision respectively; and the council shall refer these
several reports to the finance committee for
their consideration and report."

Subject of Rules.   *Rules to be Adopted.*

" The report of the finance committee on the proposed expenditures of the several committees shall be printed and only considered by the council at the meeting next succeeding that on which the said report is made, except by a two-third vote of the whole council when full ; and the report of the said committee, when agreed to or amended, shall constitute the appropriations of the council for the several services to which that report relates."

Adapted from Guelph rule 77, p. 365.

" In case of emergency or sudden injury to municipal property, requiring immediate repair, the finance committee, on the report referred to them by the proper officer or committee having supervision of such matters, may in the interval between two sessions of the council, order the expenditure of a sum not exceeding fifty dollars ; but at the next meeting of the council following such order the chairman of the committee shall report the facts to the council, and ask its approval by resolution."

Guelph rule 78, p. 365.

"All accounts and claims against the corporation and all proposed appropriations of money shall, unless otherwise specially provided for by by-law or resolution of the council, be referred to and reported on by the finance committee, and the report thereon adopted by the council before being paid, and every such resolution and report and all other resolutions and reports relating to the municipal expenditures and finances

Peterborough rule 58.

Subject of Rules.	Rules to be Adopted.

shall be duly entered in the minutes of the
council at length."

" The chairman of the finance committee shall not audit or approve of any bill or
account against the city or supplies for
services which shall not have been regularly authorized by the finance committee,
and by the council on report from said
committee."

Kingston rule 37, p. 374.

"No payment shall be made by the
treasurer (except salaries duly authorized
by law) on account of the municipality,
unless first passed and reported by the
finance committee, duly sanctioned by the
council, and on the warrant of the warden."

Adapted from Kingston rule 38, p. 374.

" No motion for the expenditure of
money shall be in order before the council
until the finance committee reports that
there are funds on hand to meet the
same."

Kingston rule 39, p. 374.

" No committee, nor any member of
this council, nor any officer thereof, shall
directly or indirectly, enter into any
contract with, or authorize the purchase of,
or purchase, any article or goods, wares,
or merchandise from any one or more of
the members of this council, nor any officer
thereof."

Peterborough rule 59.

" No officer of the corporation, nor any
member of the council, shall, on behalf of
the corporation, enter into any contract or
incur any debt without having obtained by
by-law or resolution the previous authority
and sanction of the council in that behalf."

"   60.

Subject of Rules.	*Rules to be Adopted.*
"Any breach of the regulation imposed by the preceding section of this by-law, on the part of any officer of the corporation, shall subject him to forfeiture of his office, and immediate removal therefrom."	Peterborough rule 61. " 57.
"The clerk shall notify the several printing establishments in the county, one month previous to the January session, that the council will receive tenders for the county printing for the current year not later than the third day of the said session."	Adapted from Simcoe county rule 52.
"No expenditure shall be paid by the warden or treasurer when the county solicitor has expressed his opinion, in writing, to the effect that such action would be illegal."	

IV.—NOTE ON THE MUNICIPAL SYSTEMS OF THE OTHER PROVINCES.

It is clearly impossible within the limits of this work, which is intended to be a *manual* in the full sense of the word, to give a full review of the municipal systems of all the provinces of Canada. All that it is necessary here to do is to refer my readers to the different statutes which regulate the municipal systems of the other provinces besides Ontario.

As all the councils which assemble under these statutes have rules based on the common law of parliament they will be able, generally speaking, to find all the information they require for the guidance of their ordinary proceedings in the First Part of this book, and in the notes to the rules of the councils of Ontario.

Below I give references to the municipal statutes of the other provinces to supplement the sections devoted to Ontario, and make this part of the work more complete.

1. The Province of Quebec (a).

The municipal code of the province of Quebec applies to all the territory of that province except those cities and towns (b) incorporated by special statutes. This territory is divided into the

(a) See for history of municipal system of Quebec and of the other provinces, Bourinot's "Local Government in Canada."

(b) The cities of Montreal, Hull, Quebec, Sherbrooke, St. Hyacinthe and Three Rivers are corporations by special Acts. So are the towns of the province generally. See Mathieu's Municipal Code, 1869, and Quebec Statutes.

following municipal divisions, which are governed in accordance with the provisions of this code :

(1) County municipalities.

(2) County or rural municipalities, viz.:

    (a) Parish   "

    (b) Township   "

(3) Towns   "

(4) Villages   "

The county council is composed of the mayors in office of all the local municipalities in the county. Such mayors bear the title in the county council of "county councillors." The head of the council is called the "warden," and is chosen from among the members who compose the council.

The local (c) council is composed of seven councillors elected by the electors of the municipality, or appointed by the lieutenant-governor where no election takes place.

The head of this council is called a mayor.

2. The Province of Nova Scotia.

The present municipal system of the province of Nova Scotia dates back only to the year 1879, when the Act 42 V. c. 1 (see Rev. Stat, 5th series, c. 56) was passed (d). Besides the statutes relating to county and township councils there are special statutes incorporating Halifax and several towns of the province.

The inhabitants of every county and district in the province, namely, Colchester, Cumberland, Pictou, Halifax, West Hants, East Hants, King's, Annapolis, Digby, Clare, Lunenburg, Chester,

(c) Article 19 of the Municipal Code sets forth that "the adjective 'local' when it qualifies the words 'municipality,' 'corporation,' 'council' and 'councillor,' refers indifferently to country, village and town councils, councillors, corporations or municipalities." Consequently those councils include parish, township, town and village councils, and generally every local council, except a county or city council.

(d) See also amending and later statutes, 1888, o. 1 ; 1890, c. 40; 1892, c. 48; 1893, cc. 17-22 inclusive.

Queen's, Shelburne, Barrington, Yarmouth, Argyle, Antigonish, Guysborough, St. Mary's, Cape Breton, Victoria, Inverness and Richmond are a body corporate under the name of the municipality of the respective county or district as the case may be.

Every town hereafter to be incorporated under the Act, and all towns now incorporated and made subject to the provisions of the Act of 1888 (e) are governed by a town council, consisting of a mayor and not less than six councillors.

3. The Province of New Brunswick.

The municipal system of the province of New Brunswick is regulated by a general statute (Rev. Stat. c. 99, and amending Acts), except in the cases of St. John, Fredericton, and those towns incorporated by special Acts.

In each county there is a county council which exercises all the powers of a body corporate. The head is called warden, and the members councillors. In cities, the head is called mayor.

4. The Province of Manitoba.

The province of Manitoba has adopted a very complete municipal system of local government of cities, towns, villages and rural municipalities (see Stat. of 1890, c. 51) (f). The law regulates the procedure of councils more fully than is the case in the other provinces except Quebec. The principles of the parliamentary law are made applicable to municipal divisions as far as possible.

The following councils are elected in accordance with the provisions of this Act:

A city council, consisting of the mayor, who shall be the head thereof, and two aldermen for every ward;

A town council, consisting of the mayor, who shall be the head thereof, and two councillors for every ward;

(e) N. S. Stat. of 1888, c. 1.

(f) 53 V. c. 51, amended in 1891, by c. 1, p. 4; in 1892 by c. 25; in 1893, by c. 23.

A village council, consisting of the mayor, who shall be the head thereof, and four councillors ;

A council in a rural municipality, consisting of the reeve, who shall be the head thereof, and such number of councillors to be fixed by by-law, not exceeding six nor less than four councillors.

5. The Province of British Columbia.

The municipal system of British Columbia (see Municipalities' Consolidation Act (g) c. 33, B. C. Stat., 1892) provides for municipal divisions, known as city, town, township or district. It extends to the cities of Victoria and Nanaimo, and all township or district municipalities incorporated before the passing of the Act. It also applies to the cities of New Westminster and of Vancouver only so far as it is not repugnant to or inconsistent with their Acts of incorporation, or any amendments thereto.

The councils of the cities of Victoria and Nanaimo consist of a mayor and not more than twelve and not less than seven aldermen, and in other cities thereafter incorporated of a mayor and not more than twelve and not less than seven aldermen. But the first mentioned councils may by unanimous resolution increase the number of their members to thirteen in all, including the mayor.

The council of a township or district consists of not more than seven and not less than four councillors and a reeve, but the number may be increased to eight in all, including the reeve, by unanimous resolution of the council.

The head of a city municipality is called a mayor ; of a township or district a reeve. In each case the officer is elected annually.

6. The Province of Prince Edward Island.

In this province there is no general law providing for a municipal system as in other sections of the Dominion of Canada,

(g) Amended by c. 30, Stat. of 1893.

but the legislature is practically a governing body for all municipal matters (*h*).

7. The Northwest Territories.

The ordinances of the territories (see Rev. Ord. for 1888, c. 8) make provision for the establishment of municipalities therein.

8. By-laws regulating Proceedings of Councils.

All the councils in the provinces having municipal systems have power to make, and from time to time to alter, such rules and regulations as may be requisite for the conduct and good order of its proceedings, and such by-laws touching any matters within its authority as it may judge proper. But such regulations cannot alter or change any principle of the common law, unless there is express or necessarily implied statutory authority to that effect (see *above*, p. 382, *n*).

(*h*) See Bourinot's " Local Government in Canada," p. 65.

ANALYTICAL INDEX.

[The references are in all cases to pages.]

A.

Adjournment—

a dilatory or superseding motion, 21 ; its proper form, 33

of debate, 21, 33

of the house supersedes a question under consideration, *Ib.*

motions equivalent thereto in committee of the whole, 46

rule in Builders' Labourers' National Union, No. 1, Toronto (not amendable or debatable), 97, 98

Catholic Mutual Benevolent Association of Canada (not amendable or debatable), 87

certain city councils—

Belleville (not amendable but debatable), 289

Brantford (not amendable but debatable), *Ib.*

Guelph (not amendable or debatable), 289, 291

Hamilton (not amendable or debatable), 289, 291

Kingston (not amendable or debatable), 289

London and St. Thomas (not amendable but debatable), 289

Ottawa (not amendable but debatable), 289

St. Catharines (not amendable or debatable), 289

Stratford (not amendable but debatable), 289

Toronto (not amendable but debatable), 289

diocesan synods of Church of England (not amendable or debatable), 172-174

general and provincial synods of Church of England (not amendable or debatable). 155

B.

Ballot, The—

mode of taking in diocesan synods, 178
political conventions, 76, 77
shareholders' and companies' meetings, 136
Simcoe County Council, 240

Baptist Conventions—

governed by ordinary parliamentary law, 223

Belleville City Council, rules of—See *City Councils of Ontario.*

Bills—

how introduced in parliament, 53
first reading, 53
second reading, 54
considered in committee of the whole, or in a select committee, 54, 55
reported from committee, 56
third reading, 56
clerk certifies readings thereof, 56
cannot be altered except by house, 56

See *City Councils of Ontario, rules of.*

Bishops of the Church of England in Canada—

call together and preside over diocesan synods, 160, 161
constitute upper house of general synod, 140, 141
                                        provincial synod, 143
mode of electing, 178

See *Synods of the Church of England.*

Brantford City Council, rules of—See *City Councils of Ontario.*

Breaches of Parliamentary Decorum—

rules governing, 40
words taken down, 41

Bricklayers' and Masons' International Union of America—

rules of, 102

Builders' Labourers' National Union, No. 1, Toronto—

rules of, 96, 100

By-laws—

meaning of, 109, 228
of city councils, 228, 251

	Toronto.	Belleville.	Brantford.	Guelph.	Hamilton.	Kingston.	London and St. Thomas.	Ottawa.	St. Catharines.	Stratford.
City Councils of Ontario, rules of—										
Accounts—See Money expenditure	352 353									
Adjourn, to—See Motions	....	....	....	....	....	379				
Adjournment of councils — See Meetings of council										
Admission of strangers—See Meetings of council										
Aldermen—See Committee of council—meetings of council										
Amendments—										
how to be put	294	295	295	295	295	295	295	295	295	295
in filling up blanks longest time and largest sum to be put first	294	295	295	295	295	295	295	295	295	295
only one amendment to amendment allowed	294	295	295	295	295	295	295	295	295	295
decided before main question	294	295	295	295	295	295	295	295	295	295
to be in writing	294	295	295	295	295	295	295	295	295	295
Appointments—										
voting in cases of candidates for	296	297	297	....	297	297	297	297	297	297
members not eligible for, where remuneration is payable by council...........	296	297	297	....	297	297	297	297	297	297
Appropriations and expenditures —See Money appropriations										
Auditing and auditors	357									
Bills—										
amendments in committee of the whole reported	310	313	313	313	....	313	311	311	311	313
clerk responsible for their correctness if amended	310	311	311	311	311	311	311	311	311	311
consideration in committee of the whole	310	311	311	311	311	311	311	311	311	311
date of meetings to be endorsed	310	311	311	311	311	311	311	311	311	311
first reading without amendment or debate...........	306	307	309	309	307	307	307	307	309	309
introduction of..............	306	307	309	309	307	307	307	307	309	309
may receive two or more readings in one day under certain conditions	308	309	309	309	309	309	309	309	309	309

City Councils of Ontario, rules of—Continued.

Committees—select and standing—

	Toronto.	Belleville.	Brantford.	Guelph.	Hamilton.	Kingston.	London and St. Thomas.	Ottawa.	St. Catharines.	Stratford.
City Councils of Ontario, rules of— *Continued.* *Members of council—* names voting "yea" and "nay" to be recorded	278	279	279	279	279	279	279	279	279	279
not eligible for appointment to office where remuneration is payable by council......	296	....	....	....	....	....	....	296		
not to be interested in corporation contracts	352	369	....	....	....	373				
not to disobey decisions of mayor or council on points of order, etc...............	274	275	275	275	275	275	275	275	275	275
not to interfere with officers in performance of duty	355									
not to interfere with city work	355									
not to leave seats until mayor leaves chair	280	281	281	281	281	281	281	281	281	281
not to reflect upon any vote of council	274	274	274	274	274	274	274	274	274	274
not to resist rules	274	274	274	274	274	274	274	274	274	274
not to speak beside question under debate	274	274	274	274	274	274	274	274	274	274
not to speak disrespectfully of the queen, royal family, governor-general, lieutenant-governors, etc.............	274	274	274	274	274	274	274	274	274	274
not to use offensive language against council or members thereof	274	274	274	274	274	274	274	274	274	274
one may call for "yeas" or "nays"	278	279	279	279	279	279	279	279	279	279
right of speaking on a substantive motion—reply allowed to mover	276	277	279	277	277	277	277	277	277	277
to take their places when division is called for......	300	301	301	301	301	301	301	301	301	301
transgressing rules may be ordered to leave seat for that meeting—in case of refusal to leave may be removed by police—upon apologizing may resume seat with permission of council..	274	275	275	275	277	275	275	275	277	277
when called to order to sit down—but may afterwards explain	274	275	275	275	277	275	275	275	275	275
when two or more rise at once, mayor to decide who has floor (See *Meetings of council*)	272	272	273	273	273	273	273	273	273	273

	Toronto.	Belleville.	Brantford.	Guelph.	Hamilton.	Kingston.	London and St. Thomas.	Ottawa.	St. Catharines.	Stratford.
City Councils of Ontario, rules of—*Continued.*										
Minutes of council — See *Meetings of council*										
Money expenditures—rules relating to	344 *et seq* 351	366 *et seq* 368	....	363 *et seq* 365	374	....	358 *et seq* 363	344	374	375 *et seq* 380
Motions—										
containing distinct propositions, may be divided and voted on separately	298	299	299	299	299	299	299	299	299	299
for commitment preclude all amendment until decided..	288	289	289	289	289	289	289	289	289	289
may be made to hear any member who has risen to speak	272	273	273	273	273	273	273	273	273	273
may under certain limitations, be withdrawn after read ..	288	289	289	289	289	289	289	289	289	289
must be in writing and seconded before debated or put ..	286	287	287	287	287	287	287	287	287	287
must be "proposed" or read by mayor before debated ..	286	287	287	287	287	287	287	287	287	287
notice thereof given—unless council dispenses with	286	287	287	287	287	287	287	287	287	287
on orders of the day, not disposed of, to be placed at foot of list.....................	286	287	287	287	287	287	287	288	287	287
to adjourn always in order—but second motion not allowed until a proceeding intervenes	288	289	289	289	289	289	289	289	289	289
to lay on the table	290	291	291	291	291	291	291	291	291	291
to postpone	290	291	291	291	291	291	291	291	291	291
the previous question........	292	293	293	293	293	293	293	293	293	293
to reconsider a question once decided	300	301	301	301	301	301	301	301	301	301
Orders of the day—business taken up in the order it stands upon............	284	285	285	285	285	285	285	285	285	285
general	280	283	285	283	281	283	283	283	285	285
motions on, not disposed of, to be placed at foot of list—unless otherwise determined by council	286	286	287	287	287	287	287	287	287	287
special meetings, provisions for.....................	284	285	285	285	285	285	285	285	285	285
See *Meetings of council*)										

	Toronto.	Belleville.	Brantford.	Guelph.	Hamilton.	Kingston.	London and St. Thomas.	Ottawa.	St. Catharines.	Stratford.
City Councils of Ontario. rules of—*Continued.*										
Parks and Gardens committee—										
duties of	350									
Postpone definitely or indefinitely, —(See *Motions*)										
Petitions—										
may be taken into immediate consideration, in case of urgency..................	316	315	315	317	317	315	315	315	315	315
members responsible for contents	....	315	....	....	317	....	315	315	315	315
no debate on presentation....	314	315	....	317	317	....	315	315	315	315
no letters or other appendixes thereto, permissible	312	313	313	313	313	313	313	313	313	313
presentation of	314	315	315	315	315	315	315	315	315	315
presented in previous year, provision respecting.......	316	317	....	....	....	....	....	317	317	317
read when required by a member..	314	315	315	315	315	315	315	315	315	315
referred to proper committee.	314	315	315	317	317	315	315	315	315	315
Previous Question—See Motions and Previous question in body of index.										
Printing—										
supervision of	347	368	....	363	....	....	358	....	....	375
Privilege—See *Questions*										
Property committee—										
duties of	349	....	....	364						
Public Parks, Gardens, Cemeteries and Squares	350	....	....	....	....	....	359	....	....	377 378
Questions—										
being finally put, no motion shall be made nor shall any person speak until result is declared..................	298	299	299	299	299	299	299	299	299	299
containing distinct propositions may be divided and voted on separately.......	298	299	299	299	299	299	299	299	299	299
decision of mayor conclusive as to whether a question is finally put..............	298	299	299	299	299	299	299	299	299	299
of privilege to be considered immediately...........	298	299	299	299	299	299	299	299	299	299

Councillors—

how elected members of town, township and village councils, 230, 231
make certain declarations on assuming office, 242
resignation, 232
vacancies by disqualification, etc., 233

See *Municipal Councils in Ontario, law relating to.*

County Council—See *Municipal Councils in Ontario, law relating to.*

Court of Revision—

how appointed, 247, 248

See *City Councils of Ontario, rules of; Municipal Councils in Ontario, law relating to.*

Courts—See *Church Courts of the Presbyterian Church in Canada.*

D.

Deacons' Court—See *Church Courts of the Presbyterian Church in Canada.*

Debate, rules of—
in parliament, 37-39
city councils, 272-278, 290-293
diocesan synods of the Church of England, 174, 175
general and provincial synods of the Church of England, 153-156
Methodist conference, 199-202
Presbyterian courts, 214-220
motions to close debate in—
Builders' Labourers' National Union, No. 1, Toronto (previous question to close the debate), 97
Catholic Mutual Benefit Association (previous question), 87
International Typographical Union, No. 91 (previous question), 99, 100
Iron Moulders' Union of North America (to close debate), 102
Trades and Labour Council of Hamilton (previous question), 91, 96
Toronto (previous question), 91, 93

Declarations of Office and Qualification, required from Members of Municipal Councils, 236, 241, 242
See *Municipal Councils in Ontario, law relating to.*

Delegates to Synods—
to diocesan synod, how chosen, 160
general synod   "   "   141
provincial synods "   "   149

Deputy-reeve—

members of town, township, and village councils, 230, 231
presides in case of absence or death of head of council, 246
required to make certain declarations on assuming office, 241, 242
vacancies by resignation, etc., 232, 233
votes twice under certain conditions at election of warden, 239

See *Municipal Councils in Ontario, law relating to.*

Dilatory Motions—

adjournment of the assembly or house (see *Adjournment*), 21
     debate (see *Adjournment*), 21

in committee of the whole—
" that the chairman do leave the chair," 46
" that the chairman do report progress and ask leave to sit again" (see *committee of the whole*), 46

previous question. (see *previous question*), 13-16, 36
to commit or refer in American practice, 24, 25
    lay on the table (see *lay on the table, to*), 22, 23
    postpone to a specified time (see *postpone, to*), 23
        indefinitely (see *postpone, to*), 24

all such motions, as above, governed by common parliamentary law in absence of special regulations, 26

Diocesan Synods—See *Synods of the Church of England in Canada.*

Directors' Meetings—

affairs of corporate companies administered at, under regulations or by-laws, 108, 109
agenda or order of business at, 113-115
books, 127
chairman of, 113
      signs minutes, 125
      other duties, 126
duties of, how prescribed, 111
election of directors, 110
    their qualifications, 110, 115
    number on a board, 111
example of regulations of board meetings, 112
legal principles laid down for their guidance, 115, 116
minutes of, 125
procedure at, 117
quorum of, 111, 115

District Meetings—See *Conferences of the Methodist Church in Canada.*

I.

J.

K.

L.

M.

Motions—*Continued.*

    subsidiary, 25

    substantive, 38

    Rules governing certain bodies—

        city councils, 286-300

        diocesan synods, 168-171

        general and provincial synods, 154-158

        Methodist conferences, 200-206

        parliament, 30-37

        Presbyterian courts, 215-219

    (See special references under foregoing heads in index)

Municipal Councils—

    for rules of cities of Belleville, Brantford, Guelph, Hamilton, Kingston, London, Ottawa, Stratford, St. Catharines, St. Thomas, Toronto, see *City Councils of Ontario.*

Municipal Councils in Ontario, law relating to—

    assessors, appointment and duties, 252

    auditors   "   " 253

    clerk and other officers, appointment and duties, 235

    collectors, 252

    Conduct of business in councils generally—

        ordinary meetings open, 244

        persons excluded for improper conduct, 244

        quorum a majority of the whole council, 244

        concurrent vote of three sufficient in a council of five members, 245

        head of council presides and may summon special meetings, 245

        in absence of head, clerk summons, 245

        special meetings open or closed, 245

        provisions for absence or death of head of town, township or village council, 246

        presiding officer votes as any member, 247

        in an equality of votes, the question is deemed negatived, 247

        councils may adjourn their meetings, 247

        court of revision, appointed, 247

        heads of councils, warden, mayor and reeve, 231

        high school trustees, appointed, 248

        local board of health, appointed, 251

    Meetings of municipal councils—

        election of warden, 235, 236

        first meeting, 236

        certificates of declarations of office and qualification required from each reeve and deputy-reeve, 236

N.

O.

P.

Postpone, To—

of a dilatory nature, 23

United States practice respecting—

to postpone to a specified time, 23

an indefinite period, 24

in absence of special rule, parliamentary rules prevail and motions amendable and debatable, 26

Rule in following bodies—

Builders' Labourers' National Union, No. 1, Toronto (amendable and debatable), 97

Catholic Mutual Benefit Association, to postpone to a certain time debatable and amendable ; to postpone indefinitely, not debatable or amendable, 86

certain city councils—

Belleville (amendable and debatable), 291

Brantford (amendable and debatable), 291

Guelph (amendable and debatable), 291

Hamilton (amendable and debatable), 291

Kingston (amendable and debatable), 291

London and St. Thomas (amendable and debatable), 291

Ottawa (amendable and debatable), 291

St. Catharines (amendable and debatable), 291

Stratford (amendable and debatable), 291

Toronto (amendable and debatable), 290

diocesan synods of Church of England in general (amendable and debatable), 172-174

general and provincial synods of Church of England (debatable and amendable), 155

International Typographical Union, No. 91 (amendable and debatable), 99

Iron Moulders' Union of North America (amendable and debatable), 102

Methodist conference (not amendable or debatable), 200

Toronto Typographical Union, No. 91 (amendable and debatable), 101

Trades and Labour Council of Hamilton (amendable and debatable), 91, 96

Toronto (amendable and debatable), 91

Precedence, Order of—

in case of certain motions, 200, 201

Presbyterian Church—See *Church Courts of the Presbyterian Church in Canada.*

Presbytery—See *Church Courts of the Presbyterian Church in Canada.*

Previous Question, The—

its meaning and object in Canadian legislatures, 13-16, 36

cannot be moved on an amendment, 14

but can be moved, if amendment be withdrawn or negatived, 15

when moved, no amendment admissible, 36

adjournment of house or debate admissible, 36

Previous Question, The—*Continued.*

but not, if house resolves that the question shall now be put, 36
does not stop debate in Canadian legislatures, 14
when carried, debate ceases, and vote taken on main motion, 14
if negatived, main motion superseded, and other matter taken up, 14
means the *closure* in United States practice, 15
in absence of a special rule of closure, Canadian parliamentary law
prevails, 16

Rule in following bodies—

Builders' Labourers' National Union, No. 1, Toronto (main motion not
debatable), 97
Catholic Mutual Benefit Association (main motion not debatable), 87
city and other councils, viz:—

Belleville (main motion not debatable), 293
Brantford (main motion not debatable), 293
Cobourg (main motion not debatable), 295
Guelph (main motion not debatable), 293
Hamilton (main motion not debatable), 293
Kingston (main motion not debatable), 293
London and St. Thomas (main motion debatable), 293
Mt. Forest (main motion not debatable), 295
Ottawa (main motion debatable), 293
Pembroke (main motion not debatable), 295
Peterborough (main motion not debatable), 295
St. Catharines (main motion not debatable), 293
Stratford (main motion debatable), 293
Toronto (main motion not debatable), 292

diocesan synod of Toronto (main motion not debatable), 174
diocesan synods, generally, parliamentary rule obtains and main motion
debatable, 174
general and provincial synods of Church of England (main motion not
debatable), 155
International Typographical Union, No. 91 (main motion not debatable)
99, 100
Iron Moulders' Union of North America (main motion not debatable), 103
Methodist conference (main motion not debatable), 203
Presbyterian courts (main motion not debatable), 217
Toronto Typographical Union, No. 91 (main motion not debatable), 101
Trades and Labour Councils of Hamilton and Toronto (main motion not
debatable), 91, 96

Primate of all Canada—

president of the general synod of Canada, how elected, 141

Printing —See *City Councils of Ontario, rules of.*

Privilege—

    Questions of, have precedence, 40

Privileged Motions—See *Motions.*

Prolocutor—

    chairman of lower house of general synod, how elected, 141
              provincial synod, how elected, 145
    deputy, appointed in each synod, 150
    duties of, 153
    has a casting vote on an equal division, 156
    See *Synods of the Church of England.*

Property—See *City Councils of Ontario, rules of.*

Proposed Code of Rules for Councils generally—381-399

Provincial Synod of Canada.—See *Synods of the Church of England in Canada.*

Provisional Corporations—See *Municipal Councils in Ontario, law relating to.*

Public Meetings and Assemblies in Canada—

    chairman, how chosen, 8, 9
    debate at, 13, 16
    divisions at, 69, 70
    governed generally by parliamentary law, 5, 6
    importance of, 3, 4
    minutes of proceedings, 11
    notices of, 64
    Ontario and Quebec statutes, regulating and protecting, 63
    order of business at, 9, 10
    procedure at, 66-71
    proposal of motions, 11, 12
    right of assembling in public, 61
    special rules necessary in certain cases, 5, 6
    unlawful assembling, 62

Putting the Question—

    in parliament, 41-44

Q.

Quarterly official board —See *Conferences of the Methodist Church in Canada.*

Quebec Synod—See *Synods of the Church of England in Canada.*

S.

Secretary or clerk—
minutes of, 11, 12, 83, 113, 125

Session, A—meaning of, 9

Session, The—See *Church Courts of the Presbyterian Church in Canada.*

Select and Standing Committees—
bound by order of reference or instructions, 21, 48
how appointed and governed in parliament, 21, 48-51
quorum of, 48
reports from, 21, 51
of majority alone regular, 50
signed by chairman, 51
In following bodies—
city councils, 316-341
diocesan synods of Church of England, 181-191
general and provincial synods of Church of England, 152, 157
Methodist conferences, 198, 199
Presbyterian courts, 211-214

Shareholders' Meetings—
affairs of public companies administered at, under regulations or
by-laws, 108
books, 127, 128
chairman, 126, 127
extraordinary or special, 116
minutes, 122-125
notices for, 119-122
ordinary, 116
proceedings at, 117, 118
resolutions, 127
voting, 128-136

Show of Hands—
how taken, 69, 70
the common law method, 382n

Societies—
Acts incorporating, 84
constitution of, 80, 81
election of officers, 82
organization of, 79-84
rules of, 82, 83

Synods of the Church of England—*Continued.*

Rules of order and procedure of the lower houses, viz.:—

deputy prolocutor named, 150
election of secretaries and other officers, 150
every member votes unless formally excused, 156
journal, 151
meeting, time of, 149, 151
messages from the upper house immediately read, 153
motion may be read at any time, if not interrupting a member, 156
    to postpone, lay on the table, previous question, 155
    not withdrawn without consent of house, 155
notice of motions, 154
officers, duties of, 150
order of precedence of motions, committee appointed to arrange, 152, 153
previous question (not debatable or amendable), 154
prolocutor chosen, 150
    his duties, 153
prorogation—
    of general synod, 158, 159
    provincial synod, 158, 159
question once decided not renewable except by unanimous consent, 157
    put, no further debate admissible, 156
quorum, 150
standing committees, how appointed, 152
to adjourn (not amendable or debatable), 155
    lay on the table (not amendable or debatable), 155
to suspend rules of order (not amendable or debatable), 155
vacancies in offices, how filled, 151
voting, 156
    may be taken by orders, 157
    or recorded in minutes, 157
    members must vote, 156

T.

Toronto City Council, rules of—See *City Councils of Ontario.*

Toronto Synod—See *Synods of the Church of England in England.*

Toronto Typographical Union, No. 91—
    rules of, 100-101

Town Councils—See *Municipal Councils in Ontario, law relating to.*

Township Councils—See *Municipal Councils in Ontario, law relating to.*

Voting on Questions—*Continued.*

In the following bodies—

diocesan synods of Church of England, 176-178 •
general synod of the Church of England, 142, 156
International Typographical Union, No. 91, 99
Methodist conferences, 205
Presbyterian courts, 218, 219
Trades and Labour Council of Toronto, 95

W.

Warden—

head of county council, 231
mode of election, 238, 239
provisions in case of his absence or death, 245
required to make certain declarations before entering on duties, 241, 242
resignation, 233
rule for election in Carleton county council, 240
Simcoe county council elect by ballot, doubts as to legality of this course,
382n

Waterworks—See *City Councils of Ontario, rules of.*

Words taken down—

in parliament, 41

Works—See *City Councils of Ontario, rules of.*